Drawn on Stone by J.D. Harding. From an Original Sketch by H.W. Beechey Esq.

NARROW PASSAGE OF THE NILE, BETWEEN PHILÆ AND KALAPSHE.

TRAVELS

IN

EGYPT AND NUBIA, SYRIA,

AND

ASIA MINOR;

DURING THE YEARS

1817 & 1818.

BY

THE HON. CHARLES LEONARD IRBY,

AND

JAMES MANGLES,

COMMANDERS IN THE ROYAL NAVY.

DARF PUBLISHERS LIMITED
LONDON
1985

FIRST PUBLISHED 1823
NEW IMPRESSION 1985

ISBN 1 85077 082 4

Printed and bound in Great Britain
by A. Wheaton & Co. Ltd, Exeter, Devon

PREFACE.

On the 14th of August, 1816, the Hon. Charles Leonard Irby and James Mangles, Commanders in the Royal Navy, left England, with the intention of making a tour on the continent. This journey they were led to extend far beyond the original design. Curiosity at first, and an increasing admiration of antiquities as they advanced, carried them at length through several parts of the Levant, which have been little visited by modern travellers, and gave them more than four years of continued employment.

Soon after their return to England, in the end of the year 1820, they were induced to transcribe a selection of the letters which they had addressed during their absence to their families in England, as the most convenient mode of satisfying the inquiries of numerous friends.

Among those, who by expressing themselves interested with the narrative, suggested the step which has now been taken, of printing some copies for private distribution, was a gentleman well acquainted with the Turkish provinces described in the following pages, and who has lately edited the Travels of the lamented Burckhardt through the same countries. He was not only so obliging as to suggest such corrections in the language of the original manuscript as must always be necessary in such circumstances, previously to printing, but more especially in the case of persons quite unexperienced in authorship: but he has further permitted the maps which he published in the two volumes of Burckhardt's Travels, and in the second volume of Mr. Walpole's collection, to be used in the construction of the geographical delineation, which accompanies the present volume. The only material point in which this map differs from those authorities, is in the position of a few points, in the southern part of Syria, the latitude and longitude of which have been communicated since the publication of Burckhardt's Syria, by the Earl of Belmore and Captain Corry, of the Royal Navy, who made the observations.

To these gentlemen, therefore, the authors have to express their obligations, as well as to H. W. Beechey and John Rennie, Esquires, who have kindly furnished them with five original Sketches in Nubia.

London, July, 1823.

CONTENTS.

LETTER I.

Our party and the first object of interest described. Departure in a boat from Philæ. The crew characterised, including Hassan nicnamed the blue devil. Saracenic buildings in picturesque situations. Piles of stones on elevated places, to guide the caravans from the interior of Africa, &c. Supposed boundary between Egypt and Nubia. The different natives and their languages.

Arrive at Kalapsche. Inspect the temple. Description thereof. Unusual appearance of crocodiles in this part of the Nile. Are mistaken for physicians and induced to prescribe. Found the purple acassia. Peculiar manner of taking water fowl by swimming. Bathe. Belzoni bitten in the foot by a water lizard. Trickery of a native of Senaar.

Arrive near Koroskoff. Picturesque appearance of the islands and rocks in the Nile, in that vicinity. Visited by a messenger from Halleel Cashief, requesting presents. Refused. Stop at Offidena. The natives handsome and well made, but very dark. Arrive at Derry. Apply to Daoud and Halleel Cashief, sons of Hassan, he being at Dongola, for leave to open the temple at Ebsambal. The Nubian dance. Avarice and treachery of the crew. Pass Ibrim. A sad picture of ruins and desolation. Comparative limits of former travellers in these parts considered. Arrival at Ebsambal. Renewal of application to Daoud and Halleel. Interesting appearance of the Dongola caravan, with numbers of camels laden with provisions. Remarkable appearance of the Mockatem mountains; their pyramidal form and termination. Stop opposite the village of Farras. Fine ruins of a large Nubian city. Several remarkable temples with hieroglyphics. Greek and Roman ornaments. Instance of shyness in crocodiles. Kill a torpedo with daggers. Several cameleons taken; their versatile appearances and peculiar faculties of catching flies.

Arrive at Farras. Bargain with the servants of Hassan Cashief for asses and camels to visit the Second Cataract. Arrival thereat. Fresh instances of artifice displayed by the boatmen. Consequent determination to proceed on foot. Herds of the gazelle, a nimble animal resembling the deer. Survey and description of the Second Cataract. The great extent and velocity of " the rapids." Striking and contrasted beauty of the mountain scenery. The natives' great dread of the dark. Difficulties of crossing to Elpha. Disappointment in the supply of the animals bargained for at Farras. Mutinous and desperate conduct of the boatmen. Serious interference of the natives repulsed by our firmness. Return to Ebsambal. Communication from Daoud Cashief not arrived. The crew here sued for pardon, pleading the custom of such demands upon strangers. Visit to, and description of a small temple excavated in the mountain opposite Ebsambal; curious Greek paintings, &c. Gratifying arrival of a message from Daoud Cashief at Derry to ascertain our identity as the favoured English for whom Hassan Cashief had promised to open the temple. Deceptive conduct of two natives in the promised introduction to a temple in the mountains. The crew draw their daggers on our servants; severe reproof of their sanguinary conduct, and our lives threatened in revenge Daoud and Halleel arrive; their persons described. Partake of refreshment. Give presents to the two Cashiefs. Halleel offended; sulky and inexorable at not having a gun amongst his portion similar to Daoud's. A sheep killed by Daoud to regale us, who apologises for his brother's absence and indiscretion. Artful scheme of Halleel to obtain more presents. Halleel perseveres for a gun. Gave him one of ours as a peace-offering. The Farras man, who threatened us at Elpha, suddenly annoys us. Procure his reprimand from the Cashiefs. Agree on terms for clearing the access to the temple, and proceed thither with fifty men. The exterior of the temple and its situation, enveloped in sand, described. Obstacles to our progress. Selfish song of the men. Their indolence. Contract with the cashiefs for the completion of the work. One hundred men employed. Boat's crew renew their entreaties for forgiveness. Consequent reconciliation. They work badly, and exact half the agreed terms. Despair of success. Encourage them to proceed. Complain to the Cashiefs, who promise more men. Retire disappointed to our boats. Renew our labours with fifty men only, and those idle. None of the leaders except Mouchmarr, an Arab, an elderly servant of the cashiefs present, who designated his masters as robbers, and the whole of the tribe of the Barbarins as thieves. Daoud arrives. Complain of the laziness of the men. Increased exertion promised. Remainder of the terms insisted on. Persist in a refusal. Great discontent excited thereby. Meanness of Halleel in begging Mr. Salt's pipe, the janissary's silk waistcoat, and our Greek servant's sabre, &c. All refused. Another unsuccessful attempt to get presents, by one of the chiefs, sanctioned by the cashiefs. Hassan excites us to return to Philæ to repair the boat, asserting it to be leaky; steadfastly decline till the accomplishment of our task. First day of the moon, Ramadan, or Turkish fast; total abstinence from food. Halleel's third fruitless application for Mr. S.'s pipe. His anger and abrupt departure. Farewell visit to Daoud's tent, announcing our intention of persevering to gain access to the temple. His dissuasion therefrom. Promise to apprise him in due time to share the gold, his anticipated treasure; his tacit consent. Enjoin good conduct to the crew but proceed without them to the temple. Strip, six in number, and commence, determined by our own labour to affect this Herculean task. Make rapid progress. Joined and assisted by the astonished crew. Personal inconveniences from our toils. Encourage our men. Retire to our boat gratified at the successful prospect. Unexpected visit in the night from Daoud. Exchange presents, and receive assurances of his favour and early assistance.

Vigorously proceed for our object under excessive heat. Crew refuse to work. Persevere and make great progress without them. Visited, while at work, by Halleel. Desperate affray between our janissary and Hassan. To our great joy Halleel suddenly disappears. Further artifices of the men. The Darfur caravan passes, with four thousand camels laden with gum, ivory, and ostrich feathers, on its way to Cairo. Extraordinary exactions upon them by the Mamelukes at Dongola. Description of the Jelabs conducting the caravan.

Re-commence with encreased strength, having sixty-four men. Present from Daoud of Nubian clothes, &c. His fruitless attempt to beg a pipe for his master. Renew our labours. Pleasing discovery of a seated statue, in a mutilated state, near the door. Unfinished and discouraging appearances of the exterior on further progress. Numbers of labourers offer their assistance. Retire in consequence to avoid disputes, leaving tickets for thirty only with old Mouchmarr. His infamous breach of trust in purloining ten of them. Violent quarrel among two parties for preference. Redouble our efforts, with twenty men, but only three instruments. The form thereof delineated. Observe the tracks of snakes and other reptiles on the sand. Sudden appearance of forty armed men. Mouchmarr and his party instantly fly to the mountains. Their deception and artful attempt to levy contributions. After their departure discover that they were Mahommed and Ali Cashiefs with their forces, who were engaged in war of extermination with Daoud and Halleel. Ridiculous return of Mouchmarr, with his matchlock and a few of the Ebsambal people; relates his account of the warfare. Find that Mahommed and Ali intercept our supplies.

Crew insolently withhold our ludri for their own use. Forcibly repossess ourselves thereof. About fifty men employed; annoyed by their skulking and idleness. Troublesome application of immense numbers of men. Decline their assistance, and they carry off the implements and threaten our crew. Aided by the assistance of twenty-three persons, proceed to our employment. Arrival of a Mameluke from Dongola, reporting the misery prevailing there. Half of the supplies of bread we had paid for withheld. Exorbitant increase of the price of provisions. Set to work with only two assistants and the crew. Animating song of a workman to his fellow-labourers. A spy from Daoud arrives, dissuading the men from their work. Falsely reports that the Grand Seignior had superseded the Pashaw in his government at Cairo; treat him with derision. Mouchmarr states his prohibition from supplying us with bread, or farther assistance, and takes his leave. Pursue our operations with only our sailors and Mameluke. An Ebsambal man comes to offer supplies. Refuse all assistance.

Encourage our crew for their encreased exertions. Sailors next day ask leave to go to Ebsambal to get bread. Hassan steals our doura; dispossess him of it. A milkman re-supplies us by stealth; a real luxury. The reis appears with a present of spirits distilled from dates, from the wife of Daoud. Decline the present and pay for it. Thermometer 112 Fahrenheit in the shade. Cheering indications of a door. Former apprehensions from unfinished appearances now cleared up. Hassan impudently demands pay for the crew. Mameluke departs on a raft for Cairo. Hassan sends to the cashief to apprize him of our progress. Resume our labours with the crew and two strangers, and at sunset come to the corner of the door. Sailors exult, with cries of backsheeish, and redouble their efforts in the prospect of our promised reward. Sailors beg our cook's waistcoat and the Greek's gown. Proceed to work without the crew, at moonlight, who load us with abuse; desire us to quit the boat, and threaten to leave us. Belzoni frightens them. Their abject homage on his appearance; bring up all our arms and ammunition. Hassan threatens to murder the janissary. At work by candle-light. The crew, all armed and dressed in full costume, peremptorily repeat their demands, with savage imprecations and gestures. Try to appease them; meanwhile the janissary squeezes himself through a hole and enters the temple; discovered by the crew, who now strip and work with alacrity. Hassan discloses to our cook their lawless power. Attain our primary object, and enter the temple. Obtain some statues, sphinxes, &c. of calcareous stone. Ebsambal peasants astonished at our success; anticipate the convenience of the temple as a place of retreat from the Bedouins. Contract with Hassan for bread and meat. Take internal and external dimensions of the temple. Receive a supply of provisions of one-third more than their worth. Effect the shipment of the statues and distribute forty piastres, the promised backsheeish. The splendid exterior of the temple described. Four beautiful colossal figures, above sixty feet high, sculptured in the best style of Egyptian art, and in the highest perfection. The interior consists of fourteen capacious apartments. Its stupendous and magnificent embellishments, its paintings, its sculpture, and its numerous valuable specimens of antiquity. Extreme heat of the temple, similar to the feeling and effect of the hottest vapour-bath. Visit a smaller temple, like the former, cut out of the rock. Description of it. Its colossal and other statues, some of upwards of twenty-five feet high; small female figures ornamenting the front. Its interior, consisting of three principal apartments, its antique sculpture, its ornamented walls, and other objects of exquisite beauty and interest. Start on our return. Mahommed and Ali Cashief, with their predatory band, hail us and inquire as to the money found in the temple. Call on Daoud. Another instance of his guilty duplicity. He gives us provisions. Promises to keep the temple open for Mr. Salt. Arrive at Derry. Visit, with candles, another temple cut out of the rock; its ruinous state, and dismal appearance described. A visit from Halleel, with presents. He is disappointed in expected requital.

Visit the temple at Armada, in the desert, opposite to Derry. Description thereof. In the interior are modern Greek paintings and ancient Egyptian figures. Arrive at Sabour and inspect its temple; the edifice and statues much dilapidated. Desperate conduct of Hassan, who attempts to stab Belzoni. Captain Irby wounded in the effort to disarm him. The reis and one of the crew quit the boat. Hassan returns next day, wanting us to re-land the statues and leave them behind. Admonish and threaten to bring him to account at Assuan. Mameluke rejoins us, having been robbed of his money and raft. Proceed to the small unfinished temple at Offideña. Greek or Roman figures, in entaglio, found on the walls of the neighbouring ruins. Importuned by the natives for backsheeish. Bid for a statue previously noticed, but without effect. Visit the temple of Dekki, also in an unfinished state. Traces of the artist's skill in the interior (in basso-relievo); the entrance covered with Greek commemorative inscriptions. Visit the temple of Garbe Girshe, excavated in the rock. Natives insolent, and of a murderous character. The building much mutilated, and the sculpture bad and heavy.

Inspect the temple of Garbe Dendour, built in front of a rock; small and unfinished. Pass Garbe Merie. See the ruins of a temple, with hieroglyphics. Land at Kalapsche. Proceed to the temple. The assembled natives, armed with daggers, refuse our entrance. Ask for money. Rashness of the janissary fatal to our object, nearly so to him; rescue him, and return to our boat under showers of abuse and stones. Fired over their heads to shew our forbearance. One villain frightened, by a pointed musket from his attempt to plunder the boat in our absence. Indifference of the crew. Fidelity of the Greek servant. Insolent self-will of guides and interpreters. Repass the gates of Nubia. The waters of the Nile very high. The crew ask for backsheeish for passing the rapids. Driven by the current past the two temples of Teffa. One dedicated to Isis now used as a cow-house, the other unfinished.

CONTENTS.

Visit Hindaw and various ruins in that quarter; extensive wall; stone quarries; Roman and Greek commemorative inscriptions and sculpture. Inspect the temple of Daboude, altogether unfinished, two handsome moorelithe cases of red granite adorn the sanctuary. Hassan, the Philæ murderer, deserts the boat on our approach there. Arrive at Philæ. First Cataract. Description of the edifices; their style and sculptures. French inscriptions on a pylon, indicative of the extent of their Egyptian conquests under Buonaparte. Unique symbol of the elephant in the portico of the temple. Remarkable imperfection in sculpture, in figures of Isis, on this island. Observations upon the natives of Nubia; their unprincipled habits; the country in general. Frequent appearance of ancient towns buried in rubbish. Nubians a distinct race from the Arabs; their extraordinary superstition. Curious mode of smoking. Strange manner of killing personal vermin. Their habits and costume. Their manufacture. Platters made from the date tree.

Bargain with the suspicious crew. Pay exacted in advance for conveyance down the Cataract. Receive a pilot and eight additional hands to conduct us down. Hassan disappears, dreading our report of him to the Aga. A two hours' passage down the rapids. Scenery wild and romantic. The boat strikes against the rocks. Self-imagined courage of the crew. Reach Assuan, the ancient Syene. Visit the ancient granite quarries. Examine the column there, curiously inscribed in Latin. Their ancient method of cutting pure masses of stone. The ancient road paved with granite. English translation of the inscription. Historical remarks on the origin of the quarries. Examine the mummy-cases and boxes of sacred Egyptian emblems. Curious specimens of carved-work. Assuan uninteresting, a dirty and ill-built place. The Aga visits us. Complain to him of the crew. He pronounces them notorious rascals. Their previous desertion. Visit Elephantina, celebrated by Denon. Its pleasing and luxurious appearance. Ruins of the ancient town and several temples. Engage a boat to Thebes. Inspect Koum Ombo, the ancient Ombos. Remains of two temples on a promontory of the Nile's eastern shore; description thereof; peculiar structure of one of them. Barren appearance of the neighbouring country. Observe the large fertile island of Mansouria, and a smaller one in the middle of the Nile. Saracenic ruins of brick-work. Traces of ruins of the ancient town. Extensive view from the promontory. Djibel Selsilis, mountains of the Chain; tradition thereof. Several small temples, excavated from the rocks, of calcareous stone. Statues in alto-relievo. Tasteful specimen of architecture. Numerous extensive quarries. Reach Edfoo, the ancient Appolinopolis Magna; its large temple; prodigiously high pylon. Sculptures and antiquities described. Striking contrast with the paltry modern town of Edfoo. Recent and interesting discoveries of emeralds by a French mineralogist. Stop at El Cab, the ancient

Eleethias, splendid ruins. Curious antiquities of agricultural routine and other miscellaneous objects of interest in entaglio. Another small temple. Reach Esneh, the ancient *Latapolis*. A magnificent Egyptian temple, supported by twenty-four columns, with nine capitals, obscured by modern houses. Ruins of a small temple on the site *Aphroditopolis*. Another on the opposite side of the river. Erment, the ancient *Hermontis*. Ruins of four temples visible. Highly finished symbolic representations in basso-relievo. Remains of an ancient basin and Nilometer. Arrive at Luxor, part of the ancient Thebes. Lodge in one of the temples. Magnificent obelisks. Similarity of the hieroglyphics to those at Ebsambal, and to those of Cleopatra's Needles at Alexandria.

Visit the tombs of Gourna. Deceptive practices of the natives in the concealment of the antiquities. Their party attachments to French and English travellers. Description of the tombs, and their rich and exquisite sculpture. Account of the mummy pits. the subjects therein deposited. Inspect a newly discovered magnificent tomb; its fine paintings, in fresco, and other curiosities. The valley of Gourna, and its antiquities described. Visit a temple near Medinet-Aboo. Return to Luxor. Examine the statues and temples at Memnonium. Farewell visit to the tomb of the kings. Scorpions taken by our guide. Grand view from the Lybian mountains. Remarks upon ancient Thebes.

Departure for Cairo. Stop at Tentyra; swim the canal, and revisit the temple of Isis. Astronomical table, and complete lunar system on the ceilings delineated. Egyptian mode of calculating the year. Stop at Siout. Visit Dr. Marouky and Mr. Brine. Stop at Houarti, the village of our crew; infatuation of the women to procure them families. Ruins of a city in the Mockatem. A range of catacombs and temples in the rocks. Arrive at Cairo. Mr. Salt's urbane reception of us. Shave our beards and resume our European costume. Proceed with Mr. Salt, Col. Stratton, and Mr. Fuller, to the Pyramids. Account of the Great Sphinx, &c. Return to Grand Cairo, a mean, ill-built city. Description of its wretched inhabitants. Its citadel, government, and customs. Account of the massacre of the Mamelukes. The varied appearances of the Nile, and Egypt generally. Visit the fertile island of Rhoda. Egyptian agriculture. Boulack, the port of Cairo, and its extensive commerce. Contemplate our departure. Renew our supplies of provisions, clothes, and arms. Our expenditure. Letters of introduction from Mr. Salt. Interesting tomb at Radimore, covered with beautiful paintings.

LETTER II.

DEPARTURE from Cairo. An Arab, with three camels, conducts us to Jaffa. Pass the obelisk of Mataria, the site of Heliopolis, and other ruins. Our route through the desert. Stop at a village;

proceed again at night. Howling of wild beasts. Joined at a village by a man with a loaded camel. Skirt the desert, and pass richly cultivated plains. Selahieh, the last village on the borders of Egypt. Recruit with water and provisions for the desert. Joined by eight persons on asses, on their pilgrimage to Mecca. Leave the village. Picturesque appearance of the desert. Contrast thereof with Nubia. Quails, partridges, &c. in abundance. Pass the lake Damietta and ruins of Pelusium. Desert more hilly. Many carcasses and detached bones of camels and asses, and some wells of indifferent water. Make bread. Approach a bay on the coast. Meet a small armed caravan. Backsheeish demanded and refused. Pass over a plain covered with salt. At breakfast a stranger demands backsheeish. A party of Tarabeen Arabs levy a contribution on our guides. Our arms preserve us from a like exaction. Arrive at El-Arish. Description thereof. Quit it by night, followed by an Arab, whom we request to leave us. Pass some wells, a Sheik's tomb, a Mahommedan burial place, flocks of sheep and goats, peasants and laden camels. Our arms protect us. Pass ruins, and arrive at Haneunis on the confines of Syria. Description of it and its inhabitants. Our route from Cairo. Proceed through a barren country to Esdier. Frantic grief of a woman, who had quarrelled with her husband. Proceed from Esdier to Gaza through richly cultivated plains, and thence through groves of olives and open country. Pass several villages. Arrive at Asdoud. Description of a Turkish khan. Curiosity of the natives of Asdoud. Suppose us to be doctors. Give them some balsam of Mecca. They beg some of our hair to burn, refuse it and laugh at their superstition. Their gratitude. Reasons for not proceeding from Gaza to Jaffa by way of Ashkelon. Quit Asdoud. The country open and little cultivated. Pass ruins of an aqueduct; well of poisonous water. Also Yabne the ancient Jamnia. Cross the river El Rubin. Description of Sheikh Rubin's tomb. Proceed over sand hills and along the sea beach towards Jaffa. See Ramla and Loudd on our right.

Arrive at Jaffa, the ancient Joppa. Ludicrous appearance of the British representative. His conduct. Description of Jaffa. Generosity of the Aga. Anecdote of him. Leave Jaffa, equipped, in an Arab suit of clothing, for the approaching winter. Skirt the sea-beach. Pass Arsouf, the ancient Appollonias, on the left, and arrive at Cesarea. Description thereof. Arrive at Tortura, the ancient Dora, and proceed to Athlite. Situation and description of Athlite. Pass the foot of Mount Carmel, and arrive at Caiffa, the ancient Hepha. Ascend Mount Carmel. Description of the convent. Elijah's cave, &c. Beautiful view of Acre, &c. Descend to Caiffa. Cross the brook Kishon and the river Belus. Arrive at Acre. Lodge in the convent. Description of Acre. A religious festival. Procure a firman from the Pashaw. Quit Acre, and pass on to Zib. Applied to for medical aid. Give them balsam of Mecca. Gratitude of the Sheikh's son. Leave Zib, and pass over Cape Blanco. Visit some ruins, and ascend the ladder of the Tyrians, a picturesque spot. Descend the ladder and arrive at Tsour, the ancient Tyre. Awful fulfilment of Scripture prophecies against Tyre, manifested in its present state.

Cross the Kasmia. Explore the ruins of several large cities. Cross several dry torrents and a river; its banks enriched with flowers. Pass the ruins of a city, and arrive at Saida, the ancient Sidon. Its immediate neighbourhood well cultivated. Visit the convent Mar Elias Alzo, the usual residence of Lady Hester Stanhope, with letters for her. Her ladyship absent, and residing at castle Jeba, a more elevated spot in the mountains. Forward her letters with a note. Her answer, requesting us to visit her convent. Her costume and amiable generosity. Description of Saida. Pass the ruins of an ancient town, and many sarcophagi, over the promontory of Bayruth. Descend through plantations of figs and mulberries to Bayruth, the ancient Berytus. Cross several rivers, and over a rocky promontory. Description of the nahr el Kelb. Sepulchre of St. George. Superstition of the fishermen. Cross the nahr Ibrahim, and arrive at Gebail, or Gibyle. Description thereof. Pass Batroun, the castle of Temseida, and arrive at Tripoli. Situation and description. Visit the English Consul. Visit the Cedars of Labanon and Baalbec, accompanied by Signior Guiseppe Mazoliere. Description of the road.

Arrive at Eden, and at the Cedars. Situation and description of the Cedars. Scriptural references to this country. The village of Eden identified with the garden of God. Ascend to the crest of Lebanon. Extensive view of the hills at its south-east foot, Baalbec in the distance, and the sea to the westward. Description of the Bekaa Mathooalis. Descent from Lebanon, excessively steep and rugged. Dismount, and walk the horses down to the valley. Proceed over some rugged hills covered with shrubs, to Yead. Arrive at Baalbec. Imposing grandeur of the ruins. Quit Baalbec for Tripoli. Rainy weather; stop at a village for the night; meet some peasants returning after an ineffectual attempt to cross the Lebanon; the weather very bad, with much snow. Shelter in a cave filled with peasants at the foot of the mountain. Remove to a larger one, more exposed, and kindle a fire for the night. Next morning fine weather. Ascend the mountain. Fear of the peasants to proceed before us. Approaching the summit, the snow being deep, the horses fall. Reach the summit with much difficulty. The cold excessive. Descend through a great depth of snow to Eden. Our situation thought dangerous, and public prayers offered up for our safety. Return to Tripoli. Good quality of the Lebanon wine. Leave Tripoli for Latachia. Stop at a khan near the nahr el Bered.

Arrive at Tortosa oppotite Ruad island. Description thereof. The island of Ruad, the Arpad of scripture. Cross the nahr el

Mulk. Stop at the village where Monsieur Boutin was killed. The inhabitants refuse us shelter. Bivouack in the open air. Pass Jebilee and reach Latachia, the ancient Laodicea. Its situation and port described. Detained three days by the intrigues of the Arab conductor. Arrive at Candele. Difficulty of finding Lourdee. Its situation close by the highest pinnacle of Mount Cassius. Descend the north side of the mountains. Scenery woody and wild.

Reach the banks of the Orontes near the site of the city and groves of Daphne. Description thereof. Follow the banks of the river; beautiful scenery. River meanders between high hills, and the road along precipices in the rocks. Enter the plain of Suadeah. Difficulty in finding Suadeah. Guided by a peasant across the river, up to the horses bellies. Suadeah a straggling village. Civility and generosity of the Soubash. Proceed towards Antioch. Rainy weather. Arrival at some cottages; refused admittance at three of them; our hospitable reception at a fourth; present the mistress with a gold double Napoleon. Reasons for giving it.

Arrive at Antioch—its description. Arrive at Gesir Adid, and cross the Orontes. The lake Aggi Dengis on the left. Arrive at Bourkee, the site of a Roman town. The sepulchres described. Pass several sites of ancient towns, castles, &c.; proceed over the rocky hills into the plain of Alaks. Stop at Tourneen. Arrive at Aleppo. Good fortune in the adoption of our own route, though advised by Sheik Ibrahim to take a northerly one. Arrive at Mr. Barker's, the consul-general. Find Mr. Bankes there. Wait for the Sukne caravan. Amusement during our stay at Aleppo. Idea of visiting Bagdad frustrated by a letter received by the Dutch consul. Suckne caravan arrives; dissuaded from going with it, and urged to proceed by way of Hamah and Homs.

LETTER III.

Remarks on Aleppo; its situation and buildings; decorations of the houses by Persian artists; carved-work doors, &c. Resemblance of the city to that of Antioch; neatness of the butchers' shops; its society and manners. Depart for Hamah, our good host accompanying us for two hours outside the town; his kind solicitude in our behalf; furnishes us with letters for advice and assistance to Selim, the governor's secretary at Hamah; and to Scander, secretary to the Motsellim of Homs, also to Hadgi Hassan, an old Turk, at that place, a great dealer with the Arabs. Receive also Mr. Barker's letters to the Saraffs of the Pashaw of Damascus to secure horses; also, to Acre, Cyprus, and Smyrna; to Sir Robert and Lady Liston, and other persons of consideration, at Constantinople; aids us also with printed documents, a map, and money. Stay for the night at the khan Touman, a spacious lodging, but crowded with caravans for Damascus and Latachia. Proceed next day over naked plains in company with

CONTENTS. xvii

them; stop at Sermein. View of mount Cassius covered with snow on the right. Join a caravan bound to Hamah and Damascus, and proceed therewith. Pass a ruinous Turkish fortress, enclosing a village. Custom of such circumvallations, on the skirts of the desert accounted for. Meet an extensive caravan, part of the hadj, or Mecca pilgrimage, returning from Damascus; an interesting sight. The green flag (the prophet's banner) flying; the animals, a few camels, but chiefly horses and mules, all with bells; among them, the tackterwans, a curious vehicle peculiar to the east; description thereof.

Pass many divisions of the hadj; the animals laden with the pilgrims' private speculations. History of these customs. Commercial quickness of the peasants. Observe some Roman ruins and sarcophagi. Pass the night in a very good khan. Proceed in the morning; Lebanon, a mass of snow, before us. Mount Cassius shut in by the northern extremity of the Ansarian mountains. Observe sites of many ancient towns, tanks, sarcophagi, &c. much dilapidated; an open country abounding with gazelles and game. Sleep at khan Shekune, a good khan, but crowded from the hadj. Pursue our route over the plains, parallel with the range of the Ansarian mountains. Lebanon and Antioch in sight. Descend gradually into a delightful vale, and arrive at Hamah, on the west-bank of the Orontes, a winding stream; its banks fertile and picturesque. Take up our quarters in a khan; comparative description of these buildings, in the towns and on the road side; their terms of accommodation and arrangements; also, the mode of travellers subsisting themselves. At Hamah, receive a letter from Mr. Barker, by an express messenger from Aleppo, with a firman from the Grand Seignior, empowering us to go with four servants through Syria and Cyprus, the island of the Archipelago, &c. &c. to Constantinople, and insuring us all requisite assistance and protection. Melancholy scene of traffic in female slaves; eleven of them brought from Georgia; their charming appearance; wretched diet; mode of conveyance, and unnatural treatment; witness a disgusting bargaining for one about fifteen, by a rich old Turk; agonizing grief of one of the ill-fated girls, anticipating a separation from her sister and companions; their destination, Damascus. Comparative accuracy of Bruce and Volney, as to the Georgian and Circassian women. Negociate with the Arabs to reach Palmyra; our Maltese interpreter meets with Pierre, in the employ of Lady H. Stanhope, and the bearer of a present to Narsah, the chief of the Annasee Arabs; Pierre professes his acquaintance with the Arab chiefs, his attendance upon lady Hester to Palmyra, and his negociation for Mr. Bankes, who was so injuriously treated. Embarrassed by the absence of Selim and Scander, at Damascus; resolution to wait Selim's return. Discuss with Pierre, the customary charges to travellers; his trickery and suspected treachery. A Christian from Homs offers his services; doubt his sincerity, but decide to

b

avail ourselves of them, and manœuvre with Pierre; weather-bound three days.

Pierre visits us, surprised at our not having set out for Damascus. Introduces five Arabs to bargain for conduct to Palmyra; Sheikh Salee (their chief) nephew to Mahannah, a lad of fourteen; demands three thousand piastres for convoy; treat them all with derision; they menace us with robbery; lower their terms to eight hundred, and quit us; send them an offer of six hundred, including the hire of camels; *payment on our safe return to Hamah.* Agree with us, only ' for the love of Malaka," or queen, (their title of Lady Hester Stanhope, from her liberal payment.) Send to the Aga to ratify the treaty in writing; his conditional responsibility; resist their importunities for money in advance, and depart from Hamah at day-break. Pierre follows. Cross the Orontes near the villages of Rastan, and the ancient Arethusia; description of them.

Arrive at Homs. Suspicious letter from the Sheikh Narsah to obtain money; penetrate the *trick*, resolve to walk, *and call on Narsah.* Trifling of the guide; he arrives, after three days, from his chief Mahannah with three camels. Further detention for the Motsellim's ratification of our bargain. Access to the governor prevented from the recent decapitation of the pashaw. Arbitrary proceedings of the Turkish government against suspected individuals. Make partial payment to Hadji Hassan under stipulations. The Motsellim's surprise at our confidence of safety with the Arabs. Proceed with our three camels and conductors. Our finesse to prevent probable robbery on the way.

Arrive at a Bedouin camp, and welcomed by both men and women; stop next day at another Arab camp, and equally well-received. Pursue our journey, at an early hour, in an easterly direction, but uncertain track. The Arab's economy of his time on a journey. His rapid collection of fuel to prepare refreshment. Dispatch our breakfast, in ten minutes, and proceed; quench our thirst at a neighbouring rock, under the impatience of our guides; their affected vigilance and courage. Approach the camp of Mahanna, in a valley. Observe children running down young partridges with dogs. A wild boar hunt; escape of the formidable animal with a single wound. Approach the Sheikh's tent. Old Mahannah, his two sons Sheikh's Narsah and Hamed, with chiefs from various camps assembled. Narsah's unmoved reception of us; accounted for his subsequent address. Enquires the reason of English curiosity to see Palmyra; supposes it the search for gold. Promise him the half of our chance.

Arrival of further Arab guests. Etiquette of the chiefs, and mode of salutation. Narsah questions us about Buonaparté, and the occupation of France by the allied troops. Recognize Sheikh Hamody, the person who exacted upon, and confined Mr. Bankes. His consciousness of impropriety. Regaled with roasted partridges, and bread dipped in butter and honey.

Amusing customs while eating. Evening devotions, and curious mode of ablution. Narsah's elaborate address to his circle about some land. Its soporific effects on us. Refused permission to depart in the morning, and desired by the chief to join an immense assemblage of Arabs at a breakfast banquet of rice and camel's flesh. Our portion sent to us in a separate tent, conjectures as to the course of such arrangement. Order and decorum of the feast; mode of distributing the remains to the people. Narsah summons us to his select circle. His whimsical queries as to our customary diet. Mahannah makes signs to us for money. Exchange our camels for dromedaries, and take our leave, each having his conductor mounted behind him. One of Narsah's men accompanies us as a guard on a white dromedary finely decorated. Dreadful jolting of the animals. Sleep in an Arab tent, we proceed on our destination, and arrive there in the afternoon.

Imposing effect of the ruins of Palmyra, as seen from the valley of the tombs. Picturesque beauty, and cheering contrast of the scene with the lonely desert. Examine the antiquities minutely. Survey the Arab village of Tadmor, and Temple of the Sun. Mutilated state of its chief ornaments. Our disappointment in the inferiority of the architecture and sculpture of Palmyra. Description thereof. The tombs more interesting; their merits, as works of art, compared with those of Egypt. Much salt in the vicinity, a lucrative branch of commerce. Return from Palmyra and sleep, as usual, in an Arab tent. Pusillanimity of our Arab convoy. Pass parties of Mahannah's people, armed with spears, &c. Their inquisitiveness. Reach his camp at night. Mahannah deprives our poor Arabs of the salt they had purchased at Palmyra. Scheme of Narsah to obtain a new dress from us. Declares his intention to write a letter to the KING OF ENGLAND, and charges us with one to "his dear friend Lady Hester." Their various titles, and uniform veneration of that Lady. Difficulty of obtaining a draught of water at starting. Pursue our course and get benighted. Bivouack in the open air. Timidity of the Arabs to make a fire. Lay down between the camels. Deprived of sleep from the intensity of the cold. Proceed at day break; interesting sight of the removal of a camp. Get a good breakfast, off lentiles and bread, at a small camp. Novel appearance of the ground furrowed up by wild boars.

Arrive at Homs. Pleased with our guides, give them voluntary backsheeish, and charge them with the present of a turban to the Sheikh of Tadmor. General opinions of the Arabs. Remarks on their singular hospitality, habits, manners, customs, and comparative happiness. Rest a short time at Homs; proceed through a mountainous country, rounding the point of Anti-Lebanon, and in three days view the plain of Damascus. Arrive at the convent of Terra Santa in that city. Luxuriant fertility of its vicinity and surrounding country. Sensible comforts of a bed, after thirty-eight days' privation thereof. Visit the place of the vision of St. Paul. The house of Ananias, &c. Shum, or Shem, the ancient name of Damascus. Scriptural references as to this spot, &c. Friendly offices of the Pashaw's Physician, procured by Mr. Barker's letter. Obtain another firman for the Pashalic, and a letter to the Governor of Jerusalem, for guides to Mount Sinai. Meditated route to Constantinople. Find a letter left by Mr. Bankes; with information about the ancient Abilah, his hopes of our joining him at this place. Our mutual disappointment, &c.

LETTER IV.

DEPART from Damascus, follow the road to Jacob's bridge on the Jordan, between the lakes Houle and Tiberias. Stop at the khan of the village of Sasa. Pass through a rich plain to the westward for Panias. Traces of an ancient paved way, supposed the Roman road leading to Cæsarea Philippi. Djebail Sheikh (Anti-Lebanon) on our right, a deep snow, almost impassable; a fine plain at the foot of Djebail Sheikh. A conspicuous tomb in the valley. The source of the Jordan considered. A singularly beautiful lake, called by Arrowsmith "Birket-el-Ram," by Josephus "Phiala." Further authorities as to the source of the Jordan. Fine coup d'œil. A hill to the S. W., the great Saracenic castle near Panias. The plain of Jordan, &c. A verdant country. Remarkable difference of climate from that of Damascus, &c. Cheering indications of spring. Enter Panias. Picturesque course of the river. Ruins of ancient walls on its banks. Town and environs described. Opinions as to the ancient Panias, afterwards Cæsarea Philippi; its extent, and other antiquities. Take the diversion of shooting.

Leave Panias, directed to follow the Jordan to lake Houle. Explore various fords. Cross the Jordan. Nearly lose the horses in a swamp. Reach the road to Safot at the foot of the hills. Intended day's journey shortened by the past difficulties. Stop at a village near lake Houle. Ascend an acclivity to Safot; pass some Roman ruins in a village. Grand and luxuriant prospect of the lakes of Houle and Tiberias, with part of the plain of the Jordan. Description of Safot, its castle, and fine approaches. Proceed towards Tiberias (the ancient Japhet). Pass the night at an old ruined khan, near the village of Madjdala. Dreadfully bitten and marked by a red vermin. Disgusting prevalence of other personal vermin in this country. The natives deem it " the curse of God on them." Bugs numerous, here and in Egypt. Shrubby and romantic country. Pass a picturesque cliff, with numerous caves occupied by goatherds. Arrive at Tiberias. Description of the modern town, on the lake of Gennesaret; its

CONTENTS. xxi

mural enclosure and towers. Fine reliques of the ancient town; also of the famous hot (mineral) baths of Tiberias. Their extraordinary degree of heat; experiments therein. A Turkish bath, the resort of the Jews, and a Roman sepulchre, supposed by them to be the "tomb of Jacob." Remains of Vespasian's fortifications. Description of the lake Tiberias. "The miraculous draught of fishes," and other gospel allusions considered. Lodge in the church, under an Arab priest, "identified as the house of St. Peter." Exchange the sacred roof, for the open court, on account of the fleas. Proverbial saying of the natives upon these insects. The dearth of fish accounted for. Passage of the Jordan through the lake, discernible.

Arrival of Mr. Bankes from a tour of the Haouran. Consent to accompany him on his projected tour of the Dead Sea. Mr. Bankes makes a short visit to Safot. Inspect Om Keis, (the ancient Gadara) in the country of "the Gadarenes." Leave Tiberias. Pass the site of the ancient Tanichea; ruins of a Roman bridge on the Jordan, and the village of Semmack. Cross the river Yarmack, or Hieromax. Ancient site of "Amatha." Kindly received by the sheikh of the natives inhabiting the ancient sepulchres. Lodged in a large tomb. Arrangements and description of its occupants. Scriptural recollections and identity of this spot, the Necropolis; its sepulchral and other antiquities described.

Visit the hot springs in the plain of the Yarmack. Ruins of a Roman bath at the source. Find sick persons thereat. Return to Tiberias. Occupied four days in measuring the circuit of the ancient city, and in making researches. Mr. Bankes discovers and makes a plan of a curious ancient fortification. Elaborate task of taking the measurements. Its appellation by the natives. Historical remarks thereon. Roman ruins in the village of Erbed at the foot of Mount Beatitude. Old convents of singular construction, between the village of Majdil, the ancient Magdala, and the fortress Callah-el-Hammam. Ruins of six Roman baths, of luke-warm mineral water, in the vicinity. Their form, peculiar construction, and surrounding scenery described. Swim to the Scorpion rock. Leave Tiberias. Pass an extensive aqueduct, discover traces of the walls of Tarichea. Circuitous course of the Jordan here. Pass a khan near a bridge of arches upon arches. Observe a Roman mile-stone. Pavement of the ancient road again perceivable. A sarcophagus on an eminence. A great number of Arab camps on our way. Arrive at Bysan, supposed the Bethshan of Scripture. Sacred memoranda thereof. Inspect the ruins of this great city. Its famous theatre, now filled with weeds, a primary object of interest. Remarks of Vitruvius on its peculiar structure; make a plan thereof. Discover twenty-four skulls, and other human remains in a concealed vomitory. A viper entwined in one of them. Examine the reliques of the tombs, near the Acropolis, and remaining sarcophagi. A fine Roman bridge, and near it, the paved way to the antient Ptolemais, now Acre. A dilapidated bridge. Prostrate columns of Corinthian architecture. Ruins of many subterranean graneries, and other antique remains in the suburbs. Character of the people.

Leave Bysan. Take guides for fording the Jordan. A tomb called " Sheikh Daoud," near the ford. Increased swiftness of the river here. Bathe, and ascertain its breadth. Visit " Tabathat Fahkil." Ruins of a modern village, of an ancient city, near it. Of a fine temple by the water-side, and of columns of the Doric, Ionic, and Corinthian orders. Excavations in the hills, the probable Necropolis, and the spot where Elijah was fed by the ravens. Sleep at Hallawye. Arrive at the village Cafringee in the valley of Adjeloun. Traces of a Roman town. Accompanied by the principal Sheikh to the Callah-el-Rubbat. Visit an extensive natural cave, supposed the " cave of Mackkedah." Scriptural reference thereto. Description of the castle and its antiquities. Find a Roman mile-stone in an old mosque, with fragments of Roman sculpture. Village of Eugen, Roman tombs, and sarcophagi. Extreme beauty of the country. The arbutus and other curious trees. Further traces of the Roman road. More Roman mile-stones. Village of Souf, its scenery and antiquities. Visit the ruins of Djerash. Character of the natives of Souf. Revisit Djerash escorted by the sheikh of Souf and ten armed men. Their officiousness and self-importance. Return to Souf. The natives, affected terror of the dytchmaan (enemy). Arrival of Mr. Bankes' interpreter and a soldier, with a young prince of the Benesuckher Arabs, and ten men armed and mounted. Ebn Fayes (the prince), attended by his mace bearer. Description of the party and their martial manœuvres. Negociations with them for guidance and protection on our intended route. Their refusal to go beyond Kerek, and reasons thereof. Objects of our research as connected with scripture history; conclude with the Arab guard, pay down the money, and proceed. Make further measurements and survey at Djerash. Precautions necessary in dealing with the Arabs. Pass the night at the village of Katty. The Arabs demand subsistance money. Repeat our labours among the antiquities of Djerash. Conducted to a camp of the Salhaan Arabs. Artifice of the conductors, to induce a present of one of our horses. The Benesuckhers refuse to go to Djerash. Dispatch our baggage to Katty, and proceed for Djerash. Pass a deserted village. Meditated interception of us by six Salhaans. Reinforce ourselves, and advance upon them with ridicule. Resume our operations at Djerash. Measuring, drawing, and copying incriptions. Mr. Bankes surprised at work, and robbed of his cap by an armed Arab. Great quarrel at Katty between the Benesuckhers and the villagers. The field abandoned by the former. Dishonesty, disertion of the Damascus soldier. Completion of task at Djerash. Description of its numerous splended ruins and antiquities, historical remarks thereon.

Depart for Szalt. Cross the Zerka. Pass the night at a camp

CONTENTS. xxiii

of the Salhaans. Menacing scheme of the Benesuckhers to impede our progress and extort money. The prince's prime minister, the chief rogue. The prince and his gang quit us for their own camp. Proceed to Szalt. Ruins of a large square cyclopean building in the valley Bayga. Pass some inclosed vineyards. Prospect of Szalt, and its luxuriant neighbourhood. Description of its choice fruits. Arrive, wet through. The people's reception and treatment of us. Find many Christians. Conducted to the house of one. Attempted extortion of " the minister." Dismiss the gang. Their efforts and threats to draw us to their camp. Our contempt of them. Insulted by the Mahommedan natives. Accompanied by the sheikh's son and five guards on our researches. Ruins of the village Athan, and sarcophagi in the rocks. Two old tombs at Gilhad Gilhood; adoption of one as a christian chapel. " The birth place of the prophet Elijah." Visit several ruined villages. Szalt identified as Machærus, where John the Baptist was beheaded. Conciliatory invitation from the Benesuckher prince to his camp. Our ulterior plans and determination. Quit Szalt amidst a great dispute among the people. Our interpreter found concealed and crying behind a door. Rejoined by the prime minister and two Benesuckhers; their attempt to mislead us aided by the Turkish natives. Discover the right road to Jerusalem, and proceed followed by the Arabs. View of the Dead Sea, Jericho and the plain of Jordan. The two men leave us; their supposed object. Divert our course towards the Jordan and quit " the minister." Reach its banks. Ancient tombs. Swim the river on horseback. Spoil all our papers. Misled by a labourer. Benighted and shelter in a shepherd's cave. Retrace our steps to Wady Zeit. Received by the peasants armed; mistaken. Procure a guide for Nablous. The Arabs reported to be in chace of us. Village of Bait Horage. Twenty-eight hours without food. Village of Kaffer Baiter. Old Roman tombs and tanks, dead bodies therein. Jacob's well. Nablous the ancient Sychem. Ruins of a large town, tank, and sheikh's tomb, on mount Gerizim. Visit Bethlethem and St. John's. Trick of the fire in the Holy Sepulchre at the Greek Easter. Departure with the pilgrims, the governor and an immense body of troops to the Jordan. The Procession described. Arrival at the camp near Jericho. Proceed to the Jordan. Pilgrims all bathing. Their various ceremonies described. Attended by two Arabs, bathe in the Dead Sea. Peculiar nature and effects of the water. Reach Jerusalem. Meet Lord and Lady Belmore. Serious dispute of the Friars in the Holy Sepulchre. Sepulchres called the tombs of the kings. The governor refuses permission to excavate. The Reverendissimo certifies our visit to all the sacred places at Jerusalem.

LETTER V.

Preliminary arrangements for leaving Jerusalem. Assume oriental names. Adapt our costume. Secrete our money in our belts, and depart, well armed, from Jerusalem at dusk. Party, eleven in number. Sleep at Bethlehem. Proceed for "Solomon's pools;" ascend the mountain of the Franks. The ruinous state of its walls and towers; military history thereof. View of the Dead Sea. Bethlehem, &c. Proceed by Harriatoon to the labyrinth; curiosity thereof. English names inscribed. Ruins of Tekoa, built by King Rehoboam. Track to Hebron. Pass Sipheer and its Roman sepulchral caves. Ruins of the house of the House of Abraham." Pass numerous vineyards, with antique watch-towers.

Arrive at Hebron. Hospitable reception. Description of the town and its inhabitants. Refused admission to the mosque and Tomb of Abraham. Description of the exterior. Manufactory of glass lamps. Introduction to the Jewish priest by the governour. Hospitality of the Jews, who offer letters of introduction. Visit the synagogue. Present the governour with a watch. His dissatisfaction. Contract for guides. Governour inspects our firmans, &c. Introduces our conductors. The law officers and authorities. The guides refuse to conduct us. Receive the money and watch. Depart by ourselves for Kerek. A messenger overtakes us. We re-contract and receive one Jellaheen Arab. Pass the ruins of Hagee, and two Roman tombs. Jellaheen camp of thirty tents, with harems for the women. An Arab tailor arrives; refusal, from fear, to conduct us to Wady Mousa. Agree for guides to Kerek; their avarice on the road; they leave us; they rejoin us. Delightful prospect of the Dead Sea. Pass an old Turkish ruin on a rock. Drink from a pool of green, stagnant water at El-Zowar, a man bathing therein. Enter the great plain at the end of the Dead Sea. Refresh ourselves with flour and water, and retire to rest. Disturbed by our guides in dread of the dytchmaan. Observe numerous hills and strata of salt. Mountainous margin of the Dead Sea, pass into a country of curious shrubbery. Botanical remarks thereon.

Arrive at the nahr el Hussan, or horse river. The Ghorneys hospitably entertain us; rufuse any compensation. Mistaken for soldiers of Mahommed Aga. Left them in a terrible scramble and dispute for money thrown amongst them. Great annoyance from horse flies, identified by the natives as those of the plague. The destruction of Sodom and Gomorrah. Attempt to cross the Hussan on horseback. Our horses lay down in the stream; dismount and walk down. Proceed under the mountains. See quantities of rich porphory, and various beautiful stone. Collect specimens thereof. Reach the south end of the Dead Sea, and its back-water. Pass the night in a ravine covered with the choicest odoriferous shrubs. Ascend a barren mountain; hailed by three men with a gun. Take a sketch of the fine view of the Dead Sea. Accosted roughly by the three men who remained with us. Surprised by five other armed men in ambuscade. They question us, and we proceed. Pass through a fertile country on the river Souf, Saffa. Observe the ancient mill-courses. The castle of Kerek appears. Ruins of the seraglio; a mosque of Meleh-e-daher. Approach to the fortress described. Dismount and enter. Curious construction of the town. Description of the castle and its Mahommedan architecture. A Christian church therein. Account of its supposed founder. Its paintings and sculpture. Sheikh Yousouf absent celebrating his recent nuptials. Kindly received by Abdel Khader, his son. Costume and habits of the women. Our horses and ourselves well fed, gratuitously. Meet with a great Arab traveller. His account of himself; he contrasts the privileges of this country with that of the Turks. Dine at a Turk's house on boiled mutton, without bread, a common practice, and its origin. Old Shiekh Yousouf arrives without his youthful bride; his person and manners described. Inhabitants remarkably illiterate, the Greek priest being the only person who could read. Breach of promise of the governor of Jerusalem. The Greek priest mediates and arranges for our departure and conduct to Wady Mousa, &c. Yousouf pledges himself to accompany us thither. Witness the payment of a bridal dowry. The good understanding between the Christians and Turks. Departure from Kerek. Sarcophagi. Joined by an Arab from Dejebal, who describes the fortifications and capital of Dareyah; and buried treasures. Silver preferred to gold. Horses fed on camels' milk. Shiekh Yousouf mistaken for a Wahabee. His horror threat. Refreshed with sour milk and bread at the camp of Sheikh Ismayel, Yousouf's youngest son. The ruined village of Mahannah; the Christian church. Survey various ruins. Return and sleep at Ismayel's camp. Resume our journey, and pass numerous Arab camps, and ruined sites. Arrive at that of Hamahta or Mote. Musshut, the tomb of Abou Taleb. A Roman mile-stone. Mahommedans alight and pray at the tomb of Sheikh Jaffa.

Camp of Shiekh Sahlem, commander of Djebal, and the country to Shobek. Refusal of his attempted extortion. His consequent imprecation. Adjustment of differences; accompanies us with his son to a camp of thirty tents. Visit the ruins of Dettrass. A temple and other Roman remains. Solemnities on a death in one of the harems. Pass the remains of Acoujah, a Roman fortress. Observe quantities of lava issued from the mountains. Picturesque fall of the rivulet el Hussein. Ruins of a small but rich building, on the promontory; its fine sculpture of arabesque foliage, capitals, columns, &c. Old mill-courses in the valleys. Another camp of thirty-three tents. Fresh attempts at extortion, &c. Volcanic stone, &c. Our spy-glass purloined; compelled to redeem it for two rubees. Daoud, a relation of the sheikh of Kerek, robbed of his sword. Pass the village of Bsaida, and reach the ruins of Gharundel. Columns and capitals of bad Doric architecture. A camp of Bedouin Arabs; take food with them. Discover several volcanic eminences, and quantities of lava. Trace an ancient Roman high-way of curious pavement. Ruins of square stone buildings. Three mile-stones, with effaced inscriptions. Examine some antient Turkish buildings, with Arabic inscriptions. Discover some Arabs, and divert our course. Gigantic description of Shobek. Verdant gardens of fig trees, at the foot of the hill. Pass the tomb of Sheikh Abou Soliman. Approach the town; assailed by the natives. Our safety guaranteed by the presence of Shiekhs Yousouf and Sahlem. Carried to a divan in the open air, and refreshed with dried figs; the building constructed upon the ruins of crusade architecture. Arabic inscriptions upon the Mahommedan castle. Extensive view of the before-mentioned desert and volcanos Customary salutations and manners of the natives. Alarm of Arabs, who had killed the goats of the natives. Threatened retaliation. Roman inscription on the church entrance, ascribed to the Frank kings of Jerusalem; description of its architecture.

Quit Shobek and arrive at a large Arab camp. Titular distinctions of the sheikhs. Our hospitable reception. Recognise a merchant of Hebron, who had been robbed of his goods by the Arabs. Their habits in the tents. Abou Raschid arrives and dines with us. Orders restitution of the merchant's goods. Abou Zatoun, the shiekh of Wady Mousa, violently opposes our progress there. Joined by his people and depart with violent threats against us. Abou Raschid following them, vows to enforce our advance. Joined at Sammack by a well armed and mounted host subject to him. Swears "that we shall drink of the water of Wady Mousa." Wild and romantic view of Mount Hor.

Perceive traces of a Roman way similar to the former. Alight at a camp of sixty-eight tents, in three circles on a mountain. Magnificent and picturesque views of groves, fertile fields, and camps. Mount Hor, the reputed tomb of Aaron. Distant view of Mount Sinai. Reach another camp subject to Abou Raschid. Odd dress of the natives. Warlike appearance of the Wady Mousir camp. A large deputation arrives; their conference with Abou Raschid. Ineffectual remonstrances with our opponents; and return to the camp for the night. Violent storm; the cattle seek shelter in our tents. War determined upon; Abou Raschid sends for reinforcements to Shobek, and desires the presence of Sheikhs Yousouf and Sahlem. Their arrival. Recommends pacific measures. Renewal of conferences unsuccessful. Continued arrival of reinforcements. Warlike appearance of our camp. Noble disinterestedness of Abou Raschid. Hindi, a powerful Arab chief, declares for our cause, and threatens to unite his force. Thieves and spies detected in our camp. Old Yousouf's eloquence in our favour, and conciliatory but decisive spirit.

Interesting objects of antiquity, discernible. Meditate a secret

CONTENTS. xxvii

visit thereto. Arrival of a numerous cavalcade. The chiefs alight and pay homage to Raschid. Peace proclaimed, and our auxiliary force discharged. Rejoicings of the men. Excuse themselves by having supposed us Frenchmen. Intending to poison the water. A person from the pashaw of Damascus examines our papers. His total ignorance of the Turkish language. Visited by Abou Raschid. Remains of towers; traces of a great metropolis. Depart with the deputation for Wady Mousa; contrived separation from them on the road. Arrive near the village; large encampment of the inhabitants. Outskirts of the vast Necropolis of Petra. Its various sepulchral and other antiquities ; their style characterised; historical allusions and comparisons relating thereto. Curious entablatures and inscriptions of the tombs. Awful and sublime appearance of the approach to Petra. Impressive effect of the screaming of the birds of prey. The spot where the pilgrims were murdered last year by the men of Wady Mousa; the wrapping cloak and watch of one of them offered to us for sale. A magnificent temple; unparalleled beauty of its structure; numerous colossal statues. Traditional depository of a vast treasure; Hasnah-el-Faraoun opinions as to its antiquity. Pyramids on the rocks. Pliny and Strabo's description of Petra, and its customs. Construction of the houses of Petra. Splendid ruins of the theatre, surrounded by sepulchres. Grand and capacious mausoleum. Tombs of Moses and Aaron on the supposed Mount Hor. Curious hues of the mountains. Engage an Arab shepherd as our guide. Leave Abou Raschid with our servants and horses and proceed. Visit an old Sheikh in a tomb at the top of the mountains; antiquities thereof. Prospects of the surrounding country. Observe the façade of another temple in the northern approach to the city; its majestic appearance. Reconducted by Abou Raschid from the ruins to the palace. Horticultural advantages of the city. Scriptural references thereto; depopulated state of the city. Quit the district of the tombs, and arrive at a small camp; stopped by two men rushing therefrom; friendly contention for the honour of affording us gratuitous supplies; their hospitality, and subsequent avarice. Arab character depicted. Revisit Petra, and return to the camp. Our apprehension of robbers. Proceed towards Shobek. Great inconvenience from cold. Arrive at Abou Rachid's camp, and joined by Sheikhs Yousouf and Sahlem. Raschid's mace-bearer sent with us to Shobek; quit it; pass a swarm of locusts; peculiar effect of the rock whereon they alighted; reported frequency of their appearance. Arrive at Ipseyra, or Bsaida; people surly and fanatical. Pass the village of Tafyle to the tents of Sheikh Sahlem. Entertained on our way by shepherd's boys with their double pipes. Descend into the Wady-el-Asha, and bathe in the hot spring, designated by the natives "the bath of Solomon;" scriptural reference to this spot. Kill a large black scorpion. Regaled at the camp of the father of old Yousouf's bride, and proceed to

Kerek. Pacific exchange of presents between old Yousouf and the Annasee Arabs. Desperate illness of the sheikh's brother's wife; administer to her relief. Pass the source of Ain-el-Erangee, the frank's fountain. Set out to explore the southern extremity of the Dead Sea; engage a guide; his extortion. Meet a caravan for Hebron and Jerusalem. Pass the spot of a dreadful massacre. A large herd of cattle, spoil from the Haouran.

Arrive at a prospect of the Dead Sea; remarkable appearance of its evaporation. Hebron caravan implores concealment of their route from the dread of robbers. Descend towards the plain of Ghor; its agricultural appearances. Various ruins and antiquities, probably the site of the ancient Zoar. View of the Dara, and description of the village of the infidel Ghorneys, and its inhabitants. Peculiarities of the vegetation of the Dead Sea; fine salt upon the beach. People collecting the same. Appearance and description of the promontory. Collect lumps of nitre and sulphur; observe traces of foreign travellers. Pass the strait betwixt the sea and back-water. Observe a small caravan from Kerek. Quantities of dead locusts; their extraordinary appearance. History and description of the back-water. Arrive at Sheikh Yousouf's camp; find men come to claim the cattle robbed from them by Ismayel's people; arbitrary adjudication of Yousouf. Return to Kerek. Reach Abba, formerly Rabbath-Moab, afterwards Areopolis. Ruins of Roman temples, &c. Pass the night at a Christian camp. Interesting phenomenon viewed from the southern extremity. Visit the ruins of Bait-Kerm. Remains of a large Roman palace. Lodge in the camp near it. Repeated appeals of the men for their cattle. Sheikh Harn. A conspicuous object from an eminence. Repeated prospects of the Dead Sea, and its interesting shores; ascertain its extent. Arrive upon the brink of Wady Modjeb, the ancient Arnon. The ancient road, and various relics of antiquity coeval with Trajan. Roman mile-stone of Marcus Aurelius. Pass the land of the Moabites into that of the Amorites. Reach Diban, the Dibon of Scripture. Interesting landmark. A consecrated pile of stone-work. Remains of a fine Roman bridge. Mile-stones of Severus. Pass Djebal Attarous, probably Nebo. Stop at a camp, near the ruins of Mayn, the Baal Mayn of Scripture. Take various bearings of the Dead Sea, and its vicinity. Return to the camp near Mayn. Prospect of Heshbon, and other ruins. Engage a guide to the sources of hot water. Pass immense numbers of rude sepulchral monuments of remote antiquity. Find ourselves in an ancient highway. Cross the bed of the torrent Zerka Mayn. Animals feeding, called Meddn, or Beddn. Obtain views of the Dead Sea, Frank Mount, and Bethlehem, also of the romantic valley of Calirrhoe. Stream of hot water from a high rock; its sulphureous appearance. A rapid and copious river in the bottom underneath of equal temperature. Traces of pristine buildings on the rock. Find four Roman defaced medals. Our Arab guide takes a vapour bath. Nature and properties of the springs described. Proceed to the Benesucker's camp, near Madeba. Alight at the tent of the chief Ebn-Fayes, our former companion to Djerash, (and from whom we escaped to Szalt); received by him and his brother outside thereof; their dress of handsome silk from Damascus. The elder brother plays a one-stringed fiddle, and sings "the death of his father." Supper served in an immense wooden dish, borne by three persons; agree for a guide to Oom-i-Rasass.

An immense tank at Madeba. Reach Oom-i-Rasass. Extensive christian ruins. Mr. Bankes renews his researches; is robbed by an armed Bedouin of his abba. Meet with increased numbers of camels. Reach Heshbon and find Sheikh Yousouf, the man of Szalt, and the young prince of the Benesuckhers. Prepare to inspect the ruins and the celebrated pools. Receive a message of extortion from Ebn Fayes for leave to proceed. Expostulate and produce our firman. He threatens to shoot us. Persist in our refusal of his demand, and are allowed to proceed. Heshbon wheat brought to parch during our detention. Descriptive account thereof. Ruins uninteresting. Find many human sculls and bones. Quit Heshbon for Szalt.

Arrive at Arrag-el-Emir. Grand ruins of a large edifice. Sculpture in relievo. The supposed palace of Hircan, the brother of Alexander, King of Jerusalem. Many artificial caves in the cliff near; their resemblance to stables. Arrive at Szalt. Pursue our journey, and pass the night at a camp of Benesuckhers near Amman. Examine the ruins of Rabbath Ammon (now Amman) an immense theatre and an odeum close to it. Traces of other Roman edifices and Christian churches. Pass the night at an Arab camp on the road to Djerash. Yousouf again charged with stealing the people's cattle; dismisses them by coolly pleading possession. Yousouf takes leave of us. Apology for the impositions of the natives. Cross the Zerka, the Jabbok of scripture, and return to Djerash. Complete our survey of the edifices and proceed by Rajib to the Jordan. Roman remains in a village-mosque near Katty. Wild boar shooting; these animals very numerous. Return to our bivouack. An adder found in Mr. Legh's blanket. Reach the Bysan ford on the Jordan. Proceed to Tiberias. Visit Mount Tabor; travellers names inscribed on the ruins thereof. Beautiful plain of Esdredon. Arrive at Acre. Instance of unfeeling barbarity there. Observations on the character and manners of the Arabs. Their manufacture of clothing, &c., chiefly by the women. Found many concealed dead bodies. Practice of tything to support the sheikhs. Embark in an imperial brig for Constantinople. Reasons for avoiding our visit to Asia Minor at this season of the year. Mr. Legh leaves Acre by land, for Palmyra, &c. Mr. Bankes by sea, for Egypt. Our regret at parting with such excellent companions.

LETTER VI.

Equip with Turkish travelling costume, a firman and two biruldies, for post horses. Depart from Constantinople for Scutari with a Tartar servant and another. Reasons for engaging the Tartar. Purchase of horses. Proceed from Scutari and traverse the villages of Gaobin and Bendick. Arrive at Ghiviza the Lybissa of antiquity. Cross an arm of the Marmora to Ersek. Proceed to Kisdervent, inhabited by Greeks. Pass the lake Ascanius, and reach Isnick or Tchinisli, the site of ancient Nicæa; advance to the town of Lefke. Arrive at Bilejik. Shuhut situated in a beautiful valley. Arrive at Eski Shehr. Road through open baked plains. Sidi Gazi. Many ancient fragments thereat. Pass a road-side fountain with several fragments. Stop at Khosru Khan, a miserable place, with many reliques in its neighbourhood. Breakfast at a fountain of Roman structure; its sculpture, &c. Pass two ancient cemeteries and a Mahommedan burial ground, also a Curd camp of black tents. Reach Bulwerdun. Proceed over a swampy plain and a cause-way to Isaklu, a considerable place. The road through a fertile plain, swamps and lakes in the distance.

Arrive at Ak Shehr a large town. Description of the suite of a rich Turk travelling. Proceed through a poor country and reach Ilgum, thence through a down country to Khadun Khan. Roman ruins therein. Pass two altars with Greek inscriptions; reach Ladik. Burial ground described. Road through plains. Arrive at Konieh, (formerly Iconium) the capital of a pashalic: Description thereof and its inhabitants. Proceed through plains of rich soil uncultivated; thence through open plains partly cultivated, with villages in sight, to Karabignar (near some volcanic mounds). Miserable houses, a handsome khan and a mosque in a ruinous state. Leave Karabignar, and pass a mound of conical form, surrounded by a natural fosse with salt water; ground covered with ashes and Scoriæ. Surugees return. Plan to avoid exchange of horses, pursued ineffectually. A deserted village. Observe some Turkomen's tents of singular construction.

Arrive at Erkle or Ellegria, beautifully situated. Surugees imprisioned for causing the death of a horse; with difficulty obtain one to proceed with us. Leave Erkle and enter a hilly country. Pass some fine rivulets and a village. Large patches of last years' snow on the highest parts of Mount Taurus.

Stop at Olukooshlah, a place with a khan and a few huts. Delay in procuring horses. Road now between some trees and gardens to a river's side. The mountains' production of rich grapes, sold to passengers. Scenery increases in beauty. Find fragments of breccia, porphyry, &c. Arrive at a picturesque bridge of one bold arch; ruins of another and a fountain near it. The road becomes rugged and the scenery less picturesque. Sum-

CONTENTS.　　　　　　　xxi

mits of the hills singularly pointed. Arrive at the post-house, Takehur, situated in a wild rugged place. Insolent behaviour of the Tartar, who returns to Takehur. The post-master, armed, menaces, and orders us to stop. Obliged to give up the horses. Proceed on foot. Tartar rejoins with horses and baggage. Road cut through the rock, at a place called Kolinkboaz, one of the Tauri Pylæ, or Cilicæ Pylæ of the ancients. Arrive at a guard-house and fountain; descend through a rugged road across numerous ravines. Pass a Turkish castle on an eminence. Also remains of a column of handsome porphyry. Pass an old Roman castle. Approach a considerable river, and descend into the great plain of Tersoos. Country covered with myrtle, &c. Cross the Cydnus, and arrive at the khan in Tersoos. Thermometer at 92 in the shade. Tersoos described. Its present commerce, &c. Quit Tersoos for the coast of Karamania. Proceed by the road to Kazalu. Reach an artificial mound; fine pottery and other remains on its summit Prospect over the plain; village of Kazalu. The Scala, and vessels at anchor. Plain partially cultivated with cotton. Pass the ruins of a town, having part of a building standing. On the left another artificial mound with the remains of a port. Stop at a small mill. Ground covered with dwarf wood. Proceed by various gardens of figs, &c. encompassing a village; the inhabitants sleeping in the open air under the trees. This cultivated tract very limited. Road through Dwarf Woodland. Another artificial mound with ruins. Cross a considerable stream and reach Pompeiopolis, surrounded by dark looking bushes. Ruins described. Cross several streams and bridges. Another artificial mound with ruins thereon. Country more open and boggy. Pass several places where the natives tread out the corn, and sleep on stages, elevated upon poles. Skirt the sea-beach. Quit the plain country, and cross a rocky hill. The supposed boundary between Cilicia Campestris and Aspera. Cross the mouth of a large river in a sandy bay, a bridge and village near. Large heaps of stones collected. Ruins of foundations, &c. A Roman aqueduct on a double tier of arches across the Latmus. Troughs cut in the rocks, and holes perforated to fasten the cattle to. Description of several ruins. Proceed over a stony road. Continuation of the grand aqueduct. Pass a burial place called Shedelah, and descend into a sandy bay to some wells of water, called by the natives Ayash. Some ruins described. An ancient paved way lined with tombs, sarcophagi, altars, &c. Arrive at a sandy bay and an isthmus. The great aqueduct again appears, though much in ruins, and near it the remains of a palace, &c. The ruins of Eleusa, or Sebaste. Ascend the next eminence. Baggage horse falls over a precipice. Its fall broken by the baggage. A tomb described. Rout, in the ancient paved way, to a castle and ruins. Descend into a valley leading to the sea-shore, where stands an old castle. Remains of a pier projecting into the sea, and some ruins at its extremity. Ruins of a town on a hill eastward, and on the sides of the valley to the west, remains of excavated houses. A sarcophagus on the upper part of these hills. The village of Ichuran reported to be near. Cross the foot of the western hill to a sandy bay. Another castle on a sandy island. Several springs of fresh water issue from the rocks close to the sea, the first seen since crossing the Latmus. The ruins of the ancient Corycus. Enquire for the Saffron cave of Strabo. Pursue our route over a rough road, the coast forming many bays and inlets. A small vessel at anchor in the first bay. Promontories between these bays excessively rugged, and road bad. Baggage horse falls frequently. Followed by seven natives of Ichuran, a very wild looking people, armed with knives. Our party with fire arms. The inhabitants of this country noted pirates. Passed five caves in one of the valleys. Continuation of very bad road into an extensive plain, terminating to the south in a long, low promontory. Pass the ruins of Pershendy and some others. Plain partially cultivated with cotton. Men employed spinning wool, the occupation of women in other parts of the Levant. Arrive at a miserable village, by the edge of a morass. A large building formed of ancient ruins. Continuation of bad road. A small mound with the remains of ancient buildings; and some sarcophagi near. Arrive at the Ghiuk Sooyor river, the ancient Calycadnus, and enter Selefkeh, one of the ancient Selcucias. Selefkeh, and some other ruins near it, described. Conductor taken ill. Continue our course westward. No horses to be procured at Selefkeh. Arrive at some ruins and a small bridge. Quit the plain country and pass along a rocky coast, by an extensive Necropolis of sarcophagi cut in the rock. To the ruins of another village, and further on to a bay, having a large Turkish fortress on its western promontory. A polacca brig at anchor. Converse with the crew. Pass into another bay sheltered by an island. Two vessels taking in wood. Ruins at the head of the bay and on the island. Bays sheltered by the curved projection of the point Lissan el Kahpeh.

Pass over a very high bluff, and descend among romantic cliffs and ravines into a valley. Stop at a small source of fresh water; the first seen since starting. Find an open stage placed for the accommodation of travellers, there being no inhabitants. The valley inclosed by two high cliffs; ascend with great difficulty, and examine the ruins of a Turkish castle. A commanding view of the sea, and the island of Cyprus. Observe some natives, and being unarmed, retire, and join the rest of the party. Pass a stormy night in the open air; experience violent feverish heat and thirst. Drink constantly at the fountain. Morning, the weather more serene. Valley opens on a deep bay of the seacoast. Pass over a mountainous and barren country; come to some abandoned huts and gardens. Servant's illness increases to a high fever. Advance further, and with difficulty find the track, there being no road. Arrive at Chelindreh, the ancient Celenderis. Two vessels lying in the port. Chelindreh described. Bargain for horses to proceed. The disorder, which had attacked all the party, increases. Thoughts of proceeding abandoned. Resolve to hasten to Cyprus for medical aid. Our guide, to obtain relief, blooded with the point of a nail. Party much exhausted for want of nourishment. Termination of the tour attributable to want of wholesome food, unwholsomeness of the waters, lying on the margin of the swamps, and want of sufficient covering at nights. Arrival at Cyprus. Dangerous illness of one of the party; his convalescence. Embark for Marseilles in a French brig; arrival, after a passage of seventy days; perform a quarantine of twenty, and proceed to Montpellier to recruit our health.

Some account of Cuchuk Ali, in a letter from John Barker, Esq. to the Earl of Elgin.

ERRATA.

Contents, Page xii. line	4, *for*	moorelithe *read* monolithe.
13,	27,	Sheck *read* Sheikh, *passim*.
117,	19,	" the fleece" *read* " the fluse."
127,	19,	Appolinoplis *read* Appolinopolis.
155,	10,	ΡΤΟΛΕΜΑΙΟΣ *read* ΠΤΟΛΕΜΑΙΟΣ.
222,	6,	Latachia *read* Latachia or Latakia, *passim*.
223,	2,	Selucia *read* Seleucia.
228,	13,	an *read* and.
	23,	Turkmen *read* Turkomen.
356,	26,	Goarnays *read* Ghorneys.
357,	27,	Houssan *read* Hussan.
359,	1,	el Derrah *read* el Dara, *passim*.
	11,	Saphy *read* Szafye or Ahsa, *passim*.
373,	18,	Wady el Hussein *read* Wady el Ahsa, *passim*.
378,	19,	Showbac *read* Showbec
432,	17,	Zettum *read* Zetoun.
458,	14,	Rubba *read* Rabba.

TRAVELS

IN

EGYPT AND NUBIA.

LETTER I.

TOUR IN EGYPT AND NUBIA.

Description of the party and object of pursuit.—Departure from Philæ.—Arrive at Second Cataract.—Elpha. —Ebsambal.—Open the great temple.—Derry Kalapsche.—Return to Philæ.—Pass through the Cataract.— Visit Assuan.—Thebes.—Tentyra.—Arrive at Cairo.

CAIRO, September 27, 1817.

WE arrived here on the first instant, having made a much longer trip than we had intended; the reason of this I shall explain in its proper place, and in the mean time proceed to a continuation of our narrative, from where my last letter, dated in June, concluded. I think I mentioned before, that we had joined, at Philæ, Messrs. Beechey and Belzoni; the latter is Mr. Salt's agent. Their principal object in going up to the second cataract, was to endeavour to open the great temple at Ebsambal, by desire of Mr. Salt, which Mr.

Belzoni had attempted the preceding year. The whole face of the temple, as high as the heads of the statues which are in front of it, was buried in the sand which had been blown from the desert. This sand, in the course of time, had accumulated to such a degree, as not only to fill up the whole of the valley through which it had passed, but also to form a mountain, sloping from the front of the temple, for two or three hundred yards towards the banks of the Nile. From all external appearance it is probable this temple, which is hewn out of the live rock, had been shut for many centuries, perhaps for more than two thousand years; and in that case, if it had not suffered too much in the general pillage and destruction which all the sacred edifices underwent at the conquest of Egypt, by Cambyses and other subsequent princes, it was hoped that something interesting to the antiquarian might be discovered.

We considered it a fortunate circumstance for us to have an opportunity of joining in so interesting an undertaking, and as it is adviseable that travellers should be both numerous and well armed in Nubia, the junction of us four, together with Mr. Beechey's Greek servant, an Arab cook, and a janissary, composed a tolerably strong party. We could only add one solitary musket to a pretty good stock of arms of every description which Mr. Beechey had with him. We hired a boat, which belonged to a village situated on a point amidst a cluster of date-trees, which bounds the view of the river from Philæ to the southward: the crew consisted of five men, including the reis or captain, and three boys: three of the men and the reis were brothers, and the fifth was their brother in law, having married their sister; this latter was dressed in a blue shirt, from which circumstance we nic-named him the "blue devil;" his real name was Hassan; he will be by and by a conspicuous character in this narrative. The boys were sons of some one or other of the crew, and the boat they said belonged to the father of them all, an old man who wore a green turban, as a descendant of the prophet.

In the afternoon of the sixteenth, we started with a fine, fair wind, having first settled a quarrel between two of our crew, in which one of the party was cut through the calf of the leg, to the bone: our agreement with the reis was for one hundred and sixty piastres per month, four pounds sterling; and at the end of the voyage, if they behaved well, a backsheeish or present was promised, a stipulation which always forms part of similar bargains in this country. It was expressly understood that the crew should find themselves.

As we advanced upwards, the sand hills filling up the cavities between the black granite rocks presented a most remarkable contrast, the wind having drifted it very much; the surface in many places was quite fine and smooth, reminding one, with the exception of the difference of colour, of some of the scenery in Switzerland, where the snow before it cracks, and after it has been drifted fine, presents just such an appearance. The mountains here close much on the river, and we looked in vain for that rich plain which, in Egypt, is every where to be seen on the banks of the Nile. On the heights, as we proceeded, we saw several Saracenic buildings placed in most picturesque situations; they tend very much to set off this wild species of scenery; you also observe throughout Nubia, numerous piles of stones placed on the most elevated and conspicuous parts of the mountains, to indicate the vicinity of the Nile to the caravans from the interior of Africa, as Darfur, Dongola, and other places.

Half a day's sail from Philæ, conducted us to the finishing of the granite rocks, which now gave place to those of calcareous stone, though on the river side, in most instances, their exterior still retains a black colour and a polish. The vein of red granite which begins below Assuan, and extends beyond Philæ, is supposed to continue in an easterly direction till it joins the shores of the Red Sea, keeping, nearly throughout, the same breadth; the observations which we made on our trips into the desert from Assuan, tended to confirm this opinion.

On the afternoon of the seventeenth we came to a place where the mountains close upon the river in a very abrupt manner, leaving no level land on the banks; the hills at the same time presented some very grand though rude scenery. This, by some travellers, is termed the boundary between Egypt and Nubia, though I should be inclined to agree with the French, that the first cataract is a more natural limit to the two countries; as, immediately above Assuan, you perceive not only a country quite different from that below, but even natives of a character and colour in no way resembling the Egyptians, differently clothed, and speaking another language.

This evening we arrived at Kalapsche, and as we had to wait some time while our janissary was buying provisions, we went up to inspect the temple, though we had agreed to visit the antiquities in general as we returned from the second cataract. The ruins of this edifice are large and magnificent, but it has never been finished: it consists of a large peristyle hall, (most of the columns of which have fallen, and many are unfinished,) two chambers, and a sanctuary. The exterior walls are smooth, the sculpture not having even been commenced, and in the interior it is not finished, there being in no instance either stucco or painting. There has been first a quay on the river's side, and then a flight of steps as an approach to the temple. We reserved the measurements, &c. till our return: the outer hall had several Greek inscriptions in it, some of them in tolerable perfection.

In the evening, before we stopped, we passed two crocodiles, they were on a shoal in the middle of the Nile, and retired before we got near them: they were the first we had seen since we left Philæ; indeed they are never met with near that island. On the nineteenth a foul wind obliged us to stop, when an old man came to beg medicine, thinking we were *hackim*, or physicians, a strange notion which all barbarous nations have respecting Europeans: we gave him some advice, though we declined any pretensions to the title he had given us. Bruce, in making himself acquainted with the rudiments of physic, shewed how well he judged of the proper mode of travelling in these countries; and his narrative proves how much he benefitted by this knowledge. Our denial of all knowledge of physic met with little belief among the natives, and to induce us to give them assistance, they offered two fowls for any aid we would render to their patients. On the twentieth we saw a camel swimming across the river; one man swam before with a halter in his mouth, leading the animal, another followed behind.

June 21. We this day observed, immediately opposite Duckie, two lads crossing the river, which is here tolerably wide, and pushing and towing a laden reed raft.

On the twenty-second observed the purple acassia; it bears some resemblance to a shrub, and is evidently a dwarf species of the mimosa, never attaining a height beyond a foot or fifteen inches; excepting in colour, the flower is like the yellow acassia. On the twenty-third our crew killed a snake that was basking on the river side; it was gray, with two black marks below its head. It was curious to see the precautions they used before they would surprise this reptile, which they represented as poisonous, though I did not believe it was so. We had this morning a regular wild-goose chase after an old one and four young ones; the crew jumped overboard and caught them all, though with some difficulty. I mention this merely to give you some idea how expert these people are in the water; they may almost be said to be amphibious.

June 24. This day we were opposite Koroskoff

in the morning; we purchased a sheep for nine piastres, but were obliged to send the money before they would even shew the animal; we remonstrated much against this curious method of making a bargain, but nothing would induce them to change their plan. We this day saw the calibash growing wild on creepers up the acassia-trees on the river side; our crew got three very good ones; the boys also found a sort of wild currant growing close to the water side; we tasted some, and thought them not unlike the blue-berry, though not shaped like them, being round; in size and colour they are alike.

Our custom was always to bathe morning and evening regularly, frequently oftener; this evening, while at this recreation, Mr. Belzoni was bitten in the foot, which caused him to cry out somewhat loudly for assistance; next morning he was bitten again, in the same place; this last time fetched blood, taking a piece out of the toe. The animal must have been small; he plainly felt something twisting round his leg; we all agree in thinking it must have been a water lizard. I should have told you, the other day a man hailed us and asked "if we would buy a spy-glass;" he said he was a native of Senaar: we thought it must be the property of some European who had been robbed, and therefore said we would see it first;

in consequence he came into the boat, to be carried to the village where it was, (about four hours sail above) however, on arriving there he walked off, and we never heard again either of him or his glass; the fact is, he wanted a passage, and you, I am sure, will give him credit for so cunning a method of getting one. It is by these little traits that one can judge of the character of people of this description.

June 25. We this day arrived near Koroskoff, at the point where the river reaches the southernmost point, before the beginning of the second cataract; for the ascent of the river here turns due north, and continues in that direction between ten and fifteen miles; after which it becomes S. W. and then west to the second cataract. The Nile here assumes a picturesque appearance, having several islands and rocks in the centre of it. In the evening our janissary shot a wild-goose; its plumage was beautiful, and its taste exceedingly good, though we had not the means of cooking it in a very savoury manner.

June 26. Observed the Nile to have *fallen* about one and a half foot; it is now twenty-two days since it began to *rise;* it is already above the cataract of Syene (Assuan).

June 27. We this day saw two crocodiles; our men requested us to fire some muskets to frighten them away, but were not afraid of towing the bark in the water close to the bank where we observed them; I think, from what we have noticed of these animals, that if ever they do attack people, it is but very seldom. This morning a man on horseback came down to the river side, and said he was sent by Halleel Cashief with salam alicams (compliments): he, however, seemed more intent to get something for himself; and in a moment enumerated several articles which he requested us to give him; such as coffee, snuff, gunpowder, salt, &c.; we told him we had none to spare, as we reserve those articles for Hassan Cashief, the chief person in this country, and whose favour it is necessary to gain by presents, in order to get permission to open the temple at Ebsambal, one of the principal objects of the expedition; that chief has pledged his word to Mr. Belzoni, that none but the English should be allowed to work there, on condition that he, Hassan, was to have half the *gold* that was found in it: for these people have no idea that our researches for antiquities in this country, have any other view than to get treasure; and they laugh when we tell them we are looking for stone statues, and slabs of that material, with inscriptions on them. They cannot conceive what motive can induce us to come such a distance, and expend three or four-thousand piastres to clear away an accumulated mass of sand, for no other purpose than to find some granite figures.

We now observed the water to be exceedingly muddy, and of a reddish yellow colour. We stopped a short time at Offidena with a view of purchasing a statue; but after much prevarication, we could not even get a look at it. The natives of this place are both handsome and well made, a circumstance very rare in Nubia; their complexion however was unusually dark. In the evening arrived at Derry, sent word to Daoud and Halleel Cashief, the two sons of Hassan, (who most unfortunately for us was at Dongola, and by whose absence we lost the friendship and assistance of the only honest man in the country,) that we were going up to open the temple at Ebsambal, and would thank them to send orders for us to be permitted to work; adding, at the same time, that we would wait on them and pay our respects on our return. While waiting there we had a specimen of Nubian dancing; about twelve lads assisted; the music consisted only in clapping the hands, in the doing of which, they kept very good time. I cannot say much for the elegance or gracefulness of the dance, as it was nothing more than lifting up the right foot and stamping it down again, then rising up on the left foot by the spring of the instep, and afterwards letting the feet rest on the flat sole. This was done for a backsheeish which we gave them. We also gave the reis and crew a backsheeish of ten piastres, but they said it was not enough, so we gave them fifteen. At night, when we stopped, the reis came to us to say that we were two parties, and therefore should by rights pay double the money we had agreed on for the boat. Complaint was also made that we had not given sufficient to the crew to eat; I mentioned before the agreement about their feeding themselves: it was also alleged that Jacques (an agent of Mr. Drovetti's, a Frenchman living in this country, and who hired the boat not long before us,) always gave them one third of his coffee, meat, bread, and every thing that he had; in short, they imagined that up here we were at their mercy. Now, as we had regularly fed them, and given them coffee without stint every day, we thought it time to come to an understanding, and therefore told them that the boat was at our disposal, and that it was no matter of theirs if we had two or five different parties; and with regard to food, that as they were not contented with what we had given them spontaneously, they should have nothing. We have no doubt but our janissary and the Greek servant put them up to this request, as the soldier took a poor cowardly part, and urged that we were in a savage country, and had better temporize till we were on our return, thus showing of how little use these fellows are to protect travellers.

June 28. Passed Ibrim, situated on a rude but picturesque hill of a conical shape, and of barren calcareous stone. There is not now the least vestige of an inhabitant to be seen, and it presents a sad picture of ruin and desolation. Mr. Legh, in his new publication, (a few extracts from which we have seen in the Quarterly Review for February last) says " this town was destroyed by the mamelukes;" it was the extent or limit of his voyage in Nubia: he travelled in 1813. Mr. Bankes, it appears, was the first Englishman who ever succeeded in gaining the second cataract: he travelled in 1815. I fancy he took much about the same tour of Syria that we mean to take, though we have not as yet seen his journey traced out. In 1816, Mr. Drovetti, the *ci-devant* French consul in Egypt, succeeded in reaching the second cataract, together with his two agents, Rifaud and Cailliaud; these travellers, together with Sheck Ibrahim (a real friend of ours) and Mr. Belzoni, are all that have reached thus far: Mr. Belzoni had his wife with him in man's clothes. Poor Norden, who travelled eighty years ago, could only reach Derry; his Nubian trip is rather interesting, though not very instructive. Denon went no higher than Philæ; and Pocock, who passed Norden on the Nile, only reached that isle. On the tops of the hills near Ibrim, we remarked many conical hillocks, as marks to lead the Dongola caravans (¹). This evening we saw a crocodile sleeping on the sand a considerable way up; we were within twenty yards of him, but as none of our muskets were loaded with ball we did not fire; we however made a noise to awaken him, when he rushed into the water with his mouth open, looking very savage; he was about fifteen feet long.

June 29. Arrived at Ebsambal, and unfortunately found Hassan Cashief absent; sent again to Derry, to Daoud and Halleel, for leave to begin and open the temple when we returned from the second cataract: the banks of the river between Ibrim and Ebsambal are beautifully strewed with the yellow and purple acassia, forming thick hedges, which have a very pleasing effect; a species of the tamarisk is also common here. The acassia is famous for producing the gum arabic, which is brought in great quantities from the interior of Africa in the vicinity of Darfur; the seeds of the acassia also serve for a lucrative branch of trade, being sent in the first instance to Cairo, and then shipped for Europe, where they serve as a good article for tanning. The water is now become exceedingly thick, it is not however unpleasant to the taste.

June 30. While we were at Ebsambal, the Dongola caravan passed; it was preceded by about fifty camels, carrying the provisions, &c. The conductors were armed with a sword, dagger, and spear each; they wore sandals to preserve the soles of their feet from the burning sand, which we now feel most sensibly, being obliged to stop every now and then to pour it out of our shoes. These sandals are much like those worn by the ancient Egyptians, and which are often found on the feet of the mummies at this day.

The range of the Mockatem mountains finish nearly opposite Ebsambal in a remarkable manner, terminating in a considerable number of pyramidal hills rising up from the sand, and having the appearance of a gigantic camp; some of the hills are oblong, and in the form of marquees; others are so perfectly pyramidal, that one finds it difficult to divest one's-self of the idea that they are the work of men's hands. Bruce attributes the origin of the pyramidal mode of building to an imitation of the slope or inclination of the sides of mountains. (Vol. ii. p. 33.)

July 1. Stopped opposite the village of Farras; we here examined the site of a large Nubian city, and amongst the modern stone buildings of the Arabs found several remnants of temples, with hieroglyphics; in one was a beautiful cornice and a frieze, with the winged globe highly finished. The natives shewed us some Greek and Roman ornaments, such as the spread eagle, ornamental cross, &c.; near the village are some fragments of a temple, consisting of several broken pieces of red granite pillars, also some small ones of beautiful white marble. From the appearance of these ruins, the fineness of the situation, and the rich plain of cultivated land near it, I think this must once have been a populous and flourishing city, in the time of the Greeks and Romans, as well as the Egyptians. Close to the rubbish there is a natural rock by itself, and a door leading to a very small recess or chamber, in which are two Egyptian figures, in intaglio, on the wall; one is a man, the other a woman with the lotus flower in her hand; a double row of hieroglyphics near the inner figure, and there is a niche at the further end of the chamber about four feet square.

We bathed this morning opposite a village, and

on a sand-bank in front of us, at not more than a musket-shot distant, we observed two crocodiles (timsah in Arabic); as soon as we went into the water they both walked into the river, to all appearance from fear, for they are certainly both shy and timid, and, I suspect, will only attack a single person when they can surprise him in the water, and off his guard; we saw no more of these two; at noon we saw another crocodile swimming with his nose just out of the water. We also observed, to day, a pretty large water-lizard, and a small black water-snake. To day the sand-hills have assumed a fine green appearance, being covered here and there with tamarisk; this verdure, contrasted with the dark yellow sand, forms a pleasing diversity of appearance. In the evening, while towing the boat, our sailors found a torpedo on the very brink of the river, apparently asleep; it was curious to observe their caution and timidity in approaching it; they, however, succeeded in sticking one of their daggers in his head, and by that means hauled it on shore; our Egyptian crew had done the same near Beni Hassan. We got the fish on board, and, though nearly dead, it sensibly affected my arm in laying hold of it; I felt a double shock up the arm near the elbow. It was about two feet long; had very small eyes; the belly and top of the back white; one dorsal fin, and the sides were coloured dark brown with black spots; it had no scales. Our sailors in Egypt ate the one they caught, but the present crew would not touch this, even when dead, and consequently harmless, much more eat it. They all said we avoided the shock by uttering a charm, or using some magic influence. This day one of the boys of our crew brought on board a camelion; he caught it in an acassia (called in Nubia the soont) tree, which they affect more than the date, or any other tree in this country. On coming on board, it hissed and shewed symptoms of anger, evincing at the same time a great desire to make its escape. It was then of a dirty green colour, with dark spots, and whenever it was approached it turned to a dusky brown, inflating itself at the same time. I conclude that one hue is the effect of fear, and *the other* of indifference. We had subsequently eight of these animals on board; some of them became so tame, that when the flies annoyed us much, we had only to take one of the camelions in our hand, and place it near the flies, and it would catch them with its long tongue in great numbers. One of our crew brought us some fine pieces of gum arabic which he picked off the acassia; some of the specimens were remarkably clear and large.

July 1. In the evening arrived at Farras,

when two natives with the men servants of Hassan Cashief came and made a bargain with us to procure asses and camels to go above the second cataract. One of these remained in the boat, and the other promised to meet us at Elpha on the morrow with the animals. Elpha is opposite the second cataract, and is the last habitable place to which the Nubian boats ascend.

July 2. Arrived at the second cataract, and perceiving we should have a long distance to walk to the elevated point from whence the finest view of the cataract is obtained, we requested the reis to take us higher up the river, in order to shorten the walk, but all the boatmen persisted that it was impracticable for the boat to go higher on account of the rocks; they offered, however, to take us if we would first go over to Elpha, on the opposite side of the river, and land all our effects, and then return again. We required the reason of this odd proposition, when they said, that they were apprehensive of thieves on that side of the river. We did not however like the scheme, and therefore refused it, urging them to advance higher up, as we plainly perceived we might go a good league farther without the least risk; but nothing would induce them to consent. In the mean time another boat arrived, and we perceived that our reis and his sailors were in league with those of the other boat, to force us to take their bark; but we determined to walk rather than submit to this imposition, as they wanted a high price in the newly arrived boat, and accordingly we set out. The sand was deep and the sun very hot, so that we soon found that walking in the desert is no joke; our trip occupied us about two hours, from one to three, the hottest part of the day. On the road we found innumerable tracts of the gazelle and other animals; we saw seven of the former in one lot, and three in another. They were not so timid as one would expect, and stopped to gaze on us with their ears cocked up like deer in a park; their colour is brown, not much unlike the sand, and when they are in a valley it is difficult to perceive them. We were not more than two musket shots distant from the first three we saw; when running, they appeared wonderfully light and nimble, and while on the rocky parts bounded with great agility.

The spot from whence we surveyed the cataract was a projecting cliff, about two hundred feet high, with a perpendicular precipice down to the river side; from this place, which is on the western bank, you look down on the cataract to great advantage. It presents a fine coup d'œil; the river here runs E. N. E. and W. S. W. In

EL-BUSIR, LOOKING DOWN THE 2ND CATARACT OF THE NILE.

America this would be called "a rapid," there being no fall visible, only an immense cluster of innumerable black rocks, with the Nile running in all directions with great rapidity, and much noise between them; they fill up the whole breadth of the river, which may be about two miles wide, and they extend as far as the eye can reach, altogether making a space of about ten miles of rapids; three below the rock on which we stood, and seven above. The scenery is here remarkably wild, there being no human habitation visible, excepting a fisherman's hut on one of the islands, and the village of Elpha on the opposite side of the river, in the distance. Some of the rocks have beds of yellow sand on them, and most of the islands have small trees and shrubs growing in the crevices; the verdure of these, contrasted with the sand and black rocks, produces a fine effect. In front, and on both sides, the view is bounded by the desert; to the southward are the tops of two high mountains rearing their heads above the hills, and apparently seventy or eighty miles distant. The western bank of the river is richly covered with trees and shrubs, and it is curious to observe, immediately beyond the green margin, the barren desert, without the least vestige of verdure. Having bathed and dined on bread and cheese, we set out on our return to the bark, our guides urging us to be quick, lest we should be benighted; they said the serpents and other venomous reptiles always came down by night to drink, and they were apprehensive that we should tread on them. They also said we should meet the robbers at night. These people have a remarkable aversion to being caught in the dark. I remember, when at Dendera, our servant, an Arab, hurried off and left us behind, when he thought we should be late in returning to our boat; and whenever our lights have gone out in a tomb or temple, the Arabs have always clapped their hands, and made a noise to keep their spirits up till the light returned. In the evening, after dark, we reached the boat.

July 3. In the morning at daylight we crossed over to Elpha, the way to which place leads through several intricate passages, amongst rocks and shoals, where the current runs with great rapidity. In one part we were obliged to pass close under a high bluff point with some ruined houses on it. It was not necessary to pass through this intricate passage; our boatmen took it when we were all asleep in our beds, and we only perceived our situation on awaking at Elpha. We here found that neither asses nor camels had arrived to take us up to the temple above the second cataract which we had heard off; the reason assigned for this was, that the price agreed on the day before, at three piastres for each animal, was not enough, though the person who made the agreement was there. We now endeavoured to procure beasts of the inhabitants, but they haggled so much about the price, that we could make nothing of them. While we were arranging this matter, our crew, reis and all, took their clothes, arms, and effects out of the boat, and walked off to a *sackey* *, about twenty yards distance, on the banks of river; here they squatted down amongst a considerable number of natives. We had not taken notice of this proceeding, as their clothes, &c. were all kept abaft behind the end of our cabin, and, therefore, when we could not agree for the asses, &c. we said we did not want them, and would go back to Ebsambal. With this intention we called the reis, and desired him to get the bark ready to return, but received an immediate answer, " that neither he nor his crew would come." We sent word to know the reason of their refusal, when they replied, that we must give them more money for the boat before they would come on board; they also sent word

---

* Sackey is the Persian wheel with which they raise water from the river; it is described by Burkhardt, Norden, and other travellers.

that we had never fed them, nor had we given them backsheeish, and when we reminded them of Derry, they said that was nothing.

We now threatened to take the boat off ourselves, and for that purpose rigged the oars across, but the wind being strong against us, we did not get under way. When the oars were ready we sent word to the crew to come, but they replied that they would not; that we might buy the boat if we chose, but that they would not navigate her; at the same time they said that they were people who did not value their lives a pigeon, and for half a one that they would take ours. While all this was passing, we observed the natives assembling in every direction, armed with spears, swords, and daggers; every minute they were arriving from all quarters on asses, and always going to the rendezvous under the sackey, where our vile crew had it in their power to tell any falsehoods against us without our being able to confute them, as neither our Arab cook, the Greek servant, or janissary understood the Barbarin language. Several of the Barbarins now came to see what arms we had, and took account of every thing in the shape of a weapon; for seeing affairs in this posture we had prepared for the worst, and laid out all our arms in readiness, of which fortunately we had a good stock. A message now came from the crew that they wanted money; we sent them word that they must first come and do their duty; that as soon as the boat was off from this place, they would have a backsheeish, but not one para till they had done their duty. They now sent word that we had absolutely starved them, which was no doubt what they told the natives; they also informed us by a message, that at this very place they had beaten Jacques (Rifaud) during his last voyage, (though you may remember what they said of his generosity at Derry,) and that it was done in the presence of the sheick of the place, and all the natives; and that they had made him pay fifty piastres for the stick they had broken over his head. At this moment several of the natives came down demanding backsheeish, backsheeish, in a threatening manner; we asked the reason why we should give them money? they replied, for seeing the cataract, and coming into their country. A loaded musket was now pointed at them, and they were asked if they wanted money by force or good means; on which they retired, saying la, la, la, no, no, no, evidently not liking the sight of fire arms, which they have a particular aversion to. We now told them, that if we had seen the cataract without paying, so they had seen us without giving us any thing as a recompence, though we were as novel a sight to them as their cataract was to us, and therefore we were quits.

Some of the most impudent now came down, and on being refused money said we should wait where we were till the high Nile; that we should neither go upward or downward, laughing and hooting at the same time; our villainous crew all this while sitting under the sackey, and enjoying the storm they had raised against us. To all their threats we constantly replied that we were well armed, were determined not to be robbed, and that should they come to extremities, we would certainly make a good use of our fire-arms, which we took care they should all see were pretty numerous and loaded. The asses were now brought, and the people endeavoured to persuade us to go off to the temple, evidently in the hope of plundering the boat when we were gone; we easily saw through this trick, and positively refused to go. We also told the natives that though we were few in number, we had the firman of the pashaw, and that any violence offered to us, would be sure to be well punished; those who had brought the asses now asked some remuneration for their trouble, as we had refused to hire them; this we thought reasonable, and to draw off their attention, for there were about forty of them, we gave eight piastres to be divided amongst the claimants. The division of this money turned affairs very much in our favour, for they began to quarrel amongst one another immediately.

The crew now thinking that we had given the natives backsheeish, and that they should get nothing more without danger to themselves, sent a messenger while the natives were disputing about the division of the eight piastres to say they would come and prepare the boat provided they had the backsheeish: we repeated our terms, that they should have a present when they did their duty. Seeing now they could not stir up the natives to any acts of violence at the risk of their personal safety, they returned to the boat, all armed, having their daggers fastened to the left arm above the elbow joint, the manner in which all the Nubians wear that weapon. As soon as the boat was ready they asked for the money, when we gave them fifteen piastres: before we were off, however, one of the Faras people came to be rewarded for endeavouring to hire the asses at that place, or rather for disappointing us; we gave him five piastres, which he indignantly refused, but seeing he could get no one to assist him in forcing us to give more, (for all these people are impudent and bullying for their own interest, but never for another's,) came back and said he would take the five we had already offered him; this we now refused, when he went off in a violent rage, uttering threats that we should hear more of him below. After this, we got off from this infamous place, and soon found what a trap we had been caught in; for it was with the utmost difficulty, that even the crew could get the boat through the numerous narrow passages, all of them being obliged to get out into the river, and guide her through amongst the rocks; and we were also forced to pass directly under the bluff point I mentioned before, where the natives, had we taken the boat off ourselves, would have annoyed us greatly, while they would have been sheltered behind the ruined village. Indeed our crew wished us above all things to take the boat off, that they might represent us to the inhabitants as robbers, stealing their bark: however we saw through all this.

July 4. Arrived at Ebsambal and found that no message whatever had been received from the cashiefs at Derry: this was a sad disappointment to us. Our crew now dreading the presence of the chiefs, came to beg a reconciliation, saying that they had forgotten and forgiven every thing, and hoped that we had: they said they would behave well in future—" that they were poor, and always made a practice to get all they could from passengers and strangers:"—they remarked, " that dogs, when repulsed, always made a practice of returning to get something as long as there was any thing to be had:"—this appears to be a favourite proverb amongst them.

July 6. Visited the small temple opposite Ebsambal on the south side of the river. This temple is excavated in the solid mountain; the entrance is situated on the side of a rocky precipice, which below it slopes into the river; there are some ruins of steps cut in the rock as an approach to it. The principal chamber is ten paces long, by nine wide: it is supported by four pillars, two on each side of the passage. In the centre, at the further end of the apartment, there is on each side a door-way communicating with side chambers, nine paces by four each: the sanctuary at the end of the principal chamber is six paces by four; this is the most common mode of construction in the Egyptian temples. At present the interior of this temple appears daubed all over with dirty plaster and Greek paintings, mostly representing men on horseback. Behind these, however, we easily discovered the Egyptian figures, hieroglyphics, &c. &c. in bas-relief on stucco; as most of the figures represent men with hawk's heads, we think this temple was dedicated to Osiris; and afterwards, perhaps, converted into a church of St. George. The sanctuary has been once ornamented, but the side apartments are plain: there is a small subterraneous chamber below the sanctuary, apparently intended for a sepulchre.

July 7. A message on a dromedary arrived from Daoud Cashief at Derry to see' " if we were the same English for whom Hassan Cashief had promised to open the temple;" at the same time he sent word that if we were the same persons, he would immediately come himself, but if not he knew what to do. The latter part of the message alluded to the French, who had used every effort to get Hassan Cashief to allow them to open the temple after Mr. Belzoni's first attempt in 1816; Mr. Belzoni, however, had fortunately, in Mr. Salt's name, sent Hassan and his two sons a turban each, and some other presents, after his first effort: this he did to bind them to their promise, and they certainly deserve credit for keeping it. It ought to be mentioned that Mr. Drovetti, in the early part of 1816, on his way to the second cataract, before Mr. Belzoni's arrival in Nubia, had contracted with Hassan Cashief to open the temple, for three-hundred piastres, and left the money; Hassan promising that Mr. D. should find it ready opened on his return from the falls: however, when he came back his money was returned, the chief candidly telling him he could not undertake the task for so small a sum. As Mr. D. would not go to more expense, the field now became open to any one else who chose to attempt the enterprise.

July 6. In the morning we started early with two of the natives in search of a temple which they said was in the neighbouring mountains, and stated to be about a pipe distant; for it is common among them to estimate a short journey by the number of pipes they can smoke during its performance: on our way we met two white gazelles; they were very timid, the belly and tail were perfectly white. After walking about an hour, we came to the mountains, where, having waited about two hours more, our conductors came and said, they could not find the temple, though the evening before they had described the size and every particular of it. In the evening we had a violent quarrel with the crew in consequence of their drawing their daggers on our servants; we told them that the first who should draw his dagger would be sure to be severely punished: this threat, however, had so little effect, that one of them who had murdered his own brother at Philæ, (for which reason he did not dare to go near the island ([2]), but was taken into our boat at a village above it,) said he would be the first, and swore by Alla and the Prophet that he would have one of our lives; adding, that his method was not to attack people awake, but to stab them sleeping. We however laughed at their threats, and told them they were more apt at talking of these matters than in executing them.

July 10. This day the two cashiefs arrived, Daoud and Halleel; they did not come to us, nor send any message to apprize us of their arrival, but pitched their tents, consisting of a few sticks of date, the roof covered with grass, on the sandbank at the river side: here they waited till we should make our appearance. We accordingly set out to visit these potentates; the first tent we entered happened to be Halleel's. He was a tall handsome man, about thirty-six years of age, six feet high, very corpulent, and had a fine expressive countenance, with dark eyes: his dress was a large loose white linen shirt, with long sleeves hanging down nearly two feet, an old turban and slippers. He received us with tolerable affability, and immediately conducted us to his elder brother Daoud's tent, who also gave us a very good reception. Daoud Cashief appeared to be rather taller than his brother, though not so fat. He is a man about forty-five years of age, and had a certain dignity and reserve in his demeanour that bespoke the chief: he wore a loose blue shirt. We were not long in bringing the subject of the temple to his notice, when he immediately said he would willingly give us his assistance to have it opened; pancakes of flour and butter-milk were now brought, on which we all feasted, making use of fingers instead of spoons, as these people have no idea even of the meaning of utensils of this kind. Coffee was now served, or rather a substitute for that beverage, which is not unpalatable; they call it gargadan; it is a small black grain, not unlike the English rape-seed; this they burn and pound like coffee, and it would puzzle many people who are not connoisseurs to find out the difference.

The two chiefs now dwelt much on the attempts which the French had made to induce them to consent to the temple's being opened, appearing to take great merit to themselves for having resisted all the offers that were made to them:—the presents were now brought, and given in the name of Mr. Salt ([3]): to Daoud was given a handsome gun, which at Cairo cost five-hundred piastres, a turban which cost fifty, and some other trifles, such as gunpowder, soap, tobacco, coffee, sugar, &c. To Halleel a turban was presented, and smaller articles equal in value to what his brother had received. We now took our leave, but had scarce reached our boat when we heard that Halleel was highly offended because he had not received a gun as well as his brother. We immediately waited on him and endeavoured to appease him, explaining that we were not aware of the two brothers being both cashiefs, or we would certainly have brought him a gun as well as Daoud (the preceding year when Mr. B. was in Nubia, the younger brother had not assumed the title of cashief, nor was he treated as such): we promised that if he would have patience, and confide in our word, that we would send him another gun exactly the same as his brother's; or if he preferred it, that we would give him one of our own guns; though we confessed we had none half so good as the one we had already given, and advised him to wait till we got another, as he would lose much by accepting a bad one. All was however in vain, as nothing could appease him; he sat sulky in the corner, saying, he had better guns than ours, and that he knew what to do in his own country; meaning that we should not open the temple. This was a sad and unexpected blow to our hopes; we began to despair, and seeing nothing would please him we retired. A message now came from Daoud to invite us to partake of a sheep he had killed in order to regale us; we went to his tent but found Halleel not there: we noticed this, and expressed our concern at the displeasure he had evinced. Daoud said his brother was only a boy; that he was indiscreet, and did not know what he did, and that we need not mind him. We now sent a message to him to say that we would not eat unless he came and ate with us, but he refused. Daoud now at our request went to bring him; but failing, he returned, saying, he was only a boy, and that he pledged himself we should open the temple. However, as we saw by Halleel's behaviour that he was of a mischievous disposition, and a person likely to do us great injury, indirectly, if not directly, we judged it the best policy to bring about a reconciliation. Mr. B. accordingly went himself, and after much difficulty prevailed on him to come; he, however, was still sulky, and we had scarce sat down to dinner when three strangers, apparently newly arrived, entered the tent, kneeled and kissed hands, paying their respects to Halleel before Daoud. We easily saw through this little trick, which was a concerted plan between the two brothers, to induce us to believe that each of them were equal, the one to the other, and thus to give Halleel more presents, from a supposition that his rank was equal to his brother's: the men belonged to the suite and were disguised for the purpose.

After we had retired from dinner we went to see if Halleel was still displeased, and found him as sulky as ever; our crew and Hassan having been with him from the first moment of his ill-humour, and doing all in their power to put him against us; for which Daoud had reprimanded them severely. Perceiving there was no pleasing him, that neither presents nor promises were of any avail, we returned to the boat, Daoud having pledged his word that we should commence on the temple the following morning. Late in the evening we received a message from Halleel, requesting a gun, with some powder and shot: we immediately gave him ours, which though good for nothing, was, nevertheless, the best looking in our stock. This prompt compliance calmed his anger, and we began to congratulate ourselves on the prospect of ultimate success in our projected undertaking. Daoud Cashief sent a sheep. The only remaining difficulty now was to make the agreement with the workmen. The Farras man, who told us at Elpha " that we should hear of him below," now made his appearance, and endeavoured all he could to thwart our preceedings; we, however, took him to the cashiefs and explained his conduct to them, which caused them to reprimand him, and he entirely failed in every point. After much altercation we were glad to agree for the men to work at two piastres each, per day.

July 11. In the morning the two cashiefs came on board, and we proceeded to the temple, about a quarter of an hour's row from the village. The chiefs told us we were to have sixty men, and we paid for that number, while only fifty came. We were obliged also to give them doura, as they all complained of having nothing to eat; however, we had been at such anxiety about the temple, that we were glad to give them any thing provided they would but work. As it most likely would render you more acquainted with our proceedings, and the object of our research, to give you some description of the front of the temple, I shall proceed to explain where it was situated, how formed, and the manner in which the mysterious door was hidden from our curiosity. The temple is situated on the side of the Nile, about two or three hundred yards from its western bank; it stands upon an elevation, and its base is considerably above the level of the river: it is excavated in the mountain, and its front presents a flat surface of upwards of sixty feet in height, above the summit of the sand immediately over the door, but not so much as forty on the north side, and a little more on the south; the breadth is one hundred and seventeen feet. Above thirty feet of the height of the temple, from the base, is covered by the accumulated sand in the centre, and about fifty feet on either side. You are, therefore, to figure to yourself a flat excavated perpendicular surface, fronting the river, and hemmed in by one side of a mountain of sand leaning against it; the door in the centre of this plane surface buried in the sand, which rises on each side of it, increasing the labour and difficulty of digging down to a prodigious degree; for no sooner is the sand in the centre removed, than that on either side pours down, so that to get only a foot down in the centre, we had the labour of removing the whole surface of sand which leaned against the front of the temple; this sand also was of so fine a description, that every particle of it would go through an hour-glass. Before the front of the temple are four sitting colossal figures cut out of the solid mountain, chairs and all: they are, however, brought out so fully, that the backs do not lean against the wall or front of the temple, but are full eight feet from it; and were it not for a narrow niche of the rock which joins them to the surface, from the back part of the necks downwards, they would be wholly detached.

One of the statues has been broken off by a fracture of the mountain, from the waist upwards. There were twenty-two monkeys above the frieze and cornice; of these there are not now above twelve perfect. Under the arm of one of the great figures we discovered the remains of the stucco with which they were once covered; and traces of the red paint which was once on them is discernible in many places. I think it very probable the whole front of the temple was once covered with stucco, more especially as they have used that material very liberally and skilfully in the decoration of the interior, of which I shall speak more fully in its proper place. Of the cornice over the door, which was once perfect, there is not at present more than a foot in breadth remaining, just over the corner where we entered; in the progress of our labours, you will see what is become of the rest, and its mutilation caused us some very desponding evenings, as may well be imagined, when there was so little indication of the temple being finished lower down than we could see.

This description will give you some idea of the obstacles we had to surmount, and, at the same time, of the good reasons we had to expect a magnificent interior, should we ever succeed in the undertaking.

July 11. First day, the fifty men that came

worked very badly, and we found that the burthen of the song which they sung by way of stimulating each other, was, " that it was christian money they were working for, that christian money was very good, and that they would get as much of it as they could :"—this Nubian song, though cheering to them, was not much so to us. In the evening we returned to the village of Ebsambal, and perceiving we should never make any progress with people who, being sure of their pay whether they laboured well or ill, would only work five hours in the day, we sent to the cashiefs, and concluded a bargain with them and the natives *" to open the temple "* for three hundred piastres. At this time none of us thought it would take more than four days to accomplish the undertaking, so little did we know of the real nature of our enterprize. On the morning of the twelfth, the two cashiefs and about one hundred men came and worked very well, thinking they could open the temple in one day; they requested we would not interfere in directing the labourers where to work, as it was now their own affair, they had undertaken the task, and were responsible for its execution. In the evening our boat's crew came and begged the intercession of the cashiefs to make peace; they were the more anxious for an accommodation, as by the quarrel they lost the heads, skins, and offal of the sheep which we occasionally killed. We made much ado to give in, but ultimately became reconciled; the cashiefs bursting out into a violent rage against the crew, on our remarking that no European travellers would ever come into the country again, when they heard of the usage we had received. The dispute was scarcely at an end before our sailors asked for backsheeish; this we positively refused till we arrived at Philæ, and then only on condition of very good behaviour; all came now and kissed hands in token of reconciliation. At sun-set we returned to the village of Ebsambal, when the chief of the labourers asked for two out of the three hundred piastres (though they had consented to be paid only when the temple was opened); we were, however, obliged to give one hundred and fifty, but said we would give no more till the work was finished.

July 13. Only Halleel Cashief and about sixty men came; they worked very ill, and expressed doubts as to there being any door, though they had not yet got more than four feet down. While we were endeavouring to persuade them to persevere, one of the natives, a carpenter, with an audible voice, made a speech, the substance of which was, " that they would work the whole of the present and two successive days, and if in that time they found a door, well and good, if not, that they would labour no longer." This brief effusion was received with tumultuous approbation, in which we thought it good policy to join, as neither our approval or displeasure would have had any weight with them, and it was possible our being in good humour with them might induce them to do their work more cheerfully. In the evening we returned to the village, complained to the cashief of the badness of the work, and noticed the approach of the ramadan, when it was probable we should no longer be able to get workmen, and therefore our present efforts would be useless. Both the brothers now promised us "a host of men next morning," and that they should begin early. While we were discoursing, some Mograbins on their way from Cairo to Dongola were introduced; we remarked their melancholy looks, but were ignorant of the cause. Our business being at an end, we retired to our boat after having feasted on doura cake and dripping.

July 14. Rose early, and sent to the cashiefs that we were ready, but, after waiting for three hours, they sent word to us to go and they would join by land; so busied were they in plundering the Mograbins, that our temple and ourselves were not thought of. We accordingly went, and found only fifty men doing little more than nothing, and none of the leaders or attendants present, except old Mouchmarr, an elderly servant of the cashiefs. We asked him the reason of his master's absence, when he said " that we must not think him a Barbarin, that he was an Arab, and only lived in this country by force; that both the cashiefs were robbers, and at present pillaging the caravan of Morocco; and that the whole tribe of natives were nothing but a gang of thieves." We could not help laughing at the remarks of the old man, which though true enough, would have come better from another quarter, as he himself was an old rogue, as you will perceive in the sequel. At noon Daoud Cashief arrived; the men still continuing to work without effect, we remonstrated with Daoud, but only received promises of great doings on the morrow. We returned to the village in the evening, when the men asked for the remainder of the money; this we refused, and in consequence there was much discontent evinced. Halleel Cashief now came to endeavour to persuade us to pay the money, but we persisted in refusing till they had worked the third day, according to their own promise. We were now told that if we paid the money they would come next morning and work, but if not, that not a man of them would come;

we still refused. Illeel now asked for one of Mr. Salt's handsome pipes, which the crew had told him was in the boat; having previously begged the janissary to give him his silk waistcoat, and requested of our Greek servant his mameluke sabre; this latter article belonged to Mr. Salt, was very valuable, and to save it, we had pretended it was the property of the Greek, not thinking the cashief would even beg of our servants. He had also asked the soldier for his pistols, offering him a slave in return;—all was however refused.

Tuesday, July 15. Both cashiefs came and some of the chiefs; one in particular, a stranger, was highly dressed, and we were told he was a leading character, and had much influence with the natives; that nothing could be done without him. But we had now seen enough of the character of the Nubians to perceive that this was only a trick to induce us to give the new comer some presents, and we therefore affected to take no notice of him, determined for the future to give no more than we could help. In the morning the men worked well; our crew assisted them, and behaved better, but towards the evening the work went on badly. We returned to the village; on the way Hassan told us we must go back to Philæ, in order to repair the boat, which he asserted to be leaky; we soon gave him to understand that we had no intention of returning till we had accomplished our work. Soon after dark Halleel came to the boat to ask for the pipe again, but it was refused.

Wednesday, July 16. First day of the moon, ramadan or Turkish fast, during which they do not eat or drink from sun-rise to sun-set. Early this morning Halleel sent us a water-melon, and shortly after made his appearance, begging the pipe again, which being worth upwards of sixty piastres, had greatly attracted his notice; this third attempt was evaded, and he set off in a pet, without even taking leave, mounting his horse for Derry, where he intended passing the ramadan. We now went to Daoud's tent to pay him a farewell visit previous to his departure; he asked us what were our intentions respecting the temple? We told him we were determined to work ourselves, and persevere till we came to the door; he appeared much surprised at this, and said it was impossible we could succeed, recommending us to return, and come again after the month of ramadan, doubtless in the hopes of getting more presents. To convince him of our resolution to proceed, we told him that the Nile would as soon change its course, as we our determination when once it was taken. He now asked the sailors if we had solicited their assistance, when they told him we had not mentioned the subject to them, which indeed was true; he then asked when we thought we should reach the door; we told him that was very uncertain; he said if we thought we should be only three or four days, he would remain, but if more, he must be off: we answered that we expected to be eight or ten days before our work would be over. We now promised, that whenever we should be near the door, we would give him notice, that he might be present and *get his share of the gold.* He gave a tacit sort of consent for us to proceed, and we took our leave, thanking him for what he had done for us. Amongst the warlike instruments in his tent, we observed a shield made of crocodile's skin; it was remarkably strong; one of the protuberances of the animal's back served for the boss or centre, and one of those of the tail for the hollow of the elbow. The natives assured us it would resist a musket ball; and if the skin of the living animal possesses this power, I do not see why one should doubt the assertion. In general, Nubian shields are made of the skin of the hippopotamus. At twelve o'clock we sailed for the temple, and while going took occasian to represent to the reis and crew, that now we were about to be left together, we hoped they would continue to behave well and conduct themselves peaceably, promising on our part every indulgence they could reasonably expect, provided we had no fault to find with them; they all promised to behave themselves orderly and quietly. We dined at one, and at three o'clock set off to begin our labour, going up alone and quietly that we might not wake the crew who were asleep on the beach, as we wished they should be prevented from rising high in their demands, by an apparent indifference on our part as to whether they assisted or not. We now stripped to the waist and commenced, six in number, including the Greek servant and the janissary, with a good will, and soon found that we made considerable progress; we resolved to keep to our work, and regularly to persevere from three till dark in the evenings, and from the very first dawning of the day till nine in the morning. After we had worked about an hour some of the crew came up, they appeared astonished to see us labouring without shirts, and expressed surprise at the progress we had made. They now began to assist, which we appeared to take no notice of; they worked well, and at dark we left off, having done as much as (speaking within bounds) forty of the natives would have done in a day. Our hands certainly suffered a little by blisters; I had nine on one hand, and eight on the other. We were careful to encourage our sailors, and not to expect too much from them, as their being prohibited, though under a vertical sun, from eating or even drinking, rendered their case very different from ours. We returned to our boat in high glee at the favourable appearance of affairs. We had scarcely supped and retired to bed when we heard a strange boat approaching; it proved to be Daoud Cashief on his way to Derry; he had given a passage to one of our sailors who had waited behind at the village to get bread made. He sent us a kid with salaams, and a request that we would spare him some of our small coffee-cups, which were rather handsome: we sent him two, and at the same time requested of him a ludri (a skin to contain water), which he gave us; lastly, a message came to say that he had left several of his servants behind him at Ebsambal, with orders to assist us with men, to procure us supplies and provisions, and, in short, to render us any service we might require. We thanked him, and renewed our promise of apprising him when we should be near the door, that he might not think we had any secret object in opening the temple during his absence; for they all think we expect to find money should we succeed. Daoud now departed; we gave our crew two piastres for each man, and one to each of the boys; there were six men and two boys. We told them, at the same time, that if they consented to work at similar hours, and in the same manner as we did ourselves, they should daily receive the same sum:—these conditions were acceded to apparently with great eagerness.

Thursday, July 17. Started at the dawn of day and worked hard, fourteen in number, till nearly nine o'clock, when the sun being at a considerable height, and shining directly on us, the heat obliged us to desist: we had made considerable progress, and as all our efforts were directed in the right way, we had reason to be well satisfied. The crew worked tolerably well; Hassan was on the opposite side of the river getting bread made, and looking out for a sheep. Dined at one, and at three renewed our operations: one of the crew did not come this evening; we took no notice of it, resolving to give him only half a day's pay; the rest worked tolerably well; we continued till star-light, and made great progress. At the latter part of the evening Hassan returned, having brought nothing with him; at night we paid the crew.

July 18. In the morning, at the very first dawning of day, we started to our work again, and called the crew, but as we expected from the moment Hassan arrived, they all refused to work, alleging that the pay was not sufficient; that it was now ramadan, and that they ought to have thirty piastres per day. Our janissary now informed us that they had spoken of this aloud in the night that he might tell us. Seeing them in this humour, we told them that those who did not choose to work might let it alone; at half-past eight we left off, having done nearly as much work as if they had been with us: indeed we were astonished to see what steady persevering labour would do. One of the Ebsambal men came this morning and worked very fairly, promising to bring ten more on the morrow: there came also a chief from the opposite side of the river with an offer of twenty men. We told him our terms of two piastres per day for each man, and that it was our intention to pay the money into the men's own hands, as we learnt that the cashiefs and chiefs had given each labourer one piastre only, and retained the other for themselves. At three, we renewed our operations: a few of the crew came but worked very badly;— we left off at dark.

Saturday, July 19. Commenced our labours before daylight; only two of the crew came and three other lads; the promised men from Ebsambal and the opposite side of the river not arriving: we continued working till half-past eight, when just as we were about to leave off, Halleel Cashief and his court of bullies made their appearance in a boat, and landing near our bark, came up to see what was doing. Immediately we saw them approaching we left off, and went down to our bark; Halleel and his myrmidons soon returned. Suspecting their roguish intentions, we, to avoid them, went to bathe; the men from the opposite side of the river, about thirty in number, now arrived, but without tools; this disappointed us a little. On coming out of the water, we went to visit Halleel Cashief, as a compliment, to keep up appearances; while so doing, a desperate dispute took place between our janissary and Hassan, who seeing the former was not armed, chaced him into the boat with his drawn dagger, uttering savage imprecations at the same time. Halleel made a pretence to interfere, but soon after, while we were settling the dispute, he sneaked away in his boat with all his attendants, without taking any leave; indeed he was off before we were aware, and we were very glad to find him gone.

Our Greek servant now told us he had asked for some coffee, and on being told there was none, had desired the servant to say nothing to us about his having asked for it; he was very inquisitive about the stay we intended to make, and seemed desirous we should call on him at Derry on our return, no doubt in hope of getting something more. The men worked pretty well to day; the Ebsambal man who had promised to bring his nine assistants never made his appearance; this we clearly saw was Halleel's doing. At night, when paying the men, we had a dispute with the workmen, who endeavoured to impose on us by false tickets; these tickets were slips of paper on which Mr. Belzoni wrote his name and issued them out to the workmen in the morning; on producing them in the evening they received their pay. This day the Darfur caravan, of four thousand camels, laden with gum, ivory, ostrich-feathers, tamarinds, rhinoceros horns, slaves, &c. passed on their way to Cairo: the mamelukes had made them pay nine thousand dollars (upwards of two thousand pounds) at Dongola. Some of the jelabs who led the caravan came to see our operations: they had long hair greased with oil and hanging down in ringlets; some had it plaited: they wore sandals, had each a long spear, and altogether were singular figures.

Sunday, July 20. At twilight we renewed our labours, and had sixty-four men to work; the crew stimulated them by a good example, which coupled with our own personal attendance, produced a good morning's labour; at three P.M. recommenced our operations and got on tolerably well. This evening one of Daoud Cashief's staff arrived, with some aqua vitæ, and a few dates as a present; he also brought Irby and me some new Nubian clothes; two suits cost us twenty-four piastres, or twelve shillings; double what we had given for better things of the same kind at Momfalout. In the evening our cook threw a kettle of water in the face of a bully who asked him for money in a threatening manner: this truly cook-like mode of assault unsheathed the Barbarin's sword (for the most trivial occurrence produces their drawn weapons), and it was with difficulty we could prevent some serious mischief from ensuing. At night Daoud Cashief's messenger returned, having failed in an attempt to beg a pipe for his master.

Monday, July 21. This day no men came from the opposite side of the river, but we had about forty from Ebsambal; they worked tolerably well, and brought to light the bend of the right arm of the statue, to the north of the door, which was much broken: the discovery was highly satisfactory to us, as it proved that the statues were seated, and, consequently, that we should not have to dig down so deep for the door as if they were standing figures. In the evening the men worked tolerably well, and towards the close of the day we found a projecting part of the wall roughly chiselled, uneven in its surface, and having every appearance of unfinished work. We could not see more than six or eight inches down, and it still continued the same: the projection was about four inches from the plane surface of the front of the temple, and it appeared to fill up the whole space between the two centre statues. This being exactly the place where we expected to find the door, the sudden change from a flat finished exterior, to a coarsely chiselled uneven surface, was precisely the circumstance most calculated to give the impression that the temple was unfinished, and that there was no door; indeed we could not in any other way account for an appearance so extraordinary and unexpected; discouraging as this discovery was, we nevertheless resolved to proceed with our work, and to dig down till we had ascertained beyond all possibility of doubt, that there was no entrance to the temple.

About eleven o'clock at night, a boat arrived from the opposite side; they did not make any noise, but the reis sent word that he had brought a sheep for us; the message was accompanied with the present of a water-melon.

Tuesday, July 22. At daylight we found a great assemblage of people, the boat having brought them over in the night; at the same time there arrived a considerable number from Ebsambal. As these two parties amounted to treble the number we wanted, we retired to our boat to avoid disputes, leaving thirty tickets with old Mouchmarr, with instruction to employ only that number; returning in about half an hour, we found he had only given out twenty of the tickets, keeping the other ten to himself till the evening, which would give him twenty piastres. While we were settling this with the old rogue, a violent quarrel ensued between the natives of Ebsambal and the party from the opposite shore, as to who should be employed; and after much noise and confusion, hostilities having commenced in a slight degree between the parties, the whole of them departed shouting and hooting, in number about two hundred, the stronger party not permitting the Ebsambal people to work. As they retired our crew serenaded them with repeated cries of, " barout, barout," which means powder, powder, an article they are not very partial to. In the evening we renewed our labours without any assistance, but soon had the crew and about twenty volunteers, who worked very well considering we had only three instruments, the Ebsambal men having taken away four out of the seven we had hitherto used. They were of this form,

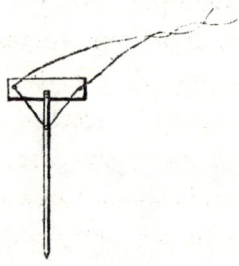

and the mode of working was to fix the implement perpendicularly in the sand, and then to pull it forward by a cord attached to it; one person was stationed at the handle to fix it in the sand, and another at the cord by which it was pulled forward. Instead of one, the Arabs generally employed from four to six men at the cord. This evening we came to the chair of the statue, but still no indication of a door; the unfinished work continuing, though the figure, drapery and all, is perfectly finished as far as we could see down.

Wednesday, July 23. It was curious to observe in the morning, on the smooth surface of the sand, drifted by the night breeze, the tracks of the snakes, lizards, animals, &c. &c. which had come down to the water's side during the night to drink; and we could plainly discern the traces of their return to their solitary haunts in the desert.

Sometimes their track indicated the presence of reptiles of considerable size; and with these proofs of their nocturnal movements, we easily accounted for the dread our guides expressed of walking near the water's side the night we returned from the second cataract. We renewed our operations at the very first appearance of day, and soon had about twenty-six workmen together with the crew; between eight and nine o'clock, as the people were working, we perceived a boat laden with men coming over from the opposite side. As soon as the Ebsambal people made them out, they all set off with old Mouchmarr at their head; the latter saying he knew who they were, and would go and treat with them, as they were coming to prevent our work. The old fellow, it appeared afterwards, was more intent on his own safety, as both he and his party went and hid themselves in caves in the mountains. Suspecting something, we sent for all our arms from the boat and waited the event. The newly arrived party now made their appearance, about forty in number, armed mostly with muskets, pistols, sabres, and pikes; they were much better dressed, and made a better figure than the attendants of Daoud and Halleel. There were two with white turbans, who appeared the leading characters; these approached in advance of their attendants, and after the usual salaams and ceremony of salute, seated themselves near us, and presented us with two sheep, which their men had brought with them. We now desired our janissary to ask them the intention of their visit, and to tell them we had nothing to dispose of, having given all we had to spare to the two cashiefs below. They replied that they wanted nothing, that they were in the employ of the pashaw, that their office was to keep order and tranquillity in the country, and that they wished to know if any obstacles on the part of the inhabitants rendered their assistance necessary, as they were ready to be of service to us, hoping that on our return to Cairo, we should not fail to speak favourably of them to the pashaw. We replied that we were going on tolerably well, and that we did not stand in need of any assistance. After sitting about half an hour, they went down to the other temple, followed by all their attendants, and soon after sent our Greek servant up with a message, " that they were at war with the other two cashiefs; that they were greater than them; that they were the governours of this country; that when the others killed one man, they could kill two; in short, that we had given a gun, shawl, soap, and tobacco, to both Daoud and Halleel, and why, they wished to know, was nothing given to them, who possessed double the authority of the brothers in this country, and could prevent our labour whenever they pleased? finally, that they must have the same, and more presents than we had already given, or that we should not open the temple." They also wished to know under what authority we acted, and desired to see our firman. We replied to these menaces by the same observations we had made on their arrival, viz. that we had already given all we had to give away; and we added, that as we had both the pashaw's and Deftarda Bey's firman for doing what we were about, any violence offered us would be sure to reach their ears. Their answer was, that they cared nothing about the pashaw: on seeing the firmans, they said they were good for nothing, being written in Turkish, not Arabic; that they had no Turkish interpreter, and that were the firmans even in Arabic, nothing but presents would induce them to permit us to proceed. The crew now thought it a favourable opportunity to ask for one of the sheep (for each of which we had given ten piastres), but we immediately refused their request, explaining, that they were mistaken if they thought it a proper time to ask gifts, when other people were endeavouring to rob and plunder us; that as soon as the banditti were gone, and we were at our own disposal, we might give them something, but never through fear of them, or to gain their favour. Soon after the two cashiefs and their gang proceeded to Ebsambal; we now learnt that they were Mahomed and Ali Cashief, that they lived a little above Derry, on the opposite side of the river, and were at war with Daoud and Halleel in consequence of their grandfather (Hassan's father) having killed some relation of Ali's many years ago. This is what the Barbarins call the " warfare of blood for blood," and it always lasts till an individual of one family is sacrificed to appease the other ([4]). Sometimes this hostility exists for many ages between families; and it is for this reason that a murderer, who is one of our crew, dares not go to Philæ or the neighbourhood of Assuan, where he committed the crime.

At three P. M. renewed our operations and had a considerable number of assistants; it was truly ridiculous to see old Mouchmarr now make his appearance, with his matchlock in his hand, and a few of the Ebsambal people. He took especial care to examine both up the river and down, to be sure that the cashiefs were well out of sight; and when he found the coast clear, he came to us to relate how his people had been in the habit of making slaves and prisoners of the other party; what numbers they had bound together and thrown into the Nile, &c.: we rallied him a little about his intercession. We found that the cashiefs had prevented many of our assistants from coming, and that they had plundered the whole country, taking two sheep from every sackey, and ten piastres from those who could not procure the animals. We also learnt that a fine of four dollars (thirty-six piastres) was to be levied on every one who came to our assistance. This evening our men worked very well; as they did not belong to Ebsambal, they knew they were out the cashiefs' reach.

Thursday, July 24. At dawn of day went to work again; as we had broken our water-jars we asked the crew for our ludri which we had lent them, but Hassan said it was ramadan, and that as they could not drink water in the day time, they wanted our ludri to keep it cool for them in the evening, and that they would return it when they got to Philæ. We gave them to understand that we liked cool water as well as they did, and desired the janissary to take the skin without further ceremony; asking them at the same time if that was gratitude for the sheep we gave them yesterday: Hassan answered, that the sheep was lean and good for nothing, or we should not have given it. This morning we had about twenty workmen, but neither Mouchmarr nor the Ebsambal men came; after we had worked about an hour a party of about thirty came from the opposite side and volunteered to assist: as they were more than we wanted, and came late, we told them we would give them one and a half piastre each if they would work; this they rejected at first, but soon returned and agreed. After they had worked nearly an hour, four other men came and solicited employ; these we refused, when one of them displaying a dirty white turban as a flag, drew all the whole party off with a shout. After about a quarter of an hour's stay, however, they returned, having been told that we could do without them: the work now went on pretty well, the armed ruffians not making their appearance. In the evening the people worked very badly, being so numerous that one skulked behind the other.

Friday, July 25. Got up at dawn of day and found one hundred men assembled, though the night before we told them that we did not want any more assistance: we explained this to them again, adding, that at most we could not employ more than twenty: they replied, that we must employ them all or none. Seeing them in this mood we returned to our boat, resolving to wait till they were all gone, and knowing that the heat of the sun, at nine o'clock, would soon drive them away. After much noise amongst themselves, and numerous ineffectual parleys, they all set off, taking all the instruments with them, and threatening our crew that if they assisted us they would acquaint Daoud and Halleel Cashief of it; thus showing that these brothers had ordered that no assistance was to be rendered us. Our sailors laughed at them, saying, they cared nothing about the cashiefs or any one else. Soon after this the whole rabble crossed the water, having a dirty white turban (the prophet's banner) hoisted. At three we renewed our work with six instruments which we had made ourselves: the crew and also that of another bark came, and assistance was also offered from a few others: we got on tolerably well.

Saturday, July 26. At dawn of day went up to our employment with the assistance we had the preceding evening, in all about twenty-three persons; our servants had another quarrel with the crew. A mameluke arrived from Dongola; he reported his countrymen in great misery at that place. He was on his way to Cairo to see his mother: his father was included amongst the mamelukes who were massacred at Cairo by the pashaw some years ago, and he had escaped with his uncle, who being lately dead, the lad was on his return to his only surviving parent. We now learned that Mahomed and Ali Cashief were gone down the river again with their plunder. In the evening renewed our operations. A man who had received money for our bread on the opposite side of the river, refused to bring it: we had a dispute in consequence, and, after much noise and confusion, half the quantity we paid for was brought, which we were glad to get. We now found the price of every thing we bought had doubled since our arrival; the natives hoped by these means to force us to relinquish our work, and, with our eyes open, we were obliged to submit to the imposition.

Sunday, July 27. At dawn of day set to work again, and had only two assistants besides the crew, who worked remarkably well: several volunteers came, but we rejected them on account of their laziness. One of our two assistants this morning sang a song to cheer up the crew; this is their constant custom when working; the words are as follows: " Oh Nubia, my country, thou smellest like a rose; when I sleep I dream of thee, and thou appearest a garden full of flowers." You may easily imagine that our ideas of Nubia, " where a flowering shrub is scarcely ever seen," were not in unison with those of our neighbour. We, however, found this a new proof of that happy disposition which nature implants in the breast of every man to be partial to his native soil, be it what it may.

> " The naked negro panting at the line,
> Boasts of his golden sands and palmy wine:
> Basks in the glare, or stems the tepid wave,
> And thanks his gods for all the good they gave.
> Such is the patriot's boast where'er we roam,
> His first, best country, ever is, at home."

At three we recommenced our operations; while we were working, arrived a spy from Daoud Cashief, who after having deliberately examined us, began by talking to the crew to draw them off from the work: he then asked old Mouchmarr, who had just arrived from the village with some bread for us, how he dared assist us; adding, that the cashiefs would cut off his head for it. This news did not appear very agreeable to our friend, who was now deterred from working as he had done the preceding day. Our young mameluke friend who understood the Barbarin language, unknown to the crew and natives, told us of this. The spy then informed us that a firman had arrived from the grand signior to supersede the pashaw in his government, and that new troops were now at Cairo. So paltry an attempt to alarm us, was answered by a hearty laugh, which made both the spy and his countrymen look very foolish, until seeing the joke went against them, they put it off by a laugh also. In the evening old Mouchmarr came to be paid for his bread, and on being asked to bring more, said he did not like to tell us a falsehood, and that he had strict injunctions against bringing any thing more, or indeed rendering us any further assistance. We further learned that the whole of the natives on both sides of the river had mutually agreed that nothing was to be sold to us. It was hinted that we might have some men to work if we chose; however, as our money was getting low, and as we had found that we did almost as much without, as with them, we sent word that we wanted nothing of them; we had three days bread, and our work had arrived at a point which would soon ascertain whether there was any door or not; we felt ourselves therefore quite independent of our troublesome neighbours. Old Mouchmarr now took his leave; it is but justice to the old man to say, that he behaved better than any of his countrymen.

Monday, July 28. Commenced our operations at the usual hour, with only our sailors and the mameluke, no Ebsambal men making their appearance; all worked pretty well. This morning no milk was brought; we affected to take no notice whatever of it, and at breakfast were particularly careful that the crew (who came down and were watching us narrowly to see what effect the want of this luxury would have) should observe no change in consequence, that they might report to the natives the poor success of their scheme. At three renewed our labours; while working, an Ebsambal man came to see what was going on; he said that if we wished it, a certain number of people would come from each sackey to assist, and he asked us if we wanted provisions; we refused all assistance. He then asked if we could live on stones? we replied, that we had a boat to go and fetch whatever we wanted, and that money would always procure something; he now said we might think ourselves fortunate in having a soldier of the pashaw's with us, as were it not for fear of the consequences, in case any thing should happen to him, the whole body of natives would prevent our work by force. We replied, that we were determined to proceed; and that even were the soldier not with us, we would persist in our undertaking. He now began to brag of the number of armed people they could muster from the neighbourhood: we, however, laughed at him, and he left us, having failed in all his designs. Our crew this evening worked very well, and we thought it good policy to tell them we noticed their exertions.

Tuesday, July 29. At dawn of day we recommenced our labours with the crew, and made considerable progress, no strangers making their appearance, the one who assisted us yesterday being deterred by the threats of the spy. In the evening, at three, renewed our work; towards the close of day the sailors requested to be dismissed, that they might go to Ebsambal to get bread for themselves. We suspected some bad intentions on their part, but said nothing: Hassan had previously endeavoured to steal some of our doura (for bread we had none), but we were too sharp for him, and made his boy give us back what he had taken.

Wednesday, July 30. At twilight we went to work again, the crew coming as usual: this morning our milkman brought us milk again, but said he was obliged to do it clandestinely. This was a real luxury, as we found, after four hours hard work on an empty stomach, that a limited ration of doura grain, dried dates, and water, to which we were now reduced, was not very sumptuous fare. The reis of the bark, who had before cheated us out of our bread, now made his appearance again with some spirituous liquors, which he said he had brought as a present from the wife of Daoud Cashief. We clearly saw this was a trick to get a present to the bearer, which is generally double the value of the article given; we therefore refused the present, but offered to purchase what he had; after some hesitation he consented:—it was the spirit distilled from the date, but without the addition of aniseed, which in Egypt makes it palatable. We generally took a little before dinner as a tonic; for without something of the kind (the average of the thermometer being one hundred and twelve degrees Fahrenheit in the shade) we found that we had no appetite. As soon as he had got his money he took himself off to the other side of the river, having evidently come to see if we yet began to complain for want of provisions. But although we had nothing to eat but doura, and only enough of that for four days, we never once mentioned the subject of provisions. This evening we came to a projection, evidently a cornice, though much broken by the shock of an immense block of stone that had fallen on it. Beneath the projection we found a plane and smooth surface, and a tablet of neat hieroglyphics, highly finished, carved thereon; the most favourable indication of a door we could possibly expect, and which much cheered our prospects.

At three we returned to our operations, and by digging down and carrying away the sand with two boxes, we removed a sufficient quantity to make out about a foot of a tablet surmounted by a torus, and one end of a broken cornice above it; which, having been broken by some accident, has evidently been chiselled away since its completion, with the design of renewing it: the furrowed surface, and the marks of the tools in all directions, though rudely done, and quite unfinished, prove this to be the case, and thus the mystery of the unfavourable appearances which had formerly given us so much uneasiness is cleared up. This evening Hassan asked, with more than usual impudence, for the pay of the crew, adding, that he wanted it immediately before it was dark.

Thursday, July 31. At twilight resumed our task; palisadoed the part supposed to be immediately over the door, by driving in piles of date-trees, and pouring at the back of them mud mixed with sand to keep the outer sand from running in between them. Just as we were going to desist from our work, some armed men came from the opposite side of the river, who had been called over by Hassan: we enquired the reason of his calling them over, when he said he wanted the boat from the opposite side, to go and get some provisions for the crew. Our sailors talked freely with the strangers; we took no notice of them; they appeared very intent on what we were doing. This day the mameluke took his departure for Cairo; he went on a small reed raft which a Nubian was conducting down the river; Hassan ran with great eagerness to send some message by the stranger; no doubt to apprise the cashiefs below of the progress of our work.

In the evening we resumed our labours with the crew and two strangers; towards sun-set we came to the corner of the door; it was rather broken. The sailors, on seeing it, expressed great signs of joy, uttering cries of " backsheeish, backsheeish," and immediately asked us if it was not true, that we had promised them money whenever we should find the door: we replied, that we certainly had promised them a present, and would give it when we had entered the temple. The fellows now began working hard to enlarge the entrance, appearing in high good humour, and occasionally repeating the favourite word " backsheeish," tyep, tyep—good, good. At dusk we had made an aperture nearly large enough for a man's body, but we could not tell whether the sand would be necessary to be drawn up from the entrance or not, which left us in great uncertainty as to the time when our labours would end; for should the temple be much filled with sand, we might have a prodigious deal of work to do yet. When we returned to the boat, Hassan told Captain Irby and myself, it was totally impossible we could ever get into the temple by palisadoing; that the sand would fall on us as fast as we dug down, and that it was like attempting to dig into the Nile; at the same time he offered to forfeit his beard if we succeeded; all the crew joined in the same assertion. But it was the only method of getting at the door, unless we cleared it altogether, which would have taken a good month more.

We resolved to begin the next morning by moon-light, and apprised the crew of our intention, that they might not think we wanted to steal in by ourselves, and thus bring away the gold unknown to them. As the day's discovery had put us all in good humour, our sailors attempted to profit by it; they asked our cook for his new silk waistcoat, and begged of the Greek his new blue gown; they did not solicit any thing further from us, thinking it best to wait till they got our backsheeish.

At moonlight on Friday morning, August the first, the anniversary of the battle of the Nile, we rose and went to work. We called the crew, but as they did not appear in any hurry to come, we went up alone with lights; while making our arrangements to begin, we heard a great noise below, plainly distinguishing Hassan's roaring voice above all the rest, and the word backsheeish frequently repeated. The Greek servant being sent down for a lamp, returned with an account that they were all abusing us, and complaining that after having worked hard for us, they only received two piastres per day, instead of four which they merited (I should here tell you that their monthly wages from the reis, were from seven to nine piastres each man). We were called christian dogs without faith, and they said we must take all our things out of the boat immediately, as they would stay no longer, having remained till they were tired, and in a place were they could get no provisions. Mr. Belzoni now went down to find our hammer which was mislaid, resolving to abstain from any argument with them; immediately on seeing him they all fell down on their kness, and began praying, bowing down, and kissing the ground according to their custom. He took no notice of them, but brought all our arms and ammunition up; the janissary also went and brought his pistols, Hassan saying in his hearing, that he must carry a soldier on his back to Derry, implying that he must murder the janissary, though it was but the day before that he came to him saying that he wished to make peace, and that what he had formerly said against him came from his warmth of temper, and not from his heart.

As soon as we had commenced working by candle-light, one of the crew came to say that we must embark immediately and depart, or land our effects and let the boat go, as they could wait no longer; we sent word that they might go whenever they pleased, but it would be to their own loss if they did, as we would pay them nothing; and that for our part we were determined to remain till our work was completed; having said this, we continued our work. The crew now made their appearance in a body, dressed in their turbans and gowns, as at Elpha; this being their custom when they wish to appear of consequence. They were armed with long sticks, pikes, swords, daggers, and two old rusty pistols, which would be more likely to kill the person who fired, than him who was fired at. In reply to our inquiry of what they wanted, they made long complaints of being badly paid, and of never having received any adequate recompence for having brought us provisions from the neighbouring villages, and for all their other endeavours to please us; that they had waited here till the last moment, and must now go down the river, all at the same time joining in savage imprecations, and scraping the sand with their hatchets and swords; the reis, who was the foremost of the party, in feigned paroxysms of anger, threw the sand up in his face, where the perspiration caused it to stick (⁵); at the same time we were accused of calling out " barout, barout," to the Ebsambal people, though it was themselves that first taught us the meaning of that word.

As all this farce was performed to intimidate us, and to extort a sum of money from us as a reward for their remaining till the temple was opened, we took care that they should see by our conduct that the scheme entirely failed; therefore, avoiding all passionate behaviour, we replied coolly and deliberately to all their lying imputations, telling them that if they studied their own interests, they would behave very differently; that this of all others was the most unlikely method to obtain any thing from us; and that as they had staid ninety-nine days, why not remain the hundredth? After several other arguments, all as useless as they were false, one of the crew stepped forward, and pretended to be a peace-maker; the janissary meantime had squeezed himself through the hole, and entered the temple during the debate unknown to them, till one of the strangers having stolen behind to see what work we had done, found it out, and apprised the crew. They now seeing themselves foiled in every way, pretended to suffer the mediator, with some reluctance, to disarm them, and then began stripping to work, laughing and repeating tyep, tyep—good, good. Berby tyep, (berby, means temple). We deemed it our best policy to suppress our feelings and appear reconciled. Hassan had told the cook that they could murder us all if they chose; that neither law or justice were known in this country; that they could, after committing the crime, fly to the mountains, where no one would pursue them; that they were not the *poor people* we took them for; that they had kept the French at bay four years; that they kept their own slaves, cattle, &c. &c. We were not told of these expressions of theirs till we went down to breakfast at ten o'clock.

We now entered the temple, and thus ended all our labours, doubts, and anxiety. This morning we built a wall to barricade the door; it was made of stones and mud, with a foundation of date trees driven in to prevent the sand from giving way. A toad crept out of the temple while we were thus employed, and hid himself in the rubbish at the entrance. We now brought down to the boat some statues of calcarious stone which we found in the temple. There were two sphinxes, emblematical of Osiris (lion's body and hawk's head); a monkey similar to those over the cornice, only smaller; and a kneeling female figure, with an altar having a ram's head on it in her lap. At three we went to work again; twa of the Ebsambal peasants came, and appeared astonished that we had succeeded. They said the country people had no idea we should have accomplished our undertaking. They appeared to think the temple would make a good hiding place for their cattle, &c. whenever the Bedouins came to rob them.

Saturday, August 2. Continued working at the wall before the door. Hassan asked for some of our money to go and purchase a sheep, stimulated no doubt by the expectation of the share they always had, viz. the entrails, skin, and head, none of the former of which the crew rejected; on one occasion I saw one of them eating that part raw, as they were skinning the animal. Reduced as we were to nothing but doura, a grain not unlike pearl barley, we told our friend it was to no purpose to bring us meat when we had no bread, and that unless he brought the latter, we did not want or wish him to bring the former; they now took the money, promising to bring us bread also. We did not employ the sailors this evening, having finished the wall. Hassan was roaring and grumbling all day about money, in hopes that his bawling would induce us to give more; we took no notice of him, determined to give the money when they had put the statues into the boat; for we now perceived there was a great difficulty made about them. We this day took all the measurements of the temple, both externally and internally; Captain Irby and I undertaking this task, while our companions were employed about their drawings. Towards the close of the evening the man brought us some cakes of doura and a sheep, for which, however, he made us pay thirteen piastres, a third more than the articles were worth.

Sunday, August 3. This morning some Ebsambal people brought us some butter and a lamb; we told them, however, that now they might keep their provisions to themselves. In the evening the crew, after much disputing with Hassan (who was against the measure), put the statues into the boat; this being the condition on which they were to receive the backsheeish. Soon after this we gave them a present of forty piastres amongst them; we had considerable difficulty in satisfying them, for the reis, on perceiving the money, snatched it up, saying *it was his share;* we, however, took it from him, and distributed it according to our original plan.

I shall now give you some further particulars respecting the exterior of the temple, and then proceed to notice the most prominent beauties of the interior. The four colossal figures in front of the temple are all of men; they are in a sitting posture, above sixty feet high, and the two which are partly uncovered, are sculptured in the best style of Egyptian art; and are in a much higher state of preservation than any colossal statues remaining in Egypt. They are uncovered at present only as far as the breast; before the recent excavations, one of the faces was alone partly visible, and part of the head-dress of the other remaining two. The face of the statue, whether taken in the front view or profile, exhibits one of the most perfect specimens of beauty imaginable; it has so far resisted the effects of time, as not to have the least scratch or imperfection; and there is that placid serenity which one admires in most of the Egyptian countenances. The face of the statue, No. 3, has a more serious aspect, the nose is not so aquiline, nor is the mouth so well turned; it is not, however, without its beauties, and perhaps a better judge would say the features possess more character than the former. The statues are not, however, without their imperfections; the necks are short, out of all proportion, and the ears are placed considerably too high, a defect very common amongst the Egyptian figures; the bodies also seem to lean rather too much forward for the natural position of a sitting figure. However, it was hardly fair to pass one's judgement on this latter defect, as being partly uncovered, they could not be seen to proper advantage.

Little or no space appears to have been left between the figures on either side, and scarcely more in the centre than sufficient for the door. Immediately above the door, which was formerly surmounted by a cornice, now broken, is a tablet of hieroglyphics, over which is an oblong square niche enclosing a standing figure of a hawk-headed Osiris, in full relief, projecting no more than the depth of the niche itself. On the head of this figure is a globe, and below, on each side of the legs, are two symbols, which appear suspended from his hands; one is a small female figure, the other a staff surmounted with the dog's or fox's head. On either side of the niche is a female figure in intaglio, presenting an offering to the Deity, and various hieroglyphic inscriptions, probably descriptive of the oblations. The cornice above the door presents a very curious appearance; it has been broken by a fall of part of the rock above, and the chisel has since been evidently employed to form the remaining part into some other shape, or to fashion it in a manner ready to admit of the building of a new cornice, or some other ornament of that description.

The interior of the temple is one hundred and fifty-four feet long, by fifty-two broad, (exclusive of the side chambers) it is comprised of fourteen separate apartments, whereof the first is a principal hall fifty-seven feet, by fifty-two; the second, an anti-chamber, thirty-seven feet, by twenty-five; the narrow chamber crossing the other two, thirty-seven feet, by nine feet eleven inches; after which comes the sanctuary, twenty-three feet seven inches, by twelve feet three inches; the rest are side apartments, whimsically placed in various directions. The interior of this temple is a work not inferior to any excavation in Egypt or Nubia, not even excepting the Tombs of the Kings; indeed the effect produced on first entering it, may be considered as more striking than any which those can afford; the loftiness of the cieling, the imposing height of the square pillars, and of the erect colossal statues attached to them, full thirty feet high; and the whole dimensions of the apartments on a much larger scale than any of the other excavations, all contribute to render the interior of this temple not less admirable than its splendid exterior.

The sculpture on the walls is not so well finished, nor the colouring so perfect as in the Tombs of the Kings, but the composition and invention of the design, and the spirited execution in the performance, may be considered as fully equal to any thing in Egypt. The extreme heat and closeness of the apartments, occasioned by the want of a free circulation of air, have contributed materially to injure the colouring, but enough still remains by which to judge of what is lost, and to convince the spectator of the original beauty of the work. The most conspicuous groups appear to represent the victories of some celebrated hero, apparently the same who is depicted at Medinet Aboo, Luxor, Carnack, and other parts of Egypt, together with the triumphant processions and consequent offerings to the deities. There is little difference in these groups, from the similar sculptures in the buildings abovementioned; the hero appears in the same manner in his car; he is of a gigantic stature, and is destroying his enemies with his arrows; the vanquished sue for mercy; the discomfiture and flight of their companions; the procession of the prisoners, and the distribution of the other parts of the groups, are likewise nearly the same. The hero himself appears to be no other, but the prisoners seem to be of different nations from those represented in other places; and it is not a circumstance of little interest to see here, painted in glowing colours, the costumes of the various tribes of the interior of Africa, at a date so remote, that one knows no where else to look for any description either of their manners or their customs. How interesting would a minute copy of these groups be to travellers in the interior of Africa! who could compare them with the customs of the present day. Some of the captives are perfectly black, and have all the characteristics of the tribes of the interior of Africa—such as woolly hair, thick lips, long sleek limbs, &c.; others are of a lighter hue, not unlike the present race of Nubians. The most common dress consists of the leopard's and tiger's skin, fastened round the waist, while the upper part of the body remains uncovered. The cap which they most commonly wear is of a construction which I do not recollect to have observed elsewhere, and appears to consist of the leaves of the palm tree, dried and cut in slips; while the workmanship is a sort of neat plaiting, apparently worked with much ingenuity. Those who wear the caps have no hair, but some are distinguished by bushy hair and beards.

In one of the groups is represented the storming of a fortress, of very singular construction, which is defended by people of the race just mentioned. On the top are seen women, among whom, one in a sitting posture, wholly divested of drapery, and of a light complexion, bears no resemblance in character or attitude to those represented in other places by the Egyptians. The hero who directs the assault of this fortress is, as usual, of gigantic stature. On the plain below are seen the peasants driving their cattle away from the presence of the conqueror, designed with great spirit of action; some of the besieged party are also kneeling and imploring clemency. The arrows are flying from all quarters amongst the defendants, and some are seen plucking them from their foreheads, arms, and other parts of the body. Large stones hurled down from above, do not in any way intimidate the attacking party. The group of twelve supplicating victims, which the hero is represented in another part as grasping with one hand by the united hair of their heads, while with the other he uplifts the axe to sacrifice them, is executed with much energy and force; and the marked difference of character in the several countenances of the various tribes they belonged to, is executed in a masterly style; the expression of agony and despair in their several features are finely traced.

In this temple we found several detached statues of calcarious stone; one of which, a little larger than life, is executed in a better style than is generally to be met with in Egyptian sculpture; the head and lower part of the legs are wanting, as well as one of the arms, but the remaining parts sufficiently attest the skill and good taste of the sculptor. The figure is an upright one, and seems to have represented either Osiris or the hero depicted on the walls. The surface of what remains is scarcely injured; but the substance of the stone is so decayed by time, that any attempt to remove it would probably occasion its total destruction. I have already described the other statues which we brought away. These were found in different parts of the temple; half a monkey at one end, and the other half at the other, and so on.

How long this temple has been buried, is a question which must ever remain unanswered; forty feet of sand had accumulated in the centre above the top of the door, before the recent excavations, which were carried no further than three feet below the top of the entrance. There is reason to suppose that the temple was deserted before any sand had collected in front of it, but there is nothing either in the interior or without, that can indicate the age in which it was abandoned. Very little sand was found in the temple compared with what might have been expected; it did not reach beyond the second pilaster, and was not much broader than the door-way. This, no doubt, is partly owing to the great depth (eighteen feet eleven inches) of the entrance. A light black substance, which seemed to be decayed wood, was found in every apartment, in some places of the depth of two feet; its surface, allowing for the difference of colour, was not unlike that of snow, when it has been frozen over by one night's frost; it cracked under the foot, leaving the impression. Many small pieces of wood were strewed about, apparently little injured by time, but which, on being touched, crumbled into dust. The wooden pivots on which the doors traversed, still remain in the upper corner of all the entrances to the different chambers; and we also found small fragments of wood in many places. Some of these appeared so perfect that we thought of bringing them away, but they mouldered at the first touch; we were, therefore, very careful in leaving what remained for the benefit of future travellers. A broken brass socket, for the pivot of a door to traverse on, was also found.

The extreme heat of the temple was such, that Mr. Beechey spoiled his drawing-book, while only copying one of the groups; the perspiration having entirely soaked through it. It has the feeling and the effect of the hottest vapour bath. In the centre of the sanctuary is a bench with four sitting statues; the one on the right is Osiris, with the hawk's head and globe; the others are human figures; two have the crux ansata ♀ in their hand. I shall send you a ground plan to convey some idea of the form of the temple, and also of the whimsical disposition of the chambers.

I will conclude this long description with a few remarks on the eight standing figures of Osiris, thirty feet high, which ornament the outer hall, and between which is the passage into the interior of the temple. These figures are as well proportioned as they are highly finished; the drapery reaches nearly half way down to the knees, and is striped like that of the figures without. The features of the countenances are perfect, and they all have the hook and scourge (the usual emblems of Osiris) in either hand, which are across on the breast. The arrangement of the statues in the ground plan is exactly as we found them.

I shall now describe what we, speaking comparatively, call the small temple of Ebsambal. The direction of the river here is W. S. W. and E. N. E.; both the temples are situated on the left bank, at the ends of the two mountains which form the valley, by which the sand which has buried the great temple found its passage. Both are cut out of the solid rock, which is of a sandy or calcarious nature. The easternmost and smallest appears to have been made before the other, as the style of the colossal statues which are sculptured in the front of it, are ruder than that of the large one, and appear to have been cut in a less advanced state of the art. The front of the temple is not perpendicular, but sloping from the top to the bottom: six square spaces are excavated in the surface, serving as niches to the same number of colossal figures, the remaining part being left in the form of buttresses projecting ten feet at the base beyond the inside of the niches:—the door is in the centre, with three erect figures, one a female (Isis) with a male on each side of her: these latter represent Osiris. On either side, between these colossal statues, are two figures of about six feet high, which reach nearly to the knees of the former; those supporting the male figures appear to represent Horus, while the others near Isis are females. The space left in the centre, and in which the door is cut, is more than twice the breadth of the other projections between the figures, and slopes on the same plane with them for about one-third of its length: it then descends somewhat more perpendicularly, and in this lower plane is the door cut, without any other projection. The points of the projecting buttresses are covered with hieroglyphics, and a single line of them extends along the top of the niches for the whole breadth of the temple, of which it forms the ornamental summit. Immediately above the door is an offering to Osiris, and on each side of it are hieroglyphics as on the other projections; a line of serpents and globes surmounts the offering, similar to what is often met with over the doors of Egyptian temples. The height of the projecting buttresses nearest the door is thirty-four feet seven inches, taken in the angle of the others thirty-eight feet, their projection at the base ten feet, that of the door only seven feet six inches; the distance between each buttress, eight feet three inches; breadth of the buttresses, four feet seven inches. The height of the female figures is twenty-four feet six inches, not including the head ornament which reaches to the top of the buttress. The male figures are twenty-five feet eight inches high, and their head dresses four feet ten inches. The height of the door-way is eleven feet six inches; width, four feet ten inches; the length of its passage into the temple, twelve feet nine inches. The whole width of the ornamented front of the temple is eighty-eight feet, and its height, in a perpendicular line, may be about forty feet.

The interior of the temple is composed of three principal apartments; the first and largest supported by six pilasters, three on each side, (surmounted with the head of Isis in the front,) is thirty-six feet by thirty-four; the space in the centre between the pilasters is fourteen feet six inches, and they are seven feet eight inches from the wall: the distance between the pilasters five feet nine inches; their dimensions three feet seven inches, by three feet three inches. The breadth of the second chamber eight feet five inches; its length is the same as the first, and also taken at right angles with the door: the sanctuary is seven feet ten inches, by eight feet nine inches: on each side of the second chamber is a small side apartment six feet square.

I shall now describe the decorations of the interior, and rather minutely, as there is more uniformity, and evident allusion to the deity to whom the temple is dedicated (Isis), than is generally met with. The interior of the porch is ornamented on each side by an offering to Isis from a human figure. Within the chamber, on each side of the entry, is a large figure, with an axe in one hand, while with the other he grasps a bow, and a kneeling victim held by the hair of the head. On either side are two human figures: that in front has a knife upheld, and appears to command the sacrifice; while that behind seems to preside over it with the lotus flower in her hand: the opposite side is the same, excepting that the figure commanding the sacrifice is Osiris.

On the left, as you enter, the wall is embellished, first, with an offering to Isis; secondly, the initiation, by Jupiter Ammon and Osiris, of a young priest; thirdly, an offering by a female figure, of a small sistrum, surmounted by the head of Isis and the serpent, together with the lotus flower, to a male figure; fourthly, an offering of a small sitting figure with the crux ansata on its knees (which are cocked up) to a male figure. On the right hand the wall is ornamented, first, with an offering of provisions to Osiris, with the scourge in his hand; secondly, an offering of the lotus flower and three water pots, pouring water on other flowers, to Jupiter Ammon; thirdly, an offering to Isis of two small heads of that deity surmounting two short handles or staffs; fourthly, an offering to Osiris of two small water vases. At the end on one side of the door is an offering to Isis of the lotus; and opposite is the same offering to a female figure. The inner chamber has offerings to Isis and Osiris, and the initiation of a priestess by two isides; the sanctuary has a small figure, in alto-relievo, in a recess at the end.

Monday, August 4. Early this morning we started on our return, and soon saw on the eastern bank Mahomed and Ali Cashief, together with the band of thieves that had attempted to plunder us: they hailed to ask if we had opened the temple, and how much money we had found in it. In the evening we called on Daoud Cashief, who protested his innocence of the transactions at Ebsambal, even before we had mentioned the subject; this was certainly not very wise in Daoud, as nothing could tend more to prove his guilt; and if further evidence were necessary, we saw amongst his train several of the principal spies and bullies that had annoyed us. It was, however, necessary to dissemble, and appear to credit him, as a contrary line of conduct could lead to no good; and after receiving a present of a sheep, goat, and some bread, together with his promise to keep the temple open for Mr. Salt, we took our leave; when near Derry we met Halleel crossing the water to be present at our interview with his brother, and thus get his share of any thing else that could be squeezed out of us: he was, however, too late. In the evening we arrived at Derry, and went to see the temple with candles. This temple is situated about a quarter of a mile from the town: it is cut in the solid rock, but is so much ruined that nothing perfect is to be seen. There has been a middling sized hall, with eight square pilasters and four terms, with standing figures in alto-relievo; the latter seem to form a sort of portico to the principal chamber. The eight outer pilasters have fallen, but those of the portico are perfect with the exception of the terms, which have all been broken off. Within is the principal chamber, seventeen paces by sixteen, supported on each side of the centre by three pilasters: this latter leads to the sanctuary, on each side of which is a small chamber surrounded with benches. At the further end of the sanctuary are the marks of four sitting statues which have been chiselled off: they appear to have resembled those of the large temple of Ebsambal. In this temple the stucco and paint is imperfect, and the whole has a black and dismal appearance; but to judge from the size and execution of the figures, &c. in entaglio, on the walls, it may once have been tolerably handsome. The dedication appears to have been to Osiris. There are boats, battles, sacrifices, &c. like those at Ebsambal.

We had just gone to bed this evening, when Halleel arrived; we sent word that we were asleep. He sent us a present of some aqua vitæ, and a miserable sheep; all these presents are paid for at the rate of double their value.

Tuesday, August 5. Early this morning Halleel came on board, when we gave him to understand what we had told his brother, viz. that we had nothing left to dispose of, having given away every thing that we had to spare. All this while he was whispering to one of our sailors, asking, no doubt, if we had any thing left, and whether it was true, that we had not given his brother any thing. He now examined attentively every thing in the cabin, but observing nothing was forthcoming, he took his leave, and we started also, glad to get rid of him and Derry too. It was here that poor Norden, eighty years ago, met with the treatment from Baram Cashief, which prevented his going farther up. This morning we visited the temple at Armada, and saw two gazelles near it. This temple is built in the desert (at least it is desert now), not far from the river, on the opposite side from Derry, and about one quarter of the way between the latter place and Koroscoff. It consists of a hall, supported by twelve pilasters and four pillars, in four rows of four each; but as a wall of intercolumniation surrounds it, the detached pilasters and pillars within the hall are only six in number. Beyond the hall is a small cross chamber, nine paces by three, and within that is the sanctuary, which is eight paces by three. The interior of the latter is daubed over with plaster, and modern Greek paintings of the twelve apostles, saints, &c. Underneath this plaster, however, the ancient Egyptian figures and hieroglyphics, &c. in bas-relief, appear; they have been executed in a very superior style, and the colouring has been rich beyond description. There is a small chamber on each side of the sanctuary. The dedication is to Osiris. The sand has drifted into, and nearly filled up the hall; some modern sun-burnt brick ruins attached to the temple may have been additions by the Greeks.

At noon we arrived at Sabour, and proceeded to inspect its temple, situated on the western bank, about one hundred yards from the river side; it is built of calcarious stone, in a plain at the foot of the mountain, at present covered with sand. The approach to it is by an avenue of sphinxes (lion's body and woman's head), having two statues in a standing position at the end nearest the Nile, all of calcarious stone. At the further end of the avenue is a pylone, with two fragments of ill-carved statues, at present thrown down; they are all full length figures, and much dilapidated. On each side of the entrance within is a peristyle space, with four terms on either side; these appear to form the hall of the temple, which being covered with sand cannot be entered. The masonry is here much ruined, and there is not one perfect figure to be found. We observed that the hieroglyphics on the back of the two statues nearest the temple were the same as those on the frieze of the large temple at Ebsambal, with the difference only of being written vertically instead of horizontally. These hieroglyphics occur on either side of the crux ansata, which occupies the centre of the frieze, on one side written from right to left, and on the other from left to right. The hieroglyphics on Cleopatra's needles at Alexandria, are exactly the same about one-fourth down; and we noticed the same characters on the two great obelisks at Luxor.

Towards the close of the evening we had another quarrel with Hassan, who drew his dagger on Mr. Belzoni, uttering savage imprecations, and saying, that all who disbelieved in the prophet were dogs. We made a great effort to get him out of the boat, but the reis and crew adhered together so much, that we could not succeed. In this country it is difficult to chastise an insult; for should a traveller so far forget himself as to use a weapon against a Nubian, he would be sure to be sacrificed, as the whole country would rise against him, and escape would be impossible*. A pistol went off twice by accident in the boat during these unpleasant disputes, but fortunately did no harm; and Captain Irby

* This part of the country has, however, been since garrisoned and taken possession of by Mahommed Ali.

had his hand much cut in wresting a dagger from Hassan, who, while foaming with rage, was in the act of stabbing Mr. Belzoni. It is not a year ago since a Russian was murdered a little above Derry; he was in company with another who escaped to Assuan; they were unfortunately unarmed. Our reis and one of the sailors quitted the boat in consequence of our last quarrel.

Wednesday, August 6. Started at dawn on our voyage; about seven the reis returned; he now wanted to land the statues and leave them behind; this we told him he should not do, and advised him to beware what tricks he played us, as we would bring him to an account at Assuan, where, at least, there is some sort of government. Our young mameluke joined us this morning, having been robbed of his money and the reed-raft which he had purchased. About noon we inspected the small temple at Offidena; which has been left in so unfinished a state, that it is difficult to make much out of it. All that is at present to be seen is a small peristyle hall, with fourteen pillars; but neither the columns, their capitals, or the sides of the hall are finished. The Greek christians had made a chapel of this temple. There are, on the walls of a fragment of some detached building, three figures, evidently not Egyptian; they are in intaglio, and are either of ancient Greek or Roman workmanship; they appear to be an Egyptian, and a Grecian priest and priestess. In the same tablet is a figure representing Isis, and Horus presenting her an offering. The people came and crowded round us here, asking for backsheeish; as they did it in a very impertinent manner, we did not give them any till we had explained to them that a more quiet mode of begging would have got them more money. We endeavoured here to purchase a statue, the same that we had attempted to buy on going up; but after being detained about two hours, we were obliged to give it up. In the evening we visited the temple at Dekki; the exterior and part of the interior of this temple have not been finished, but the basso-relievo in the interior, bears every mark of having been executed by a skilful artist; only one chamber, however, has been completed with stucco and painting. The whole building is on a small scale, but the plan is very neat; it is approached by a pylon, beyond which is a portico of two columns in front; within this are three small but distinct chambers; the centre one is narrow, with a smaller apartment on each side; one of which has steps whereby to ascend to the top of the temple. The whole building is of a narrower width than the pylon, and a wall from the exterior of the latter surrounded it. The entrance of the pylon is covered with Greek inscriptions; amongst which, several commemorate the homage paid to the god Mercury, by Greek and Roman visitors, the latter under the reign of Tiberius Cæsar. This temple, like some others in Nubia, has been subsequently used as a Greek chapel, as appears by their daubed paintings; other ruins, perhaps of a smaller town, are scattered about near the temple.

Thursday, August 7. Started at dawn, and soon visited the temple of Garbe Girshe; the natives here have a very bad character. Last year they murdered a soldier of the pashaws, and not having been punished for it, are now remarkably insolent. Seeing us all armed, and not being numerous themselves, they asked for the backsheeish in a quiet manner, and we gave them some. This temple is principally an excavation in the rock, but has been fronted by a built portico or peristyle hall; four terms on each side, and two pillars in front, in a mutilated state, remain to it; but there have been many more of the latter; and probably a flight of steps preceded by an avenue of sphinxes (a lion's body with a woman's head), as appears by fragments remaining, was an approach to it. The excavated chambers have a black and dismal appearance, and the interior ones have become the habitation of bats. The plan is not dissimilar to that of the great temple at Ebsambal, but much smaller, and the sculpture is unusually bad and heavy. The first chamber is nineteen paces by eighteen, and supported by six terms, three on each side of the centre, with alto-relievo figures of Osiris in an erect posture; but instead of the arms being across the breast, with the scourge in one hand and hook in the other, as at Ebsambal, both the insignia are here in the right hand, which is uplifted, while the left hand hangs down; these latter are executed in a most heavy and unsightly manner. On either side of this chamber are four niches, in each of which are four alto-relievo figures; the second chamber is smaller, supported by two pilasters, one on each side of the centre; beyond this is the sanctuary which is small; the altar remains in it, and four sitting statues at the further end; there is a small chamber on each side of the sanctuary, and side apartments leading from the second chamber.

Towards sun-set we inspected the temple of Garbe Dendour: this is a small edifice which has never been finished. It is built with a small portico of two columus in front, and two small chambers within it. The sanctuary at the back is an excavation in the rock, before which the

KALÁPSHÉ, LOOKING UP THE NILE.

Drawn on Stone by W. Westall, A.R.A. From the Original Sketch by J. Roome, Esq.

temple is built: it is very small and unfinished. Before the building is a portal and a square space walled in, probably intended as a quay to protect the edifice from the river near which it stands —Garbe Merie. We passed this place without stopping, there being nothing but a broken wall, with hieroglyphics, which has been part of a temple.

In the evening we landed at Kalapsche and went up to see the temple. Here we found all the natives assembled, and armed with their daggers to dispute the entrance; we asked the reason of their being assembled in such numbers, and what they wanted: they said they must be paid before we entered the temple: we asked the speaker if he meant that he was to be paid himself, or who it was that we were to give money to? they all cried out, that we must pay every one of them. Now as there were about sixty of them, and many others arriving, we thought this a bad speculation, and were, therefore, proceeding to explain to them that it was not any great object for us to see the temple a second time, since we had already inspected it; and that if they chose to let us enter, we would give them a reasonable present when we came out, otherwise that it was immaterial to us whether we saw it or not, and that we would go without seeing it.

While we were settling this, our janissary picked a quarrel with the natives, by abusing them all, calling them thieves, and saying, we would enter the temple by force: in consequence they all rushed on him with their drawn daggers, and had nearly wrenched his musket from him, when we thought it high time to fly to his rescue, and after much struggling we succeeded in restoring him his arms. We were now glad to get to the boat, being well hooted as we went down; and on shoving off, they pelted us with stones; we fired a musket over their heads, to shew them that we had ammunition though we did not choose to use it unless there was real occasion. Our Greek servant now told us that while we were up, one villain had entered the boat with a drawn sword, and was proceeding to plunder, when perceiving it was time to be serious, a loaded gun was pointed at his head, with a threat to lay him dead on the spot unless he desisted; this timely firmness caused him to quit the bark:—the crew all the while not interfering or saying a word. We commended the Greek for his presence of mind, but had not so much reason to be satisfied with the janissary, whose unseasonable rashness alone prevented our seeing the temple; this was more provoking, as further up the river such a fit of valour might occasionally have been of use.

It is a great inconvenience to a traveller in this country, that both servants and interpreters always think themselves wiser than their masters; and therefore when desired to say or do any thing, always act according to the dictates of their own judgment, never letting their employer's wishes have the least influence with them. When interpreting they never tell you half what is said, and frequently when you explain something which you are anxious should be interpreted, they answer yes, yes, I know it; never thinking of telling the other party, but taking it for granted you are speaking for their information, not for the purpose of their explaining your words to others. This evening we repassed the gates of Nubia. As the Nile was now high, and the river here much contracted by the approach of the mountains on both sides, the rocks jutting down perpendicularly into the water, our crew made a great merit of taking the boat through the rapids, with the hope of obtaining backsheeish; but, though noticing all that was going forward, we took care, by an assumed carelessness, to make them think that we were regardless of the whole proceeding, and thus we escaped an additional tax.

This evening the current drove us past the two small temples of Teffa. Mr. Belzoni, who has seen them, describes them as follows:—only one of these edifices is finished; it is dedicated to Isis, and is about twenty feet square; at present it is all dirty, being used as a cow-house (not a bad application for a temple of Isis, to whom the cow was peculiary sacred). The other, which is situated near the former (both being on the western bank of the river and near the water's edge), has never been completed; its dimensions are similar to those of that first described.

Just before dark we went to visit Hindaw; the ruins in this quarter are very extensive, but nothing can be distinctly made out as to the meaning of the buildings, which, whatever they may have been intended for, have never been finished. Beginning from the southward, the first object is a great square, situated on a bed of rock surrounded by an unfinished wall, built of immense blocks of calcarious stone. On the north side, in the middle, there is a portal similar to those by which the Egyptian temples are generally approached; the top of the door-way is ornamented with the winged globe, and a figure of Isis, in basso-relievo appears half finished on the side of it. It is not improbable that this wall (which encloses a space about half a mile each way) may have been intended to surround several temples; the space it occupies being too great to suppose that only one was intended to

Drawn on Stone by W.Westall A.R.A. From the Original Sketch by J.Bowrie Esq.

THE CATARACT OF KALÁPSHE LOOKING DOWN THE NILE.

be constructed there. Further north is an extensive quarry, from which we may conclude the stone was drawn for the building of these edifices. Within this quarry we perceived a door-way carved in the Egyptian style; and on each side is a convexity, as if it had been intended to carve out pillars. There is also a niche, with a bust of Roman execution, on each side, and forty-two very perfect Greek inscriptions, written in the time of the Romans, to commemorate the visits of various generals, and other persons of distinction who had come here to pay their vows. Mr. Bankes copied all these: to the northward of the quarry, on an eminence, is a small unfinished portico, of two pillars on each side, and two in front; the capitals are highly executed: the former combine the lotus flower with the vine, date, and doura grain; the latter have a quadruple head of Isis.

Friday, August 8. At noon we inspected the temple at Daboude; it is situated about two hundred yards from the river side, and is altogether unfinished. The approach is by three portals, after which comes the temple, consisting of a portico, composed of four columns in front, and a wall of intercolumniation reaching half way up the pillars. Within this there are two chambers and a sanctuary; the latter contains two handsome monolithe cages of red granite, between six and seven feet high, and about four broad; these are the only objects of interest which the temple contains. Towards the river side, on the banks, are the remains of a quay. This day the murderer quitted the bark, not daring to shew himself near Philæ; he did not appear ashamed of the crime which he had committed.

In the evening our crew stopped at their village, and brought a scabby half-starved lamb as a present to us; we could not forbear from laughing, as it was really the most pitiful animal we had seen in the country; and in truth it must have put them to no small trouble to find such a beast. We refused the present most stoutly, but it was all in vain; they forced it into the boat. At three, arrived at Philæ, called by Hamilton and Burkhardt, Giesiret El Berbe El Ghassir, or Giesiret Anas el Wodjoud, the first of these names means the Island of ruined Temples: not an inapt denomination. Philæ is the easternmost of a group of islands and rocks which compose the first cataract. It is about half a mile long, rather high, and being wholly covered with magnificent ruins, has a grand and imposing appearance; the lofty pylons are seen at a great distance, and produce a fine effect. The island divides the Nile into two streams, and the river, finding so great an impediment in its course, rushes by with considerable velocity. The principal edifices are approached by an avenue formed on each side by a gallery supported by columns, the capitals of all which are different with respect to each other. There are thirty of these pillars on the left, and on the right only sixteen, with cells (probably the habitation of the priests) within them; the greater part of these last-mentioned columns are finished, but there are some incomplete. These shew that the columns were first constructed and erected in the rough, and that the sculpture was finished after the erection of the column. The rough outlines which we found traced, were very curious; and, neatly as all the capitals are sculptured, the finishing artist had but a rough and coarse pattern to point out to him the style of architecture he was to pursue. The difference of the two galleries, in number of columns, is occasioned by a small temple having been situated at each end of that on the right; these temples are now entirely ruined. At the end of the avenue is a large pylon, formed by two moles; the entrance in the centre has had two lions, and two small obelisks of red granite, ornamented with hieroglyphics, before it. It is on the pedestal of one of these latter that Mr. Bankes discovered the Greek inscription; and it is on the door-way of this pylon, that the inscription announcing that this island was the termination of the French conquests in Egypt, and consequently of their travels on the Nile, is written; a copy of it, verbatim, may possibly be amusing.

"Republique Françoise, An. 6, Le 13 Mes-
" sidor, Une Armée Françoise commandé par
" Bonaparte est decendú à Alexandrie, L'Armée
" ayant mis vingt jours apres les Mamlouks en
" fuit aux Pyramids, Dessaix commandant la
" premiere Division, les a poursuivis au dela
" jusque au Cataracts, ou il est Arrivé le 13
" Ventose, 3 Mars. Les Generaux de Brigade."
" Here follow the names.

" An. 7 de la Republique, de Jes. Cr. 1799."

It was in the portico, as you approach this temple, that we noticed the elephant as an hieroglyphic; this is the only instance of our finding this symbol in the country. The abovementioned portico leads through the left end of the great pylon, after which there is a handsome court or hall, and then you enter the temple.

We here first noticed a singular imperfection or peculiarity in the sculpture of the large figure of Isis in the great pylon—she has two *left* hands; we have since observed the same singularity in other places; the French work has copied some of them. In all parts of the island, on the sides of the temples, are Greek inscriptions, commemorating the worship of Greek and Roman generals who have come to pay their vows to Isis and Serapis. Philæ is said to have been the spot where Isis was appeased of her wrath for the violence offered by Typhon to her husband; and hence we find so many temples dedicated to her in so small a compass, there being no less than four.

Before I quit Nubia, a few observations on the country and its inhabitants may not be unacceptable. At present only two English travellers have been in this country. Mr. Hamilton, Colonel Leake, and Captain Hayes visited Debode, but were prevented from advancing further by the united efforts of the cashiefs and the mameluke bey, Elfi. Mr. Hamilton's book contains the result of these gentlemens' mission into Upper Egypt. The French had penetrated only as far as Philæ, where they left the inscription before mentioned. Several years elapsed before any European travellers entered Nubia, when Burkhardt led the way, which was followed by Mr. Legh and Mr. Bankes :—the former has published. Immediately after passing the first cataract, the traveller observes the Mockatem and Lybian chain of mountains to close much on the Nile: this remark is applicable, with few exceptions, throughout Nubia, at least as far as we went; there is consequently only a narrow strip of cultivated land on either bank of the river. The ancients, to preserve the soil and prevent the rapid course of the river from washing away the land, constructed immense walls, or, more properly speaking, piers, built of huge masses of stone piled one on the other, and reaching into the river from the foot of the mountain, or rather the limit of the Nile's rising, to the point of the water's lowest ebb. These piers are invariably built at right angles with the stream, and are generally about fifteen feet wide. As they are very numerous, and as the labour and expense of their construction must have been prodigious, some idea may thence be formed of the importance that was attached to them. From the number of temples, and from the fine plains of loamy soil, now generally covered with a surface of sand, a foot thick, which makes them look like the rest of the desert, there is every reason to suppose that this country was once both populous and flourishing; at the time of the height of Egyptian power it was considered as an integral part of the state; this is evident from the figures and devices in the temples having every resemblance to those of

Egypt. Of the land of Nubia which might be cultivated, I do not suppose one fourth is made use of; this indifference in agricultural pursuits proceeds from the despotic system of the government, where the governing authorities think of nothing but making the most of their situations whilst they hold them; consequently their sole aim is to get money, no matter how it is procured. A licentious soldiery are ever ready to contribute to the oppression of the inhabitants, more especially when the fund from whence they derive their own pay and emoluments are drawn from this source; this observation applies to Egypt as well as to Nubia, only that it is more easily perceived in the latter country. The consequence is, that the date palm, the fruit of which ripens without any human aid, and which pays no duty, is here more encouraged than any other production; and dates may safely be called the staple of the country. The doura, which is the holcus arundinaceus of Linnæus, is the only grain to be met with; it makes very good bread, but they grow barely sufficient for their own subsistence; indeed, it is so prized, that they frequently preferred it to money in payment for the articles we purchased. The miri or land-tax is paid at the rate of ten dollars per sackey, consequently every sackey which the Nubians build becomes an additional inducement to the Turks to come into their country; and it is only the scantiness of the produce which keeps the pashaw from quartering his troops on them; this the crafty natives are well aware of, and take care to put no temptation in the way. The present mode of collecting the miri in Nubia, is by sending thither annually about two hundred Turkish soldiers in boats, and the money they get hardly defrays the expenses of the expedition. The duty is not paid in cash, but in doura, which they purchase back from the Turks; but they generally contrive that the soldiers do not return very full-handed. The Turks usually make Derry their head-quarters, and remain about six weeks in the country, during which time the cashiefs retire into the mountains, and the natives conceal their arms, which are always taken from them whenever they are found. I shall here observe, that in several parts of Nubia we noticed the sites of ancient towns, indicated, as in Egypt, by mounds of rubbish.

I shall now add a few remarks on the natives, as we resided longer in the country, and had more dealings with them than any other Europeans have ever had. The Nubians are a very distinct race of people from the Arabs; their dress is commonly a loose white shirt and a turban; sometimes they are uncovered, except a cloth round the waist. They are very superstitious, most of them wearing charms to keep off " the evil eye," or some other apprehended ills. These charms consist of some words written on a scrap of paper, and sowed up in leather; they are worn mostly on the right arm over the elbow, and sometimes round the neck. All the cashiefs we saw had them, and one Nubian dandy had nine of these appendages. These people think themselves very cunning in schemes to deceive strangers. Few of them smoke; instead of which they use salt and tobacco mixed, enveloped in wool, and kept between the under lip and gum; the boys commence this practice when quite young. They are all rogues, but being bred up in such principles, do not think there is any harm in being so; the opprobrious terms, harame, cadab, (thief—liar) are not considered abusive with them, as they have no notion of honesty, and cannot possibly keep from pilfering any thing within their reach; we detected our sailors at this work almost daily, but they always made a joke of it. The several districts differ much in regard to dress, and particularly in the manner of wearing the hair, some have it curled, " à la Brutus," others plaited and hanging down with great uniformity, in ringlets, to the shoulders, where it is cut off square at the bottom, and looks exactly like a mop. The latter grease their locks plentifully with oil; the former have generally a skewer sticking in their hair in readiness to disturb any animalcule which may bite too hard. There is great difference in the features and make of the several Nubian tribes: the natives of Elpha are tall and good looking; the people of Derry are hideous and deformed; the tribe at Armada are small, but handsome, and well made; they are frugal in their mode of living, subsisting principally on doura, made into flat cakes, and baked on a stone, which is heated, and some sour milk and dates. It is usual to see a courier, or man, going on a few day's journey with no other provision than a small bag of dates; they eat the offal of all the beasts they kill, not rejecting any part; and when we were at the village to which the crew belonged, the women came down eagerly to dispute for some fowls, which having died, were thrown on shore. They are great boasters, but do not appear to have any firmness; and they have a great aversion to fire-arms. They evince much outward show of religion, praying four or five times a day; and to shew their piety, they leave the sand on their foreheads, which sticks there while they are performing their devotions. They are respectful to their cashiefs, to whom are referred all their quarrels and disputes. They are invariably armed, and appear very proud of their weapons; they mostly carry a dagger on the left arm, a long pike and a sword slung across the back. The boys, when young, have weapons provided them; this they imagine shews their independence, and they acknowledge no government. They are exceedingly passionate with each other, but are soon reconciled, even after the most inveterate abuse; they adhere together, and no bribes can separate them; we never saw an instance in which we had any of them on our side, or when any thing was revealed to us. Ear-rings are common amongst the men; they usually have but one, and it is immaterial in which ear it is worn. They eat the locusts grilled, and affirm that they are good. They are considerably darker than the Arabs. The only manufacture they have has been pointed out to them by necessity, and consists of neat close-grained platters, made of the date-tree, to contain their milk and food. No earthenware is made in the country; their water-jars are brought from Egypt.

The women do not cover their faces so scrupulously as the Arabs; they are not ill-looking, are generally well made, and have good figures. They wear a brown garment reaching down to the ankles; it is thrown over the right shoulder, comes close under the left arm, the shoulder of which is bare, and has not an ungraceful appearance; they are very partial to rings and bracelets; the former are frequently worn at the nose, the latter are made of one piece of brown glass, which not yielding, and being forced on as small as possible, often causes much pain; they always go bare-footed. Young girls have a covering round their loins made of strips of leather, hanging down and ornamented with cowry-shells and beads. The hair of the women is plaited somewhat like the men's, and greased with oil. The Barabras, from their frugal mode of life, are subject to few diseases; they are all marked with one, and sometimes two scars on the spine of the back, where they have been burnt for the cure of an endemial disease, which attacks them when young; this mode of treatment, by drawing all the humours to one spot, keeps the discharge open till the patient is recovering, and experience has doubless shewn it to be often successful. A boy, while we were at Ebsambal, was in a state of cure, and accidentally injured the part which caused it to bleed; the father immediately applied a remedy, by throwing some sand, of which article there is no scarcity in the country, on the wound; this soon appeased the boy's cries and pain.

Tuesday, August 12. After about four hour's

disputing and bargaining with the crew, we persuaded them to take us down the cataract in the boat, on the condition of our paying fifty piastres, but they would not start unless we paid them every para of the money before hand. We tried to induce them to take half of the cash at first, and the other half on our arrival; but no, they must have it all. It would have been the same to us whether we paid them before or after, but knowing their character, we were afraid that when they once got the money, they would turn our things out of the boat, and take themselves off, especially as there was a great crowd assembled who would have aided them in any of their pranks. We could not help laughing when we found that however unfavourable an opinion we had formed of them, they were equally suspicious of us. Having at length supplied them with that sovereign balm, " the fleece," they prepared to depart. A pilot and eight additional hands came on board to conduct us down; just before putting off, Hassan sneaked off and disappeared, dreading the report we should make of him to the Aga. We were about two hours on our passage, which was amongst all the windings and turnings of the innumerable islands which form the rapids, for cataract there was none. The scenery was wild, barren, and romantic. Sometimes the bark was carried away pretty sharply by the stream, and occasionally, when she was roughly handled in the vortex of the current, our sailors cried out, tyep, tyep, (good, good,) and asked us whether they were not bold fellows for undertaking what they had done; at times they made such a violent noise, all speaking and bawling at once, that a person not used to Nubian manners would have thought they were all going to the bottom. The boat only struck once, but it gave her a prodigious shock, and made us fully sensible of the hardness of granite rocks; the sailors immediately began to sound the well, expecting she was bilged, but she did not make much water, and we soon got off. At the commencement, while near Philæ, we observed oyster-shells incrusted in the granite rocks, bordering on the river; some of them were very perfect and large. We reached Assuan (the ancient Syene) in the evening; Mr. Ruppell, a German traveller who was at Thebes with us, discovered on one of the uninhabited barren islands, which compose the fall, a fine tablet of red granite, with a perfect Greek inscription on it, highly interesting. As we have been on terms of intimacy with him, he has given us a copy, which I enclose to you. The stone Mr. R. takes with him to Frankfort, to be presented to the museum of that town.

On our arrival at Assuan, we proceeded to visit the ancient granite quarries in the neighbourhood: our principal object was, to examine the column which is there, and which has an inscription in Latin, not devoid of interest. Our guide lost his way at first, and took us to another part of the quarry where we found an immense granite basin, seventeen feet long, by seven wide, and three deep. It is hewn out in the rough, and is narrower at the bottom than the top; we were at a loss to imagine for what purpose such an immense basin could be intended, unless it was for a bath. The whole of this quarry was highly interesting; here we had an opportunity of noticing the manner in which the ancients used to cut the prodigious masses which one meets with throughout Egypt. It appears, that when they wanted to detach a mass, they cut niches in a right line throughout the piece they intended removing: these niches were about two feet apart, five or six inches long, and about three deep, by two and a half broad. As soon as they were finished, the block was separated by some violent blow or concussion. We met in all directions specimens of the progress of their work; some masses were but half detached, others wholly separated; here we saw an obelisk in the rough, and there a column, the whole was an interesting

scene. The ancient road, regularly paved with granite, is still plainly to be seen, though the sand covers a great part ; in the vacancies between the hills are causeways, some of considerable length, to connect the elevated parts one with the other, and thus keep a communication open with the several quarries, all these roads leading to two principal ones which conduct to Assuan. We now searched for the column with the inscription, and at last found it. The pillar is small, not being more than ten feet in length, by about three feet diameter; the inscription is tolerably perfect; an Arab, acquainted with Mr. Belzoni, told him of it, and it was seen for the first time by a traveller last year. As Mr. B. had copied the writing, we did not think it worth while to copy it. Its purport is as follows:—" To Jupiter Ammon, Kneephis
" Bona (the Good Spirit), and to Juno the Queen,
" under whose protection is this mountain, in
" which were discovered nine quarries near Philæ,
" during the happy age of the Roman Empire,
" under the most pious Emperors Severus and
" Caracala, and ——— and Julia Domna his
" august mother; and a vast number of statues,
" and large columns, were taken out of these
" quarries by Aquila, prefect of Egypt. " Cura
" Magens Opera," which Mr. Salt interprets, un-
" der his directions, Aurelius Helogabalus or-

" dered this stone to be erected in the calends
" of March." The vacant space before Julia
Domna the mother, is where the name of " Geta,"
the other brother, was erased; Caracala having
murdered him, ordered his name to be blotted
out of every inscription where it was inserted.
Mr. Salt tells us, that there is one instance of this
at Rome, and he has met another on an inscription,
discovered at the late excavation of the sphinx. I
should like to have sent the original Latin to you,
but as it was not to be got, I must be content
with what I have. You will observe the inscription
says, that the Romans *discovered* the nine quarries, *not that they made them.* One must
therefore infer that they were first worked by
the Egyptians; and as they were so numerous,
and of such magnitude, they must have been of
great consequence, and doubtless are of the most
remote antiquity. I confess I was much perplexed to think how the Egyptians could have
cut, hollowed out, and polished, such immense
blocks of the hardest stone without the use of
iron, a metal which they are said to have been
wholly ignorant of; the niches, therefore, which
I mentioned above, if not with iron, must have
been cut with brass. We examined the construction of numerous mummy cases, and boxes containing the sacred emblems of the Egyptians;

they were invariably fastened with wooden pegs, no nail of any description being visible. Some of the cases were of beautiful workmanship. Mr. Ruppell has two legs of a chair elegantly worked in the similitude of a lion's feet and paws; these specimens of cabinet-making bespeak great taste and judgment, and it is difficult to conceive that they were made with brass. The negroes in the South Sea, at this day, certainly cut hard woods shaped as clubs, and ornament them in the most exquisite style; but I doubt much if they could make cases and boxes with their flints also.

I cannot quit Syene without noticing that it is the place where Juvenal was banished by the Emperor Domitian; being sent there with the title of " Governour of the Frontier of Egypt:" he returned at eighty years of age. Assuan has nothing to interest the traveller; an immense heap of rubbish lies behind the town, which is a dirty, ill-built place.

Wednesday, August 13. This morning the Aga came to pay us a visit: he was asleep all yesterday, for as the ramadan prevents them from eating and drinking during the day, the great people invert the order of things by sleeping during that time, and sitting up and feasting all night. We complained to him of the treat-

ASSUAN, SYENE, FROM ELEPHANTINA.
Drawn on Stone by J.D. Harding.   From an Original Sketch by H.W. Pearce, Esq.

ment we had experienced from our crew; he told us that they were a notorious set of rascals; that no one would employ their boat, their character being so bad, that people were afraid to trust their goods in their hands. Our friends had not waited to be catechised for their conduct, but took themselves off the day before, after having made great efforts to persuade us to give them some more backsheeish. We visited Elephantina so glowingly described by Denon. It certainly had a pleasing, flourishing appearance, the north end being richly covered with fine crops of doura: there are a few palm-trees. The south end of the island is high, and here are situated the ruins of the ancient town, together with the temples, only one of which, dedicated to the serpent Kneephis, is in any degree perfect; it is small, with an anti-chamber and sanctuary. There are the remains of several others, so mutilated, that nothing can be made out. A high quay leads directly down into the Nile at the S. E. end. At eleven o'clock we started on our return, having hired a boat to take us to Thebes for one hundred and twenty piastres.

Thursday, August 14. Inspected Koum Ombo, the ancient Ombos. Here are the remains of two temples situated on a promontory of the Nile's eastern shore; the large one, dedicated to the crocodile (as appears by the principal offerings being presented to a deity having the head of that animal) is situated at a short distance from the river, which it fronts. The smaller one, to Isis, is close to the river side, and not far distant from the other, to the S. W. of which there is a building which appears to be part of an unfinished pylon, and which is close to the river side. There is a whimsical irregularity in this latter edifice which should not be passed unnoticed; the base is built of small blocks of stone, which gradually increase in size till you come to the top, where are the largest masses of all. The large temple consists of a portico of five columns in front, in three rows, though one at each of the outer angles is fallen. The cornice, only two parts of which are perfect, is ornamented with four winged globes. The frieze consists of a double border of hieroglyphics, rather large. The columns are of great dimensions, and have various capitals surmounted by a plinth. There are two entrances, one on each side of the centre pillars, occasioned by the unusual circumstance of an odd number of columns in front; these conduct to another ruined apartment, originally supported by ten pillars in two rows of five each; beyond these are three other apartments; the communication from the one to the other is by two large doors, one on either side, instead of a centre one which most Egyptian temples have. The cornice of the entrance, on the left, from the second to the third apartment, has an inscription in Greek, which mentions that it was written by direction of Ptolemy and Cleopatra, and that the temple was dedicated to Apollo, &c. The decorations of this edifice, in basso-relievo, are highly finished, and in a good style; amongst the figures here, we noticed the lion with the hawk's head, similar to the statues we found at Ebsambal, a union we had not before noticed. The small temple of Isis points to the south; it consists of a small portico of four columns, surmounted by the usual quadruple head of the deity, with the passage in the centre, and beyond the portico are two chambers and a sanctuary; but all the western side of the temple has fallen over into the river, and with it the chief part of the flooring of the chambers, together with a large plain altar of black basalt, which has evidently come from the sanctuary. The want of hieroglyphical inscriptions on this altar is probably the only cause why travellers have not removed it. The ornamental parts of this temple are in no way inferior to those of the larger edifice; we did not, however, notice any representations that we had not before seen. The country in the neighbourhood of Koum Ombo presents to the north and east nothing but the prospect of a barren, sandy desert; there is a small portion of land to the S. E. cultivated. Opposite to the temple, in the middle of the Nile, is the large island of Mansouria, which is highly cultivated, and a smaller island to the south, the soil of which is also good. Exclusive of the temples, the promontory of Koum Ombo has several Saracenic ruins of both baked and sunburnt brick; and the ruins of the ancient town are discernible by the rubbish of the former material. The view, as above described, is, on account of the elevation of the position, an extensive one.

Djibel Selsilis. The meaning of this term implies " mountains of the chain." The name has been given from a tradition that a chain was here drawn across the river, to prevent the irruption by water of any hostile parties from above. The principal objects of interest, are several small temples hollowed out of the rock, which is of calcarious stone. The northernmost consists of a portico and sanctuary, with three recesses in the latter, containing statues in alto-relievo; the walls have been stuccoed and painted, but at present all is so much disfigured that little or nothing can be distinctly made out.

To the southward are two more small temples, each consisting of one single niche or hollow in the rock; both their fronts have two handsome columns, together with a cornice and frieze, executed with considerable taste; the colouring having the remains of great richness. Numerous other niches with statues, &c. are interspersed near this spot. The quarries here are very extensive, and one large detached mass of stone, of considerable height, would seem to be the spot where the chain which secured the river was fastened. On the opposite side the quarries are also numerous; the vicinity of the Nile to this place, so favourable for embarking and transporting the stone, was no doubt the principal inducement to the Egyptians to establish so extensive a quarry here.

Friday, August 15. Reached Edfoo, the ancient "Appolinoplis Magna." It is situated in a fertile plain, at a short distance from the western bank of the Nile. The antiquities consist of a large temple, the plan of which appears to be the most magnificent of any in Egypt; though in point of perfection it must yield to Tentyra and some few others. It consists of a prodigious high pylon, the exterior wall of which is sculptured with a large figure on each side, sacrificing a number of human victims; and above these are two rows of figures presenting offerings to Osiris and Isis. The inside of the pylon is decorated with similar oblations; the cornice is imperfect as far as the torus, or astragal moulding, which at present forms the summit of the pylon. Within is a large and magnificent peristyle court, forming an oblong square, with a covered gallery supported by columns on each side; beyond this is the portico of the temple, presenting a front of six pillars, which continue for three rows, making eighteen in all; those in front have had a wall of intercolumniation reaching up half their height. We thought these pillars appeared to be of very large dimensions, but on measuring them found the upper part of the shaft to be six feet four inches in diameter, while those at Carnack are eleven feet six inches at the base of the column. This portico is filled with rubbish upwards of two-thirds of the way up to the roof. The frieze in front of the portico is ornamented with a row of standing figures of monkeys, in basso-relievo, and the architraves within have rows of figures of Isis sitting on a chair. The chambers of the temple are inaccessible, the rubbish which fills the portico blocking up the door. The whole of the large peristyle court, and the top of the portico, and other parts of the temple, are covered with the mud-built huts of the modern town of Edfoo. The temple is surrounded by a thick wall, about eight feet in diameter, which is continued in a line from the outer part of the gallery of the peristyle, leaving a passage between the sides of the temple and the wall. The exterior of the edifice, and both sides of the wall, are ornamented with offerings and hieroglyphics; we remarked nothing novel in the symbolic representations of this temple, excepting the horse, an animal we had not before seen in this character. The ruins of the ancient Appolinopolis Magna are high, but not extensive. The paltry modern town of Edfoo presents a striking contrast to the magnificence of the ancient buildings; from the top of the lofty pylon, the huts at its foot, and the peristyle court, are scarcely discernible as human dwellings. You here enjoy a fine view of an extensive fertile plain and the river. There is a smaller temple to the S. W. of the great one, which is nearly buried. Before I quit Edfoo, I must mention a most interesting discovery that was made a few weeks ago; a Frenchman, named Cailliaud, who understands mineralogy, has lately been employed by the pashaw to examine the Mockatem and Lybian chain in search of coal mines. His last trip was to inspect the ancient emerald mines, which are south of Cossur, at five hours' journey from the

K

Red Sea; on his way from the point opposite to Edfoo, where he quitted the Nile, he crossed a road at two days' journey from that place, which appears to be the ancient Egyptian road from Koptos to Berenice. He also found there the ruins of a temple; the road is paved with granite, and in some places is cut or hollowed out of that material. Interesting tablets, with hieroglyphic characters and inscriptions, are met with, but as he was on his journey, he had no time to examine this interesting spot. We have seen some of the specimens from the emerald mine which Mr. C. has brought with him. Our friend Ruppell, who is a good mineralogist, and who has made a valuable collection, tells us that these specimens are composed of black mica; it is of a softish, scaly substance, and may easily be separated into laminæ. The emeralds which we saw were very small, and ran in narrow strata through the other substance.

This evening, August 15, we stopped at El Cab, the ancient Eleethias. These ruins are situated on the eastern bank of the Nile, not far from the river. The city has been inclosed by a wall of sun-burnt brick, thirty-seven feet thick; the place inclosed may be a mile square. Within the great wall is another inclosure surrounding the ruins of a small temple, and other buildings much dilapidated and consequently uninteresting.

At the back of the ruins, in the side of the Mockatem, are several sepulchral grottos, two of which are well worthy of notice; the one is remarkable for a highly finished tablet of hieroglyphics, in intaglio; the other is a very interesting chamber; and as some of the groups have the merit of great originality, and at the same time are executed with good taste, we have given rather a minute description of the leading parts. On the left, as you enter, the first object of interest, is a man writing on a tablet, which he holds on his left arm; fronting him are various men driving asses, cattle, pigs, goats, &c. near to these are several hillocks of corn, and people in the act of reaping and sheafing, with gleaners, &c. following behind them. After this are three distinct rows of agricultural proceedings; the upper one begins with two men bearing on their shoulders, by means of a long pole, as brewers carry a cask, a sort of net basket shaped thus , filled with wheat in the ear; next to them are two other men, one bringing on his shoulder an empty basket, while his companion carries the pole; next is a man in an inclosed space, treading the corn with six head of cattle, their mode of thrashing. Behind these are four people winnowing the grain, by holding it up over their heads, and pouring it down for the wind to blow through it; near the last-mentioned is a man seated on the top of a high hillock of grain, and writing down an account of the quantity; afterwards are four men piling it. This group now terminates by two men depositing the corn in a square inclosure, which was doubtless the granary. The next group is a ploughing scene; there are two ploughs, each drawn by two oxen; a man walks opposite the animals, sowing grain as they advance; this he takes from a basket suspended from the yoke across the horns of the beasts. Behind him is a person driving a wheel harrow; the ploughs are preceded by four men, using a sort of pick-axe in the shape of the Greek letter alpha; this was probably to break the clods of earth; further on are four men working another plough. Below this scene is a pair of scales; at one end is a man writing an account, while another is weighing some small articles shaped thus ◯, and which we think may be the shape of their loaves, as bread is made sometimes in that form at this day in Egypt; four of these are in one scale, and many others on the shelves at the side of the wall; the weight in the other scale, is in the form of a cow couchant. Next to this are persons carrying the weighed articles into a boat, by means of a gang-board, and near to this boat are three others already laden, with men poling them. The cargo is placed in a square magazine, built in the centre of the boat, not unlike the cabin of the Thamesis; below is a boat under sail; the sail is square, with a yard at the head and foot; it is trimmed by means of a wheel, which is attached to the foot-yard, acting the part of a roller, and working on a pivot on the top of the square magazine or cabin, which is near half the height of the mast. There is a door and window to the cabin, and seven men are rowing on each side: the helms-man steers with an oar. The next group represents fishermen drawing their net, with two men carrying the fish away in baskets; and another splitting them and hanging them up to dry. Beneath this is another party catching geese with a net; after which are others employed plucking and trussing them, while one man is putting them in jars. Above are men plucking grapes, while two others are carrying them away in baskets; six others are pressing them, and others filling jars with the wine. Among numerous other groups of figures, we noticed a female, standing, and playing a harp with ten strings; the instrument is rudely shaped, and badly finished. Another plays on a wind-instrument not unlike a clarionet, with this difference, that the end is not shaped like a trumpet's mouth, but plain. As we had met most of the other groups in this chamber in other places, and have noticed them in former letters, we contented ourselves with this short account. We now visited a small temple situated in the plain, at a short distance to the N.W. The serpent Kneephis is said, by the French, to have been worshipped in this temple, though we could not observe any allusion to a serpent more than what is seen in every other temple; it consists of a single chamber surrounded by a gallery of square pillars.

Saturday, August 16. Reached Esneh, situated on the scite of the ancient Latopolis. In the centre of the town, near the market-place, is a magnificent Egyptian temple, the whole of which is however completely buried, and modern houses built over it, except the portico or anti-chamber; this is supported by twenty-four columns, in four rows of six each; the outer row in front having a semi-wall of intercolumniation like that at Tentyra. The sculpture, in basso-relievo, of this temple is executed in an indifferent style; the signs of the zodiac are represented on both ends of the cieling, but they are much inferior to those of Tentyra. The chief beauty of this portico consists in the elegant proportions of the shafts of the columns. The capitals, all of which are different, are well executed; they combine the representations of the fruit and leaves of the date, vine, lotus, &c. &c. Three miles north of Esneh there is a small temple in ruins, supposed to be situated on the scite of the ancient Aphroditopolis, and on the opposite side of the river there is another on the scite of Contra Latopolis. We visited neither of these two, as they were both reported unworthy the trouble, and time was growing precious. We had stopped at Erment, the ancient Hermontis, on our passage up the Nile in May, but as I did not describe any thing above Thebes in my letter from Philæ, I bring it in here in its place. From the state of the ruins it would appear that the city was extensive and compact: the ruins of four temples are visible, but only one at present possesses remains in any state fit to indicate what they have once been; this has but seven columns standing, each of which has a capital of different architecture from the other, the whole being composed of representations of the palm-leaf in various forms. There are two sanctuaries in the temple, both ornamented with various symbolic representations, in basso-relievo, stuccoed and painted. As we here noticed some groups which we had not hitherto observed in any other temple, we have selected some of the most singular as specimens. In the larger sanctuary are sixteen hippopotami, in two processions, walking upright; a hippopotamus presenting an offering to Horus, who is sitting on the lotus flower; various crocodiles, with hawks' heads, on square cases, either altars or sarcophagi. Two rows of three monkeys, and two of four cats; a human figure, with the Ibis's head, presenting offerings to a cat; a man bearing a globe on his shoulders; an oblong-square case ornamented with flowers all over; on the top appears twelve human heads, in four groups of three each, and below it are their feet with sandals; these last are probably men carrying a sarcophagus. A small human figure (Horus), with a hawk's head, riding between the horns of a cow (Isis), and facing Horus, who in this instance is also sitting on the lotus flower. In the inner sanctuary are two cows, with a child sucking each, the animals with their heads turned round and looking at the infants—probably Isis and her son Horus. On the cieling are two rams (Aries) with wings—a taurus and a scorpio; twelve figures in three rows of four each, with a circular head ornament, and a star in the centre, probably have some allusion to the signs of the zodiac. All the ornaments of these two sanctuaries are highly finished. Near the temple, on the east side, are the ruins of an ancient basin, in the centre of which Denon mentions, on the authority of Aristides, there was a Nilometer, but the column on which it was graduated, is not visible now; the remains of a flight of steps are still discernible from the basin up to the temple.

Sunday, August 17. Early this morning arrived at Luxor, part of the ancient Thebes, and took up our quarters in one of the temples; having settled every thing and established our house, &c. we devoted the day to a careful re-examination of both Luxor and Carnack. At the former place we carefully inspected the war scenery on the exterior of the great pylon, but did not discover any thing novel to cause further observations. We also took particular notice of the magnificent obelisks, and clearly made out that from eight to ten of the upper hieroglyphics, with the exception of their being vertically instead of horizontally written, were the same as the first characters of the frieze at Ebsambal, and the same also as the upper hieroglyphics in what are termed Cleopatra's Needles at Alexandria. We now went to Carnack and walked leisurely over all the ruins, inspecting all the paintings, sculpture, &c. but found nothing here to add to our former observations.

Monday, August 18. We devoted this day to visiting the tombs of Gourna, and as Messrs. Beechey and Belzoni had been employed for months, by Mr. Salt, in digging and making excavations in various directions among the rubbish of the ancient Thebes, and particularly at Gourna amongst the tombs, they were of course the best guides we could possibly have; it was a gratifying reflection to think that after they should have shewn us the lions, we should leave nothing behind us unseen, at least as far as has yet been discovered in this most interesting of all places. It is customary with the natives to deceive travellers, and tell them that they have seen all, before they have inspected half; and it was precisely this trick they played on us. I must give you some reason for this disposition towards misleading strangers: it may well be imagined that the population of so immense and magnificent a city as Thebes, the " city of one hundred gates," as Homer styles it, was prodigiously great; now, as the Egyptian practice of embalming was always prevalent amongst them, it is not to be wondered at, that the bowels of the earth near Gourna should contain an immense number of mummies. The natives have not been unmindful of the eagerness with which travellers inquire after papyri, and other objects of antiquity; these papyri are generally found under the arms or between the legs of the mummies, and the demand for them of late has been so great, in consequence of an opposition between the French party, employed by Mr. Drovetti, and the English, employed by Mr. Salt, that they now sell for thirty, forty, and fifty piastres each; whereas, formerly, you could get them for about eight or ten. About a dozen of the leading characters of Gourna, or rather the greatest rogues, have constantly headed their comrades, and formed themselves into two distinct digging parties, or resurrection men, designating themselves the French and the English party; these people are constantly occupied in searching for new tombs, stripping the mummies, and discovering antiquities. The directors have about three-fourths of the money, and the rest is given to the inferior labourers. They dread lest strangers should see these tombs, which to them are so many mines of wealth, and should commence digging speculations of their own—hence the care of the Gourna people in concealing them. It would be endless to describe to you all the intrigues which are carried on by the opposite parties to augment their collection; or the presents given to the Defterdar Bey, the Agas, and the Cashiefs, to attach them to either party. Lately Mr. Drovetti obtained an order from the Defterdar Bey, that the natives should neither sell nor work for the English party, and a cashief was most severely bastinadoed by the bey's orders, and in his presence at Gourna, for assisting the English. At present, things are on a better footing. Mr. Drovetti is not an amatuer, but collects to sell; he offered his museum to Mr. Salt, on his arrival, for seven thousand pounds, which he states as his price, but which most persons seem to think he will never get. He is now in Upper Egypt, and is gone in search of a temple and Egyptian road which has been reported to have been seen by the jelabs, at one day's journey, in the desert, from Madfuni, the ancient Abydus, described in a former letter.

To return to my narrative: the tombs of Gourna are situated in a valley to the S. W. of the Memnonium. Those which we first inspected are considered the best, and consist of two square courts cut in a bed of calcarious stone. There are excavations on three sides of the square, and the fourth, or south side, is that by which they are entered. The principal excavations are on the north side; these are very extensive, and we were at a loss which most to admire, the beauty of the sculpture on the walls, or the grandeur and extent of the excavations. The former is cut on the smooth stone, which is very close-grained, resembling the finest chalk, but without cracks or flaws, and rather harder; the colour is of so pure a white, and admits of so fine a polish, that stucco has been quite unnecessary. There is a harmony throughout the decorations of these tombs that we have no where else noticed; the sculpture, in intaglio, will bear the minutest inspection. The plan of the excavation, extensive as it is, is extremely singular, sometimes abruptly turning either to the right or left without any apparent cause. At the further end there is a fine quadrangular court filled up in the centre with the solid rock; you here meet with some very rich groups; and there are innumerable remains of fine statues, in alto-relievo, leaning against the wall in all directions; we could not, however, distinguish one that was perfect. The art and precision with which the decorations of these sepulchres are finished, exhibiting an endless variety of symbolic representations, in the most elaborate and highly finished style, is truly astonishing; in some places the roofs are arched, in others they are flat; here you meet with a deep well in a corner; shortly after you descend by a flight of steps. Some of the hieroglyphics are painted blue on a pale red ground; blue is very common, the colour of the stone itself serving occasionally for a fine white field. Amongst the figures, in basso-relievo, there were many quite perfect, and so minutely cut, that the eye-brows and ears, the hair, nose, lips, and the hands and nails, would bear the closest inspection; in short, throughout the whole of this mausoleum, the work of a most skilful artist is observable. I think I may safely say the examination of the principal tomb occupied us two hours.

We now went to see the mummy pits: it is impossible to conceive a more singular and astonishing sight than a tomb of this description. Imagine a cave of considerable magnitude filled up with heaps of dead bodies in all directions, and in the most whimsical attitudes; some with extended arms, others holding out a right hand, and apparently in the attitude of addressing you; some prostrate, others with their heels sticking up in the air; at every step you thrust your foot through a body or crush a head. Most of the bodies are enveloped with linen, coated with gum, &c. for their better preservation. Some of the linen is of a texture remarkably fine, far surpassing what is made in Egypt at this day, and proving that their manufactures must have arrived at a great degree of excellence. Many of the bodies, probably of the lower orders, are simply dried, without any envelopment. Innumerable fragments of small idols are scattered about; they are mostly human figures of Osiris, about two inches long, with the hook and scourge in either hand; some are of stone, some of baked earthenware, and others of blue pottery. Excepting so odd and extraordinary an exhibition, few of the common tombs, which were most likely for the poorer class of natives, are worth seeing, as none of them are ornamented in any way whatever; the bodies are stowed in compact masses, tier on tier, always crossing each other. In some instances we found the hair quite perfect. It was in a tomb of this description that some of the diggers found a beautiful net-work, composed of long blue beads, hollow, with threads passed through them; the parts of the net hanging down over the shoulders, and all emanating from a scarabæus Thebaicus, which was on the crown of the head; it was found on the head of a female mummy.

At the commencement of this year the diggers also found two remarkably fine Egyptian vases of brass, covered with hieroglyphics; they are nearly two feet high, and are the most valuable remains of antiquity which have been discovered for some years, being quite perfect. Mr. B. was fortunate enough to get them, for Mr. Salt, for one hundred and seventy piastres—£4. 5s.

We now went to inspect a newly discovered tomb, that well recompensed us for our trouble. Having crawled in through a small hole barely sufficient for the body to be squeezed in, we entered a small sepulchral anti-chamber adjoining to a tomb filled with mummies. From the finished style of the decorations of this chamber, we concluded that it must have been the tomb of some noble family; the paintings are all in fresco, and so wonderfully well preserved, that not the least scratch or stain is visible; the pure white ground of the wall not being even tinged with yellow. Amongst the groups we noticed an interesting troop of six musicians, all females, uniformly dressed in white robes reaching down to their ankles; over this, they have a sort of black, loose woollen net hanging over the shoulders, and reaching down to the waist. Their hair is jet black, plaited in ringlets, reaching down below from the outer part of the eye-lids all round the head, having at first sight the appearance of a veil. They are all walking in procession and playing at the same time: the leader has a harp with fourteen strings; then comes the guitar, which is not unlike the instrument of that description which we use at this day; then a lute, which is a handsome instrument; after this comes another girl clapping her hands, apparently keeping time; then another playing on a sort of double pipe: this instrument is played on like a clarionet, and is long and thin, both the tubes being of equal length: the procession closes with a female beating on a tambarine, which is in this shape)⎯(. The gestures of these musicians, with their uplifted eyes, would lead one to suppose they were playing some impassioned air. The preservation of this group is astonishing, the colours being perfectly fresh, and no part whatever in the least defaced. What would not the French have given for such a specimen to put in their splendid work? there is nothing throughout Egypt to be compared to it. There are also two male harpers in different parts of this apartment; both are squatted down, and playing on smaller instruments than that first described, having only nine strings each; one is playing alone, the other is accompanied by a guitar. These last-mentioned musicians are bare-headed, and have bare feet: they are apparently elderly men. There are many other groups here, but as they are like what we have before noticed in other sepulchres, we avoid entering into detail. The sacred bull (Apis) is here most magnificently ornamented, and is a handsomer animal than we have hitherto noticed. The cieling of the apartment is divided into four compartments, each of which is painted with a different device. Adjoining the chamber, by means of a small well at one end, is a tomb filled with mummies, amongst which are the fragments of a handsome mummy-case, richly painted and glazed. Some of the bodies are

L

covered with canvass, having a coat of plaster and then painted. We found some of the small ornaments of earthen ware, frequently called Nilometers, concealed in the envelope of the corpses.

The valley of Gourna ends at the foot of the Lybian mountains, where their sides present a perpendicular precipice; here are some interesting antiquities—a granite portal, discovered this year by digging; an arch, the only built one of Egyptian architecture to be seen in the country, and which, from its singular construction, I shall describe. It is well known that the Egyptians were ignorant of the regular mode of building an arch, and it is the knowledge of this circumstance which helps us frequently, in this country, to distinguish the works of the Greeks and Romans from those of their predecessors. The Egyptians built their arches in this form ▰▱▰ ; the Romans thus ⌒ . All the temples are roofed over with blocks of stone, frequently thirty feet long, but as this was the utmost extent, you consequently never meet a space between a row of columns wider than this. Their staircases, whether circular or straight, are built on the same principle as their arches, being merely firmly inserted in the side of the wall, the mason taking care to leave stone enough within, to prevent the risk of too great a weight without, injuring his work; each step is cut out of the solid stone. A painted chamber and a granite slab appear to be the other objects of interest near to this spot. It seems to have been a sepulchre, rather than a temple, and has been approached by two or more avenues. It was discovered by digging, at Mr. Salt's expence, this year; but the Defterdar Bey or governour of Upper Egypt, made them desist from their researches; there are the ruins of a small edifice below these other objects.

We now proceeded to visit a small temple to Isis, which is situated to the N. W. of Medinet Aboo; its position may be seen from Memnonium, but being surrounded by a Saracenic wall of sun-burnt brick, nothing but one portal is visible in the distance. This constitutes the approach to the edifice, and you arrive at a small portico, the pillars having capitals of the head of Isis; there is, besides the portico, a cross anti-chamber, a sanctuary, and two wings; it is altogether a neat little temple. In the evening we returned to Luxor, having previously examined the statues and temple at Memnonium.

Tuesday, August 19. Early this morning crossed the water with our janissary to pay a farewell visit to the Tombs of the Kings. One of the chief diggers accompanied us to show us two new tombs discovered by Mr. B. this year. We inspected them first, but found them quite unworthy of notice; they are situated in a small valley adjoining the great one. We now explored the other tombs, but found nothing new to add to our former observations. In the small chamber where Bruce copied the harp he gave to Mr. Burney (for his History of Music), we saw that traveller's name scratched over the very harp, which we think strong presumptive evidence that he drew it himself, though he has been accused of drawing it afterwards from memory: he is erroneous in the number of strings which he has given to it: the instrument itself is not unlike the original, though the musician is very indifferently copied. This evening we found some scorpions which our guide took up in his hand with great indifference: we remarked that he took good care always to seize the reptiles by the tail.

We returned by the way of Memnonium on foot, ascending to the top of the Lybian chain which on one side gave us a fine view of the valley and Tombs of the Kings, while on the other hand we looked down on the plain which contains the whole of the ancient Thebes, together with the Nile, to great advantage. As a specimen of Egyptian scenery, it was a splendid view. As we descended, we counted on one spot upwards of fifty mummy-pits, discernible by their mouths or entrances being open, on the sides of the hills, exclusive of an innumerable quantity of doors of grottos, sepulchral chambers, &c. &c. cut out of the sides of the mountains. We now returned to Luxor, and having seen every thing, we began to think of returning. I cannot quit Thebes, however, without a few observations; most travellers, when speaking of this ancient capital, make mention of the lines of Homer, wherein he alludes to Thebes in such glowing characters. I shall give you Pope's translation of the passage, and then add a few observations which occurred to me on the spot.

> " Not all proud Thebes' unrivalled walls contain,
> " The world's great Empress on th' Egyptian plain;
> " That spreads her conquests o'er a thousand states,
> " And pours her heroes through a hundred gates,
> " Two hundred horsemen, and two hundred cars,
> " From each wide portal issuing to the wars."

In our researches throughout the whole of the Theban ruins we could not meet with any remains of either walls or gates, unless the term is applied to the pylons and other buildings which constituted the approach to the sacred edifices. Now, if Thebes was a city which had a hundred gates, there must surely have been a wall on which to construct them; and it is not unreasonable to suppose that the walls of so extensive and magnificent a city would have been built with stone, or at least that the frames or portals of the gates would have been of that material; still no vestige of either gate or wall is to be seen; and if so many ruins of temples and their porticos remain to this day, why have we not one solitary gate, or even fragment of the wall left? Under all these circumstances, I do not think it an improbable conjecture, that it was the numerous porticos, pylons, &c. of the Theban temples, that gave to her the boasted reputation of a hundred gates, more than any real outlets that ever existed to the city. That she vanquished and subdued many states, and that the people were proud of their warlike achievements, appears from the battles so frequently traced on the walls; but we no where observed Egyptian horsemen, they being always of the enemy's party in the act of flight, and looking back with dismay on the conquering Egyptians, who are invariably in chariots. Much as has been found amongst the ruins of Thebes, I suspect there is still much more; and if the English party are not prevented from digging, it is probable we shall be continually hearing of some new discoveries.

Friday, August 21. We started early this morning for Cairo, having bargained with the reis to take us down for thirty piastres—fifteen shillings. The boat was laden with lentiles for the pashaw. We got a few mats over-head for a shade, and found the cargo a good soft place whereon to put our beds; the sailors, in the boat, offering to help us in our cooking operations, we found we did as well without as with a servant.

Saturday, August 22. This morning we stopped at Tentyra, and, as our reis said he should not start for an hour, we determined to revisit the temple of Isis*; we accordingly started on foot for that

---

* The inscription on the listel of the cornice, in front of this temple, speaks of it as dedicated to Venus, which agrees with Strabo, who says, "The Tentirites worship Venus; behind the temple of Venus is a sanctuary (ἱερὸν) of Isis." The latter still exists; it is a small temple without columns. It is curious that the French savans did not copy this inscription; either they did not see it, or, stranger still, none of them knew Greek enough to be able to copy the letters, which are considerably broken and erased, it was first copied by Colonel Leake and Mr. Hamilton. It is not surprising that the French, having failed as to the inscription of Tentyra, should have omitted others more difficult, or that they should have occupied Alexandria for three years without having been able to decypher a single word of the inscription on the column of Diocletian. Colonel Leake was the first to discover the legibility of this inscription, by making out the words ΑΛΕΞΑΝΔΡΕΙΑΣ and ΕΠΑΡΧΟΣ ΑΙΓΥΠΤΟΥ.

purpose, but when we had got two-thirds of our way, we found the canal was filled, and that we must either swim over it or return; as we were dressed in our Arab costume, the former alternative was not difficult; we therefore threw our clothes over and plunged in. We examined the temple, and did not forget the little chamber, in which we had before noticed the circular astronomical table on the cieling to be a monument of the same kind as the Isiac table which we had seen at Turin. It was in the cieling of the other half of this chamber that Mr. Ruppell discovered a complete lunar system, which had totally escaped Denon and all the other French savans. Mr. R. took an exact copy of this interesting tablet, clearly making it to contain twelve moons and a bit of another, which no doubt was meant for the odd five days, as the twelve make three hundred and sixty. As this throws an additional light on the Egyptian mode of calculating the year, it is a matter of no small interest, and reflects the more credit on Mr. Ruppell, as so many travellers have examined this chamber, and this circumstance never occurred to them. In the great

---

The joint efforts of himself and Mr. Hamilton; and Colonel Squires during several days afterwards decyphered what can be seen of the remainder. See *Classical Journal.*

French work they have put down fourteen or fifteen moons, never having taken the trouble to count them. Having returned we continued our voyage.

Tuesday, August 25. Stopped at Siout and went up to pay our respects to the hospitable doctor, Marouky—found him as friendly as ever;—stopped two hours, and pushed on.

Wednesday the 26th. Visited Mr. Brine, a grateful remembrance of whose kindness also induced us to call. We here took charge of the heads of two Egyptian mummy-cases, and other antiquities dug up for Mr Salt from a spot supposed to be the burial place of Hermopolis, near the Lybian chain.

Thursday, August 27. Stopped at Houarti. As this was the village of our crew, we were obliged to reconcile our minds to stop for three days, while they made merry with their friends and relations. We had scarcely arrived here an hour, when our reis came to ask us to lend him the two mummy-cases which we had on board. He said he should like to have them up at the village for an hour; we lent them immediately, not having any idea of his reason for borrowing them. On the following day, however, we found out, for numbers of women came down and requested them, when they alternately walked three times round them, crossing over them each time; this we found was to procure them families. From this time the women were constantly arriving, young and old, and all going through the same ceremony; they were all very serious during the performance of this mystery, and seemed to think it odd that we laughed so much. Our sailors informed us there were some antiquities at the foot of the Mockatem, about one hour and a half's distance; they mentioned temples and catacombs; we did not much believe them, but were glad of any excuse for a trip to pass away the time, and accordingly started with one of the reis's brothers for a guide. He took us to a very extensive and finely situated site of a city, which, from the state of the rubbish, must have been of some consequence; its situation is at the mouth of a valley in the Mockatem, on an elevated spot, at the edge of the cultivated plains of which it commands a fine view. The modern village of Tehene is close to it. The ruins have been much dug up by the Arabs in search of antiquities. We only found one capital approaching to the Corinthian order, most likely Roman. Immediately above the rubbish is a considerable range of catacombs and ancient temples hollowed out of the rock. One small temple of Isis is well worthy of notice, the decorations, in basso-relievo, being finished in a good style. At about a quarter of an hour's walk along the side of the mountain, to the southward, we saw a large excavated space, and on the top a frieze with a Greek inscription, the letters of which are remarkably large. It is about three fathoms long, and its size (the letters being nearly one foot long) made us believe it must be generally known; therefore we did not copy it. We clearly made out the word ΠΤΟΛΕΜΑΙΟΣ; but thinking it common, did not notice it much. We have since found that no travellers notice the site, and the inscription is not known. We have therefore given the particulars to Mr. Salt. A very old map of Danville's, on a small scale, has the site of an ancient town, under the name of Cynopolis placed nearly in a parallel of latitude with this. We now sailed, and continuing our voyage, arrived at Cairo on the 31st August.

Wednesday, September 1. Our first care now was to shave our beards, which we had allowed to grow from our first departure from Philæ, and resume our European costume; we felt as awkward at first at this change of dress, as we did when we first assumed the Arab costume. Mr. Salt received us very civilly. We found that great discoveries had been made at the pyramids and sphinx during our absence; and the first thing that drew our attention was Mr. Salt's elucidative plan of the pyramids, sphinx, and all their interesting environs. As the whole account of the proceedings is going home for publication, I shall only trouble you with a few particulars. On our arrival we found, at Mr. Salt's house, Colonel Stratton, of the Enniskillen dragoons, and Mr. Fuller: these two travellers had come from making the tour of Palestine, having lastly arrived by land from Yaffa and Gaza. They embarked at Constantinople, having first made the tour of Greece. As they had not yet been to the pyramids, we were glad to have an opportunity of accompanying them.

Friday, September 4. We went early in the morning, and Mr. Salt having lent us a copy of his newly made plan, we regularly went over the whole neighbourhood, place after place, according to the plan; we found there was nothing new for us to see, excepting a few of the upper steps fronting the sphinx. Unfortunately for us and all future travellers, they have filled up all the excavations of the sphinx, so that there is not so much to be seen now, as there was previous to our departure, the base having been perfectly cleared on one side, before we started for Upper Egypt. From the several drawings and plans which we have seen, together with the description we have heard, it appears that the indefatigable Captain Caviglia continued his operations till he had cleared all the breast of the animal; that he afterwards pursued his labours till he reached the paws, at fifty feet distance from the body; and here it was, between the two, that he discovered the small temple, views of which are given in this work. I imagine this small edifice was composed of three large, flat stones, like a similar shrine in the possession of Mr. Salt, and that the door was filled up by two smaller pieces of stone on each side of it; these sides have some fine specimens of basso-relievo, and give a fine idea of what the sphinx originally was. A man is depicted as presenting an offering to it; some inscriptions also are interesting, and one of Caracalla has the name of Geta, his brother, erased, as in the Latin inscription at Syene. The lions which were found, together with the tablets, in basso-relievo, have been sent home to the British Museum, were I hope you will see them. The great head of Memnon will please you, and when you contemplate its grandeur, recollect that Thebes has at present the remains of thirty-seven statues of equal dimensions; many greater. Beyond the small temple is an altar. To describe the other parts, I must beg you to imagine yourself fronting the face of the sphinx, at a considerable distance, and nearly on a level with the lower part of the face, and also with the ground adjoining the animal. As you advance, you find at some distance from the paws, a flight of steps which lead some depth below the paws to the base of the temple. Mr. Salt is of opinion that this descent by steps was meant to impress the beholder (after having first viewed the sphinx at a distance on a level) with a more imposing idea of its grandeur, when he views the breast in its full magnitude from below. A wall of sun-burnt brick was on each side of the steps, to prevent the sand from filling up the space. Afterwards we went all over the great pyramid, again descending to the lower chamber, which Captain Caviglia discovered, and also reinspected the well, &c. We could not shew them Colonel Davidson's chamber, as the Arabs had stolen the rope ladder which was left there. After having slept at the mouth of the great pyramid, we returned to Cairo; the excursion occupied us two days. When we were last at Cairo, a trip to the sphinx used to take two hours; we were now five hours going there, the inundation of the Nile forcing us to go more than double the distance round the edge of the canals. We went in a cangia, or rowing boat, as the canal was quite full. As we are now about to leave Egypt, I shall add a few remarks before I quit of the subject. In my last I said nothing about Cairo. All Turkish towns impress Europeans with very unfavourable ideas; the streets are invariably narrow, and the fronts of the houses look like so many barn doors. Cairo is particularly ill-built, and a stranger on arriving, after having heard so much of "Grand Cairo," can scarcely believe his own eye-sight when he finds himself in this miserable hole; and this is the more striking, as at a short distance the lofty minarets give it a grand appearance. Miserable narrow streets, the square bow windows meeting over the head, and built with unpainted deal wood; no pavement to be seen; grates substituted for panes of glass; a dirty ill-dressed populace, and women covered up like so many ghosts, may give you some idea of this metropolis. The various classes of inhabitants, such as Turks, Arabs, Copts, Jews, Franks, &c. have their respective quarters where they reside in detached societies; each quarter has its gate and porter to attend it; all are shut at eight o'clock in the evening; after which time it is customary to fee the porter to get admittance. In case of revolutions, when the troops go about robbing and plundering all they meet with, these gates become of great service. The citadel of Cairo is built on a commanding eminence; here the pashaw resides:

great merit is due to this man for the tranquillity which exists at present throughout Egypt, and could such an atrocious crime as the murder of the mamelukes be over-looked, he might be considered as a great man; this barbarous act was committed about six years ago: the unsuspecting victims, about two thousand in number, were invited to the castle to be present at the presentation of the Pelisse to the pashaw's son, Toussein, and his investiture with the command of Jidda, including the government of the sacred city of Mecca. During the ceremony, the walls and tops of the houses, the castle, &c. were lined with troops, and on a signal given, as the mamelukes were returning, the soldiers opened their fire on them, and they were all shot to a man.

Egypt at present presents a very different appearance to what it did when we went upward; the Nile having overflowed, all the villages are insulated, and being invariably surrounded with date palm-trees (which partly conceal the mudhuts) and give a pleasing and lively appearance to the face of the country. The river also, in some places, appears of prodigious width, whole plains being overflowed for many miles. We were peculiarly fortunate, having seen Egypt throughout, with the Nile at its lowest ebb, and also at its greatest elevation. There are no hedges in this country, the division of land being exactly like that of the Pays Bas. There is no freehold property, all the land being let out by the pashaw, who afterwards forces the peasants to sell their property to him only, and *at his price*. Soldiers are quartered in all the principal villages to enforce a due observance of this law. All the boats are likewise monopolized by him, and at his price. Gun-boats are stationed at the narrow passes of the river, to prevent the passage of any barks unless laden for the pashaw. The Arabs, Copts, &c. who become rich in spite of this oppressive system, are allowed but little enjoyment of their wealth; if any one of them has built a fine house, it often happens that he is desired to turn out, and give it up to some Greek, Turk, or perhaps to an European consul, and should he not immediately obey, his head is the forfeit. It is a curious fact, that no water-plants or weeds grow on the banks of the Nile; a sedgy margin is never to be met with in this country. The lotus, affecting fens and marshy places, could only flourish during the most propitious part of the year, when the overflowing of the Nile promoted its growth: hence it was so favourite a plant with the ancients; and it is generally coupled with all symbolic allusions to the river. This year the Nile has risen seventeen pics, or thirty-four feet; this is called a good Nile. Last year it rose eighteen pics, which produced a very plentiful crop. We went the other day to the island of Rhoda to see the Mekias, but the column of graduation was wholly covered by the water; so that we might have spared ourselves the trouble. The island, however, now presents a complete carpet of verdure, with beautiful sycamore trees (ficus sycamorus of Linnæus) and well recompensed us. There are no barns in Egypt: the peasant being sure of fair weather at harvest-home, the corn is immediately thrashed, and the grain is piled up in immense hills, encircled by a wall. The birds are freely allowed their share, though, during the time it is ripening, their claims are disputed by children, who are placed on elevated mud-hillocks, scattered in all directions throughout the plains; here they bawl and fling stones by means of a sling, to deter the feathered robbers from their depredations. The other day we went to Boulack, situated on the banks of the Nile; it is, properly speaking, the port of Cairo, and the busy scene it presents at this time of the year, is not exceeded by any of our quays in Europe. The large dgerms, some of forty and fifty tons, make an immense profit during the overflowing of the Nile; the stream brings them down with great rapidity, and the strong north breeze takes them up again with equal speed. It is said these boats sometimes clear half their original cost the first season; a great part of the year, when the Nile is in its bed, they are laid up in ordinary, as their great draught of water prevents them navigating at that season. We thought it remarkable that we had never met, throughout Egypt, with the remains of any thing like a pavement to their cities, with the exception of Antinoe, where we clearly made out the streets paved in many places.

Egypt begins to fill with English travellers: a few days ago Captain Bennet (dragoons) and Mr. Jolliffe arrived from making the tour of Palestine. The former is gone up as high as Assuan with Colonel Stratton and Mr. Fuller; the latter is obliged to return immediately to England. We start in a few days for the tour of Syria. Sheikh Ibrahim who travels for the African Association, and who is mentioned in Mr. Legh's publication, has been of great assistance to us with his advice, in tracing out our route, &c. This he also did for both the travellers mentioned above. Mr. Salt is very kind and attentive to us; we dine with him every day, and he has allowed us to copy his map of Syria. We intend to cross the desert on camels to Gaza; to visit the whole sea-coast up to Latachia; from thence to cross over the mountains by Antioch to Aleppo; to go to Palmyra or Damascus according to circumstances, and from Damascus to Jerusalem, visiting in our way all the curiosities to be seen in the neighbourhood of our route. We calculate that the tour will occupy us till the middle of January, when we mean to embark at Alexandria for Smyrna and Constantinople. By the time we get off for Syria, (which will be in a few days) we shall have been fourteen months absent; we have supplied ourselves with provisions, clothes, and arms, viz. two muskets and a brace of pistols, and have spent only one hundred and ninety pounds each, including our share of the boat-hire from Philæ, up to the second cataract, and back to Thebes, and also of the expenses at Ebsambal, excepting the payment of the labourers and the presents to the cashiefs. Mr. Salt furnishes us with letters of introduction to Lady Hester Stanhope, Mr. Barker, the consul at Aleppo, and all the English agents in Syria. Lord and Lady Belmore arrived at Alexandria in their yacht on the eighth instant, and embarked for Cairo on the seventeenth; we expect them daily.

Before we leave Egypt, I should inform you that we discovered an interesting tomb, opposite to Mr. Brine's, at Radimore; the sides were covered with paintings, amongst which are two groups, of a description very rarely, if ever to be met with; one of them represents the removal of a colossus between thirty and forty feet high, and seated on a chair; upwards of a hundred labourers are employed. The other drawing represents an Egyptian garden, with exotics in flower-pots arranged on the terrace, near to which is an arbour, bee-hives, &c. &c. Mr. Bankes and Mr. Beechey are the only travellers who have visited this tomb since we discovered it: the former has accurate drawings of all its contents.

LETTER II.

TOUR IN EGYPT AND SYRIA.

Departure from Cairo, through the Desert, to El Arish. Gaza.—Asdoud.—Jaffa.—Cesarea.—Tortura.—Athlite.—Mount Carmel.—Acre.—Tsour.—Saida.—Bayruth.—Gebail.—Tripoli.—Cedars of Lebanon.—Baalbec.—Tortosa.—Jebilee.—Latachia or Latakia.—Antioch.—Arrival at Aleppo.

ALEPPO, December 6, 1817.

ON the first of October, at eight A. M. we were without the walls of Cairo. We had made a bargain with an Arab for three camels to conduct us to Jaffa for thirty dollars. About eleven we passed on our left the obelisk of Mataria, the site of the ancient Heliopolis; shortly after we passed close to the ruins of another ancient city on the skirts of the desert; the only object of interest in them is a statue in a sitting posture, mutilated, but originally well executed. Our road was in the desert, but close to the cultivated plains, which extend no further from the Nile than where the soil can be benefitted by the overflowings of the river, either by natural or artificial means. This causes a sudden separation between the barren sand and irrigated land, having the appearance of a sea beach. In the evening we saw some gazelles on the right. We had left Cairo with only one camel and three asses; the other two camels we were to meet at a village in the evening. We had enlisted in our service a Maltese interpreter who mounted the third ass, while the camel carried our baggage. Arriving in the evening at the village before mentioned, we parted with the asses, and at eleven at night set out again on the three camels, with their owner and his black slave. We heard the howling of wild beasts during the night, resembling the cries of human beings in distress. We suppose them to have been jackalls.

October 2. This morning we remained several hours at a village, where our conductor bought an ass: we were here joined by a camel laden; the owners object appeared to be to profit by our protection, seeing we were armed. As the Tarabeen Arabs of the desert through which we were to pass have the character of being notorious robbers, we were not sorry to see our number thus increased; the stranger was bound to a village near Gaza. We passed, this day, occasionally through the skirts of the desert, as well as of the cultivated plains; the latter are rich beyond description, with the finest crops of doura we had seen. The retiring floods have left the land inundated with great and handsome lakes, and the soil being saturated as it were, and receiving at the same time the heat of an ardent sun, produces a very rapid vegetation. We slept this night in the desert, and on the following morning we halted at Selahieh, the last village on our road, which is situated on the borders of the cultivated plains of Egypt. We remained here a few hours to lay in a stock of water and provisions for the desert, which we entered by keeping more to the eastward. On leaving the village, at two P. M. we were astonished at the picturesque appearance of the desert covered with wild shrubs; the occasional hill and dale, gives a pleasing variety to the scene, very different from what we had been accustomed to in Nubia, where the desert deserves that appellation in the strictest sense, being nothing but a barren expanse of sand and rock, totally destitute of every sign of verdure or vegetation. The difference I have alluded to is to be attributed to the nightly dews in this more northern climate, which, though sufficient to nourish dwarf shrubs, would not be capable of irrigating a sandy soil divested of water, and consequently of every other means of moisture. Wells of brackish water are occasionally met with, which serve to sustain the numerous gazelles which we constantly see feeding in the distance. We frequently met with birds, and in some places the quail and partridge are seen in considerable numbers. We found that, although the camels are capable when grazing, and without work, of going five, six, and even seven days without drinking, it is necessary that, when travelling, they should drink at least every three days; and our driver, whenever he met with water, even if they had drank the day before, never failed to let them drink again, which always appeared to refresh them much, for the heavy sand fatigues these animals in a great degree, though they perspire but very little, which tends much to the retention of that moisture so necessary for their support; they were constantly feeding as they went along, the length of their necks allowing them easily to do so. We could not but notice the provident bounty of nature in planting the desert with vegetables of a succulent and nutritious kind. It is undoubtedly to the want of verdure in the Nubian desert, as well as throughout the interior of that of Lybia, that we are to ascribe the difficulty of exploring those parts of Africa, as every camel there must have another to carry its provisions. Our road, or rather our track, was tolerably good. At Selahieh we had been joined by a man with asses, an Arab without a nose, a free negro, and six Muggrabins, one of whom was from Morocco, another from Algiers, and a third from Tunis, all bound on their pilgrimage to Mecca. By keeping with us they secured for themselves a supply of water of which we had a good stock. They had separated from the great caravan from Morocco, consisting of ten thousand camels, which we met on our last expedition to the pyramids, when we learnt that the two sons of the emperor of Morocco were among the pilgrims. This immense assemblage had been five months on their journey when we met them.

October 4. We passed, on our left, the great lake, which is situated to the east of Damietta. We were obliged to cross several rivers and pools of salt water, sometimes up to the bellies of the camels, the arabs and asses swimming across. In the afternoon we passed, on our left, the ruins of Pelusium, but they were too far distant for us to visit them, and too many pools and lakes lay between. In the evening the desert became more hilly, with occasional clumps of palm-trees in the vallies. In one of these we remained for the night, near a well of brackish water. We saw some gazelles during the course of the day.

October 5. We had much the same country, the palm-trees, however, ceasing. We met many carcases and detached bones of camels and asses, who had probably dropped with thirst and fatigue; we also passed a few wells of indifferent water. This evening Mahomet, our camel driver, made bread; he kneaded the dough in a leathern napkin ([6]), and mixing a good deal of salt with it, made a flat round cake about half an inch thick, and baked it on dried camel's dung ([7]); it was very good. We saw several gazelles near where we slept.

October 6. In the morning we came near a bay on the sea coast. We passed, on the right, some Bedouins; saw a very fine hare; the sand became heavier, and the shrubs less plentiful; laborious work for the camels; we, however, occasionally passed through some long damp plains between the sand-hills. We met a small caravan laden with tobacco; the attendants were armed, having two pistols and some swords. They asked backsheeish of us in a very rude manner, but we refused to give it, and determined to make the best possible display of our fire-arms for the future. I have little doubt that these people use their arms to commit robberies when opportunity offers, as much as to protect themselves; indeed their insolent demand on us goes much to prove it. We still find the road strewed with bleached carcases of camels and asses.

October 7. We passed over a plain of about four miles in length, covered with thick, hard salt, resembling in appearance sheets of firmly frozen snow ([8]); the surface bore the weight of our animals without giving way in the least. While we were resting at breakfast, a man came on horse-back, and talked to the camel driver a good deal, saying, he wished to know who we were, that he was a guard, and had orders to stop all Europeans travelling without a soldier of the pashaw of Egypt. He also asked for backsheeish, but did not address himself to us; we kept our arms in sight, and he seeing we took no notice of him, shortly after retired. The road was now level, which relieved the poor animals a good deal, and we soon reached the sea beach. At three in the afternoon we arrived at El Arish. About an hour before we reached it, we stopped at some wells of fresh water, where we found a great assemblage of camels and many Tarabeen Arabs, who appeared to stop all passengers; they entered into a violent dispute with our conductors, which we did not understand, but they took no notice of us. They presently levied a contribution on the other Arabs who accompanied us, and certainly we should have shared the same fate had it not been for the appearance of our arms, as the chief followed us all the way to El Arish, surveying our baggage with the most thievish inquisitiveness (⁹). We were also passed by the man on horseback, who had visited us at breakfast, but observing that we kept our muskets in our hands, he said it was not against us that he meditated hostilities, and galloped on. At El Arish are some Roman ruins, as would appear by several marble columns we noticed; there is a very fine well of good water here. The village is situated on a slight eminence about half a mile from the sea, from which it is hidden by sand hills and clumps of palms. The principal part is inclosed within a high wall of considerable thickness, having loopholes all round for musketry, and a walk also; there is an octagon battery for cannon at each angle. Some ruined guns and old French ammunition boxes are all the warlike stores it contains. This place is remarkable for the treaty made between Sir Sidney Smith and the French army, for the evacuation of Egypt, which his superiors would not ratify. The land about El Arish is quite barren.

October 8. Soon after midnight we left this place; the morning was cold and foggy till sunrise; about an hour after, we stopped to breakfast. We begged our camel drivers to halt in a vale at some distance from the road, that our Tarabeen neighbours might not discover us. We had, however, scarcely unladen the camels, when one of our yesterday's friends came, and seated himself in the midst of us. We could not help being surprised at this fellow's adherence to us, as we were now nine hours from the place where we had first met him, and had been travelling in the dark. We requested he would take himself off, as he could have no business with us; he walked away apparently disappointed at not meeting some of his companions to assist him in plundering us. The desert was now much the same as at first, the shrubs increasing. In the forenoon we passed an extensive plain where there are wells of tolerable water, a sheikh's tomb, and a Mahomedan burial-place. In the afternoon we had occasional views of the sea. We this day passed many flocks of sheep and goats, peasants, and several laden camels. The attendants were usually armed, and eyed our baggage with a scrutinizing look, but the sight of the muskets has always had its effect on them. We saw this day some partridges, and numerous gerba, a sort of rat which runs like the kangaroo. About four we passed a temple of considerable magnitude; two pillars of grey granite are standing, with several prostrate fragments, and a large wall constructed with antique remains. At sun-set we reached the village of Haneunis. It has a long square fortification inclosing a mosque. The approach to this place is picturesque; it is seated in a valley, and its environs are prettily laid out with gardens, trees, &c.; there is but little land turned to agricultural purposes. We remarked both the houses and inhabitants to be cleaner and handsomer than those in Egypt. There are many marble fragments of columns, &c. which mark the site of a town of Roman antiquity. As we have now reached the confines of Syria, and are beginning to enter an inhabited and cultivated country, a few remarks on the mode of travelling may not be uninteresting. We had often enquired about the cheer we were likely to meet with in crossing the desert, and were always told about hardships, such as want of water, the fatiguing pace of the camels, and the total privation of every accommodation. Bruce's narrative had also led us to expect very indifferent fare. With these unfavourable prognostics we were not a little surprised to find our journey a most pleasant one. The pace of the camels we found very agreeable; the open air was the best place to sleep during the night, and even then it was rather too warm; and as for water and provision we took care to lay in a good stock of both, so that we fed remarkably well; and indeed, if I except the heat, which about noon was more than is agreeable (the skin of our noses being blistered off by it), I may safely say, I never made a more pleasant trip in my life. The pace of the camels is somewhat tedious, being little more than two miles an hour, or about the rate of Russel's waggon; but this required only some of that patience which his waggoners must needs possess. Our camels, during this trip, were only once three days without drinking.

October 9. At daylight we proceeded, the road leading through a barren country that resembled a heath. In two hours we came to the village of Esdier, prettily situated, with a view of the sea. There is here some land well cultivated and artificially watered, with the sackey, as in Egypt; the principal produce is tobacco. Beyond the village, here and there are beautiful sycamore-trees, similar to those in Egypt, in an uncultivated plain. We remained four hours under one of these trees for the purpose of drying all our things, which were wetted by the salt water on the fourth, unperceived till this day. While we were thus employed, a woman came hastily forth from the village, and seating herself on the ground, under a tree near us, bewailed most bitterly, throwing the sand over her head with frantic gesticulations which lasted about twenty minutes, when her husband, with whom we heard she had quarrelled came, and with difficulty drew her off ([10]). There are some marble remains of antiquity at Esdier. Hereabout appears to be the situation where the sea coast turns to the north. We thought we perceived a sensible change in the weather; the dews for some nights past had been very heavy; this morning the N.E. wind blew keenly, but the sky was fine and clear. From Esdier to Gaza, which latter place we reached at four P. M. are fine extensive plains prettily cultivated; and the neighbourhood of Gaza itself is richly wooded with olives, sycamores, mulberries, cedars, fig-trees, &c. &c. the country is inclosed by hedges of prickly pears, the hills gently rising to the view beyond each other, and the whole has a beautiful appearance. Excepting the less perishable materials, with which the houses are constructed, stone being substituted for mud, the town partakes of the wretched appearance of those in Egypt. The rains in winter have forced the natives to roof their houses, whereas in Upper Egypt they only lay some canvass across to shade them from the sun, that being the only inconvenience they have to guard against. We remarked that the inhabitants here were cleaner and better looking, the women being dressed in a white or blue shirt, and a white shawl thrown loosely over the head, with which those who have no other veil, cover their faces occasionally.

Being tired, and having nine days beard, we did not visit the town; we were further discouraged by our servant having been scoffed at on account of the difference of religion. The gates of Gaza, were carried away by Sampson at midnight to escape from the inhabitants ([11]) : this town was the frontier of the land of Canaan.—(See Gen. c. x.)

October 10. At four A. M. we left Gaza, the road for two hours was through beautiful groves of olives. We then entered an open country, partly cultivated. We passed some villages on each side of us, and the dry torrent Escol over a bridge of two high arches. About noon we had on our left Majudal a large village with a mosque, situated in a valley, surrounded by groves of olives. At three in the afternoon we arrived at Asdoud, the site of the Roman Azotus; near it is an antique building in the form of an open square, which we at first took to be Roman, but as the Turkish khans for the accommodation of caravans and travellers, are built much in the same manner, we are rather inclined to believe it to be a very ancient khan. I will give you a description of it, which will convey some idea of what these khans are. The inclosed court is entered by an arched passage, within which, on each side, are piazzas formed of five arches, two on each side of a larger one in the centre. On each side of the south entrance are chambers, on the right, steps to ascend to the top of the building. The chamber on the left has evidently been used as a primitive Christian chapel, as appears by an altar and a cross; and there is an inscription in some Eastern language over the door. There are other arches in ruins, partly buried, closer to the village, and a marble fragment which would appear to have once formed the capital of a Corinthian column. The natives of this place flocked round us in numbers, looking at us with wonder and astonishment, as well as every thing belonging to us; after we thought they had sufficiently surveyed us, we begged them to retire; they shewed no incivility, but said they came to look at us, because it seldom happened that Europeans arrived near this village. Some women came also, with a sick young man, apparently in a consumption, asking medical advice; we assured them we were not hackim (doctors), which they did not believe, and we luckily recollected that our Maltese interpreter had some "balsam of Mecca," which the friars say is an antidote for all distempers; we gave them some accordingly, which appeared to excite much gratitude. They, however, soon returned to beg some of our hair, saying that the smoke of Christian hair burnt while the medicine was warming would ensure a cure of the disorder*. We could not help laughing at their superstition, but they continued to entreat us; for my part I had little to spare, and Irby did not seem inclined to give any of his. Seeing we were averse to this latter remedy, they at length retired and brought us some honey and bread by way of return; this we offered to pay for, but they would not accept any thing. We had been advised by Sheikh Ibrahim to go from Gaza to Jaffa, by the way of Ascalon, or Ashkelon, but our camel conductor could not be prevailed upon to go through that place, as it is not on the direct road, and he would be liable to a penalty if he deviated from the common rout of the camels; a regulation intended, we suppose, to prevent smuggling, as Ascalon is on the sea coast. At Ascalon we should have seen part of a Roman amphitheatre, and some excavations made by Lady Hester Stanhope, in search of supposed treasure, which failed of success; but what we saw at Azotus in some measure recompensed us. This we should have missed had we gone by Ascalon; it was at Ashkelon that Sampson slew

* Mungo Park, at Dingyee, was requested by a foulah to give him a lock of his hair to make a saphie.

thirty men (Judges, xiv. v. 19). Asdoud is called Ashdod in the Old Testament (see Isaiah, xx. Jeremiah, xxv.; Amos, i. ib. iii.; Zechariah. xix.; and Zephaniah, ii.). It is called Azotus in the Acts of the Apostles, and by the Romans. Palmyra, built by Solomon by the name of Tedmor, or Tadmor, is another instance, among many in Syria, of places having regained their original names. The Arabs in that neighbourhood know nothing of Palmyra, always calling it Tedmor.

October 11. Before daylight, we quitted Asdoud; the country is open and little cultivated, though the soil is very rich, evincing a sad want of population. In the afternoon we passed some ruins, apparently Roman; they appear to have been an aqueduct to convey water to the road side, which is to the eastward of the tract we traversed; we passed also a well which our conductor told us contained poisonous water; we also passed, on our right, Yabne, the ancient Jamnia, situated on a small eminence. About noon we crossed the nahr (or river) El Rubin, close to the ruins of a Roman bridge, one great arch of which, and a part of another, only remain, overgrown with bushes and weeds, which have a pretty effect; and certainly to an amateur of the picturesque, the ruins of Syria must have a decided advantage over those of Egypt, where an arid climate totally prevents the appearance of the least spot of verdure on a ruined fabric, be it ever so old. The traveller is, however, highly recompensed for this deficiency, by the comparatively high state of preservation in which he finds the Egyptian monuments, notwithstanding their superior antiquity; and I really believe that he who has once seen Egypt, will never feel equally interested in any other country. It is this feeling that has brought Mr. Bankes back to the Nile, after having explored Greece, Asia Minor, and the Archipelago, and he is now gone a second time to Thebes. The river El Rubin, above the bridge, is nearly dry, and filled with wild flowers and rushes. Below it there is a handsome winding sheet of water, the banks of which are likewise covered with various water-flowers, and many black water-fowl were swimming on its surface; the water is bad, but not salt. On the opposite side of this river, on a small eminence, is Sheikh Rubin's tomb, surrounded by a square wall, with some trees inclosed. There are in Syria and Egypt numbers of these tombs, which the Arabs erect to the memory of any man who they think has led a holy life, for the title of sheikh is not only given to their chiefs, but also to their saints. These tombs are generally placed in some conspicuous spot, frequently on the top of some mount. The sepulchre consists of a small apartment with a cupola over it, white-washed externally ([10]); within are deposited a mat and a jar of water for the ablution of such as retire there for devotion. Sheikh Rubin, who lived many years since, appears to have been much respected, and the people to this day go to pay vows at his shrine; they also bring provisions and make festivals there; the river no doubt receives its appellation from this sheikh. Leaving the neighbourhood of the nahr El Rubin, we crossed the sand hills and came to the sea beach, four or five miles south of Jaffa, and continued coasting till we came to the back of the hill, on the opposite side of which stands the town; here we crossed over between the most beautiful gardens filled with vines and figs, prickly pears, &c. though the soil is a deep sand. We arrived at Jaffa, the ancient Joppa, about five P. M. On our right we saw Ramla, the ancient Arimathea, and Loudd, the ancient Lydda; the former is in the road to Jerusalem. There being no inns or khans in the sea-port towns, for the accommodation of travellers, we were obliged to repair to the English consuls. We found the British representative at the door of his house, and as he was a perfect original, I will give you some description of him. He was a man apparently about sixty years of age, dressed in the Turkish mode, excepting an old brown cocked hat covered with grease, and put square on his head. His beard might be of some seven or eight day's growth, and his back was ornamented with a plaited pig-tail reaching down to his middle. We found it difficult to refrain from laughing at the sight of so odd a figure, for his dress was all soiled with the drippings of soup and fat. He received us with a dignified reserve, and uttering several " favoriscas," shewed us into the apartment, which did the duties of the saloon. This room was filled with water-melons; some old English pictures decorated the walls, and an old dirty sofa, without a covering, and well stocked with fleas, constituted the furniture; numerous holes in the floor gave free access and egress to the rats. In the evening, when supper was announced, we were in hopes of something good, and as we had not tasted any thing but an early breakfast of dried fruit, we entered the room with the appetite which riding usually creates; but judge of our disappointment when we found nothing but rice and cabbage, our host observing it was " Giorno della Penitenza" (Saturday). We slept in the saloon, and got unmercifully bitten by the fleas. Next day we received some scraps of meat, but the old consul took care first to fill us so full of rice, that we could hardly find room for the better part of his feast. Jaffa, situated on the sea coast, is a small fortified town; the fortifications were in a very ruinous state, but the Aga was busily employed in repairing them. Vessels were arriving from the northward daily, with stones, &c. and he himself was in constant attendance on the operations. The Christian and Mahomedan inhabitants were obliged to take it day and day about, to work, at the sound of the drum, every morning at sun-rise. We saw the place where the French entered the town on their advance into Syria, and the hospital where Buonaparte poisoned his sick, on his retreat, to prevent them falling into the hands of the Turks. This place is now the Armenian convent, and one of the priests, who was in the town at the time, says there were *only* thirty-five men thus poisoned. About a mile without the town the French army was encamped, and it was here that Napoleon inhumanly massacred the inhabitants in cool blood, after the town was fully in his possession. The number thus slain is uncertain, but many people now in Jaffa attest the truth of the assertion. Our camel-driver being bound to Jerusalem, we sent our heaviest and most useless baggage to that place by him, and endeavoured to purchase horses to continue our route in Syria. We had great difficulty about this matter, and in consequence sent to request the Aga would lend us a soldier to assist us on the occasion, as old Damiani, the consul, was of more harm than good in the business. The Aga, however, very kindly and most positively refused, saying, he would lend us government horses for nothing, as he had also done to Colonel Stratton; he added, that an Englishman, to whom he had granted the same favour, had sent him a spy-glass three years after in return. His motive may appear to have been interested, but the following circumstance tends to prove that he is a good man: our Maltese interpreter, twenty years ago, had been in a better situation of life, and trading in a small way in cotton from Syria, was acquainted with this Aga; on some occasion he had given him a watch as a present; they never again met till the other day, when the Maltese travelling as interpreter to Colonel Stratton, was recognized, at Jaffa, by the Aga, who, seeing him in reduced circumstances, forced him to receive a sum of money, saying it was now *his turn* to give a present. The Maltese, who is an honest man, declined accepting the cash, but the other persisted in presenting it to him. This is one, amongst other instances we have met of the disinterested generosity of the higher class of Turks. As to Damiani we found him of little assistance to us; he advised us to buy a blind horse at a higher price than Mr. Bankes gave here for two sound ones. It was this that occasioned our reference to the Aga, whom we told, on his making us so generous an offer, that we feared our journey would occupy too much time for him to spare his cattle; he, however, replied, that we might keep them as long as we pleased. A neat little fountain, as you enter this town, we thought merited attention. Jaffa is the ancient Joppa: Hiram, king of Tyre, sent Lebanon cedars by sea to Joppa, for the building of Solomon's temple; and the latter had them removed by land to Jerusalem (see 2 Chronicles, c. ii. v. 16). St. Peter's vision was near Joppa (Acts, x.).

October 15. At nine A. M. we left Jaffa. We had hitherto not slept in a house, or under any cover since we departed from Cairo; as yet we had found no inconvenience from this; but as we were going to the northward, and the winter was fast coming on, we thought it adviseable to equip ourselves in a thick Arab suit, made of a sort of coarse wool or sack-cloth; it was very heavy, and at the same time very good; it cost ten piastres, little more than five shillings; a pair of coarse white Turkish breeches and red worsted turban completed our costume. The sun in the desert had browned us to a good standard colour, which very well became our dress; we thus avoided the curiosity of the natives, who used to flock round to gaze at us as if we had been wild beasts. For five piastres we purchased a woollen mat to do duty as a bed; and thus furnished, with four good hack horses under us, we felt quite independent. In the provision line, we always had a staple of bread, cheese, and onions, which served for breakfast, dinner, and supper, unless we were fortunate enough to meet with a fowl. Our road led along the sea beach. We shortly crossed the nahr El Petras. In the afternoon we passed through a wild but pretty country, and crossed the nahr Arsouf, leaving the village of that name (the ancient Appollonias) on our left. The following morning we proceeded very early, and crossing the nahr El Kasab arrived at Cesarea (see the viiith. ixth. xth. and xith. chapters of Acts). Here we stopped two hours examining the antiquities. A small part of these are inclosed within the ruins of an old wall and ditch, which appeared to be Saracenic; and on a promontory, which bounds this extremity on the south side, are the remains of a large edifice, constructed apparently upon the ruins of a Roman temple; immense pillars of granite forming the foundation of the former, placed on a bed of rocks. Here is a small bay of the coast, on the north point of which, on the rocks, are also placed many columns, apparently for the purpose of a landing-place for merchandise, &c. The Roman remains extend far beyond the limits of the walls before-mentioned, and to the north of them. Above, and parrallel with the sea beach, are the ruins of some arches and a wall, which appears to lead to the side of the hills, which now begin to approach closer to the sea than heretofore, and to the nahr Zerka where the water is fresh; this circumstance, and the wells of the town having bad water, led us to suppose these arches to have been once part of an aqueduct. There are also wells on the promontory before described, but they are now dry. Without the Saracenic walls, to the south, we found a column of marble, with a Roman inscription of the Emperor Septimius Severus, but too much buried for us to copy: Mr. Bankes has since told us it is a mile-stone, as he had it cleared for copying. About noon we arrived at Tortura, the ancient Dora (see Judges, i. 27). There are extensive ruins here, but they possess nothing of interest. We left this place at two, and at four reached Athlite, where we remained for the night. Between Tortura and Athlite are numerous quarries of stone cut out of the rock, of which the hills are here formed. The village of Athlite is situated on a promontory, nearly forming a peninsula, and apparently constructed from the ruins of a more ancient city. It is of small extent, and would appear from its elevated situation, and the old walls which surround it, to have been a citadel, as there are the ruins of two other walls without it; the other incloses a square space, the farther or southern-most end of which juts into the sea. There are three entrances through this wall, two on the east and one on the south side, and steps in various places to ascend them. The second wall approaches near to that of the citadel; but the outer one, which we may suppose to have included the remainder of the ancient town, incloses a considerable space of ground now uninhabited. There is a small bay of the coast to the south of the peninsula, which may have occasioned the construction of a town on this site, as it makes a tolerable haven for small vessels. Within the citadel the most interesting of the remains is a part of a great building which we were puzzled to make out; its form was originally a double hexagon; the half of the circumference, which is still standing, has six sides. On the exterior, below the cornice, in alto-relievo, are the heads of different animals, the human with those of the lion;—the ram and the sheep are particularly distinguished. The exterior walls of this edifice have a double line of arches in the Gothic style; the lower row larger than the upper one; the architecture is light and elegant. There does not appear to be any ancient name to this place, and from all the information that we can obtain; the ruins are no older than the time of the crusades, when the town went by the name of Castel Pelegrino. From the commodiousness of the bay, the extent of the quarries in the neigbourhood, the fine rich plains near it, though now but partly cultivated, it would seem that this place was formerly of much importance, and that the neighbourhood, though now very thinly inhabited, was once populous.

October 17. At day-light, we departed through the northernmost of the two passages in the eastern wall; here the rock has been cut away to form the road, and various circumstances combined, induced us to form an opinion that Athlite is of much greater antiquity than is represented. Passing by the part of the coast formed by the foot of Mount Carmel, we entered the bay of Acre, and in less than three hours from Athlite we were at Caiffa (the ancient Hepha); here we found the only friar at present belonging to the convent of Mount Carmel, an intelligent man (a Maltese), who, after supplying us with breakfast, attended us to the summit of Carmel, where the convent is situated. This building, now deserted, was formerly fitted with windows, beds, and every accommodation; it was pillaged and destroyed by the Arabs after the retreat of the French army from the siege of Acre; the latter having used it as a hospital for their sick and wounded, while their operations were carrying on; and in the places where the poor fellows were lain, the numbers still remain by which they were arranged. The friar shewed us a cave cut in the natural rock where the prophet Elijah had his altar (see 1 Kings, xviii. 17, and following verses). In front of this are the remains of a handsome church in the Gothic style, built by the Empress Helena at the time she made her pilgrimage to Jerusalem. Those objects are in the upper part of the convent, which is of a square form, inclosing an open court. From Mount Carmel there is a beautiful view of the bay of Acre, the mountains at the back, the Mediterranean, &c. Near the convent are some prostrate columns; we found an immense scorpion here amongst the rubbish; there is a well of excellent water in the court of the convent. Mount Carmel is of very inconsiderable height, and now quite barren, though at the north-eastern foot of it are some pretty olive yards. On mentioning to the friar our suspicions of the ruins of Athlite being partly Roman, he suggested the idea that it might have been called Athla as the present name Athlite resembles it much in sound. Returned from Mount Carmel, and left Caiffa at three in the afternoon, and following the coast of the bay of Acre, shortly passed on over to the right of the brook Kishon were Elijah slew the worshippers of Baal after he had proved to them the existence of the true supreme being, by the miracle he had wrought on Mount Carmel. We soon after crossed the mouth of the river Kishon, and subsequently the river Belus; we reached Acre at sun-set, and were shown to the house of Signor Malagamba the British agent. All the rivulets we have hitherto passed in Syria, are fordable, in the Autumn, close to their junction with the sea, where the counteraction of the streams of the rivers, which are rapid, and the surf of the sea, form sand-banks or bars; the water is generally fresh close to their junction with the ocean.

October 13. We found Signor Malagamba more useful to us than Damiani; as he had no room to lodge us in, we took up our quarters in the convent, where we met with a most handsome reception from the " Padre Superiore." We ate our meals with the worthy consul, whose house is in the same khan as the convent. Acre is a strong fotified town. Since the French siege, in 1799, the Turks have doubled the walls which inclose the town. We were shewn the breach made by the French army, now entirely repaired, except the spent shot holes. The situation of Acre is delightful; the principal objects in the town are the mosque, the pashaw's seraglio, the granary, and the arsenal. A great religious festival was solemnized by the Turks while we were at Acre: the mosques were brilliantly illuminated at night, and the next day we went to see the pashaw's finest horses; they were splendidly caparisoned with the most gaudy trappings of leopard's skins embroidered with gold and silver. The animals themselves were ill made and good for nothing, the whole being more for show than use. Acre was the Accho of the Old Testament, which, together with Achzib, Dor, Sidon, and some other places of the sea-coast of Syria, were never completely subdued by the Israelites (see Judges, i. 31.) Gaza, Ekron, and Ascalon, further to the southward, were subjugated (same chap. v. 18). We here procured a firman from the pashaw, having travelled thus far without any authority from the Syrian governments. We found this firman worded very strongly in our favour; it was addressed to all the Agas in the pashalic of Acre, and our horses were ordered to be furnished with fodder, &c. free of expense wherever we might go.

October 20. At one in the afternoon, we quitted Acre, going over the plain of that name. There was nothing remarkable to be seen but the extensive aqueduct by which the town is supplied with water. We stopped at Zib, the ancient Achzib (see Old Testament, Judges, i. 31); the inhabitants were dressed for the Mahomedan feast, and crowded round us with curiosity. All their sick came for medical aid, but we had nothing to give them but the balsam of Mecca, which had been so useful at Ashdoud; the shiekh's son amongst others had his hand most terribly burnt, and he evinced much gratitude for the assistance we rendered to him and the rest of the villagers. He offered our interpreter a considerable sum of money, which the other refused. A small medicine chest, with Reece's or some other book on the subject, would be a truly valuable article in the trunk of a traveller in these countries, and would be a sure means of conciliating a stranger with the natives; it was by a judicious application of a trifling knowledge of medicine, that Bruce made his way so well in Abyssinia.

October 21. We were mounted and on our route at daylight, and in about an hour's time we reached and ascended Cape Blanco; the descent on the north side, by its numerous windings, reminded us of the mountain roads of Switzerland, but these were not half so good as the very worst European road we ever met; the sea dashing against the rocks below us had a fine effect. About three hours before we reached Tsour, the ancient Tyre, we observed some ruins on a small eminence on our right; we stopped to visit them, and found they consisted of the remains of a large city, and the ruins of a temple in a most dilapidated state. Two columns, much defaced, are only standing; in the lower part of the capital of one we distinguished the Echinus moulding: the whole has been composed of the natural stone of the country, which is calcarious and very porous. Beyond this town we distinctly traced the remains of the great ancient paved way towards Tyre, and afterwards we ascended what is called the ladder of the Tyrians; it is a picturesque spot, the road being cut in the side of the perpendicular cliff on the sea shore, several hundred feet above the level of the water. This, according to Maundrell (page 52), was the work of Alexander the Great. Descending hence into the place below, we passed the rubbish of another ancient city, and some picturesque rivulets, and arrived at Tsour at one in the afternoon. Here we put up at the house of an Arab who called himself a Christian archbishop; he was not at home, and at first his wife was unwilling to receive us, as we were very roughly attired as Arabs; but our conductor assuring her that we were persons travelling for pleasure, she behaved to us with great civility and attention. The establishment was a very humble one, as might be expected in so mean a place; the prophecies of the fall of Tyre in Isaiah, Jeremiah, and Ezekiel, seem to be fulfilled in the present appearance of Tsour, there being no vestige remaining of the ancient city (so called from Tiras the son of Japheth) but mere rubbish. The city, formerly built on an island, is now on a peninsula; the isthmus which Alexander caused to be made for the prosecution of his attack on the city, has now the appearance of being the work of nature. The port is much choaked up with mud, and the walls and castle are visible, but I should strongly suspect they are not the same which existed at the time when Tyre was in its glory.

October 22. At sun-rise we proceeded on our journey, seeing the remains of the ancient aqueduct. In the morning we crossed the mouth of the Kasmia; the banks of this river are very picturesque; it proceeds from an extensive valley between the mountains, and has pretty windings. There is a bridge with one arch over it, a little below which, it encloses a small island. We continued our route through a country nearly barren, very thinly populated, and very uninteresting, with mountains on our right destitute of either beauty or vegetation. We passed through the ruins of five or six large cities, now mere rubbish, and only distinguishable as sites of towns, by numerous stones much dilapidated, shewing marks of having been cut square with the chisel, with morter adhering to them, and fragments of columns. The only place marked in the map in this quarter is the ancient Sarepta or Zarephath, remarkable by the miracle wrought there by Elijah (see 1 Kings, xvii. 9. and ensuing verses). In the afternoon we crossed several dry torrents, and a river by a bridge of five arches; the banks of all these streams contain quantities of wild-flowers, amongst which is the oleander in full bloom and beauty. As we approached Saida we observed that the sides of the hills were covered with vineyards, but they have not at all a lively appearance. Half an hour before we arrived, we passed the ruins of another ancient city, also a fragment of another granite column, and a Roman inscription in the time of Septimius Severus; see Maundrell, who, as well as Mr. Bankes, copied it, and found its purport to be like that near Cesarea— a mile-stone. The immediate neighbourhood of Saida (the ancient Sidon) is pretty; it derived its name from Sidon the first born of Canaan (see Genesis, x. 15). The plain at the foot of the hills is entirely appropriated to extensive and shady groves and gardens, with narrow and pretty lanes between them. There is no English consul or agent at Saida, we therefore went to the convent but found no friars there, and the church was shut up. The French consulate had entire possession of all the apartments, either for themselves or friends: the French consul himself was on a tour to the Holy Land. We had seen him at Acre; he was then going to Nazareth, and seemed to be a genteel person; his wife was with him. We had some difficulty in obtaining a room in this convent, but at last we got one belonging to one of the absent servants. The French vice-consul now came and visited us, and shortly after retired. As we are now come into the neighbourhood of Lady Hester Stanhope, a few observations will be necessary. As we were entrusted with a letter from Mr. Salt, a packet of English letters from Acre, and a book from Jaffa, we deemed it our duty to wait on her, and therefore set out for her usual residence, an old deserted convent in the mountain about one hour and half distance from Saida, called Mar Elias Alza; but her ladyship was removed on account of the heat to a more elevated spot in the mountains, called Castle Jeba: we therefore forwarded the letters, &c. together with a note requesting her ladyship's permission to wait on her. The following morning we received a letter, saying, that she had made her mind up not to receive any more Englishmen, with the exception of officers of the army and navy, " all fine fellows," as she was pleased to express herself; at the same time she strongly dissuaded us from undertaking the trip to Palmyra, and recommended us to make a short tour of fifteen or twenty days round the vicinity of Saida, and then to return and pass twenty days with her in her convent. This, at the present season of the year, with the winter and rainy season fast approaching, would have been the most impolitic plan we could have pursued, and therefore we returned a polite answer declining her civilities with as good a grace as we could. She is always dressed in the Turkish costume as a man; her generosity we heard spoken of in all directions. Saida possesses as few relics of its ancient magnificence as Tyre. The port, if ever it was extensive, is now small and nearly filled up with the accumulation of mud. The castle, connected to the main by a bridge, is an old building, but the same remark which I made on the ancient edificies at Tyre is applicable to those of Sidon, viz. that they do not appear to be of equal antiquity with that city in the time of its splendour.

October 25. At nine A. M. we left Saida over a wretched rugged road, and an uninteresting country; we met occasionally the remains of the ancient paved way. In the afternoon we passed the ruins of an ancient town and burial ground; here are many stone sarcophagi, some never opened; their lids are very high and massy, and terminating in an angle. A little beyond them are two arches in the mountain's side, the ruins either of a bridge or an aqueduct. Shortly after, we quitted the sea coast and passed over the hills which form the promontory of Bayruth; here is a fine view of the plain, covered with groves of olives, and of several villages on the mountain's side. Descending, we passed through plantations of figs and young mulberries for the silk-worm, and from thence through gardens neatly inclosed by walls where we met occasionally with fragments of antiquity. We entered Bayruth at dusk; there is an ancient bath, with fragments of granite columns, &c. within the town. Bayruth is the ancient Berytus; it was here that St. George conquered the dragon, &c.: it is a fine situation, and like all the other towns of Syria that we have seen, has pretty environs on account of the rich gardens, &c. at the back of it; but these beauties are always confined to particular spots, for an hour's ride usually conducts you again into an uninteresting and rocky country. There is a fine view of the sea from the marina, and the jetty is built on foundations of ancient granite columns. At Bayruth we were at the house of Mr. Laurella, the English agent, a very good fellow.

October 26. At two in the afternoon we left Bayruth, the road being for a short time very pretty, with gardens on each side of us. We soon crossed the nahr El-Sazib previously joined by the nahr El-Leban, or River of Milk, from its foaming when overcharged with water. It is a pretty rivulet; the bridge has six arches. From hence the road led along the sea beach until we came to a rocky promontory whose ascent reminded us of the ladder of the Tyrians, though it is neither so high or picturesque; on reaching the summit, we saw below us on the other side the nahr El-Kelb, or River of the Dog, running beautifully through a deep chasm in the mountains, and a very neat bridge over it, which

Maundrell describes as being a bow-shot from the sea. The banks are planted with vines and mulberries. There is a Roman inscription on a tablet carved out of the rock on the side of the road we descended; this was copied by Maundrell one hundred and twenty years ago, and appears to record the construction of the passage by the Emperor Antoninus. Near the bridge is also another inscription in the Arabic language. We passed the night at the mouth of the river; at daylight the following morning we moved, going along the sea-shore, and in an hour's time ascended a rocky point of a small bay inhabited by fishermen. At the foot of this promontory, close to the sea, are the remains of a chapel cut out of the rock, which we were informed was the sepulchre of St. George (see the note on Bayruth). The old fishermen, whose cottage is situated on the promontory above the chapel, were so superstitious as to believe, and endeavoured to persuade us, that the water of the sea near this spot is a cure for all distempers, and that numerous people came hither for the purpose of being healed by them. We had here a good view of the grand convents of Harissa Soummaar, romantically situated on the summit of the mountain. The valley at the end of this bay is cultivated and studded with cottages. Proceeding along the sea beach we passed a Roman arch constructed with large stones over a dry torrent; from hence the road led over rugged rocks, till we came to the bridge over the nahr Ibrahim, the ancient Adonis. The bridge is of a single arch, and handsome, and the river, like the nahr El-Kelb, proceeds from a deep chasm between the mountains, but the level land near the bridge is more extensive than that of nahr El-Kelb. We now proceeded by the sea-coast to Gebail. On our way we crossed over one of those *natural bridges,* over a torrent now dry, spoken of by Volney, who describes them thus : " In many places the water meeting with inclined beds, has undermined the intermediate earth, and formed caverns," or natural arches. We reached Gebail, or Gibyle, at two in the afternoon, and stopped at the convent of Maronites, a poor miserable set of people who make a merit of never eating meat, &c. At Gebail, without the town, there are many Roman ruins, and a bridge with many granite columns; within, the modern edifices are, in some instances, constructed upon ancient foundations, particularly the castle, and there is another ruin near the seashore. The Roman name of Gebail is marked in the map, as Byblus ; but in Ezekiel, xxvii. 9. it is called Gebal, and is mentioned as furnishing the fleets of Tyre with caulkers.

October 28. We went from Gebail to Tripoli, which we did not reach till dusk, though we started at daylight. We saw nothing of interest except what appeared to have been a Roman temple, and we passed over a very rugged and bad road until we passed Batroun, the ancient Botrys. Here the road turned to the right through a fine valley between the mountains, in which we noticed an old castle standing on a high rock; it is called Temseida, and may have been constructed to defend this pass; we thought it a picturesque object. The hills on the south of the vale are covered with shrubs, and by the road's side are plantations of mulberries, vines, &c. A small river, which we occasionally crossed by bridges, takes its winding course through the valley. Leaving the valley, we passed to the north over the mountains by rugged paths, bordered by the myrtle and other wild shrubs, until we again joined the coast. When about an hour's distance from Tripoli, we passed through some very rich inclosed gardens. At sun-set we arrived, and not being aware that there was an English consul in the town, took up our quarters in the convent, with Padra Hermenigildo. Tripoli is the neatest town we had seen in Syria, the houses being all well built of stone, and neatly constructed within. It is seated at the foot of the mountains, at some distance from the sea-shore, and is surrounded by luxuriant gardens, producing innumerable oranges and lemons. The town is commanded by two old castles on the heights at the back of it, built in the time of the crusades. The port, an indifferent one, is near an hour's distance, on a low point of the sea-coast; there is a village there, but the anchorage is open, being only a little sheltered by the Pigeon Islands. Maundrell (quoting Strabo) says that here were anciently three cities; one subject to Aradus, a second to Tyre, and the third to Sidon, which is the origin of the name of Tripoli; there are other square towers, apparently of the time of the crusades, all the way from the port towards Tripoli. On the second day of our arrival we received a message from the English consul, expressive of his regret that we had not come to his house; we immediately waited on him, and explained the circumstance to his satisfaction. He was a fine old man, nearly eighty years of age, and well remembered Bruce, who stayed some days at his house; we were quite delighted with the affable and sensible conversation of this good man.

On Thursday, at four in the morning, we left Tripoli, for the purpose of visiting the cedars of

Lebanon and Baalbec. Signor Giuseppe Mazoliere, the son of a late French merchant of that name, whose son is the sheikh of the village of Eden, accompanied us, at the request of the padre of the convent. The ascent from Tripoli is gradual; the first object of interest is the aqueduct and bridge over the nahr Kavdas, or Abouli river. These structures are overgrown with bushes and weeds, and the river runs in a picturesque manner under them in two channels. Leaving this place, the road is good, through cultivated plains and groves of olives, passing occasionally beautiful vallies watered by branches of the river. Afterwards the road becomes very rugged, steep, and irregular, the whole way to the village of Eden, passing between two conspicuous points of the mountain. Eden is delightfully situated, by the side of a most rich and highly cultivated valley. It contains between four and five hundred families, who on the approach of winter descend to another village only an hour's distance from Tripoli; the families were in the act of removing to their winter habitations when we arrived; and on our return from Baalbec, all those who had not previously quitted their summer quarters descended with us. They have an Arab catholic bishop, a church, and several priests; there is another village, probably in the same diocese, lower down in the vale. We arrived at Eden about two o'clock, which, including stoppages, makes it ten hours from Tripoli.

Early on Friday morning, we set out by moonlight for the cedars, and arrived a little after daylight. The ascent from Eden to the cedars is but little; the distance, allowing for the windings of the road, which is very rugged, and passes over occasional hill and dale, may be about five miles. On the right, higher up the mountain, is a larger and deeper vale than that of Eden, with the village of Beshiri in the bottom; this valley is very rich and picturesque. It is surrounded by lofty mountains, and is watered by a winding stream. It reminded us of the vale of the Dive in Savoy, and its " Pont de Chevres." The famous cedars of Lebanon are situated on a small eminence, in a valley at the foot of the highest part of the mountain; the land on the mountain's side has a sterile aspect, and the trees are remarkable by being altogether in one clump; from this spot the cedars are the only trees to be seen in Lebanon. There may be about fifty of them, but their present appearance ill corresponds with the character given of them in scripture. There did not appear to be one tree amongst the whole which had much merit, either for dimensions or beauty; the largest amongst them would appear to be the junction of four or five trunks into one tree; according to Maundrell this is twelve yards in girt; but we are much more inclined to agree with Volney than with Maundrell, in the description which these travellers have respectively given of the cedars of Lebanon. Numerous names carved on the trunk of the greater trees, some of which are as far back as 1640, bear testimony to the curiosity of individuals to visit this interesting spot, which is nearly surrounded by the barren chain of Lebanon, in the form of an amphitheatre of about thirty miles circuit, the opening being towards the sea. We thought the *tout ensemble* more represented the Apennines at the back of Genoa, than any other mountain scenery we had witnessed. Mount Lebanon and its cedars are so frequently alluded to in scripture, that it would be almost an endless and useless task to make extracts; but it appears to us that they are no where so remarkably noticed, as in the glory and fall of Assyria, in the xxxi. of Ezekiel; in the 16th verse you will observe, "All the trees of Eden, the choice and best of Lebanon," which would seem to infer that the boasted cedars were always near the same place in which the few remaining ones now are, as they are not more than five miles distant from the modern village of Eden.

In a former part of my letter, relating to Joppa, I mentioned that the cedar of Lebanon was used in the construction of Solomon's temple; in the 2nd Chronicles, ii. 8. are the words, " Send me also cedar-trees, fir-trees, and algum-trees, out of Lebanon," which clearly implies, that quantities of not only cedars formerly grew on this mountain, but also that other kinds of wood were found there, which now are no more to be met with, unless the walnut-tree of the present day, which is in very high perfection at Eden, is the algum-tree of the ancients. In the first book of Kings, chap. vi. and vii. describing Solomon's temple, it also appears that much cedar was used in this edifice. With respect to the village of Eden, this also appears to be the same with the garden of God, so called throughout the whole of the xxxi. chap. of Ezekiel, particularly in the 8th and 9th verse; but by reference to Genesis ii. verse 8, the position of the garden of God, in Eden, where Adam and Eve were placed, seems very uncertain, for from the 10th to the 14th verses you observe, " A river went out of Eden to water the garden, and from thence it was parted and became into four heads:" the river of Ethiopia (the Nile) appears to be one of the four, and the Euphrates another. Maundrell makes no extracts from scripture concerning Lebanon; I dare say, because he thought it would be useless, as it is mentioned in so many different places. Volney is also silent on the subject, I mean as far as respects quotations. Eden is called Aden by the natives at this day; but to proceed:—We here hired a guide to conduct us over Lebanon into the valley of Bekaa Mathooalis, in which Baalbec is situated. Leaving the cedars about an hour after sun-rise, we ascended to the crest of Lebanon, where we had an extensive view over the hills at its S. E. foot into the valley, with Baalbec in the distance; we beheld also to the westward the sea for a considerable distance. Altogether it was not a bad view, but certainly not deserving the commendations which Volney bestows on it. Lebanon, it appears in the Syriac language, signifies white, which this mountain is, both in summer and winter; in the former season, on account of the natural colour of the barren rock, and in the latter by reason of the snow.

The valley of Baalbec, or of the Kasmia, or Bekaa Mathooalis, has an excessively rich soil, but it is put to little advantage, being very partially cultivated, and having no trees except in the immediate neighbourhood of Baalbec itself, which are chiefly the fig and the walnut. The valley is bounded on the N. W. side by Lebanon, and on its S. E. by Anti-Lebanon; its breadth may be about ten miles, while its length from N. E. to S. W. extends as far as the eye can reach. The Kasmia has its source to the north of Baalbec (see Volney), and running through the plain, discharges itself into the sea a little to the north of Tyre. How deplorable that so luxuriant a spot, with a fine loamy soil, should lay waste and desolate! and what ideas of former wealth and magnificence do the splendid ruins of Baalbec call to the mind. The inhabitants of the mountain are nearly all of the church of Rome; but those of the Bekaa Mathooalis are a particular sect of Mahomedans, differing from the Turks in general; they are more hostile to the Christians than any of the natives of Syria; but to return:—In descending from the summit of Lebanon the road was excessively steep and rugged; we dismounted and walked our horses down it; the sides of the mountain abound in partridges, all red-legged, and other game. At the S. E. foot of this part of Lebanon is the source of a fine clear rivulet, which finally unites with the Kasmia. From hence we proceeded over some rugged hills covered with shrubs; a species of oak, the myrtle, and the almond-tree, are all remarkable. Mr. Mazoliere told us they have a tradition that there were formerly gardens here, and the almond and pear-trees seem to confirm the idea.

Crossing these hills, you come, near the plain, to the first village, after leaving the cedars. Late in the evening we arrived at Yead, a village about an hour's distance from Baalbec; the horses having been on route from two o'clock in the morning, without any food, about fifteen hours, which caused us to blame our guide much, as we might have brought fodder with us from Aden, had we known how uninhabited the country was through which we had to pass. But the guide seemed intent only on his own interest, and when we, hearing of the distance to Baalbec from the cedars, threatened to return to Tripoli, on account of the horses, he, fearing to lose his money for the trip, declared there were several villages in the way where we could refresh the animals.

November 1. Early this morning we arrived at Baalbec, and employed the whole day in visiting the antiquities; the preceding day had been excessively fine, the sky being so clear that scarce a cloud was to be seen, but on Saturday evening they collected much on Lebanon and the tops of the other hills, and the natives announced to us the approach of bad weather. We took dimensions and made remarks of every thing at Baalbec, but as Wood, and Dawkins in particular, as well as Volney, have given correct descriptions, illustrated with plates, it would be superfluous here to enter into minute detail. I cannot help, however, making a few observations on one mass of ruins, the imposing grandeur of which particularly struck us. I allude to that remnant of a colonnade where there are six columns standing; the beauty and elegance of these pillars are surprising; their diameter is seven feet, and we estimated their altitude at between fifty and sixty feet, exclusive of the epistylia which is twenty feet deep, and composed of immense blocks of stone, in two layers of ten feet each in depth. The whole of this is most elaborately ornamented with rich carved work in various devices. We imagine these pillars to have been the remains of an avenue of twenty columns on each side, forming an approach to the temple. The space originally included by these pillars was one hundred and four paces long, by fifty-eight broad. We were much pleased with the architecture and sculpture throughout, though now much disfigured by the ruins having been once converted into a fortress. There are remarkably large stones used in the building of the various edifices, and in the S. W. part of the elevated walls on which they stand, we measured a single stone of sixty-six feet in length, and twelve in breadth and thickness. The whole of these buildings, together with the walls, are of coarse marble, excessively hard. In the construction of the pyramids and temples in Egypt, we never noticed a single stone of more than thirty feet in length, and these were most of calcarious or sand stone, excepting some few of granite. The inhabitants of Baalbec, although much prejudiced against Christians, were to us quiet and well disposed, and seemed less curious and inquisitive than the natives living near any antiquities we had visited. We left Baalbec on our return on Sunday at mid-day, but the afternoon turning out very rainy, we stopped for the night at a small village beyond the opposite side of the plain. We observed, when it cleared away in the evening, that considerable quantities of snow had fallen on the mountains, which may give some idea of the vast height of Lebanon; and as a farther proof, when we crossed the mountain the preceding Friday, we found several patches of last year's snow, which, though melted on the general surface of the mountain, still remains in some places, near the summit, throughout the year ([13]), though the weather was perfectly clear, with the sun shining all the time, and the heat was oppressive.

November 3. Monday, the morning was foggy but calm, and the sun breaking out with force at times, we hoped the haze would clear away and that we should have fine weather; we accordingly proceeded on our return to Tripoli, but had not gone far when we met some peasants returning to their village, after having made an ineffectual attempt to cross Lebanon, where they said we should meet with very bad weather, and much snow. In fact, the N. E. wind began shortly to blow with violence and excessively cold, with such heavy showers of sleet, snow, and rain, that we were obliged to take shelter in a cave at the foot of the mountain for the whole day. We found here many peasants, who had made ineffectual attempts to cross, but as we had a difficulty in getting room for our horses, the cave being small and nearly filled before we arrived, we removed to a larger though more exposed one, being little more than a projecting cleft of the rock, where we got ourselves and our horses also under a roof, and made a large fire for the night ([14]). The next morning being fine we began to ascend; the peasants with their cattle were unwilling to make the first trial, as they knew it would be difficult to find the road on account of the depth of snow; at the same time they were aware that the second party could always profit by the traces of the first. We met with no difficulty until we came nearly to the top, when losing the road, the snow being very deep, and the sides of the mountain steep, our horses all fell with us, and were partly buried; being obliged to dismount, we had considerable trouble in reaching the summit: the cold was excessive, and having on loose linen Turkish breeches, and shoes without any stockings, we felt it severely. In descending the opposite side, the snow was also very deep, and we found it adviseable to push on lest we should be caught in a fog, which the appearance of the weather seemed to threaten; we reached Eden in safety about two in the afternoon; the weather had again set in thick and hazy; shortly after we began to descend. We were informed at Eden that the bishop had publicly offered up prayers for our safety, and that people are prohibited from crossing Lebanon after the first of November; but I much doubt the truth of the latter assertion; none of us received any injury by the weather except Mr. Mazoliere's servant, whose legs were much chapped and cracked by the cold, he having never been in the snow before.

On Wednesday, November 5, with fine weather, we returned to Tripoli; the natives of Aden with their wives, children, and baggage, descending at the same time; the first part of the descent was in some places so steep and difficult, that we observed the peasants held on by the tails of their horses to prevent them from falling. On our arrival at

Tripoli, we understood that they also had experienced very bad weather on the coast. Young Mazoliere was very civil, he supplied us with accommodation, and an excellent supper the first time we stopped at Aden; but on our return, his relations had retired from the place. We got delightful wine there; that of Lebanon has always been esteemed, even in the time of the Bible (see Hosea, xiv. 7). We were treated with the greatest kindness by the Padre Hermenigildo, and we dined one day with the consul, when we found that Mr. Bankes had sent his trunk there from Cyprus, previous to his own arrival. Wet weather detained us at Tripoli until the afternoon of the ninth of November, when we went as far as the nahr El-Bered, or Cold River. We passed the night in a khan, a place appropriated to the use of travellers, which Maundrell very well describes in the first and second pages of his book. The map places here a village named Orthosa, the site of the ancient Orthosia, but there is nothing now about the nahr El-Bered but the khan above alluded to. There is a difficulty, in some instances, to distinguish Roman ruins from these khans, as both the Romans and the Turks seem alike partial to the mode of building with arches. The next day we went as far as

Tortosa, nearly opposite the island of Ruad, where stood the famous city of Aradus. There are Roman remains at each of these places; the walls of Tortosa are constructed on the ancient foundation cut in the rock, and the remains of the castle after you enter the gates are ancient. There are also some old sepulchral caves by the road side; they serve to shew that the Romans, as well as the Egyptians, had burial places of this description; but the difference of climate between this country and Egypt has destroyed all remains of stucco or painting, if ever they were thus decorated, which we have reason to believe they were, as **Mr. Bankes** told us he saw a Roman cave with fresco painting in it near Saida. The island of Ruad, according to Maundrell, is the Arvad, Arpad, or Arphad in scripture (see Ezekiel, xxvii. Jeremiah, xlix. Isaiah, x. 2 Kings, xviii. and xix. and Genesis, x.). In the first of these, it appears that Arvad and Sidon supplied the fleets of Tyre with seamen.

November 11. We went as far as the nahr El-Mulk, which having crossed by a bridge, we stopped for the night at a village about half an hour's distance from the river, the huts of which appeared to be temporary habitations, being constructed of reeds and straw, there are Roman ruins at the mouth of the nahr El-Mulk. We had hitherto been always in the habit of sleeping in the open air, when we arrived at an Arab village in the night; but now, the month of November being far advanced, we wished to discontinue the practice, and accordingly asked for shelter, which was refused, unless each of us four would consent to sleep in a separate habitation. This we knew was the place were Monsr. Boutin, the French traveller, was killed, and not being pleased with this mode of proceeding, the natives assuring us that they could not find room for all four in one hut, we bivouacked in the open air as usual, the night being fine and clear. The following morning we found, close to where we slept, an empty uninhabited hut, which appeared to have done duty as a barn; our heads were against one end of it, and had they any civility, they might have offered it to us. In the night a man came to endeavour to persuade us not to lie where we were, saying, that the wolves would destroy us; we, however, had more apprehension of the two-legged wolves stealing some of our things, and told our informer we had our fire arms ready, and should keep a good look out for these animals. In the morning our bread and part of a ham which Padre Hermenigildo had given us were missing, but we suspected the dogs, with which all Arab villages abound, had taken our meat, for pork is an abomination to the Turks.

November 12. In the afternoon we reached Latachia. Two hours from where we slept is Jebilee, the ancient Gabala, where are Roman ruins, the principal of which is the remains of a fine theatre at the north side of the town. The whole journey from Tripoli, with one exception in the neighbourhood of Markab, a village inclosed in ancient fortifications, and seated on the top of a square mountain, near which the coast is rocky, is along a vast rich plain at the foot of the Ansanar mountains, which are of no considerable height, and are said to be inhabited by Pagan tribes; the plain is watered by many rivers, and there are also several torrents now dry. These rivers are generally pretty, their banks are covered with myrtle, oleander, wild vine, fig, &c. Though the soil is rich it is very partially cultivated and thinly peopled; the principal produce near Jebilee is cotton, which the natives were gathering in as we passed. The city of Latahcia was founded by Seleucus Nicator, under the name of Laodicea, in honour of his mother; he also founded three other cities in this neighbourhood, viz. Selucia, now Suadeah; Antioch; and Apameia, now Famiah. Latachia is seated on the N. W. side of Cape Ziaret, an elevated projection of the coast; in the neighbourhood are gardens planted with olives, figs, &c. in the manner of all the towns of Syria. The port, which is half an hour's distance from the town, is very small, but it is better sheltered than any we have seen on this coast. There is a fine old castle projecting into the sea at the point of a bed of rocks; the Marina is built upon foundations of ancient columns. There are, in the town of Latachia, an old gate-way and other antiquities; there are also sepulchral caves in the neighbourhood, but as they have no paintings, we did not think it worth while to visit them. Mount Lebanon was in sight the whole way from Tripoli, and was the only mountain on which we could see snow; Mount Cassius was before us. The Christian natives of Latachia and of all the pashalic of Aleppo to the north of Latacha, are mostly of the Greek church, speaking the Arabic language; but I must refer you to Volney for a general description of the different tribes and religious sects that inhabit Syria; as he deals largely and scientifically on the subject. We lodged at the house of the English agent, Signor Moses Elias, a very excellent man. We were detained here till the fifteenth, by the intrigues of the Arab conductor, who affected to be unwell, and who had previously at Acre, Bayruth, and other places, tried all in his power to oblige us to send him and the horses back to Jaffa, thus occasioning us a good deal of trouble and inconvenience.

November 16. We went as far as the village of Candele; the road was along a fine plain until we came near it, when crossing some hills we descended into the valley of that name. The village is seated amongst the sand hills to the west of the vale, and we had some difficulty in finding it. The next day we were continually passing over hills richly wooded, with numerous narrow intricate roads, which occasioned us to lose our way several times, by which means we lost so much time, that the night had set in, without our finding the village of Lourdee, whither we were bound; and we were on the point of giving up the search, and bivouacking in the wood, when luckily some dogs barking, indicated to us the vicinity of the place, which is in an elevated situation, and immediately by the side of the highest pinnacle of Mount Cassius, in the middle of a plain.

November 18. We were employed in descending the north side of these mountains, the scenery still continuing woody and wild; we this day also lost our way several times. In the afternoon we reached the banks of the Orontes, at the place where commences the picturesque part of the river, and, immediately below the spot where the chart was marked, the site of the "city and groves of Daphne." Mr. Barker has visited the site, and from him we learn that there are still to be seen the grand sources of water which composed the celebrated fountain. In some instances, Mr. B. says, the water boils up as thick as a man's body, and that *jet d'eaux* might be made here of that thickness, of upwards of fifty feet high. We now began to follow the banks of the river, and were astonished at the beauty of the scenery, far surpassing any thing we expected to see in Syria, and, indeed, any thing we had witnessed even in Switzerland, though we walked nine hundred miles in that country, and saw most of its beauty. The river, from the time we began to trace its banks, ran continually between two high hills, winding and turning incessantly; at times the road led along precipices in the rocks, looking down perpendicularly on the river. The luxuriant variety of foliage was prodigious, and the rich green myrtle, which was very plentiful, contrasted with the colour of the road, the soil of which was a dark-red gravel, made us imagine we were riding through pleasure-grounds. The laurel, laurestinus, bay-tree, fig-tree, wild vine, plane-tree, English sycamore, arbutus, both common and andrachne, dwarf oak, &c. were scattered in all directions. At times the road was overhung with rocks, covered with ivy; the mouths of caverns also presented themselves, and gave a wildness to the scene; and the perpendicular cliffs jutted into the river upwards of three hundred feet high, forming corners round which the waters ran in a most romantic manner; and on one occasion the road wound round a deep bay thus ⟨sketch⟩, so that on perceiving ourselves immediately opposite the spot we had so recently passed, it appeared that we had crossed the river. We descended at times into plains cultivated with mulberry plantations and vines, and prettily studded with picturesque cottages. The occasional shallows of the river keeping up a perpetual roaring, completed the beauty of this delightful scene, which lasted about two hours, when we entered the plain of Suadeah, where the river becomes of a greater breadth, and runs in as straight a line as a canal. By the time we entered the plain it had become moon-light, and we had difficulty in finding Suadeah. A peasant at last shewed us a place where the river is fordable just up to the horses bellies, for there is no bridge. We found Suadeah to be a straggling village, consisting of unconnected cottages, situated in a plain chiefly inclosed with mulberry and lemon plantations. We put up at a house appropriated for the use of travellers in general, and which we found the best place we have yet met with. The soubash of the place, a sort of petty governour, was in the house, and treated us with wonderful civility, ordering us a good supper, feeding our horses, and in the morning he refused to let us pay a para; and whatever may be the generally received character of the Turks, we have always met from them the greatest civility and attention. All he asked for was a little gunpowder; we gave him a little, but had unfortunately given nearly all our stock to young Mazoliere at Tripoli.

November 19. In the morning we pursued our journey towards Antioch, being in a hurry, and understanding that the ruins of the ancient Seleucia, which are near the sea, (Suadeah being half an hour's distance from it) possess no particular interest. The weather turned out very wet this day, and after we had been on route about three hours, being two hours' distance from Antioch, we perceived some cottages, and being thoroughly wet, through baggage and all, we requested shelter. The two first cottages had only women in them, whose husbands being absent, they did not dare receive us; at the third we went to, the men were willing to admit us, but the women would not hear of it, and expressed their refusal in a violent and ill-natured manner; during the time we were soliciting a shelter, was it only in a cow-house, the rain was pouring in torrents, and we making a pitiable appearance, being perfectly soaked. Seeing no intreaty could succeed, we gave them the kat-ack-harack, the Arab expression of thanks, an tried another cottage, where we were admitted without the least hesitation. These cottages are long buildings of a single room; the cattle occupy one end, and human inhabitants the other. They have extensive plantations of young mulberries for the silk-worms, and looms for manufacturing their produce. The occupants of the hut, who consisted of the proprietor, his mother, wife, brother, and children, were of that tribe of Mahomedans which Volney designates as Turkmen; they were uncommonly kind, placing us near a large fire, giving us good beds and coverlids, and making us join them in a humble supper of doura and wheat boiled. It rained a great deal the whole night, and we were detained till noon on the following day, when we proceeded to Antioch, giving these people eleven piastres, and a double gold Napolean, value forty-four piastres, as an ornament for the wife, besides paying for the horses, corn, &c. The women in this country ornament themselves with money according to their circumstances; the poorer class with paras, and the higher orders with sequins of eleven piastres each, and gold roubees of two and a half each. We gave this present as much to reward the goodness of our host and his wife, as to make the ladies in the other cottage vexed and ashamed of themselves. We also thought that a few piastres thus disposed of might benefit other travellers coming after us, and who might find themselves in the same predicament. Antioch is beautifully situated on the left bank of the Orontes, at the foot of a hill; there is a good-looking bridge over the river, and some of the heights are picturesque. The present town, which is a miserable one, does not occupy more than one-eighth part of the space included by the old walls, which have a fine, venerable appearance, having square towers every hundred yards, with occasional turrets for looking out; these are the works of the Roman and Greek emperors. Antioch is said to have contained between eight and nine hundred thousand inhabitants. The plain of

Antioch is considerably elevated above that of Suadeah. We were concerned to find ourselves at Antioch without having visited the ruins of the city and groves of Daphne, but this was impossible without a guide, and there was no procuring one. The houses of Antioch, Suadeah, Lourdee, and their neighbourhood, are roofed and tiled, without terraces, differing in that respect from most of the towns of Syria. There are many sepulchral caves in the side of the hill at the back of Antioch. This town is celebrated in the Acts of the Apostles, xiii. " Paul and Barnabas embark at Seleucia (the present Suadeah, and the port of Antioch) for Cyprus;" at Antioch we were lodged in a khan.

November 22. We went as far as Gesir Adid, four hours' distance, near a bridge over the Orontes. Our road was through a barren plain, bounded to the north by mountains, with a view of the lake called Aggi Dengis at their foot. Rain prevented our leaving this place till noon on the following day, when we went as far as a place called Bourkee, the site of a Roman town of considerable dimensions; the ancient sepulchral caves of which are cut in the side of the mountains, and serve the present natives for their habitations. We took up our abode in an old, deserted mill, in ruins, and which a small rivulet had served to turn.

November 23. We passed over some rocky hills into the plain of Alaks, supposed to be that in which Aurelian conquered Zenobia. We passed many sites of ancient towns, castles, tanks, temples, &c. all of the lower empire, and very uninteresting; on one occasion we counted eleven sites in a rich plain, with a fine loamy soil, now left desolate and uninhabited. So much for the Turkish government, and their mode of encouraging agriculture, the arts, &c.! The eastern part, however, of the plain of Alaks, which is nearest Aleppo, has a few villages, the inhabitants of which, in considerable numbers, were collecting their cotton as we passed them. We stopped at Tourneen, the easternmost of the villages above alluded to.

November 25. About three in the afternoon we arrived at Aleppo, passing through an open country, with a thin surface of soil, well tilled in most parts, but destitute of trees or variety, as indeed is the case all the way from Antioch. We had been recommended by our departed friend and adviser Sheikh Ibrahim, to take the route to the northward of Aggi Dengis, as it would have conducted us to the mountains and ruins of St. Simon, which, however, are all of the lower empire, and, as we have since learnt, totally uninteresting, being very like those we saw by the road we went. We have further reason to rejoice in having taken the road we did, as the Curds who inhabit the mountains were in rebellion against the pashaw, who had sent a military force to quell them shortly before our arrival; we have since heard that the chiefs escaped, but example has been made by the death of about twenty of the prisoners, some of whom, I am sorry to say, are supposed to have been innocent. The pashaw hearing this, is said to have been much affected, and recalled his troops, saying, that as the chiefs had escaped, and the natives had submitted, he did not wish the business to be carried any farther.

On arriving at Mr. Barker's, the consul general, we found Mr. Bankes there, and were glad of the opportunity of meeting this celebrated and indefatigable traveller; he was on his way to revisit Egypt and Nubia, having some idea of penetrating from the second cataract into Abyssinia. We mutually gave each other all the information we possessed; Mr. B. on Asia Minor and Greece, and we on Egypt and Nubia. He paid us the compliment to say he wished he could contrive that we might travel together, as he heard we were the only travellers he had met that go after his method. We found him a most sensible and entertaining person; he has now been five years on his travels.

December 22. We still remain waiting for the arrival of the Sukne caravan, which brings kali from that place to Aleppo, from which it is five days' distance, and Palmyra is two more days' off. The kindness we have experienced in this hospitable mansion, merits our sincere gratitude. I fear we shall be a little spoiled when we turn out for Palmyra in a new Arab costume; for here, independent of the society of Mr. B. and his amiable family, we have had every comfort and luxury we could imagine. Our amusements have varied in the most delightful manner, sometimes we went out shooting, the gardens near Aleppo abounding in woodcocks, &c.; twenty a day is not thought very good sport : I have killed altogether one dozen, but never more than three in one day. We coursed the gazelle and hare alternately, the greyhounds in this country being very swift and strong. We were indulged one day with a hawking scene. The cheapness and plenty of game is astonishing; every day we have had either, woodcocks, or partridges, wild-geese, or ducks, teal, the bustard, or wild turkey, joli notes, &c. and to crown all, the porcupine, which is a delicious animal, resembling both in appearance and taste, the pig and hare. We thought the flesh of the gazelle well flavoured, although Bruce abuses it; the white species is supposed to be the best. The porcupine inhabits holes in the rocks, and they are so quick of hearing, that it is very difficult to shoot them, as they never quit their holes till dark, and even then with the greatest circumspection; the people wait patiently for hours in the cold, near the holes, till the animal makes its appearance; they commit much mischief in the gardens near the city. We had an idea of visiting Bagdad, for the purpose of seeing the ruins of Babylon, but as Mr. Massick, the Dutch consul here, had recently received a letter on the very subject, from a friend, wherein mention was made that there is nothing whatever to be seen, we gave it up, as also did Mr. Bankes, who had the same intention; I inclose you the copy of the letter. Mr. Barker has resided nineteen years as consul general in this place, and we find his advice and assistance of the greatest use. As we came into this country with only one hundred and fifty pounds, which Mr. Salt supplied us on our bills, we had made up our minds to return to Cairo, to get our letter of credit, and also to increase our stock of money for Asia Minor, Greece, &c. but Mr. Barker imagining some such motive was the cause of our intended return to Egypt, most kindly anticipated us on this head, and without our even hinting the subject, insisted on supplying us with whatever money or letters of credit we wanted; this will entirely prevent the necessity of our going to Egypt again, and will assist us much. I shall say nothing of either Aleppo or its environs, reserving that for the subject of a future letter. We are anxious to have done with travelling in the Mahomedan countries, and again to enjoy the comforts of Switzerland and Italy. There is a great sameness in all Turkish towns, and the want of inns, theatres, museums, picture galleries, libraries, promenades, evening parties, and the ever handy and comfortable caffé, are privations which an European must ever regret. We have a firman from the Grand Seignior coming from Constantinople, Mr. Barker having written for it on our arrival here; it will be useful in Asia Minor.

December 24. The caravan from Sukne arrived this day, and we shall soon be off. We are to send the outlines of our tour to Lord Belmore for his guidance, but this we defer till we get to Palmyra. His lordship very kindly offered us a passage in his brig to any parts which might lie in his way, should we be enabled to embark with him from Syria; but there is no chance of this.

December 29. We were to have set off this evening for Palmyra, by way of Sukne, when a merchant from Bagdad, a great friend of Mr. Barker's happening to drop in, strongly dissuaded us from the measure, and urged us to go by the way of Hamah or Homs, as the Annasee Arabs are in the neighbourhood of Palmyra. We had thought the cold had driven them to the southward, towards the banks of the Euphrates, but as it appears there yet remain two tribes of them, Homs is recommended as the best place to start from. In consequence we propose moving from hence in two or three days for Damascus, visiting Palmyra on our way; this will be a considerable saving of time to us.

LETTER III.

Departure from Aleppo to Sermein.—Marah.—Hamah. —Homs.—Camp of Mahannah.—Palmyra.—Return to Homs.—Arrival at Damascus.

In the Convent of DAMASCUS, February 17, 1818.

In my last letter from Aleppo, I think I mentioned that we were going to Palmyra by way of Sukne. We found, however, that the natives of that place were not capable of conducting us with safety to Tadmor, and that, moreover, they asked as high a price as we had any idea of giving to the Arabs, whose protection would have insured the accomplishment of our object. Thus circumstanced we prepared for our departure for Hamah, which place as well as Homs is only four days' distant from Palmyra, and we had sanguine expectations of succeeding in our project from either one or the other of these towns; besides the chance I have just noticed, we had two other strings to our bow, viz. to push on to Cariateen, which is only one day from Tadmor, and thence to steal there before the

Arabs were aware of our intention; or to take Turkish post-horses and an escort from Damascus, and go in spite of the Arabs; this last plan, however, would have been a very expensive one. But before I proceed further, I shall add a few remarks upon Aleppo. The city is pleasantly situated in a hollow surrounded by sloping hills, which are very uninteresting, having no trees, and the land having no inclosures. The houses of Aleppo are built of stone; the streets are narrow and ill paved, except the Bazars which are all roofed over with arches of the same construction as the houses, and are lighted from above. Thus you can walk all over the town on the terraces of the houses; the arches I have mentioned connecting the streets one with the other. The Franks avail themselves of this mode of communication to visit each other during the time of the plague; we made visits half a mile distant in this manner. The Franks and Christians have their separate quarters here, the same as in all Turkish towns. The city is surrounded with gardens, watered by small rivulets drawn from the main stream which supplies the town. We visited some Turkish houses, and were much struck with the beauty of the cielings of the apartments, which are decorated by Persian artists; they are very curiously gilded and painted, but to describe them in writing would be difficult and uninteresting. The decorations in carve-work, on the doors and window-frames, are also extremely curious. We assisted Mr. Bankes in tracing some of them from copies on paper which were lent him. The neat private steam-baths and fountains are worthy of notice. The society of Aleppo is good: the men and women make separate parties to the baths, where they have coffee and refreshments, and pass the evening. The walls of the city resemble those at Antioch; Volney describes the castle and other particulars, and as a description of a town is at best but a dry subject, I shall refer you to him for further particulars. The neighbourhood of Aleppo abounds in game, and we were struck with admiration at the neat and cleanly appearance of the butcher's shops, which are equal to those of London.

January 3. We started for Hamah, our kind and estimable host, together with his brother, accompanying us on horseback for two hours outside the town. Such had been his solicitude in our behalf that he furnished us with letters to Selim, the governour's secretary at Hamah, and to Scander, the secretary to the motsellim of Homs; he likewise gave us a strong letter of recommendation to Hadgi Hassan, an elderly Turk at Homs, who has great dealings with the Arabs. All these people were requested to render us every assistance in their power to get to Palmyra. We had besides other letters from Mr. Barker to the Saraffs of the pashaw of Damascus, urging them to assist us in getting post-horses, should we be obliged to go in that manner. In addition to these, he gave us letters to Acre, Cyprus, and Smyrna; to Sir Robert and Lady Liston, and to several other people at Constantinople. He lent us Maundrell's Travels in Syria, and a good map of Asia Minor and Greece, and furnished us with money.

At sun-set we stopped at the khan Touman, a spacious lodging, but which was filled to excess with the caravans for Damascus and Latachia. On the following morning we proceeded at daylight in company with them, our road lying over naked plains partly cultivated. About three in the afternoon we stopped at Sermein; there are several villages in this quarter, and a few clumps of olives, otherwise the country is destitute of wood. Mount Cassius, whose summit was by this time covered with snow, was in sight on our right.

January 5. We proceeded at sun-rise, intending to go with the Latachia caravan as far as Shogher, and thence follow up the banks of the

Orontes to Hamah; but being late, and seeing a caravan on our left, we branched out in that direction, joined it, and found that they were in the straight road to Hamah, and that they were bound to that place and Damascus; we therefore continued with them. About ten we passed a ruined square Turkish fortress enclosing a village. Many of these places, on the skirts of the desert, are walled in, as one would suppose to afford them protection against the Arabs. Shortly after we met a very extensive caravan, being part of the hadj or pilgrimage to Mecca on their return from Damascus—an interesting sight; they had the green flag, the prophet's banner, flying ([15]). There were few camels, the animals being mostly horses and mules, and having all bells attached to them, they made a merry, ringing noise ([16]). There were amongst them several tackterwans, the only species of vehicle in the east, which supplies the place of four wheel carriages; we had seen one of them in the great Morocco hadj, which arrived at Cario in September last; it resembled a sedan chair, supported before and behind, with horses instead of men; but those which we saw this day differed from it, one being a species of tent-bed placed crossway on the back of a mule, and the other resembling two childs' cradles, fitted like panniers on the back of a camel. These tackterwans are enclosed with curtains, and are generally used by women or sick people. Nearly the whole of this and the next day, we passed divisions of the hadj; all the animals were laden with some private venture of the pilgrims, as they always make a commerce of this expedition; if you read Volney you will see in what estimation even the Turks hold the man who has made a hadj. They have an old adage among them to this purport, " Beware of thy neighbour if he has made a hadj; but if he has made two, quickly prepare to leave thy house:" the keenness with which all the peasants, near the khans bargain for every thing they sell seems to agree with this remark. We saw this day some few Roman ruins, and sarcophagi formed of the stone of the country, apparently of the lower empire. At two P. M. we stopped for the night at Marah, and slept in a very good khan. The ensuing morning we proceeded as before. Lebanon, now a mass of snow, lay before us; and Mount Cassius was shut in by the northern extremity of the Ansarian mountains. We passed several sites of ancient towns, tanks, sarcophagi, &c. every thing much dilapidated and uninteresting, excepting that they served to shew that the neighbourhood was better peopled in former times than it is at present. The country was still nothing but open plains, without a single tree, being inhabited by numerous gazelles, partridges, hares, bustards, &c. We passed the night at Khan Shekune situated near an artificial hill, several of which we had seen during the day; they resembled those on Salisbury Plain, and other parts of England. We found the khan good, but very full of people, occasioned by the return of the hadj already mentioned.

January 7. Our road was still through open plains partially cultivated, parallel with the range of the Ansarian mountains; Lebanon and Anti-Lebanon in sight before us; about three in the afternoon we arrived at Hamah. The approach for the last hour was pretty enough, descending into a vale through which the Orontes takes a winding course, the banks of which are cultivated, wooded, and laid out occasionally in gardens on one side, with perpendicular chalky cliffs in some parts on the other. Here are immense wheels or sackeys turned by the stream of the river, to raise the water for the irrigation of the soil. Hamah is the Epiphania of the Greeks and Romans, though it is, no doubt, the site of the ancient Hamath mentioned in various parts of scripture ([17]), together with Damascus, Lebanon, and other contiguous places, it took its name from the sons of Canaan, fourth son of Ham, the son of Noah, which makes it of very high antiquity. Hamah is delightfully situated in a hollow, between and on the sides of two hills, near the west bank of the Orontes, but in itself presents nothing worthy of notice at this day. We took up our quarters in a khan, and as these buildings in the towns differ considerably from those on the road side, I will give you a description of the former. Like the latter, they surround an open square, but are differently constructed, being meant for travellers and merchants to lodge in during the time they remain in the towns to dispose of their merchandise, or settle any private affairs they may have to transact; whereas the khans on the road side are only intended for a night's lodging, and security for the traveller and his animals. In these the squares are formed in open piazzas in which men and animals indiscriminately take up their abode, there being no division into apartments, cells, or any detached chamber whatever; for this accommodation no payment is required. The khans in the towns, instead of the open piazzas, are furnished all round with two stories of small apartments, each chamber, or rather cell, being about twelve feet square, with a door (the key of which is given you), and an iron-barred window with wooden shutters but no glass. I suspect they were originally intended as a gratuitous lodging for travellers, the same as those on the high-roads and in the villages, but as they have only one small entrance, and are thereby the most secure places in the towns, the lower rooms are generally filled with merchandize of the different resident proprietors. In front of these are arched piazzas for the horses, mules, &c. &c. and also a balcony or terrace, with wooden railing, fronting the upper row of cells, which are all totally unfurnished, being nothing but bare walls; and for a mat to lie on, cooking utensils, fuel, &c. these must be the care of the occupier. There is a porter who generally rents the khan, and in the day time attends the gate, which is locked up at night; he makes his profit by the fees from travellers, and also by the merchandize which is lodged within. We paid two piastres (1s. 5d.) for admittance, or as it is termed for the key of our room, four paras (one penny English) per day for the lodging, and one para per day for each horse. As for provision we always got that from the market, and cooked in our own room, making excellent soup, roast, &c. Our principal meat was mutton, as the Turks do not eat much beef, and therefore it is never good. While at Hamah we received a letter from Mr. Barker by an express messenger from Aleppo, together with a firman from the grand Seignior, which Mr. B. had written for to

Sir Robert Liston shortly after our arrival in the latter end of November. This firman empowers us to go with four servants through Syria, Cyprus, the islands of the Archipelago, Smyrna, Adana, Karaman, Karahissar, Kiutaya, to Broussa, and from thence to Constantinople; we are to be treated in the most friendly manner, offered every assistance, security, and protection, according to the imperial capitulations, and furnished with all necessary escorts whenever occasion may require. We witnessed a melancholy scene the few last days we were here: there arrived one evening four shabby-looking, ill-dressed Turks, attired somewhat like soldiers, and an elderly knave better clad, though no better looking than the others. These people brought with them eleven Georgian girls, the remnant of between forty and fifty, as we were informed, whom they had stolen or kidnapped from their parents on the confines of Georgia; they were brought to be sold as slaves or mistresses to such wealthy Turks as could afford to bid high sums for such unfortunate victims. These poor girls were lodged in the cells contiguous to ours; they were mostly between fifteen and twenty years of age; two were younger, being about twelve. They were all exceedingly pretty, with black sparkling eyes, rosy cheeks, long black hair, and very fair complexions, giving a very strong contradiction to the account which Volney writes of the Georgian and Circassian women, where he says "that their fame for beauty arises more from the fancy of travellers, heightened by the difficulty they have always found to get a sight of them, than from any real merit they possess in this respect." The prices which were demanded and offered for these girls, is the best proof of the estimation in which they are held by the Turks, especially when it is known that these people are allowed a plurality of wives. We were present at the bidding for one girl by a rich Turk, when fourteen purses, each purse being five hundred piastres (18*l.*), were demanded, and although he offered ten, they would not abate one para; the poor girl, who was about fifteen, standing up all the while, and hearing the disputes about her purchase. They were all taken out four different times, and conducted through the town to the rich Turkish houses to be viewed and bid for, the same as any other merchandize; and on two occasions considerable parties of the principal inhabitants came to our khan, and examined and bid for the unhappy creatures at the door of their cells; they being obliged to stand up in a row, while their several merits were discussed by the rival bidders. We saw several candidates for purchasing, of upwards of fifty years of age, while the friendless object of his choice was only fifteen. The diet of these poor unfortunates, considering their sex, was of a character with the rest of their treatment, consisting only of a loaf of bread and a small piece of cheese twice a day; and although we were buying oranges, at only two paras (a halfpenny) each, we never saw one amongst them all. Whenever the owners went abroad they locked their charge up in the cells, and carried away the key. Being returned from one of their tours through the town, we heard some bitter lamenting in the cell next to ours, and found that it proceeded from one of the young girls being about to be sold, and consequently separated from her sister and companions. The mode of conducting these girls from town to town is on horseback; in this manner they had been brought from Georgia, being exposed for sale at all the principal towns as they came along; they were now destined for Damascus, where it was thought a good mart would be found for them; they set out on their melancholy journey two days before we did. Bruce has given some account of the Georgian and Circassian women, which you can read and compare with this; I think in this instance he comes much nearer the truth than Volney.

Nothing else of consequence occurring while we were at Hamah, excepting our negociations with the Arabs, in order to reach Palmyra, I shall now describe them; shortly after arriving, our Maltese interpreter, in conveying our letter of introduction to Selim, the governour's secretary, met at the house of the latter a man named Pierre, of Dar-el-Camar, in the employ of Lady Hester Stanhope, by whom he had been sent, as he said, to fetch two horses that had been presented to Lady H. by the governours of Homs and Hamah; he was also charged with a present of one hundred piastres to Narsah, the chief of the Annasee Arabs. Pierre, who returned with our interpreter, said that he had accompanied Lady Hester to Palmyra and was acquainted with the Arab chiefs, and that it was he who made the bargain for Mr. Bankes, who was obliged to pay one thousand two hundred piastres, besides being sent back once by Narsah, and kept in confinement by Sheikh Hamed, his younger brother, at Palmyra, by which he extorted two hundred piastres from Mr. Bankes. Selim, as well as Scander, being both absent at Damascus, we were at some difficulty how to proceed, but resolved, however, to await the return of Selim, as Pierre expected he would be back in a few days. We had much conversation about the

Arabs with Pierre, and about the prices which travellers had at different times paid for visiting Palmyra; for although we were determined to go *coute qui coute*, we still determined to dispute and fight as hard a battle as we could, pretending at the same time to be very indifferent about it. We soon saw that if this man assisted us, he would at least make us pay as much money as he could, for he talked of two, three, four, and even six hundred piastres as nothing. We, however, told him that four hundred was the utmost we would pay, and informed him of our knowledge of Sir William Chatterton and Mr. Leslie having visited Palmyra, by Cariateen, for only one hundred piastres, while the Arabs were employed in making extravagant demands of Mr. Bankes. Pierre, on hearing this, observed, "that if Sir W. C. and Mr. L. had gone in this manner, they had stolen to Tadmor." Perceiving that he was not inclined to make for us a moderate bargain, we were undetermined what course to pursue; as we made no doubt that he would at all events give information to the Arabs of our arrival, and of our wish to visit Palmyra. In the meantime a Christian who lives at Homs came to us, asserting, that there was no difficulty in getting to the object of our wishes, and that he was acquainted with two others of his sect at Homs, who with himself would answer for conducting us upon asses, at a moderate price, and without any danger from the Arabs. We did not place very implicit confidence in his account, particularly as we knew that our departed friend, Sheikh Ibrahim, had been robbed and stripped in his first attempt, and we had Mr. Bankes' fate also before us; but as time was passing away, and we were doing nothing, we decided on going with the above-mentioned Christian to Homs, telling Pierre, and every body else to whom we spoke on the subject, that we had given up all idea of going to Palmyra, in consequence of the expense attending it, and had decided on pursuing our journey to Damascus and Jerusalem.

January 16. We had intended to set out in the morning. It however turned out very wet weather that day, and we did not accompany the man, as we had no idea of getting wet through on such an uncertain excursion; but we promised him to follow whenever it became clear weather. During the afternoon Pierre visited us and appeared to be much surprised that we had not set out for Damascus; we told him that we were solely prevented from quitting Hamah by the rain. He made no further observation, but shortly after retired, and in about half an hour more returned with five Arabs whom he said he had brought to us that we might make a bargain with them for going to Palmyra. The chief of these was Shiekh Salee, nephew to Mahannah, a lad about fourteen or fifteen years of age, very dirty and ill-dressed, with a sheep skin cloak: he sat down in our room with great composure, as did his four companions, three of whom were blacks; while smoking their pipes, they examined every thing in our apartment with great attention, but we had purposely hid whatever was likely to attract notice, or give an idea of riches. Their first demand was three thousand piastres, at which we burst out into an immoderate fit of laughter; they then came down to two thousand, but we remained fixed at four hundred: at last they lowered to eight hundred. The lad now made signs that we should be robbed; we shewed all we meant to take with us, and said it was not worth fifty piastres, which indeed was true enough. He then made signs that we should have our throats cut; we told him that neither he, Mahannah, nor any of his tribe would dare touch a Frank, furnished as we were with the imperial firman, which he knew we had, though they do not care much for the Grand Seignior; it was not a little remarkable to hear such threats from a boy only fourteen years of age. At last they quitted us altogether, saying, they must have eight hundred or none: after some deliberation, seeing they were gone in earnest, we sent to give them six hundred as our ultimatum, the hire of the camels which were to carry us included; *but nothing to be paid until our safe return to Hamah.* After much prevarication, during which they endeavoured to make us pay for the camels extra, they at length consented to our terms, as they said, "for the love of the Malaka" or queen, for such they were pleased to call Lady Hester Stanhope, who gave five hundred pounds for this trip; had we paid them as much money, no doubt they would have called us two kings, for like the Nubians flus (money) is their idol. The next morning we sent to the Aga to have the treaty ratified in writing. They now demanded three hundred piastres in advance; we positively refused paying a para until our safe return; and, finally, the Aga declined being responsible unless Mahannah or Narsah sent a written document to say we might pass safely. Thus the affair remained till the morning of the nineteenth, the Arabs having, however, come to us once in the mean time, to endeavour to prevail on us to give them three, two, or even one hundred piastres in advance; but as the smallest sum paid before hand would have placed us in some measure in their power, and rendered our journey uncertain, we persisted in refusing.

January 19. We removed to Homs, no message from Mahannah having arrived; Pierre followed us. We left Hamah at dawn of day, and arrived in about eight hours, the road leading still through rich plains destitute of wood. There is only one variety, viz. about half way we crossed the Orontes, now diminished in breadth to a paltry stream; the river here winds much through a chasm. There is a bridge of thirteen arches, and the water being kept up for the purpose of turning a mill, together with a cascade which it forms, a khan, the village of Rastan, which stands near it, and a few trees on the immediate bank of the rivulet, altogether make it rather a pretty spot. Rastan stands on an eminence near the bridge, and the ancient Arethusia adjoins it, presenting a sight of more interest than we had lately been accustomed to, though nothing remains perfect; part of the walls, the line of the streets, and the pedestals of some columns being alone remarkable. Settled in a khan at Homs. We had, on the twentieth, some conversation with the Christian we had seen at Hamah; but it appeared evident he was undertaking a business he did not know how to

execute. In the evening one of the Arabs who had visited us with Shiekh Salee, came with a letter from Sheikh Narsah, who, he said, was encamped one day's journey from Palmyra; this letter stated, " That Narsah had heard of our
" arrival in Hamah, and of our wish to visit
" Tadmor; that he expected by the twenty-
" fourth, that the Fidon and Isbaah Arabs, under
" Shiekh Haleel, and who were at war with the
" Annasees, would be removed from the neigh-
" bourhood of Palmyra, and that at the expi-
" ration of that time he would come to Homs
" with three camels to conduct us." This story we had afterwards reason to believe was a fiction, to persuade us of the absolute necessity of his protection; in the mean time he desired we would give the bearer twenty piastres; upon this we made great difficulties, as our departure not being yet completely settled, their remained some chance of our being cheated out of it; and we had an idea that if we shewed an easy compliance in giving money, we might soon receive an order for some thousands; in short, finding how tardily affairs were going on, we resolved to set out the next morning and walk, determining to call on Narsah on our way. To this plan the Arab consented, and every thing was agreed on, he swearing the most sacred oaths that all

should go on well, and that we should have one ass to carry our bread, water, and sheep-skin coats.

January 21. This morning the man appeared again, saying, he could not take us, as he feared Narsah would cut off his head for having undertaken the business without express orders; therefore after much prevarication, this last arrangement also terminated unfavourably, and the Arab set off a second time for the camp of Mahannah, to bring the camels as soon as possible, and apprize his chief that we had removed to Homs. In the afternoon it came on to blow hard, with continued squalls of snow, sleet, and rain, and as we were to have set off that morning on our walking trip, we were not sorry of our failure in this instance. As the bad weather continued without intermission night and day till the twenty-fourth, in the evening, when the man returned from Mahannah with the three camels, we could not arrange for starting till the twenty-sixth, as the motsellim (governour) being busy taking an inventory of the decapitated pashaw's effects, could not ratify the bargain. For an account of the arbitrary proceedings of the Turkish government towards suspected individuals, I refer you to Volney. In this instance, the sufferer had been appointed to the command of the hadj, and had set off from Constantinople. While he was on his return from Mecca, a khat-sherriffe was dispatched from the capital, ordering his head to be cut off and sent immediately to Constantinople; his sentence was carried into execution before he reached Damascus ([18]). We hear that this man was accused of intriguing with the Russians against the state. We paid three hundred piastres into the hands of Hadji Hassan, as part payment to the Arab sheikhs, but it was agreed that they should not themselves receive any portion of it till our safe return to Homs. Sheikh Narsah's order was, that we should pay all before starting; but we persisted in refusing, and moreover, we made the Arabs consent, before ample witnesses, that no further demands were to be made upon us, exclusive of the six hundred piastres, on any pretence whatever. The motsellim, who like all the Turks, had a great, and as you will observe in the sequel, unnecessary dread of these people, observed, "why will you trust yourselves amongst the Arabs, suppose they should destroy you?"

January 26. At one in the afternoon, after nineteen days' negociation, either at Hamah or Homs, we were on rout with our three camels and as many conductors, with two skin bottles (see Judges, iv. 19, " a bottle of milk), into which they had run the melted butter, bought with Lady Hester's present. We proved to them before departing that we had not a para in our pockets, thus preventing any temptation to pilfer; all our baggage consisted of a sheep-skin coat, the woolly side in, and the other side coloured red with ochre, and greased to keep out the rain ([19]). We went five hours, our guides singing nearly the whole time a favourite Arab song. Arriving at a Bedouin camp, we had some scruples about entering a tent, expecting they would have had many objections against receiving us; instead of which, to our surprise, we were welcomed by both men and women; the latter smiling, said, we were Frangi (Franks), and retired to their part of the tent to prepare supper.

January 27. Being regaled with a breakfast, we proceeded at eight and marched till four in the afternoon, stopping at another Arab camp, where we were again well received.

January 28. We started at dawn of day, and met with many dwarf trees, of which the country had hitherto been destitute; it now resembled a heath with a plentiful stock of aromatic shrubs, and occasional hill and dale. We followed no particular road or track, but our general direction appeared to be east. We had this morning a striking instance of the value the Arab sets on his time, and of his impatience to accomplish a journey when once undertaken. Suddenly one of our party quitting us, hastened on in advance, and was soon out of sight; shortly after, on coming up with him we found he had collected brushwood and made a blazing fire; presently some butter was melted and sweetened with honey. In this we dipped our bread which we had brought; and what with the Arab's voracious mode of eating, and these time-saving measures, our breakfast did not detain us above ten minutes. The same hurry was subsequently shewn on our wanting to drink some water from a small crevice in the rock close to us; we were prohibited and told there was plenty before us; but as the camps were hours in advance to our knowledge, we were not to be controlled, and dismounting, quenched our thirst. The soil was excessively rich, but we saw no water, and all species of cultivation had ceased a few hours from Homs. We could not help laughing at our principal guide, who with a rusty old match-lock and *no powder*, pretended to be very vigilant in reconnoitring from all the heights for harami (robbers), while we knew that he and his companions were of the most timid nature, and that to their knowledge we were going with the sanction, and under the protection of their own chiefs, who commanded the whole country. At noon we saw a wild boar, so large that we at first took him for an ass. About four in the afternoon we opened the valley in which Mahannah's camp was pitched. The Arabs were obliged to inquire before they could find out the direction of the camp, and as they had only been absent a few days, some idea may be formed from this circumstance of the difficuly of attacking the tribes in the desert. As we approached, we beheld a very animated and busy scene; the girls were singing, and the children busied in running down the young partridges ([20]) with dogs, as they were as yet only able to fly a short distance at a time. Presently we heard a hue and cry from all quarters, and soon perceived a large wild boar, with his bristles erect, beset by all the dogs; every body running eagerly to the pursuit. He was found behind one of the tents; they chased him all through the camp, and two Arabs on horseback, with spears, soon joined in the pursuit. The animal, however, kept both men and dogs at bay, and finally got off with only one wound. We now approached the sheikh's tent and found Mahannah with his two sons, Sheikhs Narsah and Hamed, together with about thirty Arab chiefs of various camps seated round an immense fire; Sheikh Narsah was leaning on a camel's saddle, their customary cushion; he did not rise to receive us, although we afterwards observed that he and the whole circle rose whenever a strange sheikh arrived. We attributed this cool reception to the low estimation he held us in, in consequence of the unusually small sum we had paid for visiting Palmyra, and from the plainness of our dress and appearance. All the assembly kept up a most profound silence, while Narsah alone addressed us. Mahannah, his father, was a short, crooked-backed, mean-looking old man, between seventy and eighty years of age, dressed in a common sort of robe; his son, Narsah, to whom he had, in consequence of his age, resigned the reins of government, was a good looking man about thirty years of age, with very dignified and engaging manners. He had the Koran open in his hand when we arrived, as we suppose to give us an idea of his learning. He was well dressed with a red pelisse and an enormous white turban; we observed much whispering going forward between Narsah and every stranger that arrived, evincing a distrust of those near him, and all our guides were separately questioned in the same manner, as we suppose to learn whether we had much money or not; he also asked us why the English wished so much to see Palmyra; and whether we were not going to search for gold? We told him he should have half of any we might find there. It appeared they had only arrived the day before, as they are constantly shifting their quarters, in order to provide food for their numerous camels, sheep, and goats; the scarcity of water and dryness of the pasturage prevents them from having cows and oxen. As the evening advanced, the Arab guests increased to the number of fifty, all giving way as new faces arrived; their mode of saluting their chiefs is by kissing either cheek alternately ([21]), and not the hand as in Nubia. Narsah questioned us about Buonaparte and the occupation of France by the allied troops; I suspect his knowledge of these matters proceeded from his correspondence with Lady Hester Stanhope. Inquiring after Sheikh Hamedy, a handsome young man apparently between twenty and twenty-five years of age, with evident confusion in his countenance, acknowledged himself as the person; at the same time remarking that we had probably heard a bad account of him, but that the reports to his prejudice were not correct; this man confined Mr. Bankes a day, and obliged him to pay two hundred piastres exclusive of the one thousand two hundred he paid to Narsah for visiting Palmyra. Some of the partridges which the children had caught, were now brought in; they roasted them on the fire, and part was given to us; Sheikh Hamedy *throwing* a leg and a wing to each of us. They afterwards gave us some honey and butter together, with bread to dip in it ([22]), Narsah desiring one of his men to mix the two ingredients for us, as we were aukwardat it; the Arab, having stirred the mixture up well with his fingers, shewed his dexterity at consuming as well as mixing, and recompensed himself for his trouble by eating half of it. Both at sun-set and at eight o'clock, the whole assembly were summoned to prayers, a man standing outside the tent and calling them to their devotions, in the same manner as is done from the minarets of the mosques of Turkish towns; each man rubbed his face over with sand, a heap of which was placed in front of the tent for that purpose, to serve as a substitute for water for their religious ablutions; we could not but admire the decorous solemnity with which they all joined in the divine worship, standing in a row and bowing down and kissing the ground together ([23]). An immense platter of roast mutton was then brought in for supper, with pillaw of rice; the assembly fed apart, while a separate portion was brought for Narsah and us. We observed the elderly men gave their half-gnawed bones to those around them, and were told that they have a complimentary adage in favour of him who doeth so. A black slave was perpetually pounding coffee from the moment we entered the tent till we went to sleep, and as he began in the morning at day-light, and was constantly employed, it would seem that the consumption in this article must be considerable. Late at night Narsah began to address the whole circle of sheikhs, who we found had been convened in order that they might hear his request, that some portions of grazing land, called "the Cottons," might be delivered up to him. Being tired with the length of his discourse, we removed to a corner of the tent and fell asleep; we heard afterwards that his harangue lasted till three in the morning. On the following day we wished to proceed according to a promise which Narsah had given the preceding evening, Alla Raschid (by his head), lifting up his hand at the same time ([24]), to let us depart before sun-rise; but as the chief had sat up so late he did not make his appearance till about ten o'clock, when instead of letting us go, he desired we would follow him; and presently proceeding to a small vale contiguous to his tent, we found the Arabs assembling from all quarters and following us in great numbers. We were quite at a loss to know the meaning of all this; at first we thought it was intended to shew off the numbers of his people; presently, however, we came to a tent, and found an immense feast of rice and camel's flesh prepared for the whole assembly. We were conducted to a smaller tent apart, and had our share sent to us; we were in doubt what object the sheikh had in thus separating us; whether it was meant as an accommodation to us that we might eat more comfortably and freely by ourselves, than in the midst of so great a concourse of people, or whether he thought we were not fit society for him. Our dress was certainly of a much meaner description than that of any of the sheikhs; and as throughout the east a stranger is generally estimated according to the dress he wears, it is probable that our homely appearance had some weight with Narsah on this occasion. We found the meat both savoury and tender, being part of the hump, which is considered the best; there was little fat, and the grain was remarkably coarse; however we made a hearty breakfast. The feast was conducted with much order and decorum; the sheikhs fed apart in a double row, with several immense platters placed at equal distances between them, and a rope line was drawn round to keep the people from pressing in. Narsah was at the head of the row, with a small select circle, amongst whom we were called after we had breakfasted, he having perceived us amongst the spectators. When the sheikhs had finished, the people were regaled with the remains; independent of which, portions (see Esther, ix. 19, " sending portions") were distributed to the different tents of the camp, which consisted of about two hundred; this latter arrangement was for the women and children ([25]). We believe that several camels were cooked from the immense quantities of meat we saw. This feast was no doubt intended to give weight to the proceedings of the former evening. We were here asked whether Christians did not not eat pig's flesh; and answering in the affirmative, were questioned if we did not also drink sow's milk, as they do camels ([26]); this, however, we stoutly denied. Mahannah made many signs for money, both for himself and Sheikh Alli, a very handsome little boy about five years of age, the son of Narsah; the Arab sign for money is rubbing the fore finger and thumb together. About eleven we set out, our camels were changed for dromedaries of a heavy sort, which set off with us at full trot up hill and down dale, each of us having his Arab conductor mounted behind him. We had now an addition to our party; one of Narsah's men, who was called a guard, accompanying us, mounted on a white dromedary, decorated with tassels, and armed with another old match-lock gun. We continued till four o'clock in the afternoon, and slept in an Arab tent as usual. We found the pace of the animals, on level ground and up hill, good enough, but in descending we were dreadfully jolted.

January 30. At dawn we proceeded, our new guard had endeavoured to make us start at midnight, but we would not submit to this, as the nights were very cold and frosty. We trotted this day at the same rate as the preceding, and were jolted and bruised almost beyond endurance. At two in the afternoon we arrived at the object of our wishes; our useful guard having previously lighted the match of his gun and gone through the motions of loading *without ammunition.*

On opening the ruins of Palmyra, as seen from the Valley of the Tombs, we were much struck with the picturesque effect of the whole, presenting altogether the most imposing sight of the kind we had ever seen; and it was rendered doubly interesting by our having travelled through a wilderness destitute of a single building, and from which we suddenly opened upon these innumerable columns and other ruins on a sandy plain, on the skirts of the desert; their snow-white appearance contrasted with the yellow sand produced a very striking effect. Great, however, was our disappointment, when on a minute examination, we found that there was not a single column, pediment, architrave, portal, frieze, or any architectural remnant worthy of admiration. None of the columns exceeded in diameter four feet, or in height forty feet; dimensions but ill calculated to give an idea of the sublime, at least according to Longinus. Those of the boasted avenue had little more than thirty feet of altitude; the epistylium is in no instance ornamented with any carved-work, excepting now and then an ill executed cornice. The plates of Wood and Dawkins are certainly well executed, but they have done but too much justice to the originals; taken as a *tout ensemble*, these ruins are certainly more remarkable, by reason of their extent, (being nearly a mile and a half in length), than any we have hitherto met with, and they are, moreover, less encumbered by modern fabrics than any we have witnessed; for exclusive of the Arab village of Tadmor, which occupies the peristyle court of the Temple of the Sun, and the Turkish burying place, there are no obstructions whatever to the antiquities. Take any part of the ruins separately, and they excite but little interest; and altogether, we judged the visit to Palmyra hardly worthy of the time, expense, anxiety, and fatiguing journey through the wilderness, which we had undergone to visit them. The projecting pedestals in the centre of the columns of the great avenue have a very unsightly appearance; there is also a great sameness in the architecture, all the capitals being Corinthian, excepting those which surround the Temple of the Sun. These last are fluted, and when decorated with their brazen Ionic capitals, were doubtless very handsome; but the latter being now deficient, the beauty of the edifice is entirely destroyed. The sculpture, as well of the capitals of the columns, as of the other ornamental parts of the door-ways and buildings, is very coarse and bad; although the designs are generally correct in the work of Wood and Dawkins, we found that the execution of the sculpture is far inferior to what might have been expected from the engravings. The three arches at the end of the avenue nearest the Temple of the Sun, so beautiful in the designs, are excessively insignificant; the decorated frieze thereof, although handsome in the plates, is very badly wrought; and in this instance, even the devices are not striking; they are not to be compared to the common portals of Thebes, although the Egyptians were unacquainted with the arch. Every thing here is built of a very perishable stone; if it deserves the name of marble, it is very inferior even to that of Baalbec; and we are inclined to think the ruins of the latter place are much more worthy the traveller's notice than those of Palmyra. We suspect that it is the difficulty of getting to Tadmor, and consequently the few people that have been there, that has given rise to the great renown of the ruins of Palmyra. We give the preference to Baalbec, not only for the general superiority of the sculpture, but also for the extraordinary massive structure of the buildings; and while the columns of Baalbec have nearly sixty feet in height, and seven in diameter, supporting a most rich and beautifully wrought epistylium of twenty feet more, the pillars being built of only *three* pieces of stone; the smallest columns at Palmyra (three feet and a half in diameter and thirty feet high) are formed of six, seven, and even eight parts; although those which surround the peristyle court of the Temple of the Sun may be about forty feet high, and four feet diameter, are formed of only three and four stones; there are in the centre of the avenue four granite columns, each of one single stone, about thirty feet high; only one is still standing. We found the Tombs very interesting; their construction is different from any thing we had elsewhere seen. They consist of a number of square towers, three, four, and five stories high; they are situated without the walls of the ancient city. The best remaining are on each side of the valley which leads to Homs and Hamah. These towers are not ornamented on the exterior, with the exception of a tablet whereon is a Greek inscription (certainly copied by Wood and Dawkins) and a few figures in basso-relievo over the door. There are generaly five sepulchral chambers one over the other, and on each side are eight recesses, each divided into four or five parts, for the reception of corpses; the lower chamber, in some instances, fronts an excavation in the side of the hill contiguous to it. The best of these lower apartments which we saw are very handsome, the sides being ornamented with sculpture and fluted Corinthian pilasters, though the walls were plain white stucco, without any figures or emblematical representation. The cieling, on which the paint is still very perfect, is ornamented like that of the peristyle court of the Temple of the Sun at Baalbec, with the heads of different heathen deities, and disposed in diamond-shaped divisions. We were much interested by the remains of some of the mummies and mummy cloths, which appear to have been preserved very much after the manner of the Egyptians, only that the gum had lost all that odour, resembling frankincense, which we noticed in Egypt. We found a hand in tolerable preservation; but after all, you must not imagine that these sepulchres are in any way so interesting as those of Egypt. You here look in vain for those beautiful paintings, &c. which so well pourtray the manners and customs of the ancients. Over the inside of the door-way, we saw a tablet in basso-relievo, of seven or eight standing figures dressed in long robes, with their hands on their breasts; we suppose them to have been priests; and we also noticed a sarcophagus, with the sides ornamented much in the same manner. We observed the marble folding doors, still erect, of some of the grander tombs situated in the town; these latter are much dilapidated; the doors were carved in pannels, but ill executed and unpolished. The lines of the streets and foundations of the houses of Palmyra are very distinguishable in some places. We agree with Mr. Bankes, that many of the small square rows of columns which Wood and Dawkins suppose to have inclosed temples, were no other than the open court of private edifices which inclosed fountains; and Mr. B. was more led to suspect this, from there being one of only four columns, which never could have inclosed a temple or solid building within it. These ideas were suggested to him by his having noticed similar remains at Pompeii. Passing down the great avenue of columns there is a door-way standing on the right hand, and within it are the remains of the building it belonged to, having an Hebrew inscription on the architrave, interesting on three accounts; first, as the foundation of Tadmor was by Solomon; second, as Zenobia is said by some to have been of the Jewish religion; and third, as Bishop Riddle sets down two thousand Jews at Tadmor in his day. This was a discovery of, and information we received from, Mr. Bankes. There is at Palmyra a tepid spring of mineral water, having a strong sulphureous taste and smell; a subterraneous aqueduct supplied the town. There is a great quantity of salt in the desert adjoining Tadmor, which forms a lucrative branch of commerce to the present natives. After the complete work of Wood and Dawkins, I need not trouble you with any further remarks on Palmyra.

January 31. Having finished our examination of the ruins, we started at two, and continued till ten at night, when we slept at an Arab tent as usual. After dark the Arabs implored us not to sing for fear the robbers should hear us, and appeared to be as fearful in their own desert, as it was possible for a stranger to be.

February 1. We moved at sun-rise, and did not reach Mahannah's camp until dark in the evening; we were conducted back by another road, and met with two parties of his people on horseback, one of seven and the other of twelve, mostly armed with spears; we also met a small party on dromedaries richly caparisoned ([27]), and as we thought purposely sent to shew his power; they asked us in passing how much we had paid for visiting Palmyra, taking it as a thing of course that we were obliged to give money; our change of road naturally gave some mystery to our proceeding. On our arrival at the camp, old Mahannah came out of his tent and began feeling the saddles, and took from the poor Arabs all the salt which they had purchased at Palmyra. We were pretty well received by the chiefs; Narsah had on the old robe this time, and the father the new one. We soon found out the meaning of this, when the former asked our interpreter to request that we would give him a new dress; but the latter said it was a thing impossible, as we had made our bargain for six hundred piastres only. We begged, and obtained a promise to depart early in the morning, Narsah saying, he had only to write a letter *to the King of England,* which we were to take with us; he sent one to his dear friend Lady Hester, with whom they all seem to be enchanted. They call her " El Malaka," (the queen);

some say she is "Bint-el Sultan" (daughter of the king), and others favour her with the appellation of the Virgin Mary ([28]).

February 2. In the morning we were detained until nine o'clock, and had very much difficulty in procuring a draught of water before starting; but we absolutely refused to move without it ([29]). In consequence of this detention we were at the end of the day's journey benighted, and had a bitter cold bivouack in the open air, the Arabs being afraid even to light a fire. We however managed to lay down between two of our camels, which, from their kneeling posture, kept some of the cold air off, sleeping was out of the question, as it was freezing hard, with a strong, cutting wind ([30]). The following morning, at dawn, we were on route; we saw twenty-three white gazelles, and witnessed the removal of an Arab camp; the moveables being all placed on the camels' backs; the women with their children slung over their shoulders, and the flocks following, presented altogether an interesting sight. We breakfasted at a small encampment off a thick mess of lentiles and bread, highly seasoned with pepper, and very good ([31]). Towards noon we passed a valley, grubbed up in all directions, in furrows, by the wild boars; the soil had all the appearance of having been literally ploughed up ([32]). In the evening we reached Homs; we were highly satisfied with our conductors, and one would have had difficulty in finding such good guides in any part of Europe, we therefore gave them each twenty piastres, as voluntary backsheeish, although, when the agreement was made, we particularly stipulated that six hundred piastres should include all our expenses. One of these men had received twenty more for carrying the message to Narsah, as before mentioned. We also sent a turban of twenty piastres value to the shiekh of Tadmor for his civilities to us, and gave one hundred piastres to Pierre, so that our whole expenses in visiting Palmyra amounted to eight hundred piastres, two hundred of which consisted of voluntary gifts.

I shall now close this long story with our opinion of these Arabs: their behaviour to each other, whatever may be their conduct to others, presents an amiable picture of domestic harmony and comfort, and is in unison with all the ideas the poets have formed of the peaceful contentment of the pastoral life; in fact, they are a nation of shepherds, and I question much if in our most polished circles, divested of the empty pomp of dress and finery, you could meet with more dignity of deportment or urbanity of manners than you find in the humble tent of the

Arab. It appeared to us that all the good amongst them was centred in the lower orders; the chiefs monopolizing to themselves all that cunning and roguery which renders them contemptible in the eyes of a stranger. An Arab, on arriving in a strange camp, goes to the first tent that comes in his way; he does not wait to be asked in, but without any ceremony makes his camel lie down, unloads at the entrance, and entering the tent with the simple salutation of salaam alicam (peace be between us), sets himself down by the fire, no matter whether the host be at home or not. Should the latter be present, he immediately puts fresh wood on, and begins to burn and pound coffee, generally offering his pipe to his guest in the mean time. His wife, or wives, after spreading mats, if they have any, for the stranger to sit on, retire to their part of the tent, which is divided in the middle by their sack of corn, and whatever other effects they have, prepares the dinner or supper according to the time of the day, without any order being given by the master, but as a matter of course; in the mean time the host chats with his guests, generally about their flock, &c. such being their principle concern. The coffee being ready, the landlord pours out for every one his cup, helping himself last; as soon as the meal is prepared, which generally consists of a large wooden bowl of either camel's, goat's, or sheep's milk, boiled wheat and milk, lentil soup, or melted butter and bread to dip in it; the landlord pours water alternately for his guests, who therewith wash the right hand, begining with one, and going regularly round the circle ([33]). The ablution finished, every one commences; the host retires, not eating with his guests, but welcoming them with frequent repetitions of coula, coula (eat it all, eat it all). The repast being finished, the attentive master again washes the hands of his party, and then eats himself of what remains. On two occasions we arrived at a camp late at night, and halting before a tent, found the owner, with his wife and children, having arranged their carpets, &c. for the night, had just retired to rest, when it was astonishing to see the good humour with which they all arose again and kindled a fire, the wife commencing to knead the dough and prepare our supper ([34]), our Arabs making no apology, but taking all as a matter of course, though the nights were bitter cold. Surely this was a noble instance of Arab hospitality. It was a pleasing sight to see them bring in their flocks at night, which always slept close to the tents of their owners; several Arabs, together with numerous dogs, remaining outside as guards. The lambs (for it was the lambing season) were placed inside the tents, in a small fenced place, to screen them from the inclemency of the night air, which was nearly as cold as you would experience it in England at that season, always freezing hard. The first care in the morning was to let their young charge out to their mothers, when it was not an uninteresting scene to observe the numerous ewes recognizing their offspring by the smell alone; the lambs not being gifted with the sagacity of their mothers, were all willing to suck from the first ewe they met with. In short, it would appear that these people having few wants are unacquainted with many cares, and are thus ignorant of the greater part of the troubles and difficulties which are experienced in more civilized society. Every Arab having a tent of his own, is thus possessed of a freehold, which has nothing to do with either rents or taxes, and the shrubs of the wilderness serve him spontaneously both with food for his flocks, and fuel for his fires ([35]). The labour of tilling and reaping is unknown to him, though much judgement and foresight is necessary in his periodical migrations with his flocks, which must be regulated and timed with such due regard to the seasons as to consume the verdure while they are advancing, and at the same time to leave the land fallow sufficiently long for its recovery before they return; a minute attention to this, being with them what our systematic mode of husbandry is with us. They contrive to be near their southern boundary in the winter, and consequently at their northern limits in the summer. They are frequently obliged to pitch their tents at six and eight hours' distance from the wells, and then it is that their camels are of incalculable utility to them. They are unacquainted with the miseries of blighted crops, or those other disappointments to which the farmer is so liable. Their behaviour to us was the same as towards each other, and I suspect that their character for robbing and pilfering, arises from the conduct of some few of the worst part of the community, who infest the high roads, than from any dishonesty of the generality of these people. The dread which the Turks have of the Arabs appeared to us quite unaccountable, as during the whole of our trip we did not see more than half a dozen old matchlock guns, and about eighteen spears. Narsah was imprisoned a short time ago for some tricks he had been playing in this city. The pashaw wanted to cut off his head, but a strong remonstance from the merchants of Aleppo and Bagdad, setting forth the disastrous consequences which would attend the execution of this man, from the vengeance of the

Arabs, procured his release, and instead of losing his head he was dismissed with a present of a robe and some backsheeish. Scriptural authority, however, is not wanting to prove the comparative independence in which these people lived ([36]).

February 7. Requiring a little rest on our return from Tadmor, we remained at Homs till this morning, when we travelled for about seven hours, passing over rich plains, and rounding the point of a mountain which we took to be the end of Anti-Lebanon.

February 8. We went nine hours through a mountainous country.

February 9. We went seven hours, passing through several deep, dry torrents. We stopped at a khan in a plain, and found the mountains very barren, uninteresting, and partly covered with snow.

February 10. Leaving this plain we again entered a hilly country, when arriving at the brow of a descent, the extensive and beautiful plain of Damascus opened on our view, with the town surrounded by woods, amidst which were several villages; the land was highly cultivated; to the eastward the plain extends as far as the eye can reach; in other directions it is bounded by hills, with Lebanon very conspicuous above them all. In about two hours we had descended into the plain, and in five more arrived at the convent of the Terra Sancta in Damascus. The last three hours the road was extremely beautiful, passing through rich olive groves and gardens, generally inclosed by walls of sun-burnt brick, and surrounded and irrigated by streams of water, partly natural and partly conducted by art. We were here very sensible to the comforts of a convent, having never slept on a bed, or with our clothes off, since we left Aleppo (thirty-eight days ago). Our time has been occupied in writing our letters, and in visiting different parts of the town, such as the place of the Vision of St. Paul outside the eastern gate; the place where he was let down the wall in a basket; the house of Ananias; the street called Straight, &c. all alluded to in the ninth chapter of the Acts of the Apostles. For a decription of these places, as well as of the town in general, I must refer you to Maundrell, who describes every thing in Damascus that is worth notice. The Turks call it Shum, or Shem, and the friars of the convent think it was originally founded by Shem, the son of Noah; the earliest information we have of this place is in the time of Abraham ([37]).

We shall proceed to the Holy Land in a few days by Panias, near to which place is the source of the Jordan; thence crossing the bridge of Jacob.

we go to Nazareth, Tiberias, Nablous, Jericho, and Jerusalem. In consequence of a letter from Mr. Barker, we have received great assistance from Monsieur Chaboceau, physician to the pashaw of this place, and through his assistance we have got another firman for the paschalic, and a letter for the governor of Jerusalem, from whom we wish, if possible, to get guides to conduct us to Mount Sinai. Whether we succeed or not in getting to Mount Sinai, we shall return by Jerusalem to Acre, and then embark for Cyprus, whence we proceed for the coast of Asia Minor, beginning by Tarsus, which will conduct us to Smyrna, the site of Troy, and finally, Constantinople. We find by a letter left here for us by Mr. Bankes, that he quitted Damascus on the 10th of January, with an escort to make the tour of the Hauran, and passing to the eastward to cross the southern point of the Dead Sea to Jerusalem. He was so good as to wait here in hopes of our joining him, but a letter from Mr. Barker mentioning our detention at Aleppo, and our final plans of Palmyra, obliged him to give up his design. He left us some information about the site of the ancient Abilah, as well as some inscriptions he found proving it so, at five hours' distance from this town. But we have neither the time, intelligence, books, or money, to enable us to follow this excellent traveller through his researches. We hope to meet him at Jerusalem.

LETTER IV.

TOUR IN SYRIA.

Departure from Damascus.—Arrive at Panias.— Safot. —Tiberias.—Om Keis.—Callah-el-Hammam.—Erbed. —Bysan.—Tabathat Fahkil.—Hallawye.—Cafringee. —Callah-el-Rubbat.—Adjeloun.— Eugen. —Souf.— Djerash.—Szalt.— Athan.—Gilhad Gilhood. — Bait Forage.—Kaffer Baiter.—Nablous.—Arrival at Jerusalem.

JERUSALEM, April 30, 1818.

I HOPE our Damascus letters have reached you, which will have accounted for our proceedings up to the latter end of February, on the twenty-third of which month we left that delightful city for the source of the Jordan. About noon we quitted the plain of Damascus, over a slight eminence into another, through which runs a fine stream, but the plain being destitute of wood, has less beauty than that we quitted, though the soil is rich. About four in the afternoon, we stopped at the khan of the village of Sasa. Hitherto we had followed the road from Damascus to Jacob's

Bridge, at that part of the Jordan which lies between the lakes Houle and Tiberias.

February 24. We passed to the westward for Panias. The first part of the road led through a fine plain, watered by a pretty, winding rivulet, with numerous tributary streams, and many old ruined mills, from whence we began to ascend over a very rugged and rocky soil quite void of vegetation, having in some places traces of an ancient paved way, probably the Roman road leading from Damascus to Cæsarea Philippi; as we ascended we had the highest part of Djebail Sheikh (Anti-Lebanon), on our right; we found the snow in some places of considerable depth, and difficult to cross with our horses. The road now became gradually less stony, and we found flocks of goats browsing on a rich verdure, in places from whence the stones had been cleared away and piled up in great heaps. We also came to a few shrubs, which gradually increased in number, size, and beauty, until we had descended into a very rich little plain at the immediate foot of Djebail Sheikh. There is a conspicuous tomb in this valley, and a rivulet which appears to take its source at the foot of the mountains, passes along the western side of the plain in a southerly direction, when its course turns more to the westward, and rushing in a very picturesque manner, through a deep chasm, covered by shrubs of various descriptions, it joins the Jordan at " Panias ;" it is marked in Arrowsmith's chart as the real source, which is the reason why I have given you this tedious detail, for the source of the Jordan is a subject of much dispute; the fountains at Panias, which are by far the most copious, though not the most distant from the Dead Sea, where the river terminates, are generally called the source ; an opinion in which we both agree. From this plain we ascended up its southern side, and after passing a very small village about one o'clock, we saw on our left, close to us, a very picturesque lake, apparently perfectly circular, of little more than a mile in circumference, surrounded on all sides by sloping hills richly wooded. The singularity of this lake is, that it has no apparent supply or discharge, and its waters appeared perfectly still, though clear and limpid; a great many wild-fowl were swimming in it. It appears that this lake has only been remarked by Burkhardt and Seetzen, those who have gone from Damascus to Panias having taken the route by Raschia and Hasbeya; Arrowsmith's map notices the lake by the name of the Birket-el Ram (according to Seetzen). Josephus (Jewish Wars, b. 3. c. 10. § 7.) mentions it under the name of "Phiala" (cup), in allusion to the shape of the lake. It was supposed by the ancients to be the real source of the Jordan; a passage in the Jewish historian notices, that they threw straw into the lake, which came out at the *apparent source* at "Panias." But this is impossible, for to arrive at Panias, its discharge must pass under the rivulet which Arrowsmith points out as the true source. On quitting Phiala, at but a short distance from it, we crossed a stream which discharges into the larger one which we first saw; the latter we followed for a considerable distance, and then mounting up the hill to the S. W. had in view the great Saracenic castle near Panias, the town of that name, and the plain of the Jordan as far the lake Houle, together with the mountains on the other side of the plain, forming altogether a fine *coup d'œil*. As we descended towards Panias we found the country extremely beautiful, great quantities of wild-flowers, and a variety of shrubs just budding, together with the richness of the verdure of the grass, corn, and beans, shewed us all at once the beauties of spring, and conducted us into a climate (although the difference of latitude is comparatively trifling) quite different from that of Damascus, or of the country which we had passed through since we left that city. About five in the evening we entered Panias, crossing a causeway constructed over the rivulet, which as before stated, flows from the foot of Dgebail Sheikh. The river here rushes over great rocks in a very picturesque manner, its banks being covered with shrubs and the ruins of the ancient walls, but whether the ruins are Saracenic or not I cannot say. The present town of Panias is small, the ground it stands on is of a triangular form, inclosed by the Jordan on one side, the rivulet on the other, and the mountain at the back; from this compressed situation, we think the ancient Panias, afterwards Cæsarea Philippi could not have been of great extent. Ancient authors (see Josephus' Jewish Antiquities, b. xv. 10. § 3.) mention a temple built by Herod, but we could find no trace of such an edifice. The apparent source of the Jordan flows from under a cave at the foot of a precipice, in the sides of which are several niches with Greek inscriptions.

Copied from Burkhardt, by permission of Col. Leake.

The neighbourhood of Panias is very beautiful, richly wooded, and abounds in game; as we had seen a variety of birds the preceding evening, we employed a part of the morning of the twenty-fifth in shooting, but had poor sport, though we saw plenty of partridges, wild ducks, snipe, &c. Having been directed to follow the Jordan to the lake Houle, we endeavoured, on leaving Panias at eleven o'clock, to perform this route. The beautifully wooded country does not continue more than two miles, when we entered into open but rich plains. We found the ground very marshy, after winding about to find fords over the numerous streams which water the plain, we crossed the Jordan itself; but the country on the other side was as full of marshes and swamps as that we had left, and in several places we nearly lost the horses; at last we succeeded in reaching the road to Safot, which runs at the foot of the hills on the other side of the plain, and to have taken which, in the first instance, we ought to have passed round the north end of the whole valley. Loss of time in these bogs occasioned our arriving no further on our journey this evening, than a village by the side of a hill in the neighbourhood of the N.W. end of lake Houle; the banks of this lake are very low, the hills not approaching it in any part.

May 26. We ascended from hence to Safot, the plain which we had quitted was literally covered with wild geese, ducks, widgeon, snipe, and water-fowl of every description. Mounting up to Safot, there is a village at the foot of the steep ascent, in which are a few Roman ruins. As we ascended, the lakes of Houle and Tiberias opened to us with much grandeur, and part of the plain of the Jordan added to the beauty of the scene. The country in the mountains is generally cultivated. The situation of Safot is extremely beautiful; the castle is on a small hill, standing by itself; the town appears to consist of four distinct villages at the foot of it. The approach is very fine, and the country abounds in olives, vines, and almond trees, which are now in blossom. The lake of Tiberias is visible from some part of the town, which, from its elevated situation, Maundrell thinks is the same alluded to by our Saviour ([38]). Its ancient name appears in Arrowsmith's map as Japhet. We were detained by rainy weather at Safot until the afternoon of the twenty-eighth, when we proceeded for Tiberias, but only reached an old ruined khan, about two miles to the north of the village of Madjdala by the lake's side, that night. Here we were dreadfully bitten by a red sort of vermin which is the annoyance of camels in this country; it was soft like a maggot. In the morning we found ourselves studded all over with deep crimson spots, from which it would appear that there is much venom in the bite of this disgusting animal. I shall take this opportunity of remarking, that a traveller in these countries, however much the very thoughts may shock him at first, must make up his mind, and reconcile his feelings, to being constantly covered with lice and fleas; we kill every day from ten to twenty of these guests, which are always to be found on every mat or cushion used in the country. These nauseous visitors seldom get into the head, but crawl about your shirt and clothes. Every native you see in the country is covered with vermin, and if you ask why they have such a plentiful store, while we are comparatively so little annoyed by them, they tell you " it is the curse of God on them." The other day I cut my foot, and our Arab Seys, (the same that has accompanied us all the way from Yaffa,) who is always washing himself, and is a very cleanly person, tore off a small piece of the sleeve of his shirt for my hurt; the piece was about three inches long, by two wide, and before using it, I killed three lice and two fleas on it; this will speak more than all I can say on the subject. Bugs are also very plentiful, and in Egypt our rooms were full of them.

March 1. Our road this day was generally on a descent, passing through a beautiful and wild country covered with shrubs of various descriptions, and crossing occasionally over valleys and rivulets. About four miles from Safot there is a picturesque cliff, the sides of which are perforated with a great number of caves, at present inhabited by goatherds; we supposed them to be ancient sepulchres, as indeed have other travellers who have not thought them, from their ruined appearance, worthy of examination; but Mr. Bankes, who leaves nothing unexplored, inspected them a few days afterwards, and pronounces them to be only natural cavities. About eight o'clock we reached Tiberias, having travelled about two hours along the side of the lake; we had occasion to observe that more pains appeared to have been taken to construct the road where it was very rocky, than in most parts of Syria which we had visited. The modern town of Tiberias is very small; it stands close to the lake of Gennesaret, and is walled round with towers at equal distances. At the northern extremity of the ruins are the remains of the ancient town, which are discernible by means of the walls and other ruined buildings, as well as by fragments of columns, some of which are of beautiful red granite. South of the town are the famous hot baths of Tiberias; they consist of three springs of mineral water; we had no thermometer, but we found the water too hot to admit of the hand being kept in it for more than fifty seconds; we endeavoured to boil an egg but without success, even out of the shell. Over the spring is a Turkish bath close to the lake's side, which is much resorted to, particularly by the Jews, who have a great veneration also for a Roman sepulchre, which is excavated in the cliff near the spot, and which they take to be the " Tomb of Jacob." Beyond the baths a wall runs from the lake to the mountain's side, which rather perplexed us when we were taking the measures of the ancient walls of Tiberias; but it has since appeared evident that the walls did not extend so far to the south, and that this was the fortification of Vespasian's camp, as appears from Josephus (see Jewish Wars, b. 3. c. 10. § 1.), who places it in this position. The lake of Tiberias is a fine sheet of water, but the land about it has no striking features, and the scenery is altogether devoid of character. It appeared to particular disadvantage to us after those beautiful lakes we had seen in Switzerland; but it becomes a very interesting object, when you consider the frequent allusions to it in the gospel. We were lodged as Frank travellers usually are, in the small catholic church, which is under the direction of an Arab priest; this they tell you is the identical house of St. Peter; but after we had been there a few days, we observed that one of the stones of the building had part of an inverted Arabic inscription on it, which proves it to be of much more modern origin; Doctor Clarke, however, seems to believe the assertion of the natives. We found this church so full of fleas, that we preferred a small open court in front of it for our lodging. The natives have a saying, "that the king of the fleas has his court in Tabaria;" if he has, his subjects are extremely numerous. We here lived on fish, which are most excellent; there is not much variety, but the best sort is the most common; it is a species of bream, equal to the finest perch. It is remarkable that there is not a single boat of any description on the lake at present, and the fish are caught with casting nets from the beach, a method which must yield a very small quantity compared to what they would get with boats. I imagine this to be the reason why fish are so dear, as to be sold at the same price per pound as meat. It was on this lake that the miraculous draught of fishes took place ([39]). There is a current throughout the whole breadth of the lake even to the shore; the passage of the Jordan through it is observable by the smooth state of the water's surface in that part.

March 2. Mr. Bankes arrived after having made a complete tour of the Haouran, and passed round the lake of Tiberias. He proposed that we should join him in a tour, which he contemplated beyond the Jordan, and round the Dead Sea to Jerusalem; he had expressed a wish to this effect at Aleppo, and had left a letter at Damascus to the same purport. We accordingly embraced the opportunity of accompanying him; though it is due to Mr. Bankes to notice here, that we had ourselves totally abandoned all idea of making the tour of the Dead Sea, as a hopeless undertaking, notwithstanding we had our poor friend Burkhardt's notes to aid and assist us; Mr. B. was, however, resolved to make the attempt alone if we could not have joined him: while Mr. Bankes made a short visit to Safot, which he had not yet seen, we determined to inspect Om Keis (the ancient Gadara), in the country of the Gadarenes [40].

March 4. We quitted Tiberias at eleven, and following the shore of the lake till we came to the site of the ancient Tarichea, proceeded to a ford of the Jordan, situated close to the ruins of a Roman bridge, a few hundred yards from the lake's discharge, thence we passed by the village of Semmack (Arabic for fish) at the south end of the lake, and turning to the southward, in about half an hour crossed the river Yarmack or Hieromax, a very pretty stream, tributary to the Jordan. There is a small ancient site in this position, but it contains nothing of interest; the map marks it " Amatha." From hence we ascended the mountains by a very steep road, and before sun-set arrived at Om Keis; we were very kindly received by the sheikh of the natives who inhabit the ancient sepulchres; the tomb we lodged in was capable of containing between twenty and thirty people; it was of an oblong form, and the cattle, &c. occupied one end, while the proprietor and his family lodged in the other; it was near this spot that the people lived in the tombs during the time of our Saviour ([41]). The walls of the ancient Gadara are still easily discernible; within them you find the pavement of the city very perfect; the traces of the chariot wheels are still marked in the stones. We found the remains of a row of columns which lined the main street on either side; two theatres, in tolerable preservation, are within the walls, and without them, to the northward, is the Necropolis; the sepulchres, which are all under ground, are hewn out of the live rock, and the doors which are very massy, are cut out of immense blocks of stone; some of these are now standing, and actually working on their hinges, and used by the natives; of course the hinge is nothing but a part of the stone left projecting at each end, and let into a socket cut in the rock; the face of the doors were cut in the shape of pannels. From hence we had a fine view of the lake of Tiberias.

March 5. In the morning we descended to the N. E. into the plain of the Yarmack, to visit the hot springs there; they are not so hot as those of Tiberias. One of them is inclosed by palm-trees in a very picturesque manner; it is of great depth, and its surface is covered by a species of red moss, somewhat resembling sponge before it has been purified: this the natives told us they apply to their camels when they have a certain cutaneous disorder. The ruins of a Roman bath are at the source; we found several sick persons at these springs who had come to use the waters. Hence we followed the Yarmack until we came near to the place where we had crossed it the preceding evening, and returned by dusk to Tiberias. From the sixth to the tenth, we employed ourselves in measuring the circuit of the ancient city, and in making researches in the neighbourhood. Mr. Bankes had discovered a curious ancient fortification, situated to the west of Magdala on the north side of the entrance of a ravine;

there is a high perpendicular cliff, which from its projecting situation and steep sides, forms a natural barrier on two sides of a triangle, the other side being defended by a wall of rough masonry, with numerous projecting turrets. Mr. B. made a plan of it; we were two days in taking the measurements. The natives call it Callah-el-Hammam, (Castle of the Pigeons,) but no ancient authors, that we have seen, give any clue to its origin. It may possibly be the ancient "Jotapata" where Josephus was taken; and the city demolished by Vespasian (see Jewish Wars, b. 3. c. 7. § 3.). It is certainly very antique, and Mr. B. thinks prior to the time of the Romans; in which case the Bible will be as good authority as any to search for a fortified camp in this direction. The village of Erbed, in which there are a few Roman ruins, stands in a plain at the foot of the Mount Beatitude, on the opposite side of the ravine. There are some curious old convents in the side of the cliff, on the left in going from the village of Majdil (the ancient Magdala) to the Callah-el-Hammam; these convents are very singular, being built several stories high in the perpendicular cliff, with galleries, &c. About two miles south of Majdil are the ruins of six Roman baths of mineral water, but only of a luke-warm temperature.

The baths are circular (from fifteen to twenty feet in diameter,) inclosed with a wall about twelve feet high within, and six without; at present there is no apparent means of ingress or egress. The spot where they are is now very picturesque, being close to the lake, and overgrown with shrubs, weeds, and wild flowers; the water is very clear, and about six or seven feet deep, with pebbles at the bottom; there are also fish sporting about in them; the spring discharges itself into the lake, subterraneously, through the wall. We swam to the Scorpion Rock mentioned by Josephus, but found no scorpions on it.

March 10. In the forenoon we left Tiberias, and observed, in following the borders of the lake, one of the circular towers with part of the wall of the ancient town on that side. We left the hot baths about noon; drawing towards the southern extremity of the lake, we observed, on our right, at the foot of the hills, an extensive aqueduct, and at the entrance are traces of the walls of Tarichea, which appears to have been situated on two eminences, one on the right of our road, and the other bordering on the discharge of the lake, by the Jordan; this latter appears to have been artificially surrounded by water on the other sides. The Jordan winds extremely here, but has little current. The ruins of the Roman bridge (alluded to in going to Om Keis) had ten arches : the road continues from hence through rather a naked country, with occasional views of the river. About three o'clock we came to a khan near a bridge; they are both rather picturesque objects; the bridge consists of an arch in the centre, with small arches upon arches on the sides. About one hour beyond this, we observed by the road side a Roman mile-stone, but there were only two or three distinct letters visible on it. Farther on, the pavement of the ancient road is perceivable, and about two miles from Bysan we saw a sarcophagus on the brow of a slight eminence on the right of the road; hence we crossed a small stream and ascended to Bysan about dusk; during the latter part of this day's journey we remarked a great number of Arab camps. Bysan is supposed to be the Bethshan of scripture, afterwards called Scythopolis, the largest city of the Decapolis, and the only one on that side of the Jordan. It was to the wall of Bethshan, that the body of Saul was fastened after he was slain ([42]).

March 11. We employed ourselves in inspecting the ruins. The principal object is the theatre which is quite distinct, but now completely filled with weeds; it measures across the front, as well as we can remember, one hundred and eighty feet, and it has this singularity above all other theatres that we have ever seen, viz. that those oval recesses half way up the theatre, mentioned by Vitruvius as being constructed to contain the brass sounding tubes, are found here; as Mr. B. had not lately read Vitruvius, we were quite at a loss what use to apply these very curious cells to; there are seven of them, and Vitruvius mentions that even in his day very few theatres had them. We were lucky enough to find this useful author in the library of the convent while at Jerusalem. We were very careful in taking a very correct plan of this theatre, attending to every minute particular.

We found twenty-four sculls and other bones in one of the most concealed vomitories; in one of the sculls a viper was basking with his body twisted between the eyes, presenting a good subject for a moralizer. The other remains are the tombs, which are interesting enough; they lie to the N. E. of the Acropolis, without the walls; the sarcophagi remain in some of them; we were interested in finding the niches, of a triangular shape, for the lamps; some of the doors were also hanging on the ancient hinges of stone, in remarkable preservation. Two streams run through the ruins of the city, almost insulating the Acropolis; there is a fine Roman bridge over the one to the S. W. of the Acropolis, and beyond it may be seen the paved way which led to the ancient Ptolemais, now Acre. The plains extend in this direction to the sea-coast, without any intervening mountains. On the other side the walls of the town cross the rivulet (a little below where both unite in one stream) in a singular manner; one high arch in the centre, with a smaller on each end of it, appear to have formed a bridge, and on the outside the wall of the city was continued on the edge of the bridge. It would appear as if the centre arch had been blocked up by a grating, allowing the stream to pass through; the outer part of the other two smaller arches was walled up. On the hill near this arch the ruins of one of the gates of the city are very distinguishable, and amongst the remains are prostrate columns of Corinthian architecture. The Acropolis is a high circular hill, on the top of which are the traces of the walls which encompassed it. The people are a fanatical set.

March 12. At eight o'clock in the morning we left Bysan. Near the town are the ruins of many subterranean granaries ([43]). Taking guides for fording the Jordan from an Arab camp, we reached its banks in one hour and twenty minutes; we observed them to be very prettily wooded, although the more distant parts of the plains are quite destitute of trees. Near the ford, at about half a mile to the south, is a tomb called " Sheikh Daoud," standing on an apparent round hill resembling a barrow. The stream of the Jordan is here much more swift than in that part near the lake of Tiberias; the depth at the ford reached above the bellies of the horses. We measured the breadth, and found it to be one hundred and forty feet; we bathed here. From the Jordan we turned to the right of the path to see " Tabathat Fahkil," which we reached in about half an hour; here the ruins of a modern village stand on a hill, bearing E. S. E. from the Acropolis of Bysan; and in a plain to the west of it are the ruins of a square building, with a semi-circular end, which appears to have been surrounded by columns; on the east and south side of the hill are considerable ruins of some ancient city which must have been of great extent. The situation is beautiful, being on the side of a ravine, with a picturesque stream running at the bottom. As this place appears to be as ancient as the ruins of Scythopolis, and full two-thirds of its size, it appears unaccountable that history should not mention a place so near " the principal city of the Decapolis" as this is; we searched for inscriptions, but in vain. The ruins of a fine temple are situated near the water-side, and amongst the columns are discovered the three orders of architecture, Doric, Ionic, and Corinthian; the river passing to the south, finally communicates with the Jordan. Crossing the rivulet, and following a path to the southward, we were conducted to a small plain very thickly set with herbage, and particularly the mustard plant, reaching as high as our horses heads; looking from thence to the eastward we observed several excavations in the side of the hills; these are probably the Necropolis, for Mr. Bankes was informed of several tombs in that direction, resembling those at Bysan and Om Keis, which information was confirmed at Hallawye. Finding no path this way, we re-crossed the rivulet, and proceeding to the north rejoined the track from the Jordan, which we had originally quitted to visit Tabathat Fahkil; from hence we began to ascend, passing through occasional hill and vale, well wooded, the country gradually increasing in beauty. On our left we saw the spot where Elijah was fed by the ravens ([44]); there are many villages in this direction.

March 13. We slept at Hallawye. In the morning we continued our route, and passed through the most beautiful woodland scenery, with the gall oak, wild olive, arbutus, &c. &c. in great luxuriance, and a variety of wild flowers, such as the cyclamen, crimson anemone, &c. on a rich soil. We arrived in three hours at a village called Cafringee, situated at the southern extremity of the valley of Adjeloun ([45]). There are sufficient fragments amongst the rubbish and buildings of Cafringee, to judge that there was once a Roman town or some edifice on the spot. We remained here about an hour, and then sending our baggage by the vale to the village of Adjeloun, proceeded, in company with the principal sheikh of the neighbourhood, to the Callah-el-Rubbat, situated on an eminence, an hour's distance, to the N. N. W. About half way up the hill we were shewn a great cave, the most extensive natural one we had seen in Syria; this, supposing the valley to be the same with that alluded to in Joshua, ch. x. may be the " cave of Makkedah," in which the five kings hid themselves and were buried ([46]). The Callah-el-Rubbat commands, by its elevated situation, a most extensive view of the plain of the Jordan, the lakes Asphaltes and Tiberias, and a vast tract of country in every direction. Indeed, for several days we had constantly this castle in view from all quarters ([47]); unluckily for us the weather was too hazy to admit of our profiting much by our situation, but we fully examined every part of the castle, which is entirely of Turkish architecture, and has an Arabic inscription in one of the centre stones. The building is constructed out of the rock, which they have excavated to form the moat round it. There are some tanks near the castle; we now descended to the village to pass the night. We found at Adjeloun, in the court of an old mosque, a Roman mile-stone, and in the building itself, several fragments of Roman sculpture. The next day we went to Souf. Half an hour from Adjeloun, we passed through the village of Eugen; here are some Roman tombs, and two sarcophagi cut in the live rock. From hence, towards Souf, the road led through a narrow and picturesque valley, with a fine view of the Callah-el-Rubbat behind us. This vale opens at the further end into a plain, whence the road passes through a woody, uneven country, extremely beautiful. We here observed the arbutus of unusual dimensions and great beauty; one tree was about six feet in circumference, and in some instances the Valonia oak and arbutus andrachne were growing grafted together, probably from the acorn or berry of either having accidently dropped into some crack, in the stem of the other, and taken root. The Roman road is discernible beyond this situation as you advance into a plain near Souf; we saw likewise three Roman mile-stones near to each other; it is about two hours and a half's journey from Adjeloun to Souf.

Souf is a small village situated on the side of a hill; in the vale below it is the source of a stream which runs through the valley. At the fountain is an imperfect Greek inscription, and in the ruins of a church in the village a mile-stone, together with an altar having a Greek inscription. At three in the afternoon, we went with three armed natives of Souf to Djerash. We took the shortest road over the hills one hour, and after taking a general view of the ruins, returned to Souf by a valley to the N. E. of that place. This latter road is very beautifully wooded, having a picturesque stream, with its banks covered with the oleander. We found the natives of Souf a very rude set of people, constantly annoying us with stories about the dytchmaan or enemies, alluding to the Salhaan Arabs, who are encamped near Djerash; but it was evidently done with a view to induce us to have a strong escort from the village every time we went to Djerash, which as they asked two piastres per man each trip, was well worth their pains. In consequence of these remonstrances, we went on the 15th to Djerash again, accompanied by the sheikh of Souf and ten of his people. We employed ourselves in taking measures of one of the temples; our attendants annoyed us in the meantime with officious remarks on their use in protecting us against the

Arabs; two of these arrived, armed with pikes, during the day, but they were very quiet; they were on horseback. We returned to Souf rather early in the afternoon.

March 16. It rained hard; but had it been fine, the natives of Souf refused to attend us any more to Djerash, telling us the old story of their terror of the dytchmaan. In the afternoon the interpreter and soldier of Mr. Bankes arrived, with a young prince of the Benesuckher Arabs and ten of his men, all of the Benesuckher tribe; the prince, named Ebyn Fayes, was attended by his mace-bearer; the mace was of iron, hollow, and about two feet long. They were well mounted and armed, and as they galloped down the hill, firing their pistols and manœuvring with their spears, they made a curious and interesting appearance. Mr. B. had dispatched the interpreter and soldier from Adjeloun to the Benesuckher camp, for a guard to conduct us to the several places lying east of the Jordan and Dead Sea which we wished to visit: he had a list of places which Burkhardt had visited, and a note of his route by Kerek and Wady Mousa, intending to pass from the latter to the south end of the Dead Sea, and by Hebron to Jerusalem. The interpreter, however, could only make a bargain with these people as far as Kerek, as they said they were at war with the tribes beyond that place, and could go no further. As the places beyond Kerek were the most difficult to reach, there seemed to be little hope of performing the whole of the journey under their protection; we, however, kept them for the present, hoping if we reached Kerek with them, to pursue the further object of our journey by other means; as the natives of Kerek are mostly Christians, and in the habit of making their pilgrimage to Jerusalem by that route. Volney mentions a report by the Arabs, " that there are to the S. E. of the lake Asphaltes, within three days' journey, upwards of three hundred ruined towns absolutely deserted;" several have large edifices with columns. " This was the country of the Nabatheans, the most potent of the Arabs and of the Idumæans, who at the time of the destruction of Jerusalem were almost as numerous as the Jews." (See Josephus.) Our lamented friend Sheikh Ibrahim, in his notes, tells us, that three days south from Kerek are the ruins of Petra, the capital of the ancient Arabia Petræa in the Wady Mousa. Here are wonderfully fine temples cut out of the rock, and more than two hundred sepulchres, to use his own expression. Since the death of the poor sheikh, no European living has seen this place, or indeed the others to the S. E. of the Dead Sea.

Hebron is the ancient Kiriath Arba, and is said to be of higher antiquity than Memphis; to see the site of such a place, exites no ordinary degree of interest. Abraun or Hebron, is the place also where Abraham died. I should now add, that the bargain which we had made with the Arabs was to conduct us safe to Kerek for one thousand piastres; Mr. B. unfortunately paid the whole of the money before hand, and to this unfortunate step, we owe all the tricks they afterwards played us.

March 17. We quitted Souf with our Arab guard, and passed the day in taking further measurements at Djerash. We took this day the length of the main street, the Ionic oval, the length from the S. W. gate to the Circus, which is outside the town to the south, and the dimensions of the stadium and the triumphal arch near it. It was this day that the Arabs got Mr. Bankes to pay *all* the money in advance; and from that moment commenced a regular train of impositions and falsehoods on their part, which in the end induced us to leave them and to abandon the journey. In dealing with these Arabs one should never pay them a para in advance, but make a bargain *that they are to receive nothing till they have completed their contract.* They are a cunning set of people, who behave well when they are kept in check in this manner, but when once paid before hand, they continue to teaze you for more and more, and having received the whole of their agreement, consider you as completely in their power, and do as they like with you; perhaps few people, since Lady H. S. spoiled the market for Palmyra, have succeeded so quietly with them as we did in going to that place; and this was certainly owing to our persisting in not paying a para till the agreement was fulfilled. In the evening we went to Katty, a village one hour distant to the W. N. W. of Djerash, in a beautiful situation, and passed the night there; the Arabs here made a demand for money to feed themselves, and we agreed with them for thirty piastres per day.

March 18. This morning we went to Djerash again; we measured this day the walls of the town, and the principal temple. Some of the Salhaan Arabs appearing in the distance, our Benesuckher friends galloped off to parley with them, and we were constantly teazed about the dytchmaan. We went this night, by the desire of our conductors, to a small camp of the Salhaans, lying one hour and a half to the S. E. of Djerash, although they had been continually calling them their enemies. On our way they tried to persuade Mr. Bankes to give a horse to the Salhaans; this request took place in a valley about half an hour distant, and was made in a very mysterious manner; on Mr. B.'s refusal they at first stopped to go somewhere else, but finally conducted us to the camp, and said they would give up one of their own horses, and even went through the ceremony of parading their present before the tent we were in. We never ascertained whether the animal was really given, but we rather suppose that it was an attempt to induce us to part with one of our horses.

March 19. We went in the morning to examine a place called Reashy, but found nothing there of consequence. The Benesuckher Arabs refused to go to Djerash excusing themselves by saying they had fear of the Salhaans; we were very anxious to finish the plan of Djerash, no person having ever published on these antiquities; and, indeed, they were unknown to Europeans until Mr. Seetzen, discovered them in 1806. I believe Mr. B., Sir W. Chatterton, Mr. Leslie, Sheikh Ibrahim, and Mr. Buckingham, are the only Europeans who have seen them. The Arabs were now told that Mr. B. would give up the researches he had intended to make on the banks of the Zerka in favour of Djerash; we accordingly set out in that direction with three of the Arabs, the remainder proceeding with our baggage from the Salhaan camp to Katty. In our way we ascended to Nebi Hood, a village situated on the summit of a hill S. S. E. of Djerash; the village is at present deserted; we found a Greek inscription on an altar in the court-yard of one of the houses. We were going from hence to Djerash, when one of the three Arabs who accompanied us, and had advanced a little in front, returned to inform us that six of the Salhaan Arabs were waiting near Djerash to intercept us. We accordingly returned to join some more of the Benesuckher party, after having first reconnoitred ourselves. We soon met the remainder of our escort on their way to Katty, and therefore proceeded with them all, and had a parley with the six Salhaans, who after some conversation, in which they said that " they wanted heads not money," told the Benesuckhers that we had *their* permission to remain at Djerash till the afternoon of this day. Our Benesuckher friends and ourselves laughed heartily at them, as the circumstances of their being enabled to bring only six armed men to intercept us, was no great proof of their force. We endeavoured to finish with Djerash this day, but though we were at work till dark (Irby and myself measuring, and Mr. Bankes drawing, copying inscriptions, &c.), we could not complete our work : in the course of this day Mr. Bankes was robbed of his cap by an armed Arab, who, having concealed himself amongst the ruins of the great theatre, stole on him unperceived while he was drawing. We passed the night at Katty; just as we arrived a great quarrel ensued between the Benesuckhers and the villagers; the scene of action was on the house tops. It is a custom in the country, that travellers are fed gratis for one night; and there is in every Turkish village a room to lodge them in. European travellers generally, on departing, make a present to the servants, at least equivalent to what has been consumed. I mentioned before that we had given the Arabs thirty piastres per day to feed themselves; these cunning fellows, however, wanted to force the villagers to feed them, although they had been there before on the night of the seventeenth, and as the poor people had to feed the horses gratis, as well as the men, it came very hard on them. We paid for every thing *we* got, and we assured the villagers that the Benesuckhers were provided with money to pay for all *they* had. Perhaps a more curious battle never took place, for although there was much appearance of anger and rage, and the greatest noise and confusion imaginable, men, women, and children, all mixed together pell mell, nevertheless all were cautious to avoid blows, and the affray ended to the advantage of the poor natives, the Benesuckhers retreating from the village; we remained.

March 20. We went in the morning to Djerash

to finish our operations; a very singular circumstance here took place. Mr. B.'s soldier of Damascus, whom he had always found very useful and attached, had within the last two or three days very much altered his manners and conduct, and exhibited strong proofs of fear, both in words and actions; on our way to Djerash he told us frequently that the Arabs would strip us all of every thing, and while Mr. Bankes was taking a copy of an inscription near the north gate of the city, the soldier very slowly, without making any further observations, walked off, and was never seen any more. On the preceding evening he said he had received information of some Damascus troops having arrived at a town a few hours' distant, and asked permission to depart in the night to procure them for our protection; however, he did not then go, as the villagers persuaded him to the contrary; we, of course, imagined that this was his object in setting off, and that finding the report false, he had returned to Damascus. Two spy-glasses were found missing, which Mr. B. had with him, to make presents of; we did not, however, suspect him of any roguery in this respect, although he certainly took the interpreter's gun, leaving his own, which was worse. This theft we afterwards heard was proved; the Arabs denied having taken the telescopes. It was two o'clock in the afternoon before we had completed our operations at Djerash, which place I will now add a few remarks on. It has been a splendid city, built on two sides of a valley, with a fine stream running through it; the situation is beautiful. The town has been principally composed of two main streets, crossing each other in the centre at right angles, like Antinoe. The streets have been lined with a double row of columns, some of which are Ionic and some Corinthian; the pavement is exceedingly good, and there is an elevated space on each side for foot passengers; the marks of the chariot wheels are visible in many parts of the streets. Djerash, supposed to be either Pella or Gerasa, but in some respects answering to neither, can boast of more public edifices than any city we have seen. There are two theatres, two grand temples, one, as appears by a Greek inscription, dedicated to the sun, like that at Palmyra, and not unlike that edifice, being constructed in the centre of an immense double peristyle court. The diameter of the columns of the temple is five feet, and the height of just proportions; the capitals are Corinthian and well executed. One singularity in this edifice is a chamber under ground, below the principal hall of the temple, with a bath in the centre. Five or six inferior temples are scattered about the town; and a magnificent Ionic oval space of three hundred and nine feet long, adds greatly to the beauty of the ruins. The scene of the larger theatre is nearly perfect, presenting a singularity very rarely to be met with. There are two grand baths, and also two bridges crossing the valley and river. The temples, and both theatres, are built of marble, but not of a very fine sort. Three hundred yards from the S. W. gate is the Circus or Stadium, and near it is the triumphal arch. The cemetery surrounds the city, but the sarcophagi are not very highly finished; upwards of two hundred and thirty columns are now standing in the city. There is to the N. E. about two hundred yards distance, a very large reservoir for water, and a picturesque tomb fronted by four Corinthian columns; near it is also an aqueduct. These ruins being overgrown with wood, are objects of considerable interest. There are numerous inscriptions in all directions, chiefly of the time of Antoninus Pius; most of them are much mutilated; but the one I alluded to about the Temple of the Sun, was on the propyleum of that edifice, which has been a grand piece of architecture. On the whole we hold Djerash to be a much finer mass of ruins than Palmyra; the city has three entrances of richly ornamented gateways, and the remains of the wall, with its occasional towers, are in wonderful preservation.

At two o'clock in the afternoon, having completed our operations, we set out in a S. W. direction for Szalt; we observed pieces of columns apparently unfinished. In an hour and twenty minutes we crossed the Zerka. The Zerka is a small stream winding prettily in a narrow valley, which is not so well wooded as its neighbourhood; there are the ruins of a small building on the front of the hills near the ford. Ascending from the rivulet, we passed some small sites of towns, possessing nothing of interest; and at five in the evening, we arrived at a camp of the Salhaans, where we passed the night.

March 21. This morning we proceeded, but shortly coming to a cross-road, the Benesuckhers said they could not reach Szalt that day, but would conduct us to a camp of their own; although we knew that Szalt could be only a few hours' distant. We positively insisted upon being conducted to Szalt, which after much altercation, in a lonely valley, they consented to do, if we would give two hundred piastres to each of the sheikhs of Szalt, Heshbon, and Kerek, and also to themselves five days' advance of the thirty piastres per day for their food. All this was positively refused, excepting the thirty for the present day; and after much altercation, the Benesuckhers evidently endeavouring, both by their threats and the place they had chosen, to frighten us into a compliance with their demands; the dispute ended by our going to Szalt, accompanied by the prime minister (as we termed him) of the young prince, the chief of the party. The minister is a very great rogue; he is not an Arab born; we thought he had much the appearance of a Levantine, of some European extraction.

It was he who put every bad idea into the minds of the prince, and the rest of the Arabs, who were mostly very young men, and not so well versed in the art of cheating as himself. We did not succeed in getting to Szalt, until the interpreter, and the Arab Seys who took care of our horses, impelled by fear from the gesticulations of the opposite party, had given the Arabs sixty piastres, for which we told them they must themselves be the sufferers. The prince and his gang now quitted us for their own camp, as they said they could not enter Szalt, because they were at war with the inhabitants. On leaving them we crossed over some small hills into a spacious valley called Bayga, in which are the ruins of a large square cyclopean building ([48]), perhaps a fortress; on quitting which, we ascended to the westward over some rugged rocks, and thence descended into, and passed through some picturesque vallies most beautifully wooded. From these vallies we again passed over some barren soil, and descending again, went by some vineyards, inclosed with stone walls ([49]), on our left; whence turning round a point to our right, we had the first view of Szalt, not ten minutes' distant from us, the castle is situated on the top of a hill, on the sides of which is the village, nearly surrounded by a valley and by high hills, forming a very picturesque object. The neighbourhood abounds in vineyards and olives; we found the finest raisins here that we had seen in Syria. The inhabitants of Szalt are numerous, and more than one-third of them are Christians. We arrived, wet through, both ourselves and baggage; the people shewed us great attention, drying our clothes before the fire. We first went to the travellers' room, but were soon after conducted to the house of a Christian. Bad weather continued the whole of the next day, but on the twenty-third the weather became fairer. In consequence of the treachery of the Arabs, we wished to quit them, and if possible to get the natives of Szalt to conduct us to Kerek. The minister made some extravagant demands, however he was paid up to the day, and told, his services and those of his comrades were no longer wanted. He now tried all he could to induce us to consent to go to their camp, but this would have been a very imprudent course to have taken; finding that he could not either by good or bad words prevail on us to go, he said that his companions would take care that we did not stir from Szalt, until we consented to his scheme, and went off in a huff. To shew how little we feared these threats, we took a walk of two hours, and returned in the evening. Some of the Mahomedan natives of Szalt insulted us on our return. We wished next day to go to Amaun, but the son of the sheikh of the town told us his father was gone to the Arabs, and that he could do nothing till his return.

March 24. This morning the shiekh's son and five other guards accompanied us to visit some places in the neighbourhood. The first was a village called Athan, situated two hours' distant to the N. N. W. There is a ruined village here; we saw nothing of antiquity; but in ascending from it we observed some sarcophagi cut out of the live rock. We afterwards went to a place called Gilhad Gilhood, where there are two old tombs; one of them has since been used as a Christian chapel, the natives say it is the birth-place of the prophet Elijah. There are some sarcophagi cut out of the rock, and other antique remains. We visited, in all, five ruined villages, which serve at least to shew that the country lying five or six miles to the north of Szalt, was once more populous than it is at present. Szalt has been thought to be the ancient Amathus, but we are more inclined to believe it to be Machærus where John the Baptist was beheaded. The country in general is extremely beautiful and woody. On our return to the town we found a black messenger from the Benesuckher prince, inviting us to go to his camp and adjust our differences, but we had determined, if on the following day the natives of Szalt refused to conduct us to Kerek, to recross the Jordan and proceed to Jerusalem, where we could adopt other measures for carrying our plans into execution.

March 29. In the morning, at nine o'clock, we quitted Szalt in the middle of a great dispute amongst the natives, whether they should or should not deliver us up to the Arabs; the tops of all the houses were covered with women and children to see the result of the fray. On quitting the house, our interpreter was missing, and after waiting some time, we found him concealed behind the door crying bitterly. The first object we saw was the prime-minister whom we had not seen since the twenty-third; he was in company with the black and another Benesuckher Arab, and mounting their horses they immediately joined us, and endeavoured all they could to persuade us to go the wrong road, in which they were joined by all the Turkish natives of the place, who kept bawling to us that we were going wrong. Fortunately, when walking out one day, we had made inquiries, and had discovered the right road to Jerusalem; and, therefore, in spite of all their remonstrances, we took the road we knew to be right. The plan of the prime-minister was, doubtless, to lead us to the Arabs' camp and there detain us till they had got what they wanted. As we ascended the hill, followed by the Arabs, we soon got a view of the Dead Sea, the neighbourhood of Jericho, and the plain of the Jordan. We had given out that our intention was to pass through Jericho on our way to Jerusalem;' but having deviated from the right path shortly after we began to descend, we had an idea of passing on to Bysan. One of the Arabs quitted us on the brow of the hill; and when they saw that we had ceased to keep the road to Jericho, the black man went also. Both these people had, no doubt, for their object, to give information to the prince and his party of the track we had taken. A little after mid-day, when we had nearly descended into the first part of the plain, to the minister's surprise and vexation, we turned short off to the ford of the Jordan, which we saw in the distance, and quitted him, notwithstanding his numerous remonstrances; indeed, had we continued long in the track we were going, we should soon have been amongst some of the Benesuckher camps, as we had shortly before passed five or six small camps, but of what tribe we did not know. We now pushed straight for the Jordan, and reached its banks about two o'clock. At the foot of the mountains we observed some very singular, interesting, and certainly very ancient tombs, composed of great rough stones, resembling what is called "Kitt's Cotty House in Kent." They were built of two long side stones, with one at each end, and a small door in front, mostly facing to the north; this door was cut in the stone. All were of rough stones apparently not hewn, but found in flat fragments, many of which are seen about the spot in huge flakes; over the whole was laid an immense flat piece projecting both at the sides and ends. What rendered these tombs more remarkable was, that the interior was not long enough for a body, being only five feet; this is occasioned by both the front and back stones being considerably within the ends of the side ones. There were about twenty-seven of these tombs, very irregularly situated. The plain, from the foot of the mountains, is about half way pretty level, but barren; thence it becomes very rugged, consisting of a quantity of hills, vales, and deep chasms, in a dry soil, of a very white appearance and of a saltish nature; this continues to within a quarter of a mile of the river's bank; whence the rest is a rich, flat plain to the margin of the river, which is in the bottom of a deep ravine, beautifully wooded, and so overgrown, that the stream is not seen till you are close to it. The Callah-el-Rubbat bore N. E. half N. from the ford. Hereabouts it would be interesting to search for the twelve stones put for a monument of the Israelites passing the river ([50]). The water was too high for us to search, and indeed we were not very much at our ease, with the idea of the Arabs being in chase of us. We were detained till nearly three o'clock before we could cross the river, which, to our surprise, was very much swollen; an Arab, on horseback, arrived shortly after us, and as he had no baggage, was well mounted, and likely to be acquainted with the ford, we requested him to cross first, that we might profit by his example; but like the peasants on Mount Lebanon, he refused to lead the way. We therefore crossed one at a time, the rest directing the progress of the one passing, from an eminence on the banks; the stream was exceedingly rapid, and so deep, that we were obliged to swim our horses, which, with our fire-arms, baggage, and ourselves on their backs, was no easy task. We all, in consequence, got completely wet through, and all our papers, pocket books, &c. were totally spoiled. From the river we pursued a direction W. N. W. for two hours, into a rich valley; there was no road or track. On the right we passed a great cave, with an artificial door; a labourer misinformed us, and directed us up the course of a deep, dry torrent in search of a village. After wandering in vain till dark, we came to the termination of the valley, and saw no signs of any path or habitation. It now came on to rain hard with thunder and lightning, and we were glad to take shelter for the night in a cave used occasionally by the shepherds ([51]).

March 26. At day-light we were forced to retrace our steps, and return to the valley we had left, which we found was called Wady Zeit (Oil Valley); it has a village called Agrarba, which we did not see. On entering Wady Zeit, the peasants all came out, armed with six muskets and their instruments of agriculture. Seeing six people mounted, issuing out of an uninhabited valley, so early in the morning, they had mistaken us for Bedouins. We got from them a guide for Nablous. From these people we learnt that the Arabs had crossed the Jordan the preceding evening in chase of us, and failing to get any information, had returned to the other side of the river. We, therefore, owe our escape to the circumstance of having lost our way. We observed that this rich valley ends abruptly at the foot of the hills to the westward. We followed the principal road, which led us out by a ravine, to the S. W., and continued in this track till about eleven o'clock, when we crossed over the hills to the westward. About half an hour after mid-day, we reached the village of Bait Forage, situated by the side of a rich extensive plain, having six other villages on its borders, many olive yards, and much corn. We were glad to get some breakfast here, after an abstinence, with the exception of a few dirty raisins, which we found in the bottom of one of our hourges, of twenty eight hours, since our leaving Szalt. We remained till two o'clock, and then proceeded for Nablous, about two hours' distant. In twenty minutes we arrived at a ruined village called Kaffer Baiter, about which are several old Roman tombs and tanks. In one of the former we found some dead bodies concealed, with the mouth closed with rubbish. From thence we went to Nablous, the road leading us by Jacob's Well, a short distance from which a valley in a southern direction, unites with the one in which Bait Forage and the six others are situated. Maundrell says, these rich valleys are supposed to be " the portion of land given by Jacob to his son Joseph." Nablous is the ancient Sychem; we went to the summit of Mount Gerizim, and found the ruins of a large town, with a tank, near a conspicuous sheikh's tomb.

March 28. We quitted Nablous, and reached Jerusalem on the twenty-ninth. For an excellent description of Nablous, and also of every thing that the pilgrim is shewn at Jerusalem, I must refer you to Maundrell; we took his book in our pockets, and visited every place which he mentions, most of them three different times; once by ourselves, once as Ciceroni to Lord Belmore and his family, and once in the same capacity to Mr. Legh, the same who published his Journey in Nubia. We have been to Bethlehem and St. John's, were in the sepulchre at the Greek Easter, and saw the celebrated trick of the holy fire, &c.

May 1. We set off with all the pilgrims, escorted by the governour, and a body of troops, for the Jordan. The sight was most impressive. The immense number of Christians from all quarters, the various costumes of Greece, the Copts from Egypt, the Abyssinians from Æthiopia. Some of the pilgrims on camels, with double cradles on their backs; some on mules, in cradles also; some on horses; some on asses; amounting to about five thousand, presented a most curious and interesting scene, winding along the road amongst the hills, in a line as far as the eye could reach, and sometimes appearing through different openings in the mountains, in two or three divisions. In the evening we arrived at the camp near Jericho. We could find no remains of the Hippodrome which Josephus places here.

May 2. At two this morning we started by torch-light for the Jordan, which we reached at seven o'clock A.M. Here we found all the pilgrims bathing in the river, men, women, and children, all mixed together. They immersed their clothes in the river, and collected boughs off the trees, and bottles of the water to take home, in commemoration of their pilgrimage. Maundrell mentions all these circumstances with much fidelity. We now went, attended by two Arabs, to the Dead Sea, and bathed in it; the water was as bitter and as buoyant as people have reported; those of our party who could not swim, floated on its surface like corks; on dipping the head in, the eyes smarted dreadfully, and we were much surprised to observe, on coming out of the lake, that the water did not evaporate from the body as is the case on emerging from fresh water, but adhered to the skin, and was greasy to the feel or touch. At night we reached Jerusalem. To morrow,

May 6. We start with two Arabs to make the tour of the Dead Sea, and search for the sites of the cities that are known to have stood in that direction. Our party will consist of Mr. Legh and his attendants, Mr. Bankes and his, and Captain Irby and myself. We shall muster altogether eleven people, including two Arabs; we have plenty of arms. We calculate that the trip will take us about three weeks; we have all dressed ourselves as Arabs of the desert, to excite less observation. Lord and Lady Belmore and their party have been here about three weeks; they came from Cairo by land, having taken the same route that we took. Their party is very strong, and they had a famous Arab chief's brother to protect them. They are all now attiring themselves as Arabs, and are going to visit Baalbec, Damascus, &c. after which they embark in their yacht for Europe. The friars of the convent had a serious dispute in the Holy Sepulchre the day before yesterday; they were performing one of their ceremonies, when the Greeks attacked them, and wounded several. There has been much disputing before the governour in consequence, and this letter will go with the Tartar who carries their complaints to Constantinople

In Maundrell's time there was a similar fray between the Greeks and Latins; and the jealousy has existed ever since. In short, seeing how well this author has described every thing worthy of notice in this part, we abstain from any particulars, and only beg you to remember that there is not any one object mentioned in Maundrell's publication that we did not carefully examine. When this tour is over, we embark at Acre for Cyprus, and thence follow the route mentioned in former letters. I cannot, however, quit Jerusalem without mentioning a singular adventure we had here. There is amongst the sepulchres which travellers have designated as " the Tombs of the Kings," an excavated vault with an oblong portico, thus:

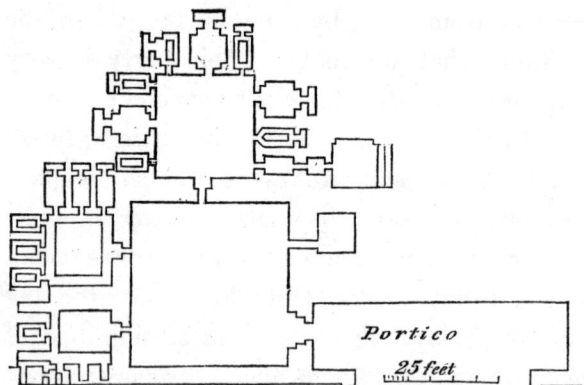

the only visible entrance to this tomb is at one end of the portico, while from its construction there is every reason to suppose that a corresponding entrance would be at the other end, which is now filled with rubbish. Mr. Bankes was so thoroughly convinced of this, that when at Constantinople he used every exertion to procure a firman authorizing him to excavate and ascertain the fact, but in vain. We now endeavoured to obtain permission from the governour of Jerusalem to dig there ourselves; but failed also in this instance. Now, as we could not procure any legal authority to commence our labours, we determined on prosecuting the undertaking secretly in the night, and accordingly purchased privately some pickaxes and implements of husbandry. Late in the evening we quitted the town singly, from different gates, to avoid suspicion, and assembling at the rendezvous after dark, found we mustered a working party of ten persons, viz.—Messrs. Bankes and Legh, Captain Corry and ourselves, together with five servants, including two of Lord Belmore's sailors, whom his lordship had allowed to assist us. We divided our party into two watches, and worked hard four hours at a spell during the whole night, digging and clearing away the rubbish. We were obliged to spare one of the servants as a centinel near the road side, to apprize us of the approach of any one. In the morning we had got down about ten feet, when we came to an immense block of stone, apparently in the very spot where we expected to find the entrance to the tomb. As we were unable even to move this mass, we returned to the city tolerably fatigued, having been obliged, for want of spades, to clear away the rubbish with our hands. The next day Captain Corry, Mr. Bankes, and Mahomet his janissary, by the advice of Lord Belmore, succeeded in breaking the stone by heating it, and pouring cold vinegar on it; but shortly after this was done, our proceedings were discovered by some Turks, and reported to the governour, who put a very effectual stop to our exertions, by ordering the whole of the portico to be walled in.

We send you a certificate from the reverendissimo, of our having visited all the sacred places at Jerusalem.

LETTER V.

TOUR TO PETRA, AND ROUND THE DEAD SEA.

Departure from Jerusalem to Bethlehem.—Hebron.—Albaid.—Jellaheen Camp.—Pass south end of the Dead Sea.—Arrive at Kerek.—Mahanna.—Medin.—Hamahta or Mote.—Gharundel.—Shobek.—Petra.—Mount Hor.—Return through Shobek.—Kerek.—Ghorney's Village.—Rabbath Moab.—Beit Kerm.—Diban.—-Medeba.—--Oom-i-Rasass.—--Heshbon.-—Arrag-el-Emir—Szalt.—Rabbath Ammon.—Djerash—Katty.—Rajib.—Tiberias.—Mount Tabor.—Arrive at Acre.

CONSTANTINOPLE, September 12, 1818.

OUR last letters, dated Jerusalem, in the beginning of May, will have apprized you of our intended tour round the Dead Sea and to Petra. We were then on the point of setting off; but before I quit the former place, it will be necessary to inform you of the obstacles which presented themselves, and the difficulties which we had to surmount before we commenced our journey. It had for some time been the wish of Mr. Bankes to undertake this tour, as the only two Europeans who had ever been at either Kerek or Wady Mousa (Valley of Moses or Petra) are both dead, viz. Sheikh Ibrahim and Mr. Seetzen. Both these travellers, indefatigable as they were, performed this trip alone and in disguise, and were consequently obliged to conceal their papers, and make all their observations by stealth, which must necessarily have rendered their remarks very brief and cursory, compared to what they would have been had the writers being unrestrained. Seetzen travelled as an Arab, calling himself Moosa, but never reached so far as Petra.

Although we are of opinion that Mr. Bankes, solely, could not have succeeded in accomplishing this journey without his junction with Mr. Legh and ourselves, still he has the merit of being the first person travelling as a European, who ever thought of extending his researches in that direction; and from his profound knowledge of ancient history, as well as his skill in drawing, he was by far the best calculated to go on such an expedition. To give you an idea of the difficulties which the Turkish government supposed there would be for an Englishman to go to Kerek and Wady Mousa, it is necessary to say that when Mr. Bankes applied at Constantinople to have these places inserted in his firman, they returned for answer, " that they knew of none such within the Grand Seignior's dominions;" but as he and Mr. Frere, the British minister, pressed the point very much, they at length referred him to the Pashaw of Damascus (who equally averse to have any thing to do with the business), passed him on to the governour of Jerusalem. This latter tried all he could to dissuade us from the undertaking, though Mr. Legh gave him a handsome spy-glass to induce him to assist us. He advised us to apply to Mahommed Aga, the governour of Yaffa; as the communication between Egypt and Mousa, being usually through Gaza, which is under Mahommed Aga's government, it was supposed that he would have the greatest influence over the Arabs about Wady Mousa, as possessing the means of punishing them for any bad acts they may commit, either by stopping their supplies from Egypt, or by making prisoners of such of their people as come within his reach. The governour of Yaffa, however, not only evaded the affair altogether, but by way of putting a stop, if possible, to our journey, ordered back the horses which he had lent us. Another visit to the governour of Jerusalem seemed to promise as little as the preceding; we all four called on him; on this occasion, a former motsellim, who had been twenty years in office, and was sitting with the governour, pledged himself to us that the Arabs are a most savage and treacherous race, and to prove it, added, that they think Frank's blood a good medicine to cure their women with when sick, and that they would make use of our's for this purpose. All that we could procure from the governour was a promise to write to the sheikh of Kerek to apprise him of our coming, and when we went with the Greek pilgrims to Jericho and the Jordan, the governour sent a man to us, whom he thought fit to call the sheikh of Kerek, congratulating us on the obstacles to our going to that place having been overcome. This man, however, was no sheikh, and we suspect the motive of the motsellim for sending the counterfeit, was to obtain another present. Finding that there was no getting any of the public authorities to compromise themselves for our safety, or indeed to render us any assistance, we determined to proceed, trusting to our numbers and force, and to try our fortune with the sheikh of Hebron. Each of the party procured a Bedouin Arab dress of the most ordinary description, and we all bought horses for the journey, except Mr. Bankes, who was already provided with them. Our party consisted of Mr. Legh, having with him an interpreter, a Tartar from Constantinople, and a seyes (hostler). Mr. Bankes had with him a soldier of the pashaw of Egypt, and ourselves a Christian Arab servant. We had for our guide a cultivating Arab, dwelling near Jericho, named Mahommed, and a man belonging to Hebron. We took the precaution of having as little baggage as possible with us, sending the greater part to Acre with one of Mr. Legh's servants. We each gave ourselves an Eastern name for the journey; Mr. Legh was called Osman; Mr. Bankes, Halleel; Captain Irby, Abdallah; and myself, Hassan. Our dress consisted of a frock and drawers of very coarse linen; the frock being fastened round the waist by a red, leathern girdle, about four inches broad. The head-dress was a handkerchief of mixed silk and cotton, coloured with broad stripes of alternate red, green, and yellow; this was doubled into a triangular form and thrown over the head, to which it was attached by a double girdle of brown worsted rope. One corner of the handkerchief hangs down over the back of the neck, and the remaining two cover the ears, and come down over the shoulders; these latter, when the weather is cold, the Arabs tuck up under the chin, and cover the whole face with the exception of the eyes. Over all we had the woollen abba, which we had long worn, and which we procured at Yaffa; it is described in the Aleppo letter. For arms, we had amongst us six muskets, one blunderbuss, five brace of pistols, and two sabres. Our money, consisting of small gold coins, was concealed in leathern belts round the waist next the body.

May 6. We left Jerusalem two hours before dark in the evening, our party consisting of eleven persons, all mounted. We slept at Bethlehem.

May 7. At eight this morning we proceeded for " Solomon's Pools," and thence down the valley towards the Mountain of the Franks, which we ascended; we found it hollow on the top, with walls round it, and four towers, all much in ruins. This post is said to have been maintained by the Franks forty years after the fall of Jerusalem; though the place is too small ever to have contained even half the number of men which would have been requisite to make any stand in such a country; and the ruins, though they may be those of a place once defended by Franks, appear to have had an earlier origin, as the architecture seems to be Roman. From the Mount of the Franks we could see part of the Dead Sea, and the situation of Kerek on the other side of it. We took from hence the following bearings by compass; Abou Jane, a village on the right, between Bethlehem and the Frank Mountain, West.—Bethlehem, N. W.—St. Elias, N. N. W.

We now proceeded to see the labyrinth. On approaching it, we left our horses at the ruins of a village called Hariatoon, and proceeded on foot by the side of the cliffs on the southern side of a deep and picturesque ravine to the mouth of the cave, which runs in by a long, winding, narrow passage, with small natural chambers or cavities on either side. We soon came to a large chamber with natural arches of a great height, from this last there were numerous passages leading in all directions, occasionally joined by others at right angles, and forming a perfect labyrinth, which our guides assured us had never been thoroughly explored, the people being afraid of losing themselves. The passages were generally four feet high, by three feet wide, and were all on a level with each other. There were few petrifactions where we were; nevertheless the grotto was perfectly clear, and the air pure and good ([52]). In the large chamber we found some broken pottery, by which it would seem this place had been once inhabited, probably serving for a place of concealment. We observed a few English names written with charcoal. We now returned to the horses, and proceeded to the southward, to visit the ruins of Tekoa. They stand on a slight eminence, commanding several bursts of the Dead Sea, and cover a considerable extent; this place was built by King Rehoboam, and is coupled with Bethlehem ([53]). We could not find the remains of any distinct temple or public edifice, though there are a few fragments of columns. From Tekoa we passed through a plain of cultivated land, and thence all the way to Hebron, through a much prettier country than that near Jerusalem, the sides of the hills being richly studded with shrubs and dwarf trees in full verdure; the prickly oak, arbutus, and Scotch fir, were most prevalent. About five o'clock we passed a village called Sipheer by the side of a well cultivated valley; there are about nine Roman sepulchral caves near this village. From hence we crossed a rugged road into another plain, where are the ruins of a small old convent; the Jews call this "the House of Abraham." We now ascended considerably, and passing between numerous vineyards, with a watch-tower in each, some of which appeared to be antique ([54]), we reached Hebron at dusk: according to Moses, this place vied with the best cities of Egypt in antiquity ([55]). "Hebron was built seven years before Zoan in Egypt." Josephus makes it not only older than Zoan, or Tanais, but also than Memphis. Here Abraham, Sarah his wife, and Isaac died ([56]). We had this day passed many camps of cultivating Arabs, and found them all very civil; towards the evening some of them invited us to pass the night in their tents. The sheikh of Hebron received us very kindly. We were lodged in a small praying-room attached to the khan; it was furnished with mats and carpets for us, and we were presently served with a beverage we never saw before in the east,—" warm rice milk with sugar;" it was given before the coffee, and in the usual small cups. The Turks of Hebron having little intercourse with Europeans, are extremely jealous of Franks, not one of whom is allowed to live in the town, and I believe very few travellers have ever visited it; in consequence we found it impossible to gain admission into the mosque, in which is said to be the " tomb of Abraham." The lower part of this building is very curious, evidently antique, being formed of great stones, some of which are upwards of twenty-five feet in length; it has sixteen pilasters on each side, and eight on either end, without capitals, excepting a sort of ornamental summit which extends along the whole building, and is a species of cornice. Above this is a continuation of modern masonry, The approach to the entrance of the edifice is by a long flight of steps between it and other ruined buildings which stand on its S. E. side; the buildings being constructed lengthways, N. E. and S.W. I imagine, however, that these outside walls only inclose the court which surrounds the mosque, and are not part of the mosque itself. The town of Hebron is not of large dimensions, though its population is great; the country is cultivated to a considerable extent all round it. The streets are winding, and the houses unusually high. We visited a manufactory of glass lamps, which are exported to Egypt. We were told by the governour of Hebron, that there is a regular party of pilgrims who set out from thence every year, without any escort, depending entirely on their own strength; they contrive to fall in with the great Damascus hadj near to or at Mecca, which is at the distance of thirty days. From a merchant of Cairo we ascertained the existence of great ruins at Abdi, in the Desert, to the south, about three days' distance.

The governour of Hebron made no difficulty the first evening about our going to Wady Mousa, Kerek, &c. saying, " it was an easy matter, and he would undertake it." On the seventh, however, difficulties began. We visited, after dinner, the house of the Jewish priest; there are one hundred Jewish houses in Hebron; we found their quarters excessively clean, and neatly whitewashed; that of the priest was particularly so; it had a very nice divan, and commanded a fine view of the country; they were very civil, and offered us letters to the places we were going to. The governour now made a motion to retire, that his presence might not prevent our drinking wine, but we declined it. We were now shewn the synagogue. On our return to the khan, a watch was given to the governour by Mr. Bankes; he took it without making any remark at the time, but shortly after retired, when a man arrrived to say, that the motsellim was not content with his present, and had given it to the Jewish priest. Soon after, however, another person made his appearance, saying, they wished to arrange the bargain for paying the guides, &c.; three hundred and fifty piastres were offered, but immediately rejected, as three thousand five hundred would have been at the first offer. After a second visit, however, to the Jew's house, where we again found the governour, four hundred piastres were paid down, and we were to proceed the following morning. After supper the governour called at the khan; he appeared to be shuffling a good deal, altering the order in which the different places were to be visited, but as he did not make any material change, *still placing Wady Mousa before Kerek*, we did not much care about it. He looked at all the firmans, boyourdees, &c. but did not appear to pay as much respect as is usual to the firman of the Grand Seignior. On observing Mr. Legh's Constantinople Tartar, he said, but in a good humoured way, that a few years ago, if a Tartar had come to Hebron, he would have had his head cut off, but that it was not so now. We requested to proceed on our journey early in the morning, but he said that arrangements could not be made for our departure till an hour after sun-rise, and soon after he left us.

May 8. The governour did not make his appearance till after eight o'clock, bringing with him the three men who where to be our conductors and the Jew priest. He was shortly after followed by his brother, who had previously desired to know, in an indirect manner, why he had not received a present as well as his kinsman? Lastly came all the law officers, and heads of authorities; these, together with the motsellim, advised us to go to Kerek direct, and not to Wady Mousa. The governour, however, told the guides that there were four hundred piastres for them if they chose to take us; but these people, who had, in all probability, previously received instructions to the purpose, declined conducting us. Finally, seeing there was no dealing with such people, we mounted our horses and left the town; but in justice to the governour, it should be mentioned that he not only returned the four hundred piastres but the watch also. When we had got outside the town we held a consultation together, and finding it impossible to proceed alone, without a guide to shew us the road, we sent into the town to say we would consent to visit Kerek first, in the mean time we retired to a neighbouring olive-yard; by the return of the messenger, the governour sent to say, " he would have nothing at all to do with our concerns." A man on horseback, however, offered to shew us the road, and we accordingly proceeded with him, but had scarcely advanced half an hour, when two men came galloping, and hallooing after us; upon which we stopped in a corn field, and sent Mr. B.'s soldier, Mahommed, into the town, as the governour wished to communicate with us; this was about mid-day. Towards two o'clock, Mahommed the Arab, who had accompanied us from Jerusalem, quitted us; about three o'clock, Mahommed the soldier returned with one of the Jews, the sheikh having consented to send us to Kerek, with a letter to Sheikh Yousouf. We likewise received for a guide one of the Jellaheen Arabs. In return for this, the motsellim demanded three hundred piastres, or the watch and two hundred: the watch and one hundred and fifty were given, as the former was of more value than they imagined; two roubees (five piastres and half) were given to the Jew, and he begged one for the governour's brother; a roubee is less than two shillings value. We now proceeded; the country was ugly enough, but tolerably well cultivated with corn. We passed several ruined sites; one of them, which they called Hagee, stands on a hill, and has a large square building, which appeared partly perfect; we had also another on our right, and a column which was too far off to be visited; we afterwards passed two Roman excavated tombs, with porticos in front, not very interesting; there are two ruined sites near them, to one of which they probably belonged. About five o'clock we reached a well where we gave our horses water, as the camp where we were to sleep was ill provided; they called this well " Al-baid;" there are two pools; one is small with green water, the other a fountain in the live rock. There is an ancient site N. W. of it, with a wall of large construction, and some good masonry; there are slanting passages cut in the live rock, leading to caves which have probably served for tombs.

We reached a Jellaheen camp of thirty tents about dusk; it was situated on the summit of a hill, an unusual position, as they generally pitch their camps in vallies. The harems, or parts of each tent allotted to the women, were covered in front, and they all appeared particularly veiled. We found these people uncommonly poor in appearance, though they had plenty of sheep, goats, and camels; the camp was placed in a desert country, the cultivated land having ceased about the well Al-baid. We had mutton for supper, but were obliged to find our own coffee. An Arab journeyman tailor arrived, and was employed making coats of sheep-skins, which he dyed red with ochre or some such substance. These people said that in years of scarcity they retired to Egypt. Our course from Hebron to this camp was in a south-easterly direction.

May 9. We wished to make a bargain with the Jellaheens for conducting us to Wady Mousa; but nothing would induce them to consent. After much bargaining, they agreed to take us to Kerek, if we would give seventy-five piastres to the chief, and ten to each of five guides, who were to accompany us with muskets. Though these people had for a long time refused to accept this sum, still, when it was agreed to, they all began fighting who should go. After we had descended from the camp, we offered five hundred piastres if they would conduct us to Wady Mousa; but nothing could induce them to consent. They said they would not go if we would give them five thousand piastres! observing, that money was of no use to a man if he lost his life, and that the people of Wady Mousa were a treacherous and cruel race, and always attacked strangers by firing at them from rocky eminences, which concealing the hostile party gave the others no chance. Seeing that all our endeavours were fruitless, we ceased to press the subject. We had left the camp about eight, and at nine we arrived at a well where we watered our horses. We remained here about half an hour and then proceeded, when our conductors began their tricks, by saying they would go no further unless we gave them five hundred piastres, the sum which we had offered if they would conduct us to Wady Mousa; after much altercation, seeing that nothing would bring them to reason, we said we would go alone, which they defied us to do. We, however, left them, taking a course in the desert about S. E. by compass, and trusting to our good fortune to meet with some Arabs or tents in our way. We had proceeded in this manner till eleven o'clock, when one of the guides appeared in the rear, waving his turban, and making all possible signs for us to stop; in about half an hour two of them joined us; we were greatly rejoiced to see these people return, but affected to be quite indifferent about it, to prevent further roguery. We now proceeded a little more to the south, and about mid-day had a delightful prospect, from a slight eminence to the left of the road, of the southern extremity of the Dead Sea, together with the back-water and plain at the end of it. From this view it appeared evident that the lake Asphaltis must be of much less length than is usually supposed, or than all the ancient authors have made it out to be. We now began a continued descent into a deep, barren valley, and did not get to the bottom till near five o'clock, passing with considerable difficulty over a path so rugged, barren, and full of great stones, that we were obliged to lead our horses; at last we reached the ruins of an old Turkish fort, standing on a single rock to the left of the road; to the right there is a pool of green water, tolerable for horses, but of which we were glad to drink, though an old man was stripped and washing himself in the middle of it at the time; it was about fifteen feet wide; we filled our skins. Further on the same side, the cliff is excavated at a considerable height with loop holes; possibly meant for a post from whence a sentinel might see all passengers, and apprise the castle of their approach. It would appear that this was a sort of "barrier" where duties were levied on the passers by; they call the place El Zowar. From hence we passed through a pretty, gravelly ravine, with bushes of the acassia tree, and another bearing a small stone fruit, resembling in taste a dried apple; the Arabs call it "doom," though it is a very different tree from the doom palm. About six we entered the great plain at the end of the Dead Sea; for about a quarter of an hour we had a few bushes, and afterwards found the soil sandy and perfectly barren. On our right we had a continued hill of a sandy soil, running in a S. E. and N. W. direction towards the middle of the plain. At dark we stopped for the night in a ravine at the side of this hill, much against the wishes of our guides, who strongly urged the want of water, and the dread of the dytchmaan, as inducements to make us proceed. We collected a quantity of wood which the Dead Sea had thrown up at high water-mark, and endeavoured to make a fire in order to bake bread, as we had flour. The wood was, however, so impregnated with salt, that all our efforts were unavailing, and we contented ourselves with drinking the flour and water mixed, which though not very palatable, still served to appease our hunger. All night our guides, not being able from fear to sleep themselves, endeavoured to prevent us by alarms of the dytchmaan.

May 10. In the morning, at the very dawn of day, we proceeded across the plain; for the first half hour we had still the before-mentioned sand hill on our right. We found, exclusive of the saline appearance left by the retiring of the waters, several large fragments of clear rock-salt lying on the ground, and on examining the hill, we found it composed partly of salt and partly of hardened sand. In many instances the salt was hanging from cliffs in clear perpendicular points like icicles, and we observed numerous strata of that material of considerable thickness, having very little sand mixed with it. Strabo mentions "that to the southward of the Dead Sea there are towns and cities built entirely of salt;" and although such an account seems strange, yet when we contemplated the scene before us, it did not appear very improbable. The torrents, during the rainy season, had brought down immense masses of salt, and we observed that the strata were generally in perpendicular lines. Leaving this hill, the plain opens considerably to the south, and is bounded at the distance of about eight miles, by a sandy cliff, from sixty to eighty feet in height, which runs directly across and closes the valley of el-Ghor, thus forming a margin for the uttermost limits of the Dead Sea to the southward, when the waters are at their greatest height. We were told that the plain on the top of this range of cliffs continues the whole way to Mecca, without any interruption of mountains. It appeared to us that the mountains to the westward of the Dead Sea gradually decreased their height to the southward, while those to the eastward continued to preserve the same altitude as far as the eye could reach, and appeared to be of a reddish colour, resembling granite. Leaving the salt hill, our track led for an hour and a half across the barren flats of the back-water, now left dry by the effects of evaporation. We passed six drains into that part more contiguous to the main sea, where the water still remains; some were wet and still draining, others were dry. These had a strong marshy smell, similar to what is perceivable on most of the muddy flats in salt water harbours, but by no means more unpleasant. I imagine this to have given rise to the unfavourable reports of the ancients, of the disagreeable smell of the waters of the Dead Sea. The water on the main body of the lake is perfectly free from any smell whatever. We now entered into a very prettily wooded country, with high rushes and marshes; leaving these, the variety of bushes and wild plants became very great, some of the latter were rare and of remarkable appearance. Occasionally we met with specimens such as none of our party had ever seen before; a botanist would have had a fine treat in this delightful spot. Amongst the trees which we knew, were various species of the acassia, and in some instances we met with the dwarf mimosa; we saw also the doom mentioned above, the tamarisk, and the plant which we saw in Nubia, and which Norden calls "the oschar." There was one curious tree which we observed in great plenty, and which bore a fruit in bunches, resembling in appearance the currant, with the colour of the plum; it has a pleasant though strong aromatic taste, exactly resembling mustard, and, if taken in any quantity, produces a similar irritability in the nose and eyes to that which is caused by taking mustard. The leaves of this tree have the same pungent flavour as the fruit, though not so strong. We think it probable that this is the tree our Saviour alluded to in the parable of the mustard seed, and not the mustard plant which we have in the north; for although in our journey from Bysan to Adjeloun, mentioned in the Jerusalem letter, we met with the mustard plant growing wild, as high as our horses heads, still, being an annual, it did not deserve the appellation of a tree; whereas the other is really such, and birds might easily, and actually do take shelter under its shadow. We passed the wild cotton plant amongst an infinity of others that we neither knew how to name or describe. In about half an hour we arrived at the little river, which is marked in the map, and improperly placed as Futlet; the people told us it was the "Nahr-el-Hussan," or horse river; there was plenty of corn cultivated in the open grounds between the bushes. Our guides told us not to talk, lest we should be discovered by the natives; but this was what we wanted, in order to get something to eat, the flour and water of the preceding night not having been very satisfying. We soon met some of the natives taking in the harvest; they were a wild looking people, and wore leathern aprons reaching to the shoulders, a dress we had never seen before; they addressed us with great civility, and on our telling them we were soldiers of the Aga of Jaffa, going to Kerek, they said they wished that more would come amongst them, as they were much oppressed by the Bedouin Arabs, whom they described as a bad set of people, caring neither for God nor the saints. They took us to their bivouack in the thicket, saying that their village was some way off, and that they were only remaining here to take in the harvest. They gave us to eat some doom, dried and pounded into a sort of coarse meal and mixed with butter; we found it exceedingly good; about half an hour afterwards they brought us bread, butter, and milk. We were annoyed here with large horse flies, which were in great numbers, and some of our animals were streaming with blood. We were told at Kerek, that these flies were " a plague sent by the Almighty at the destruction of Sodom and Gomorrah;" and that no Turk when praying, is allowed to kiss the earth in the customary manner there. These people are called Goahrnays, and differ materially, both in manner and appearance, from the Arabs, as well as from the natives of the towns; they adhere to one place of abode, and cultivate the land in its vicinity. They do not live in tents like the Arabs, but build huts of reeds, rushes, and canes; they construct their buildings contiguous to each other, and form their villages in the shape of a square, with only one entrance for the cattle, which are thereby prevented from straggling, and are kept more collected for protection during the night. These people treated us very hospitably, which they would naturally do, taking us to be soldiers of so powerful a man as Mahommed Aga; but we never heard any other than a bad character of them ever after. Before we left them, they threshed out some corn with great sticks for our horses. The women commenced the labour, but as they could not work *and hide their faces* at the same time, the men dismissed them and did the work themselves. On our taking leave, we offered them a handsome reward for what we had had, but they absolutely refused, and held out for a good quarter of an hour, notwithstanding all our intreaties; at last we threw the money amongst them, when a most furious battle took place about the sharing it out. We could not refrain from laughing most heartily at so odd a scene, and at eleven, left them fighting and beating each other most furiously. We now crossed the Houssan, our horses smarting from the bites of the unmerciful flies, and, unable to resist the refreshing influence of the water, quietly laid down in the middle of the stream, leaving us no alternative but to dismount and walk out. We proceeded along the foot of the mountains which bound the east side of the plains, and continued in this manner till near five in the afternoon, our track being rugged and barren in the extreme, with innumerable fragments of red and grey granite; grey, red, and black porphyry; serpentine stone; beautiful black bazalt, breccia, and many other kinds of stone scattered in every direction, all fragments from the neighbouring mountains. Hereabouts it may be presumed the ancients procured materials for the numerous handsome columns which one meets in Syria, and which now adorn the Turkish baths, mosques, &c. Mr. Seetzen, who was a geologist, if he passed over this ground, must have been highly gratified. Our two companions each made a collection of all the specimens they met; some of these were beautiful, and well adapted for vases or other ornaments. We found that the chain of mountains under which we were passing, was chiefly composed of sand stone and bad marble, together with the various kinds of minerals we have just alluded to. At five, we had reached the tongue of land, which lies between the south end of the Dead Sea and its back water, and from hence we began to ascend the hills on our right. At six we stopped in a beautiful shady ravine, watered by the river " el-Derrah," whose banks are covered in profusion with the palm, acassia, aspine, and oleander, in full flower and beauty, perfuming the whole place, and rendering it a most delightful spot, particularly when contrasted with the desert appearance of its neighbourhood. I will here insert the relative distances of the principal objects we passed this day. Two hours and a half from the western cliff of the Ghor to Rahk, the first salt water drain; half an hour to Saphy, the nahr-el-Hussan; three hours from Saphy to the Honey river, nahr-el-Assel; from thence two hours to Mare; and two more to el-Derrah. We passed the night here; Mr. Bankes took a sketch of the spot, as well as another of that part of the Dead Sea which is seen from it.

May 7. This morning, shortly after the rising of the sun, we began to ascend the mountain; the road was very rugged and stony, with hardly a vestige of vegetation. The rocks were of a dark sand stone. On our left we had a deep ravine. Three men shouted from a height, and asked " where we were going to?"—they had only one gun. About eight o'clock we reached a commanding point, where the road turns in its ascent; here we had an excellent bird's-eye view of the south end of the Dead Sea and the backwater. The delay which it required to take a sketch of it, gave time to the men who had hailed us to come up; two were blacks; they accosted us very roughly, examining us with great scrutiny. They were armed, but still we were as strong as they were. Mr. B., Captain I., and myself were alone, with our Christian Arab servant, Mr. Legh and his party having gone on before; the strangers remained with us. As soon as the sketch was finished we began to ascend to the rest of our party, and in our way were surprised by seeing five other men armed with muskets, peeping from behind a rock at some distance from the road; after hesitating a moment, they came forward and questioned us about where we were from, and the place of our destination, &c. By this time we had joined Mr. Legh and the rest of the party; and having satisfied the curiosity of these people, we proceeded on our journey.

Our road now was on a sort of terrace scarped out on the side of a romantic ravine, with vast fragments, each as large as ordinary houses, which had been detached from the sides of the precipices, and were lying below in confused heaps; some were only just cracked off, and not yet fallen. About a quarter of an hour after meeting the strangers, we came to a small deposit of water, under an olive tree; here some of the same men we had left behind came up with us again, and called out loudly to us to come and eat bread with them; but as we did not like either their appearance or suspicious conduct, the rest being visible in the distance running to join their comrades, we continued our route. As we advanced we began to find ourselves in corn fields, with cattle grazing in the valley on our left, through which the river Souf Saffa runs towards the Dead Sea; we observed the ancient mill-courses, but the river itself was hid by the richness of the vegetation on its banks, especially the purple oleander in full blossom. The castle of Kerek now opened on our view, but not any part of the town, which lay behind the castle. The ruins of the castle on this side, that is the N. W., present two principal features; a great mass at the south angle of the town, and more towards the north, a great building called the Seraglio of Meleh-e-daher. Between these two is the only gate of entrance on this side— the west. It is no more than a plain, narrow arch, with an Arabic inscription over it. This entrance is very singular, the arch being fitted to the mouth of a natural cavern, or passage in the rock, which leads with a winding course *through* a high ridge of the natural rock, and has thus been made to serve as the principal avenue to the fortress. The form of the hill on which it stands is not advantageous on this side, being rather long, and the buildings upon it straggling. High as the town stands, it is commanded on every side. In our approach we descended moderately into the narrow valley at the foot of the castle hill, where runs a stream with a narrow line of gardens on its banks, in which we observed olives, pomegranates, and figs, with some vegetables. The ascent from hence is steep and toilsome to a great degree; we all dismounted, entering at the cavern gate already described. We soon found ourselves within the walls, with the seraglio on our left hand; the houses do not come very close upon that part of the fortification, though there are ruins and foundations every where, seeming to announce a greater population formerly. There are the remains of a mosque with pointed arches, and an octagonal minaret, with a band of black stone carried round it; the whole is much in ruins. Over the door-way is a pointed horse-shoe arch, like that at the khan at Bysan, and amongst the ornaments is the cup repeated several times. The houses are of one story, terrace roofed, and so constructed that the roof at the back is in many of them not above the level of the ground; in many instances you may pass over the houses, even on horse-back, without being aware of it; some have a little court before them. The principal chamber in the best buildings has two arches thrown across it, on which rest the rafters, not squared and very smokey; a small hole in the centre serves as a vent for the smoke; and immediately under it, in the centre of the room, is a circular hearth with a rim raised round it. In the recesses between the opening of the arches are raised platforms which serve as shelves; there are also receptacles for corn, with bung-holes in the manner of casks, for taking it out. The walls are daubed with rude paintings in red and black; we observed particularly an attempt to represent a horseman, and in another instance a kneeling camel, with a man mounting ; this will give you some idea of them. There is not a vestige of antique work in the castle; but considered as Mahommedan architecture it is good, especially at the south end, where the live rock has been cut down in order to detach the ridge from the fortified hill to which it was by nature joined; it is probable, that the hollow, furnished materials for the building above, as at the "Callah-el-Rubbat," &c. Two sides are left standing up across this artificial ravine in the manner of walls. The most remarkable thing that we observed was a christian church within the enceinte of this part of the castle; it is very ill constructed with small stones, and some pillars are laid horizontally into the masonry, forming quite a contrast to the Mahommedan work, which is of large, well cut stones, laid in regular courses. This church has small narrow windows, and a circular end and arched front, resembling that at Tiberias, which is called the house of St. Peter, but which is evidently posterior to the first Mahommedan conquest, as there is an Arabic inscription built upside down into the present walls. It is probable, therefore, that both are the works of crusaders; and as Godfrey de Boulogne took Kerek, and called it Mons Regalis, it is likely he or some of his successors may have built this church. There are remains of paintings of large groups of figures on the stuccoed walls; one seems to have represented a king in armour, another the martyrdom of some saint, by twisting out his bowels; and there is an imperfect inscription with letters of the Gothic form; the castle seems to be more ancient than the church. We found a few remnants of antiquity; first, a small column of deep coloured red granite, well polished but ill shaped; secondly, another of grey granite; and thirdly, not far from it, close to a well, a great wing of sculpture in basso-relievo, bearing much resemblance to those which we used to see attached to the globe in Egyptian buildings. We could form no conjecture what it was; there is no trace of the globe; possibly it was the wing of a Roman eagle; its length was seven feet, and breadth four. Near the mosque are three capitals, resembling no regular order of architecture, but similar to some that we saw at Hamah. We found two Greek inscriptions, but neither of them interesting. The place is well supplied with water by numerous cisterns. Sheikh Yousouf was absent at a camp about half a day distant, passing the honey-moon with a young Arab wife he had just married; we were very well received by Abdel Khader the sheikh's son. Few questions were asked, and less attention excited than might have been expected. There was a merchant from Damascus; the distance on a swift dromedary is five days, but the ordinary travelling is ten; another merchant was present from Hebron. The women here do not cover their faces at all, or keep out of sight; the utmost they ever conceal is the point of the chin. We sat and conversed familiarly with several of them. We were well fed, horses and all, for nothing. Amongst our company was a man who represented himself as a great traveller; he had been to Tripoli, Aleppo, Mardyn, and Cyprus; he had never been to Constantinople, and said he had no desire to go there, because he had heard that a man could not beat out his pipe without burning the house down, and that justice was so strictly administered, that persons ran the risk of having their heads cut off while they were talking in the streets. It appeared that few if any of them knew the name of the present sultan; it was also a curious example of the liberty of speech in these remote corners, that our traveller added, " that they respected the sultan because it was their interest to do so, on account of commerce, &c. but as to the pashaws, they were no better than themselves, and that it was a degradation to stand in a humiliating posture with the head stooped, and the hands hidden before one of them, when here, a man might loll at his ease in his own house, and stand or lie in whatever posture he pleased." We were invited out to dine one day at a Turk's house, and treated to a boiled sheep, without bread or any thing but the meat itself; this custom we first observed at Szalt, and to our great annoyance found the same practice on the east side of the Dead Sea, &c., not only amongst the Arabs, but in the towns and villages. It appears that the Wahabees made an attempt on Kerek, and were encamped for several days on the heights south of the town; one of them was sent in to parley, and the inhabitants boast of having killed about forty of them, from the loop holes of the castle, with their muskets.

May 13. Towards the evening, Sheikh Yousouf arrived without his bride; he was a fine looking old man, apparently nearly sixty years of age; he had lost his front teeth, and his beard was white. Upon being told the motive of our travelling in these mountains, he asked rather roughly " whether this was the country of our fathers;" but we soon found him to be a plain, blunt, honest old man, of very few words. Only one man in the town could read, and he was the Greek priest. He read to Yousouf the letter from Sheikh Eysah of Hebron, without which we have reason to think we should have had a much colder reception. It appears that the governour of Jerusalem deceived us, and never wrote to Kerek at all. We got the Greek priest to be a mediator in arranging the business with Yousouf, and as we had for once to deal with an honest man, we had not much trouble; for in fact the negociations the next morning were hardly closed, before the horses were ordered to be in readiness. Four hundred piastres were paid down as the price of a safe conduct through several places, specified in a list, as far as Wady Mousa, to the south, and Szalt, to the north; but the old man could not undertake to free us from some incidental tributes on the road. Yousouf pledged himself to accompany us through the whole journey. During our stay at Kerek, we saw the dowry of a young woman going to be married paid at the sheikh's house; it amounted to about one hundred piastres, in white Constantinople money. This I believe was only what she was to wear as her head ornament, as the ladies here decorate their foreheads with dollars and different kinds of money; sometimes they hang down to both ears, and must really be a great weight. The amount of a dowry is sometimes as high as four purses! There are about as many Christian inhabitants in Kerek as Turks; the former boast of being the strongest and bravest, and are able to produce four hundred men bearing arms; they are on very good terms with the Turks, and appear to enjoy equal freedom with them. It was said that at the time of the French invasion in 1799, there was a project for disarming the Christians and driving them out, which the present sheikh prevented. We saw, and were recognised by several of the suspicious people we had met on our road the day of our arrival; they asked us why we did not stop to eat with them? but their concealment, and the manner in which they first came upon us, looked as if they meant no good.

May 14. In the afternoon we set out from Kerek to the southward; we descended into the ravine which surrounds the place, having the main body of the castle close on our right hand, the base of which is here a slanting casing of the rock, as at Homs, Aleppo, &c. From hence we passed up the side of a narrow ravine to its very end. On each side there are caverns and wrought tombs, in one of these, which had all the appearance of a natural grotto externally, we observed places for sarcophagi; it is probable that the whole is the burying place of the ancient town. In this ravine is a spring of water, with a small Turkish building. Here we were joined by an Arab from Djebal who had been forced away by the Wahabees, and had lived and served with them; almost all his fellow-townsmen had been put to death. He was upwards of a month at Dareyah their capital, which he describes as being larger than Kerek. The houses are all built with mud, and the fortifications with mud and palm trees; there are cannon on the walls, and an immense treasure buried and concealed. He said that the Wahabees prefer silver very much to gold, for which no reason was given. He confirmed the relation of their horses being fed at times entirely on camel's milk. He was mounted on one of that breed, a light leggy horse, very different in appearance from those of the Arabs; he seemed to think the Wahabee sect very general, and said, jokingly, that Sheikh Yousouf was one, which the other denied with apparent horror. We ascended into a country of downs, with verdure so close as to appear almost turf, and with corn fields at intervals; the rock did not appear much, though the surface was sprinkled over with stones. In an hour and a half we reached a camp belonging to the people of Kerek under Sheikh Ismayel, Yousouf's youngest son. After taking some leban (sour milk) and bread, we proceeded to the N. W. about a mile, across some corn land, to a ruined village called Mahanna. The ruins are mostly of ordinary buildings, but it is evident that one them was a Christian church; another ruined site to the westward was called Dgellgood. The following ruined sites are visible from this point: Machad. Arti-Musshut, (which is the single building supposed to be tomb of Abou Taleb) Harnahta or Mote, Toor, Howeeh, and Marrowhich. We now went due east for an hour to Medin, from whence we could see the following ruined sites, most of them on slight eminences; Imriega, E. by N., Hadad, Shirsee, Behlanah, Suhl, and Nehkill; in short, the whole of the fine plains in this quarter, are covered with sites of towns on every eminence or spot convenient for the construction of one; and as all the land is capable of rich cultivation, there can be little doubt that this country, now so deserted, once presented a continued picture of plenty and fertility; hereabouts, I think, must be the quarter alluded to by the Arabs, when they made the report to Volney, which we have quoted in page 310 of this volume. Having finished our survey of the neighbouring ruins, we returned to Ismayel's camp were we slept.

May 15. This morning we were off before sunrise; the same downs continued, with numerous Arab camps in various directions, the ruined sites being still in numbers all around us. In about a quarter of an hour we came to the site of Hamahta or Mote, which last name, signifying death, it acquired from the circumstance of all its inhabitants having been exterminated by Abou Taleb, whose reported tomb "Musshut" is a building upon arches which appears to stand in a small enclosure, and is less than half a mile distant to the W. S. W. Near this spot, on another site, is a Roman mile stone, inscribed in Latin, the number of miles is thirteen, but the rest is indistinct; it may have been thirteen miles from Rabath Moab. In about a quarter of an hour from Mote we reached the tomb of Sheikh Jaffa; here the Mahommedans of our party alighted, and entered the tomb to pray. Mahommed the soldier reported, that within there are two dark granite columns well polished. A quarter of an hour farther we reached the camp of Sheikh Sahlem, who commands, or has influence at Djebal, and over all the country as far as Shobek. This man asked us two hundred piastres in lieu of thirty, which old Yousouf said was all he would require; we refused it, and Sahlem persisting, we mounted and retired to a distance. Upon our leaving the tent he expressed a wish " that we might be struck with lightning before we reached Kerek," and added, " that had not Sheikh Yousouf been present with us, he would have had our money by force." Finding, however, that he did not follow us, we sent back to offer one hundred and fifty piastres; the bargain was struck, and the money counted into his hands. He mounted his horse, and accompanied us, together with his son, a fine young man; in about half an hour he brought us to another large camp of his tribe of thirty-three tents. Having remained a short time here, we proceeded, unattended, about two miles off, to visit the ruins of Dettrass. At the foot of the hill are many cisterns; the ruins are indistinct and of no interest, except three piles of buildings which appear to be of Roman architecture; one was evidently a temple; the others, though large, are so much ruined that it is impossible to ascertain what they have been intended for. While we were examining these ruins, the people from the neighbouring camps flocked round us in considerable numbers, but were very civil. We returned to our camp in the evening, and observing that all the old women, and many of the young ones, had their cheeks covered with blood and scratches, we enquired the reason, when they told us they had mourned the day before for a death in one of the harems.

May 16. We recovered the track which we had quitted, where it falls into a deep ravine, having a very steep descent, with wild rocky sides. At the extremity, where we turned out of this track to follow a more rapid and deep descent into the Wady-el-Hussein, we saw upon our left hand, on the height, the remains of an ancient fortress, which seems to have commanded the pass; it is of dry masonry and large stones, and is no doubt antique; they give it the name of Acoujah. As we proceeded downwards, there was on our right hand a great quantity of lava and black volcanic stone, which seem to have issued from the side of the neighbouring ridge of mountains. We presently reached the little rivulet called el-Hussein at the bottom of the ravine; it has in some parts pitted for itself a very deep channel in the live rock, and there are occasionally some small though picturesque water-falls from ten to fifteen feet in depth. The oleander, as usual upon the banks of most streams in this country, was in great beauty and profusion. From hence we began to ascend a more steep acclivity than that we had come down. It is observable that the sides of this valley, el-Hussein, are more destitute of verdure than the plains above. We continued our course up a slanting hollow, in which we noticed the stones gathered into heaps, and converted into fences ([57]), in a manner which seemed to denote an abandoned cultivation, and we observed a field or two of corn near a little spring. A little further, upon the point of a sort of promontory of high land that stands between the fork of two vallies, are the ruins of a small but rich building; little or nothing is left entire, but all the fragments are lying in confusion. There are rich Arabesque borders of vines and foliage, much in the taste of Diocletian's buildings at Palmyra, or the triumphal arch; the capitals are not of any regular order but fanciful, and loaded with ornaments; the execution is sharp and neat. The temple appears to have fronted S. S. W. and there were apparently four semi-columns attached to the front wall, three feet five inches in diameter; amongst the fragments are pieces of columns of a smaller diameter. There are other vestiges of building near, but nothing that gives reason to suppose there ever was a town. The great dark mass of volcanic matter which we passed, bears from these ruins N. N. E., it is called Elabahn, the name also of a clear spring issuing from the rock a little south of it. There are old millcourses in the low ground. The ascent still continued for a short distance, when we reached the level of the high plain in a S. S. W. direction. There were reapers at harvest who informed us that the chief persons of the town of Djebal were encamped; this induced our two sheikhs to turn to the southward, out of the great track, towards the encampment. At one in the afternoon we reached a camp of thirty-three tents, having travelled six hours this day. A feeble attempt was made here to extort money from us, under pretext that the sheikh was independent. Upon our mentioning our intention of visiting their village, Djebal, which was two hours' distant, objections were raised against it; we therefore left it for our return. There were some small specimens of volcanic stone in the valley near to the camp, but not in any great quantity. Near this we visited some uninteresting ruins called el-Hagre. Some person in this camp secreted a spy-glass which had dropped from Mr. B.'s pocket; after confessing that it had been found, and was in the camp, they attempted to force him to give an extravagant reward; this was obstinately refused; and by the intervention of Sheikh Yousouf it was recovered with difficulty for two rubees. We supped as usual on mutton without bread.

May 17. After we had set out, Daoud, a relation of the sheikh of Kerek, missed his sword, and rode back for it, but the rogues refused to restore it to him. Passing to the southward, in about half an hour we saw the village of Bsaida about a mile distant. About and beyond this village there are hanging woods of some extent, but the trees are small and stunted. From hence, in three hours, the descent becoming more considerable as we advanced, we reached the ruins which are called Gharundel. They are situated on the slope of a hill, and their extent is very considerable. Towards the centre of the ruins are the remains of two parallel rows of columns, of which three are standing in one row, and two in the other; their diameter is two feet; none have capitals. There are also, near to this spot, fragments of columns of three feet diameter; the capitals appear to be bad Doric. A spring of water runs close below these ruins from Gharundel. We passed up a valley to an Arab camp; they were Bedouins of the tribe of Hadjeyah. While we were eating with these people, there was an alarm of an enemy having made an attempt to carry off some of their flocks; the women cried out and waved their scarfs from the top of the hill. We rode up, but saw nothing of the offenders. Our road was S. W.: a white line in the desert, at a considerable distance to the left, as far as the eye could reach, was pointed out as the hadj road to Mecca. We noticed three dark volcanic eminences, very distinguishable from the sand; the lava that had streamed from them forms a sort of island in the plain. Close on the right of the road was another volcanic mount, covered with scoriæ of a reddish colour, and in substance extremely light; there was much black porous stone below it. Soon after we found an ancient Roman high-way paved with black stone; the edges, and a line down the middle, were paved pretty regularly. On the right, at intervals of about a mile and a half, are ruins of square stone buildings; there was a cistern in one; they were probably intended for the use of travellers. Proceeding in a direction parallel to this road, we saw, towards the S. W.

a large mass of ruins, called el-Gaig, they offered no interest. We found three mile-stones; the last only was erect; all the inscriptions were effaced by time and the climate. From one of these stones we turned off, about a mile from the road, to examine some buildings, but found them Turkish; one had an Arabic inscription over the door, which appeared ancient. Some crosses were scrawled about the door, and these signs are three times repeated + λII. Seeing some Arabs in the distance to the south, we returned to our companions, who had advanced just a Roman mile on the road, and were waiting at another mile-stone. We still followed the road till we came to the edge of a deep vale; here we deviated to the right and descended, the original road continuing straight on the height. At the S. W. end of the vale rises a hill, upon which stands "Showbac," like a gigantic mound; at its foot the ground is terraced out in gardens, and thickly planted with figs, now in full verdure. There are numerous caves in the side of the hill. Nearly at the bottom of our descent we passed a sheikh's tomb, called "Abou Soliman;" from thence passing a ravine, or dry torrent, we approached the town on its N. E. side by a zig-zag path, which seems to be the only one leading to it. It appeared, in ascending, that almost all that side of the castle-hill has once been covered with buildings. Our coming seemed to excite considerable alarm amongst the natives, who stood on the walls shouting and throwing down stones. We entered at an iron gate, when the inhahitants seeing Sheikhs Yousouf and Sahlem with us, received us very civilly, some crying out, " Go and get bread and fire-wood for these poor fellows, who are come to lodge a night amongst us." We were carried up to a sort of divan, in the open air, constructed upon what seemed to be the ruins of a church of crusade architecture, standing due east and west. The tower of the castle has Arabic inscriptions, which appear to be Mahommedan. The three doors of the supposed church are square topped, and the centre is under a pointed arch, and has more the air of Mahommedan than Christian architecture. We had a boundless view from hence, comprising the whole skirts of the desert, with the volcanos which I have mentioned above. They brought us figs split and dried, of a very green colour and delicious flavour, tasting nearly like the fresh fruit; they told us they were on the trees when the pilgrims arrived at Damascus; this was in December. We observed much kissing in the salutations; each party generally kissed the right cheek first, once, and then the left four or five times ([58]). They evinced their good breeding by suppressing their curiosity as to the motive of our journey, whence we came, &c. though evidently labouring under the greatest anxiety to know every particular. Shortly after our arrival we had an alarm of Arabs; thirty men, with guns, immediately ran out; others were driving in the flocks in great haste; they returned in about an hour, saying, the Arabs had killed forty of their goats, but that they would find an opportunity of returning the compliment; we, however, doubted the truth of this story. The name of Showbec, or Shobek ([59]), occurs among those who sealed the covenant. After a diligent search for inscriptions, we found one in the architrave of the principal door; it is in Latin, and though imperfect, Mr. Bankes made so much of it out, as to leave no doubt that it was a work of one of the Frank kings of Jerusalem. One of their principal strong holds, somewhere in this direction, was called " Mons Regalis;" this might either be Kerek or the place in question; though Miletius, extending their conquests still further, says, that this name was applied by them to Petra, and, relying upon some passages in Diodorus Siculus, says, that it seems to have borne that name in the historian's time. The most remarkable circumstance is, that while the interior parts of this church are in the pure Gothic style, resembling that of the same age in Europe, the ornaments of the inscribed door-way are of the genuine eastern taste, exhibiting that border of convex fluting which is common in Turkish buildings; the pointed arch itself inclines slightly inwards at the bottom, in the manner of a horse-shoe. The construction also has more of the Oriental than the Norman style; the transome, in lieu of consisting of a single stone, being composed of many, irregularly locked together by dove-tails and angular inequalities. In the walls, at the gates of Antioch, are similar examples, and certainly of the time of the crusades.

May 18. Quitting Shobek, we wound by a spiral road into the valley which surrounds it, and observed that the road had been artificially deepened, and in some parts cased with masonry. From thence we ascended to the S. W. and soon came to a brook which contributes to the watering of the gardens below Shobek, but is not the only supply. Upon the two parallel ridges, between which our road led, we noticed stones arranged in fences and gathered into heaps, denoting the boundaries of former fields and gardens; and near the spring there appeared the remains of a village. Our course continued much in the same direction, between west and

S. W. for about a mile, gently ascending till we arrived at a large Arab camp, situated upon high ground, with still higher about it. Here we expected to have found the Sheikh "Mahommed Abou Raschid," that is to say, Mahommed the father of Raschid, which latter is the title he goes by. Most of the sheikhs have some denomination of this kind to distinguish them. "Mahommed Aga," for instance, is called "Abou Nabout," (the master of the mace or stick;) and in Sir Sydney Smith's transactions at Acre, his principal coadjutor, the pashaw, was surnamed "Dgezar," which in Turkish signifies the "Cutter." Shobek, and the great district about it, is commanded by Abou Raschid. He was absent on our arrival, but messengers were dispatched to acquaint him with our coming. From this camp another was in sight to the southward, and beyond it a hill thinly scattered with trees. We were hospitably received. A merchant whom we had known at Hebron came in, complaining that he had been robbed of twenty-eight pieces of merchandise, which he had brought to sell amongst the Arabs; they had lain hands on the goods in their tents, and refused to give them up. At particular seasons of the year the inhabitants of these tents are in the habit of passing to Cairo, whence they carry on the charcoal trade between that city and Suez; they said it was a five days' journey from hence to Suez. In passing into Egypt they usually take the road to Gaza, though they seem to be fully aware of the shorter way; it is, therefore, only for the sake of security. At Shobek there was a small caravan to set out the morrow of our departure; the owner of it offered to carry us to Cairo in eight days, computing two to Gaza, and eight thence.

May 19. About noon Abou Raschid arrived. He was a middling sized man, with very marked features, having a dark complexion, very dark beard, black piercing eyes, and aquiline nose; his age might be about thirty. He was full of life and spirits, but rather a man of few words, and plain, unaffected manners. We had always heard him spoken of in great raptures in the camp, ever since our arrival. Having dined with us, the Hebron merchant pleaded his cause before him, when he presently gave orders " that his goods should be restored to him." On our part, he very soon came to terms with us, assuring us that he would willingly conduct us to Wady Mousa for nothing, for the sake of Mahommed Ali, Pashaw of Egypt. Soon after a great dispute and tumult arose in the tent, Abou Zatoun (the Father of the Olives), the sheikh of Wady Mousa declaring, with violent gestures, and swearing " by the beard of the prophet," and " by the honour of their women," that we should not go forward; and seeing that, notwithstanding his violence, both Abou Raschid and ourselves were preparing our horses, he quitted the tent, uttering threats and execrations, and rode off for Wady Mousa, determined to prevent our going. All the Wady Mousa people also quitted the camp, joining in their chief's hostility to our advance, repeatedly exclaiming, " Let the dogs go and perish if they please;" and swearing we should neither drink of their water ([60]) nor pass into their territory. While this was passing, our good old man Sheikh Yousouf's resolution was shaken, and both he and Sahlem of Djebal strongly urged us to return and give up the business, representing all future perseverance as fruitless. Abou Raschid twice dismounted to answer the arguments of his people, or to overcome their opposition, as they had surrounded him in numbers, imploring him to desist, and asking him " why he risked himself for the mere gratification of our curiosity, who were only Christians." The sheikh seeing that all his arguments had no effect, seized his spear and sprang on his horse, exclaiming, " I have set them on their horses, let us see who will dare to stop Abou Raschid." We presently descended in a south by west direction, through a ravine whose sides, rocky as they are, have at some time been terraced up and cultivated. The Wady Mousa people rode in a parallel line with us, keeping on the high ground on our left. In about half an hour (four o'clock) we reached a source that issues from the live rock, and is called Sammack; here we were joined by a host of people, all armed, and subject to our sheikh, some were on horseback and some on foot; two double-mounted dromedaries also arrived. Sheikhs Yousouf and Sahlem still remained behind at the camp we had left. Abou Raschid, on the coming up of his people, took an oath ([61]), " By the honour of their women," and " by the faith of a true Mussulman," that we *should* drink of the water of Wady Mousa, and go whithersoever he pleased to carry us. Thus were both the rival chiefs oppositely pledged in their resolution respecting us. To the honour of Abou Raschid it should here be said, that as yet he had not received, or even stipulated for any pecuniary or other reward whatever. As we advanced down the ravine, a wild and romantic view opened to us, terminated by the peaks of the black and rugged ridge of Mount Hor, the same that is alluded to in Scripture, and by a boundless extent of desert view, which we have hardly ever seen equalled for singularity and grandeur. We turned up out of this valley to the eastward, and remarked as we quitted it, that there were two small masses of ruins upon two opposite points which command it: they were, perhaps, forts. Our way leading through a circular plain covered with corn, and bushes of white-thorn just coming into blossom, conducted us to a valley with the sides prettily studded with turpentine trees, so clustered and grouped together, as to give it a very parkish appearance; here we perceived traces of a paved way, constructed similarly to that we had quitted when we were descending into Shobek, and which we thought to be a continuation of the same. At sun-set we alighted at a camp of sixty-eight tents, pitched in three adjoining circles, on the highest point of a pass; our whole journey this day was S. W. three hours. The pass just mentioned was not between two mountains, but on the highest summit of one of them great part of these heights being so steep as to be almost inaccessible, except by the beaten tracks. One of these precipitous falls of ground was close to our camp to the westward; it commands a most magnificent view, in which the fore-ground is a circular, but uneven hollow, in part cultivated, with several circular camps pitched in different parts of it, and the little village of Dibdeba, with a grove of fig-trees about it, bearing S.W. The dark ridge of Mount Hor, which appears to be altogether composed of a sort of sparry flint, broken into masses and seamed with wide crevices, with scarcely any verdure to vary its deep purple colour, forms the boundary of this hollow to the southward, and also to the westward, with that high peak, upon which is the reputed tomb of Aaron, (the Arabs call it Nebi Aaroon, Prophet Aaron) rearing itself above all the rest in the middle of the picture. This craggy ridge does not, however, terminate the landscape; the mountain from which we viewed it being considerably higher, and commanding a boundless view beyond it, over a whitish expanse of country, which is varied here and there with other coloured ridges rising like islands upon it, or jutting forward into it like promontories. The violent rains of the night of the twenty-first and twenty-second supplied the feature of water to this varied landscape, forming a glittering line in the distant plain. S. W. by S., as far as the eye could reach, is a range of mountains, in which the natives pointed out Mount Sinai. We were told it was at the distance of four days; they also reported " Agaba," an inhabited place on the Red Sea, as distant a day and a half from us; and Mahn on the hadj road one day off. A place which the Arabs call Gereye was likewise mentioned as being four days' to the eastward, or S. E., where are very extensive ruins.

In front of our tent there passed an ancient road; no remains can be traced of pavement, but merely two parallel lines of low, dry wall, set at the distance of about twenty-five feet apart.

May 20. We followed the road in its passage downwards to the S. W. for half an hour, when we reached another camp, subject, in some measure, to our chief; we had passed over the sites of two others abandoned by the adverse party during the night; these sites are always distinguishable by the fires and bed places of the Arabs; the former are marked by little holes filled up with ashes, the latter by stones laid in oblong circles, with dried heath and dead boughs laid on them.

An eminence, about S. W. of this last camp, commanded a view over Wady Mousa, bearing south; it seemed an inconsiderable village, in a low situation, with a few fig trees about it. Nebi Aaroon and Dibdebar were also visible from this point, but we were admonished to go to the brow of the precipice, only one at a time, and were afterwards prohibited altogether. There were some very odd-looking people in this camp, some of the men having long hair of a tawny colour, plaited in small plaits, very much in the Nubian manner, but without grease, and a handkerchief of a brown colour, instead of the usual gaudy stripes, confined, in lieu of the plain cord, by a brown, flat band, worked in with patches of coloured woollen, and standing up above the head; their sandals, which however are not peculiar to them, as we had observed them in many other instances, are simple and curious, having a thong coming up on each side of the foot from the sole, and another between the toes; a single tye fastens them on. The women had a peculiar way of plaiting their braided hair across the forehead, which had the air of a formal wig. The female children had the same leathern aprons ornamented with shells, &c., which are in use in Nubia.

From the break of day we had been apprized that the adverse party were fully prepared to stand to their word in opposing us; that they had removed several of their camps, and that a large part of them had abandoned their village of Wady Mousa to occupy a height which commanded it. We could see the tents which they had pitched there, as the distance from our advanced camp was very moderate; they had also moved their cattle with them. Messages, sometimes of persuasion, and oftener with threats, were continually passing; a small detachment of the hostile party passed our tents, but refused to eat in them; they were suffered to go on, unmolested. In the afternoon a large deputation arrived, sufficient to fill the whole tent; a conference was immediately commenced with them; they never personally appealed to us; but carried on the conversation with Abou Raschid only. It was in vain that the authority of the sultan or of the pashaws was dwelt upon in our favour; they got rid of the firmans, by insisting that they did not understand Turkish, and after having a boyourdi of Sali, pashaw of Damascus, delivered into their hands, they said it was a fabrication of the Jews, who are the pashaw's ministers. Not argument only, but even artifice and falsehood were employed in our favour; our friend Abou Raschid asserting that we had with us a person on the part of Soliman, pashaw of Acre, (our servant was the person whom he pointed out as such) and a letter from the governour of Yaffa; which, however easy to have procured, we were not provided with. The adverse party, in some of their conferences, insisted much on seeing something under the hand of the last-mentioned governour, whose recommendation, we have reason to think, would go farther in this country than that of any other person. It was however in this instance only captiously asked for, on the presumption that we had it not to produce.

Abou Raschid urged repeatedly, that in the

event of their not complying, we could use our influence with the several pashaws to cut off their communication entirely with Mahn, Gaza, and Egypt; and he insisted upon our taking down the names of the refractory chiefs, which were, Abou Zatoun (Father of the Olives,) sheikh of Wady Mousa, and commanding the Howetatt Arabs; Kali Phee, of the same place; Lehaddineh Hinde, and the adherents of even Ebn Jarzee, who was himself rather disposed to our side. Our champion advised us, in the presence of these people, to instigate Mahomed Ali to lay hands on some of them whenever they should come to trade at Cairo. These people said on their first coming, "that we were very lucky in the protection of the chief who accompanied us, for otherwise we should never have returned." They pretended to believe that we had a design of poisoning the water.

In the evening there was a very loud thunder storm; and as all that could be said or threatened seemed to have no effect upon our opponents, and as there was neither food for us nor forage for the horses in the tents, we returned, and slept at the same camp as on the preceding night. It was the full of the moon, a dismal cold rain came on, which, for the space of two or three hours, penetrated the covering of our tent, and until a trench was dug along the inside of the back curtain, it flowed in upon us from the high ground; the goats and sheep were continually encroaching, and at last even a cow.

May 21. A thick fog prevailed, so that even the opposite side of our camp was not visible; we heard very noisy councils in the adjoining tents, and it was soon after announced to us, that " war was positively determined on," as the only alternative of our not being permitted to see what we had desired, and to drink of the water. Messengers were dispatched to the camps, under Abou Raschid's influence, and to Shobek, to apprise them of the circumstance, and to request immediate reinforcements; the presence of Sheikh Yousouf aud Sahlem was also required. A poor matronly woman, in the other half of our tent, was looking over the partition with her child in her arms, shedding tears occasionally, and throwing in arguments of dissuasion. It was in vain that we agreed to give up Wady Mousa altogether, and declared that we had no desire to taste of the water; the antiquities, which are distant from the village, being the only object of our curiosity. Our chief, who was a man of few words, stood always to his point, and declared that we should not only see the place, but *even bathe* in the waters; and, that if fair means could not compass this, he had sworn to accomplish it by force.

The messages which arrived in the course of the morning from the opposite party, were only a renewal of protestations and oaths against our entering their territory; and they even threw out menaces of cutting off our return from where we were; thus situated we could not but compare our case to that of the Israelites under Moses, when Edom refused to give them a passage through her country ([62]). The circumstance must likewise have occurred nearly in the same place, as the death and burial of Aaron on Mount Hor ([63]), whose tomb was now before us, would seem to confirm. About mid-day, when the weather was somewhat clearer, we perceived a number of armed men, some mounted, coming up the valley from the north-eastward; the horsemen were Sheikhs Yousouf and Sahlem, with their own attendants, and some few others with lances; the total number of these was seven; the infantry followed, with their match-locks and muskets, to the amount of upwards of sixty. They drew up into something like a line near the camp, and approached it shouting, the women answering with their usual screams of exultation from the tents, lee, lee, lee, lee, &c. ([64]), but they were not suffered to stand exposed in the way; such as had come out being rudely warned back into their tents by the men. The sheikhs of Kerek and Djebal were conducted, each by separate openings, into the camp, to the tents allotted to them; we found them dispirited and discomposed at what had happened, and at the consequences which were likely to ensue. They reminded us of their having dissuaded us from pressing the matter any farther at the camp where we had last parted, and in their conferences with Abou Raschid gave him such advice as might be expected from persons of their years ([65]); old Yousouf particularly, like Nestor in the Iliad, dwelt much upon what had passed in his youth, and upon wars in which he had engaged and had found reason when too late to repent of. He told his stories with a great deal of grave action; but his counsels had more effect upon the rest of his audience, than on the spirited young Arab to whom they were addressed, who continued staunch in his determination of waging war ([66]), and could not be induced even to shift his ground so far as to confine his demands in our favour to the sight of the antiquities only; strenuously persisting that, as we had put ourselves under his protection, we should go wherever he was pleased to carry us.

A deputation arrived from the enemy, and the old sheikhs tried every argument that experience could suggest to induce them to permit us to go forward; they were denounced as rebels in the case of non-compliance, and the consequences were painted in the strongest colours. No effect was produced by these conferences. Our party was continually gaining strength by armed persons dropping in from various directions until night. The reinforcements were distributed amongst the different tents, and rations were refused to such as had not brought guns or spears. The camp now began to assume a very warlike appearance; the spears stuck in the sand, the saddled horses before the tents, with the arms hanging up within, altogether had an imposing effect ([67]). Perceiving that such a concourse of strangers must distress the camp, we begged to be permitted to pay for our food and that of our horses, but Abou Raschid would not hear of it; all was gratuitous, and our animals had abundance.

One circumstance seemed to turn in our favour; Hindi, an Arab chief of very poor and ordinary appearance, and almost blind, was represented to us, as a man of great power and influence, who could command two thousand guns; and though this was probably an exaggeration, yet from the effect which his interference appears to have had in the sequel, it seems probable that he is a chieftain of considerable power.

He had been upon ill terms with Abou Raschid, yet from the time of our first conference with him at the advanced camp, he had seemed disposed to favour our pretensions, and to dissuade the hostile party from their obstinate opposition, more especially as he professed great respect for the written orders of the Turkish government. On the other hand, it was said that there was a strong party among his adherents inclined to prevent his co-operation; however, towards the evening of this day, he made a solemn peace with our chief, and passsed into the enemy's quarters, with the intention of bringing all his men to act in concert with Mahommed Abou Raschid, in open war against them in case of their persisting another day. Some communication was also made by letter, but in whose name we did not learn. The answer was expected, but did not arrive this night. Towards dark there went a rumour throughout the camp, that our opponents had given in, and that we should be at liberty on the morrow to go where we pleased. We laid down with this impression on us, and it was pretty general throughout all the camp. Our chief seemed proud of matters having been brought to a favourable end so soon, and said exultingly, " that there were some who had the talent of carrying their point with saying very little, while others who made a great noise were obliged to give way, and behaved like cattle."

The same dismal weather continued; about midnight there was a cry of thieves in the camp, and it was found that they were very quietly sitting at our fire ([68]); but as there were some of our people not yet asleep we lost nothing. In the morning we heard that two spies had also been detected in the camp ([69]), but it did not appear that any further measures had been pursued against them, than their dismissal.

May 22. The fog was still thicker; we were surprised to find that this weather was not deemed unusual or out of season. It was announced to us that the men of Wady Mousa did not adhere to their agreement, but in the plainest terms had declared, " that they would oppose us by main force, and that we should pay with our lives for any attempt that we should make to advance within their limits." It appeared that they had even thrown up some sort of fortification about the well. Upon our declaring that we did not wish matters to be pushed to extremities, and again persisting in confining our desires to the sight of the antiquities only, Mahommed would hardly listen to the bearer of the message, and scarcely came to see us during the whole day.

Armed reinforcements in small numbers were continually dropping in. For the last two days, since the negociations had been pending, we had seen so very little of our friend Abou Raschid, that we feared he was displeased; and it appeared that he had avoided us from the moment we had offered to abandon our object rather than to proceed to extremities.

May 23. In this predicament we found ourselves this morning; the result of Hindi's declaration was expected with impatience, and almost every one seemed to think that it must have great weight with the enemy. We however heard that their party had also had an accession of two neighbouring tribes of Arabs who had declared against us. Old Yousouf was this day unusually eloquent in our favour giving out that we were believers in Mahommed, and that our only motive in wishing to advance, was to pay our devotions at Aaron's tomb, thus giving a very plausible turn to the motive of our Journey; when asked " if we were of the true faith," he always replied " they are English." He recapitulated the list of the documents with which we were furnished, roundly asserting that we had recommendations from Yaffa and Egypt, though he knew that we had them not, and he attached much importance to the presence of our soldier and Tartar from Constantinople. He mentioned all the places we had visited in the country, particularly Palmyra and Szalt; adding, that this was the first time we had been stopped. He dwelt again, in the true character of an old chieftain, on the events of wars that had happened in his early days. His drift was to carry matters by fair means if possible, and to restrain the impetuosity of Abou Raschid, whom he warned of the usual effects of hasty measures, and, for the first time alluded to an old grudge which the people of Wady Mousa bore towards him, on account of the fate of three or four of their fellow townsmen whom he had beheaded at Kerek. The tone, however, of old Yousouf was considerably changed, and he seemed not altogether so adverse to hostilities as he had hitherto been; he said, " I too could bring out the men of Kerek," and he spoke of their numbers and courage, but he did not pledge himself to bring them out.

In the course of this morning it had been discovered that one of the ruins which we were in quest of was in sight from our mountain; it proved to be that which we called the palace; it was discernible through a narrow strait formed by two craggy cliffs, which gave it a very picturesque appearance. By following the brow of the mountain we gained a sight also of the theatre cut out of the live rock, and of several of the tombs. Though they were at a considerable distance we could make them out pretty well with the help of a spy-glass; this sight was a great encouragement to us, as it appeared possible to reach the spot without passing at all near the enemy's quarters; and we began to concert among ourselves some means of getting there secretly in the night, should all other expedients fail. While we were deliberating on this subject, we saw a great cavalcade entering our camp from the southward. There were many lances and mounted Arabs, and we observed that there were some amongst the horsemen who wore richer turbans, more gaudy colours, than is usual amongst Bedouins or peasants. As the procession advanced, several of Abou Raschid's Arabs went out, and led the horses of the chiefs by the bridles into the camp. The whole procession alighted at the tent of our chief, and kissed his turban; this was the signal of pacification. Peace was immediately proclaimed throughout the camp, and notice was given that the men bearing arms who had come from a distance, many of whom had dropped in that very morning, were to return to their repective homes.

Our late opponents were now willing to consent to our setting out that afternoon; but by the general wish it was deferred until the next day. We heard music and singing in several of the tents. One of the chiefs of the party who had been adverse to us, came very shortly to pay us a visit; amongst other things, he said in his excuse that he had misconceived the object of our journey; having supposed us Frenchmen who came with a design of poisoning the water; they dissembled the real motive of their change of conduct, which there can be little doubt was fear, and imputed their concessions entirely to their respect for the sultan and the pashaws. To make the matter more formal, there came a person who was in the employ of the pashaw of Damascus, with two attendants, to read and examine our papers. It proved, however, that he was wholly unacquainted with the Turkish language, and in consequence confined himself entirely to the boyourdees of the two pashaws, which he declared to be satisfactory and sufficient, although, in point of fact, they were altogether foreign to the question, being addressed to persons and places in quite a different part of the country. This man, in recompence for his decision, in the course of the evening attempted, through old Yousouf, to lay claim to some remuneration, but Yousouf fought off his pretensions, by asserting, that for his own part he had not *seen* the colour of our gold;

which was so far true, as the four hundred piastres were deposited in the hands of the Greek priest at Kerek.

In the evening we were visited by Abou Raschid, who was in high spirits; the weather had been considerably clearer this day, but it was still much colder than might have been expected at this season of the year. During the day we had explored the high land to the eastward of the camp, and found it covered, upon both its sides and on its summit, with lines of dry wall, and solid masses of the same. The former appeared to be the traces of former cultivation; the solid ruins seemed to be only the remains of towers ([70]) for watching in harvest and vintage time. The whole neighbourhood of this spot bears similar traces of former industry, all which seem to indicate the vicinity of a great metropolis.

May 24. The morning was less unfavourable than those which had preceded it. Soon after sun-rise we set out from the camp; there were in all about fifty persons, amongst whom were the deputation from Wady Mousa and the men of Damascus, who had passed the night in the tents of our chief. The first part of our road was the same which led to the advanced camp where we had been on the twentieth; but before we reached that spot we turned off from it in an

E. S. E. direction, constantly descending. As we got lower down, we passed into a rocky and steep defile, where the footing is extremely bad, and the passage so commanded from the sides, and intersected by huge masses of sand-stone detached and rolled down from above, that it was obvious that a very small force would be capable of holding it against a great superiority of numbers. Towards the lower extremity of this pass the path branched off two several ways; it had previously been whispered to us by our chief, that we should not seem to take any notice of it, but let the men of Wady Mousa go their way, while we should follow one of our own party, who would go forward and guide us in a different direction. When we reached the point of separation, the others not being apprized of this determination, said all they could to induce Abou Raschid to ascend to their tents, and came even to high words with him, but they could not prevail, he having sworn an oath, that neither we nor himself should eat or drink at their expense, or within the limits of their territory. Some few even followed us for a time, hoping to persuade us to turn back with them, but before we reached the valley of Wady Mousa they had all withdrawn.

Our defile brought us directly down into this place, whose name had become so familiar to us; it is, at the point where we entered it, a stony but cultivated valley of moderate size, without much character or beauty, running in a direction from E. to W. A lesser hollow, sloping down to it from the southward, meets it at an angle; at the upper end of the latter valley is the village seen over stages of hanging fruit-grounds and gardens, which are watered by a spring. At the point of junction of these valleys a source issues from the rock and forms a brook, to which the other is contributary; to this Abou Raschid pointed, with a sneer of exultation, as we crossed it, observing, "there is the water about which there has been so much contention and dispute." It flows towards the westward, and is, in point of fact, the head of the stream which Pliny has dignified with the name of a river. We approached no nearer to the village than this point, but as the distance did not exceed a quarter of a mile, we could plainly perceive that there was nothing ancient there; that the houses were mean and ragged, and not more than forty or fifty in number. On the summit of a broad, green hill, rising above it, we could not only distinguish the large encampment to which the inhabitants had retired on the night of the twentieth, but could plainly see them collected in great numbers on the brow looking down and watching us.

Some hundred yards below this spring begin the out-skirts of the vast Necropolis of Petra. Many door-ways are visible, upon different levels, cut in the side of the mountain, which towards this part begins to assume a more rugged aspect; the most remarkable tombs stand near the road, which follows the course of the brook. The first of these is on the right hand, and is cut in a mass of whitish rock, which is in some measure insulated and detached from the general range. The centre represents the front of a square tower, with pilasters at the corner, and with several successive bands of frieze and entablature above; two low wings project from it at right angles, and present each of them a recess, in the manner of a portico, which consists of two columns whose capitals have an affinity with the Doric order, between corresponding antæ; there are, however, no triglyphs above. Three sides of a square area are thus enclosed; the fourth has been shut in by a low wall and two colossal lions on either side of the entrance, all much decayed. The interior has been a place of sepulture for several bodies. On the front are little niches and hollows cut, as if for the reception of votive offerings. Farther on, upon the left, is a wide façade of rather a low proportion, loaded with ornaments in the Roman manner, but in a bad taste, with an infinity of broken lines and unnecessary angles and projections, and multiplied pediments and half pediments, and pedestals set upon columns that support nothing. It has more the air of a fantastical scene in a theatre than an architectural work in stone; and for unmeaning richness, and littleness of conception, Mr. Bankes seemed to think, might have been the work of Boromini himself, whose style it exactly resembles, and carries to the extreme. What is observed of this front is applicable, more or less, to every specimen of Roman design at Petra. The door-way has triglyphs over the entablature, and flowers in the metopes. The chamber within is not so large as the exterior promises; it has a broad, raised platform round three sides, on which bodies were probably disposed. Immediately over this front is another of almost equal extent, but so wholly distinct from it, that even the centres do not correspond; the door-way has the same ornaments. The rest of the body of the design is no more than a plain front, without any other decoration than a single moulding. Upon this are set, in a recess, four tall and taper pyramids; their effect is singular and surprising, but combining too little with the rest of the elevation to be good. Our attention was the more attracted by this monument, as it presents, perhaps, the only existing example of pyramids so applied, though we read of them as placed in a similar manner on the summit of the tomb of the Maccabees, and of the Queen of Adiabæne, both in the neighbouring province of Palestine. The interior of the mausoleum is of moderate size, with two sepulchral recesses upon each side, and one in form of an arched alcove at the upper end; a flight of steps leads up to the narrow terrace upon which it opens. The subjoined cut may convey an idea of some of these singular excavations.

The sides of the valley were now becoming precipitous and rugged to a high degree, and approaching nearer and nearer to each other, so that it might rather deserve the name of a ravine, with high detached masses of rock standing up here and there in the open space. Of these the architects had availed themselves. In some instances the large and lofty towers are represented in relievo on the lower part of the precipice, and the live rock is cut down on all sides, so as to make the resemblance complete. The greater number of them present themselves to the high road, but there are others which stand back in the wild nooks and recesses of the mountain. All seemed to have been sepulchral, and it was here that we first observed the features of a sort of architecture that was new to us, and is, perhaps, not elsewere to be found.

To erect quadrangular towers for sepulchres, seems to have been the fashion in several inland districts of the east; they abound at Palmyra, and are seen in the valley of Jehoshaphat near Jerusalem, &c.: but the details and ornaments of these, universally betray an imitation of Roman architecture, whilst at Petra they bear all the marks of a peculiar and indigenous style; their sides have generally a slight degree of that inclination towards each other, which is one of the characteristics of Egyptian edifices, and they are crowned with the Egyptian torus and concave frieze. A very remarkable superstructure rises above as a parapet. Two corresponding flights of steps are represented in relievo, ascending in opposite directions, from two points near the centre, thus ⌐⌐ ; they are connected together by a horizontal line drawn between the uppermost steps, and there are usually from four to six. At the angles are pilasters; in many instances they have a considerable diminution upwards; the capital is very peculiar, and appears like the rough draft of an unfinished Ionic capital as it comes from the quarry. It is, however, almost universal on these tombs, and may be called the *Arabian order* of architecture. An entablature and frieze, little differing from the Ionic or Corinthian, rests upon these pilasters; above that is a blank space, in the nature of a low attic, which is finished with the Egyptian torus and frieze, bearing the superstructure which I have described. There is one single example, near the theatre, of an upper door-way opening in this attic, to which there is no visible access; there may possibly, however, be some stairs in the interior; the lower door-way is unluckily choaked, so that we could not ascertain. In some instances the pilasters are multiplied to four in the front, and are rounded instead of being angular. What is the least peculiar in the details of these Arabian elevations, is the decorations of the door-ways, which have in many instances a pediment not distinguishable from those of the Romans, and in others a plain horizontal architrave with the same character in the mouldings. It is remarkable, that in very many instances the whole frame and ornament of the door has been of separate pieces, and grafted on upon the solid rock. Sometimes there are cavities for pegs or rivets which would seem to have fastened these decorations in metal or in wood; in others they seem to have been of marble or some finer sort of stone, let into grooves, which shew, in the hollow, their exact form. We were at a loss to account for the apparent conformity of this single member of the building to the rules of the Greeks and Romans; it seems too strong to be accidental; and if we suppose the imitation to have taken place so far back as the first Macedonian expedition into this country, it will still make the tombs, by many ages, more recent than it is probable that many of them really are; since, from the days of Rekem, King of the Midianites, who passes for the founder of Petra, to those of Alexander the Great, there must have been a long suite of kings, and these monarchs probably had tombs. Yet if the form of the door-ways be judged decidedly posterior to that period, it is so general, that few if any of the larger sort will remain for that early dynasty. If we bring them still later, and suppose them a Roman innovation, the difficulty is increased, because we must then believe a much greater lapse of ages to have passed in a flourishing kingdom, without any considerable monuments, when architecture was not unknown. It is possible such of the door frames as were not cut in the solid, may have been added afterwards, but this does not appear very probable, nor does it entirely remove the difficulty; especially, as in some instances in the higher parts of the design, broad bands seem to have been attached in a similar manner, which very probably were charged with inscriptions.

It is surprising, amongst such a multitude of tombs, to find so few with any inscription to record, for whom they were constructed; we only met with two instances; one was on the tomb, which had a door in the attic already mentioned, as being near the theatre; it is much mutilated, the other, which we copied, is on the left hand side of the track leading towards Dibdebar, on a large front of pure Arabian design, with four attached columns; and in this monument the architect, from failure, or a defective vein in the sand-stone, has been obliged to carry up the lower half in masonry, so as to meet the upper, which is sculptured on the face of the mountain, where also there were flaws, and here pieces have been let in to make up what was defective; these last remain, but the whole substruction has disappeared entirely, and the upper part is left hanging from the rock above without any base whatever. This is not the only proof that is to be found, among the remains at Petra, that those who wrought on the live rock, contrary to the necessary practice of builders, began their work at the top. To return to the inscription; it is upon an oblong tablet, without frame or relief, but is easily distinguished from the rest of the surface by being more delicately wrought; there projects, from each of its ends, those wings in form of the blade of an axe, which are common both in the Roman and Greek tablets, and which would seem to have been in their origin, for the purpose of receiving screws or fastenings, without encroaching on the part inscribed; thus ◁▭▷. This original purpose seems to have been particularly kept in view in the present instance, since, although the whole is in the solid, there is upon each side a stain of metal, which must be the effect of studs of bronze actually driven in, to give the whole tablet the appearance of a separate piece. The letters are well cut, and in a wonderful state of preservation, owing to the shelter which they receive from the projection of cornices, and an eastern aspect. None of our party had ever seen these characters before, excepting Mr. Bankes, who upon comparing them, found them to be exactly similar to those which he had seen scratched on the rocks in the Wady Makootub, and about the foot of Mount Sinai. He subsequently found a passage in Diodorus Siculus, wherein he speaks of a letter written by the Nabathæi of Petra, to Antigonus, in the *Syriac character;* though this, perhaps, is no proof that the Syriac was in use with them, since they may have chosen that language only, as more familiar to the court they were addressing. The tablet has five long lines, and immediately underneath, a single figure on a larger scale, probably the date; the very same occurs at the bottom of the Hebrew characters on the tomb of Aaron. The interior of the tomb we have been describing has two chambers, with recesses for bodies, but no peculiarity worthy of notice; the front is crowned with a double flight of steps in the usual form. In many instances, in lieu of two flights diverging from each other, they are brought to meet in the form of pyramids, being reduced to a much smaller scale, and repeated in the manner of battlements, thus to the number of three, or five entire, with the half of one at each extremity. We have preferred collecting into one view, the most remarkable features of these tombs, before we advance further; without confining ourselves strictly to those which are met with in the approach from Wady Mousa to the city, in order to generalize the description, and avoid interrupting the narrative by alluding to them as they present themselves, which is the case not only in every avenue to the city, and upon every precipice that surrounds it, but even intermixed almost promiscuously with its public and domestic edifices. To return to the description of the eastern approach to Petra: as we advanced, the natural features of the defile grew more and more imposing at every step, and the excavations and sculpture more frequent on both sides, till it presented at last a continued street of tombs, beyond which the rocks gradually approaching each other, seemed all at once to close without any outlet. There is, however, one frightful chasm for the passage of the stream, which furnishes, as it did anciently, the only avenue to Petra on this side. It is impossible to conceive any thing more awful or sublime than such an approach; the width is not more than just sufficient for the passage of two horsemen abreast, the sides are in all parts perpendicular, varying from four hundred to seven hundred feet in height, and they often overhang to such a degree, that without their absolutely meeting, the sky is intercepted and completely shut out for one hundred yards together, and there is little more light than in a cavern.

The screaming of the eagles, hawks, and owls, who were soaring above our heads in considerable numbers, seemingly annoyed at any one approaching their lonely habitation, added much to the singularity of this scene ([71]). The tamarisk, the wild fig, and the oleander, grow luxuriantly about the road, rendering the passages often difficult; in some places they hang down most beautifully from the cliffs and crevices where they had taken root; the caper plant was also in luxuriant growth, the continued shade furnishing them with moisture.

Very near the first entrance into this romantic pass, a bold arch is thrown across at a great height, connecting the opposite sides of the cliff. Whether this was part of an upper road upon the summit of the mountain, or whether it be a portion of an aqueduct, which seems less probable, we had no opportunity of examining; but as the traveller passes under it, its appearance is most surprising, hanging thus above his head betwixt two rugged masses apparently inaccessible. Immediately under it are sculptured niches in the rock, destined probably for statues; and we suspect that by careful inspection inscriptions might be found there; but the position in which they are viewed is disadvantageous, and the height so great that it would require a good glass to distinguish them. Farther down, upon a much lower level, there is an object frequently repeated in sculpture along the road side, which we were at a loss to explain: an altar is represented in a niche, upon which is set a mass of a lumpish form, sometimes square and sometimes curved in its outline, or rising in other instances to a sharper or obtuser cone; in one instance three of them are coupled together in one niche. It might possibly be a representation of the god Terminus, or perhaps one of the stones which were objects of worship amongst the Arabs, down to the time of the coming of Mahommed. The number of these representations on the face of the rock is very considerable; in some instances there are many, almost contiguous, with Greek inscriptions on them, all of which are too much defaced to be of use in explaining their object. The ravine, without changing much its general direction, presents so many elbows and windings in its course, to which the track, of necessity, conforms, that the eye can seldom penetrate forward beyond a few paces, and is often puzzled to distinguish in what direction the passage will open, so completely does it appear obstructed. The exact spot was not pointed out to us, but it is somewhere amidst these natural horrors, that upwards of thirty pilgrims from Barbary, were murdered last year by the men of Wady Mousa on their return from Mecca. The wrapping cloak of one of them was afterwards offered to us for sale at Ipseyra, and one of their watches at Zaphoely. Salvator Rosa never conceived so savage and suitable a quarter for banditti. The brook has at this season disappeared beneath the soil, but the manner in which its occasional overflowings have broken up the antique pavement, and the slippery passes which the running of the waters have made, by polishing the live rock where it had been cut away to form the road, sufficiently prove the necessity of providing another course for its waters. A trough, carried along near the foot of the precipice upon the left hand side, was destined to confine the water, and to convey it upon a higher than the natural level to the city. At a considerable distance down the ravine this water-course crosses over to the opposite side; and towards its extremity may be traced passing along at a great height in earthen pipes, bedded and secured with mortar, in horizontal grooves cut in the face of the rock, and even across the architectural fronts of some of the tombs, which makes it probable that it is posterior to them.

We followed this sort of half subterranean passage for the space of nearly two miles, the sides increasing in height as the path continually descended, while the tops of the precipices retained their former level. Where they are at the highest, a beam of stronger light breaks in at the close of the dark perspective, and opens to view, half seen at first through the tall narrow opening, columns, statues, and cornices, of a light and finished taste, as if fresh from the chisel, without the tints or weather stains of age, and executed in a stone of a pale rose colour, which was warmed at the moment we came in sight of them with the full light of the morning sun. The dark green of the shrubs that grow in this perpetual shade, and the sombre appearance of the passage from whence we were about to issue, formed a fine contrast with the glowing colour of the edifice. We know not with what to compare this scene; perhaps there is nothing in the world that resembles it. Only a portion of a very extensive architectural elevation is seen at first, but it has been so contrived that a statue with expanded wings, perhaps of victory, just fills the centre of the aperture in front, which being closed below by the sides of the rock folding over each other, gives to the figure the appearance of being suspended in the air at a considerable height; the ruggedness of the cliffs below setting off the sculpture to the highest advantage. The rest of the design opened gradually at every pace as we advanced, till the narrow defile which had continued thus far, without any increase of breadth, spreads on both sides into an open area of a moderate size, whose sides are by nature inaccessible, and present the same awful and romantic features as the avenues which lead to it: this opening gives admission to a great body of light from the eastward. The position is one of the most beautiful that could be imagined for the front of a great temple, the richness and exquisite finish of whose decorations offers a most remarkable contrast to the savage scenery which surrounds it.

It is of a very lofty proportion, the elevation comprising two stories. The taste is not exactly to be commended, but many of the details and ornaments, and the size and proportion of the great door-way especially, to which there are five steps of ascent from the portico, are very noble. No part is built, the whole being purely a work of excavation, and its minutest embellishments, wherever the hand of man has not purposely effaced and obliterated them, are so perfect, that it may be doubted whether any work of the ancients, excepting, perhaps, some on the banks of the Nile, have come down to our time so little injured by the lapse of ages. There is, in fact, scarcely a building of forty years standing in England, so well preserved in the greater part of its architectural decorations. Of the larger members of the architecture nothing is deficient excepting a single column of the portico; the statues are numerous and colossal. Those on each side of the portico represent, in groups, each of them, a centaur and a young man. This part of the work only is imperfect, having been mutilated, probably by the fanaticism of early Christians, or Mussulmen, directed against idolatry, and particularly the human form. In the upper tier the figures are females, two are winged, and two appear to have been dancing or much in action, with some instruments lifted above their heads, of which that on the left hand seems to be the Amazonian bipennis. Unfortunately the centre figure, which was doubtless the principal one, is too much defaced for her attributes to be determined; nor is there any thing in the ornaments that could enable us to discover to what divinity the temple has been dedicated. The principal chamber of the interior is large and remarkably lofty, but quite plain, with the exception of the door-frames and architraves, of which there are three; one at the farther end, and one at each side, all opening into small and plain cells. There is also a lateral chamber on each side, opening from the portico, of a rude form. The centre of the superstructure, which comprises the second story, is a circular elevation surrounded by columns, with a dome surmounted by an urn. This latter has not escaped, or failed to excite the covetousness of the natives. We heard of it as the deposit of a vast treasure, " Hasnah-el-Faraoun," (Treasure of Pharoah,) as far as Jerusalem; and that it has been repeatedly aimed at by musket-shot, there are evident proofs in the marks of bullets in the stone. No one, however, seems to have succeeded in arriving at it by climbing, which would indeed be a difficult task; the green stains on either side would lead to the supposition that the handles had been of bronze. It is doubtful whether one of the perforations, by a musket-ball, does not shew that the urn is hollow. Above the monument the face of the rock is left over-hanging, and it is to this that the excellent preservation of its details is to be ascribed. The half pediments, which terminate the wings of the building, are finished at the top with eagles, which, combined with a style of architecture differing little from the Roman, can leave no doubt that this great effort of art is posterior to the time of Trajan's conquest.

Some of the heights whose steep sides inclose the area in front of the temple, are rendered accessible, though with great difficulty, by flights of steps cut in them; we found the ascent, in some instances, so steep and slippery that we were obliged to take off our shoos, and also to use our hands nearly as much as we did our feet. Some small pyramids hewn out of the rock are on the summit of these heights; and we discovered a much higher conical point of mountain, to whose summit there is a regular spiral staircase of ascent, cut with great care and neatness, the same point possibly on which we could distinguish from another quarter, a single pillar or obelisk; we first observed, also, from the heights above the temple, the great vase which crowns another monument to the N. W. The wide space which constitutes the area before the temple is about fifty yards in width, and about three times as long. It terminates to the south in a wild precipitous cliff, rendered accessible by the steps above-mentioned to the N. N. W.; the defile assumes, for about three hundred yards, the same features which characterise the eastern approach, with an infinite variety of tombs, both Arabian and Roman, on either side. This pass conducts to the theatre, and here the ruins of the city burst on the view in their full grandeur, shut in on the opposite side by barren, craggy precipices, from which numerous ravines and valleys like those we had passed, branch out in all directions; the sides of the mountains, covered with an endless variety of excavated tombs and private dwellings ([72]), presented altogether, the most singular scene we ever beheld; and we must despair to give the reader an idea of the singular effect of rocks, tinted with most extraordinary hues, whose summits present us with nature in her most savage and romantic form, whilst their bases are worked out in all the symmetry and regularity of art, with colonnades and pediments, and ranges of corridors adhering to the perpendicular surface. The short notice of Petra, by Pliny, is as follows: " the Nabatæi inhabit a city called Petra, in a hollow somewhat less than two miles in circumference, surrounded by inaccessible mountains, with a stream running through it. It is distant from the town of Gaza, on the coast, six hundred miles; and from the Persian gulf one hundred and twenty-two." 6th book, 28 c. Strabo says " the capital of the Nabatæi is called Petra; it lies in a spot which is in itself level and plain, but fortified all round with a barrier of rocks and precipices; within, furnished with springs of excellent quality for the supply of water and the irrigation of gardens; without the circuit, the country is in a great measure desert, and especially towards Judæa. Jericho is at the distance of three or four days." He adds, that one of the royal lineage always resided at

Petra, and had a sort of counsellor attached to him who was entitled his brother; he premises their laws and customs.

It will be seen that these two ancient geographers, in characterising the position of the city, not only agree with one another, but will be found sufficiently conformable to the reality, though, strictly speaking, the situation can neither be called a valley with Pliny, nor a plain with Strabo; yet it is certainly both low in position, and level in surface, when compared with the crags and precipices that surround it. It is an area in the bosom of a mountain, swelling into mounds and intersected with gullies; but the whole ground is of such a nature as may be conveniently built upon, and has neither ascent nor descent inconveniently steep. Within the actual circuit of the city there are two mounds, which seem to have been entirely covered with buildings, being still strewed over with a prodigious quantity of loose stones, tiles, and fragments of ancient ware, of a very light and delicate fabric. The bed of the river, taking its course to the N. W., flows between these two spots; the water has now sunk beneath the surface, and perhaps creeps through the rubbish which ages have accumulated in its bed; great part of it seems to have been arched over in the same manner as the stream at Philadelphia. In the low ground, on the left bank of the stream, seem to have been some of the principal edifices; the first, to the N. W. from the theatre, was an archway of a very florid architecture with pilasters having pannels enriched with foliage, in the manner of Palmyra: the whole is much ruined. The arch was the introduction to a great pile of building, standing nearly at right angles to it. This building had a door on one side; on the three others, it was decorated with a frieze of triglyphs, and large flowers in the metopes. Beams of wood are let in at intervals between the courses of the masonry, and continue to this day, a strong proof of the dryness of the climate. The front had a portico of four columns; this part is much fallen into ruins. The interior of the edifice was divided into three parallel chambers, and there seem to have been several stories. This interior economy made us suspect that it was not a temple, but rather a palace or some private edifice. Whatever may have been its nature, it seems to have been destined to the same purpose as the ruined building at " Bait-el-Carm," which we afterwards saw from our camp above Dibdebar, and which is the only considerable work of masonry existing at Petra. Upon the summit of the other mound there is a mass of ruins of some solidity, but no very definite shape. The Nubian geographer, climate three, says that the houses of Petra were excavated in the rock; now, that this was not universally true, is evident from the great quantity of stones employed in the lesser kind of edifices which are scattered over the whole site; but it is also true, that there are grottos in great numbers, which were certainly not sepulchral, especially near the palace; there is one in particular which presents a front of four windows, with a large and lofty door-way in the centre. In the interior, one chamber of about sixty feet in length, and of a breadth proportioned, occupies three of the windows and the door; at the lower end, the fourth window seems allotted to a very small sleeping chamber, which is not brought down to the level of the floor of the great apartment, but has a chamber below it of the same size, receiving no light but from the entrance. This, which seems the best of all the excavated residences, has no ornament whatever on the exterior; and the same applies to all the other excavations of this nature. The access to this house is by a shelf gained out of the side of the mountain ([73]); other inferior habitations open upon it, and more particularly an oven, and some cisterns. These antique dwellings are close to an angle of the mountain, where the bed of the stream, after having traversed the city, passes again into a narrow defile, along whose steep sides a sort of excavated suburb is continued, of very small and mean chambers, set one above another, without much regularity, like so many pigeon-holes in the rock, with flights of steps or narrow inclined planes leading up to them. The main wall and ceiling only of some were in the solid; the fronts and partitions being built of very indifferent masonry with cement.

Following this defile farther down, the river re-appears, flowing with considerable rapidity; though the water is plentiful, it is with difficulty that its course can be followed, from the luxuriance of the shrubs that surround it, and obstruct every track. Besides the oleander, which is common to all the water-courses in this country, one may recognise among the plants which choak this valley, some which are probably the descendants of those that adorned the gardens, and supplied the market of the capital of Arabia; the carob, fig, mulberry, vine, and pomegranate line the river-side; a very beautiful species of aloe also grows in this valley, bearing a flower of an orange hue, shaded to scarlet; in some instances it had upwards of one hundred blossoms in a bunch.

Amongst the niches for votive offerings in the mountain's side, some of which are cut to the height of thirty feet, are pyramids and obelisks; and in one instance there is an altar between two palm trees. The position of the theatre has been mentioned; it is the first object which presents itself to the traveller on entering Petra from the eastward. It is entirely hewn out of the live rock; the diameter of the podium is one hundred and twenty feet, the number of seats thirty-three, and of the cunii three. There was no break, and consequently no vomitories. The scene, unfortunately, was built, and not excavated; the whole is fallen, and the bases of four columns only remain on its interior face. The theatre is surrounded by sepulchres; every avenue leading to it is full of them, and one may safely say, that a hundred of the largest dimensions are visible from it. Indeed, throughout almost every quarter of this metropolis, the depositories of the dead, must have presented themselves constantly to the eyes of the inhabitants, and have almost out-numbered the habitations of the living; there is a long line of them not far from the theatre, at such an angle as not to be comprehended in the view from it, but which must have formed a principal object for the city itself.

The largest of the sepulchres had originally three stories, of which the lowest presented four portals, with large columns set between them; and the second and third, a row of eighteen Ionic columns each, attached to the façade; the live rock being insufficient for the total elevation, a part of the story was grafted on in masonry, and is for the most part fallen away. The four portals of the basement open into as many chambers, very dissimilar, both in distribution and arrangements, but all sepulchral, and without any communication between them. In one were three recesses which seem to have been ornamented with marble, or some other extraneous material. Almost contiguous to this extensive front, is another somewhat smaller but equally rich, whose design has a great analogy, especially in the circumstance of the half pediment, and the circular lantern in the centre, to the beautiful temple of the eastern approach. Though a general symmetry pervades this piece of architecture, yet there are irregularities observable in its doors and windows, which may be explained by the circumstance of their opening into apartments no way connected with each other, and intended apparently for different families. A little further to the S. E. an area is gained upon the slope of the mountain, by excavating it, so as to form three sides of a square; two of these have been formed into Doric porticos; the third, which is the loftiest, as being that which abuts against the body of the mountain, is occupied by a lofty front, decorated with four engaged columns of the same order, but without triglyphs. A pediment surmounts the frieze, supporting an urn, in all respects similar to that on the temple of the eastern approach. A door-way, with a window over it, fills the centre, and there are three windows in the attic, the centre one of which exhibits two half-length figures in basso-relievo. In the approach to this tomb there were arched substructions of great extent, now fallen into ruins. It is surprising to reflect that monuments of so vast a scale should be executed subsequent to the Roman conquest, since after that period we can look upon them as no more than the tombs of private individuals. Whence should come so much wealth, and such a taste for magnificence after the country had lost its independence, it is difficult to conceive; it is possible, however, that a trade by the Red Sea with India, or even the caravan trade with the spice country, may have imported such riches into the place, as to give the inhabitants the same fondness for ostentation and ornament, observable at Palmyra, which owed its wealth to the same source. Yet to consider a mausoleum of upwards of seventy or eighty feet high, with lateral porticos, and flights of terraces upon arched work leading up to it, as the effect of vanity of some obscure individual in a remote corner of the Roman Empire, has something in it surprising and almost unaccountable. The interior was disposed of in one large and lofty chamber, having six recesses, with grooves in them at the further end.

On the establishment of Christianity these six recesses have been converted into three, for the reception of the altars, and the whole apartment has been made to serve as a church; the fastenings for the tapestry and pictures are still visible in all the walls, and near an angle is an inscription in red paint, recording the date of consecration. These were the only vestiges of a Christian establishment that we were enabled to discover throughout the remains of Petra, though it was a metropolitan see.

Diodorus Siculus has a long account of the expedition sent by Antigonus against the Nabatæi; he mentions that their riches were very great in gold and spices, and that such of them as were feeble and infirm were left ἐπί τινος Πετρας, which he calls afterwards a place of prodigious natural strength, but without any walls; and distant two days' journey from any inhabited place. In the second expedition, it is said there was but one way of access to it, which was artificial. The loftiness of the post is afterwards mentioned. It is difficult to apply this description to Wady Mousa. Upon some of the high points of rock that rise about the skirts of the city, and tower above them, the remains of walled forts are visible from below; and as it is probable there was an acropolis, it must be looked for in some of these.

Two days were spent upon these ruins, from day-break until dusk, and yet it will be seen by what has been said, that this time was very insufficient to complete an examination of them. It was impossible to remain any longer, for although Abou Raschid attended personally with us the whole time, yet having forced us to decline visiting Abou Zettum in so abrupt a manner, and having but few attendants, he was never at his ease, and constantly urged us to depart. On the first afternoon, we undertook the ascent to the little edifice, which is visible from all the country round, upon the very highest and most rugged pinnacle of this range of mountain, and is called "the Tomb of Aaron." The Tomb of Moses has been so grossly misplaced by the Mussulmen, who shew it half a day's journey beyond Jordan to the westward, that we might look with some suspicion to one assigned to his brother, were it not that Josephus expressly says of the place of his decease, that it was near Petra (⁷⁴). Compare also Mosera with Mousa, and it seems that the monument and the ruins mutually authenticate each other; we had no doubt, therefore, that the height which we were going to ascend, is the Mount Hor of Scripture. The base of the highest pinnacle of the mountain is a little removed from the skirts of the city to the westward; we rode to its foot over a rugged and broken track, passing in the way many sepulchres, similar to those which have been described. A singular monument presents itself upon the left hand; an obtuse cone, produced by the coils of a spiral, is represented as standing on a vast square pedestal or altar, the whole being obtained out of one of the peaked summits of the rock. Not far from thence, close to the way side, is the same representation in relievo, within a niche which we have remarked upon in the eastern approach, the form of the recess which surrounds the altar rising into the figure of a sugar-loaf. No where is the extraordinary colouring of these mountains more striking than in the road to the Tomb of Aaron which we followed, where the rock sometimes presented a deep, sometime a paler blue, and sometimes was occasionally streaked with red, or shaded off to lilac or purple, sometimes a salmon-colour was veined in waved lines and circles, with crimson and even scarlet, so as to resemble exactly the colour of raw meat; in other places there are livid stripes of yellow or bright orange, and in some parts all the different colours were ranged side by side in parallel strata; there are portions also with paler tints, and some quite white, but these last seem to be soft, and not good for preserving the sculpture. It is this wonderful variety of colours observable throughout the whole range of mountains, that gives to Petra one of its most characteristic beauties; the façades of the tombs, tastefully as they are sculptured, owe much of their imposing appearance to this infinite diversity of hues in the stone.

We engaged an Arab shepherd as our guide, and leaving Abou Raschid with our servants and horses, where the steepness of the ascent commences, we began to mount the track, which is extremely steep and toilsome, and affords but an indifferent footing. In most parts the pilgrim must pick his way as he can, and frequently on his hands and knees. Where by nature it would have been impassable, there are flights of rude steps, or inclined planes, constructed of stones laid together, and here and there are niches to receive the foot-steps cut in the live rock; the impression of pilgrims' feet are scratched in the rock in many places, but without inscriptions. Much juniper grows on the mountain, almost to the very summit, and many flowering plants which we had not observed elsewhere; some of these are very beautiful; most of them are thorny. On the top there is an overhanging shelf in the rock, which forms a sort of cavern; here we found a skin of extremely bad water, suspended for drinking, and a pallet of straw, with the pitcher, and the other poor utensils of the sheikh who resides here. He is a decrepit old man, who has lived here during the space of forty years, and occasionally endured the fatigue of descending and reascending the mountain. The tomb itself is enclosed in a small building, differing not at all in external form and appearance, from those of Mahommedan saints, common throughout every province of Turkey. It has probably been rebuilt at no remote period; some small columns are bedded in the walls, and some fragments of granite, and slabs of white marble are lying about. The door is near the S.W. angle, within which a constructed tomb, with a pall thrown over it, presents itself immediately upon entering; it is patched together out of fragments of stone and marble that have made part of other fabrics. Upon one of these are several short lines in the

Hebrew character, cut in a slovenly manner; we had them interpreted at Acre, and they proved to be merely the names of a Jew and his family who had scratched this record; it is not probable that any professed Jew has visited the spot for ages past, perhaps not since the period of the Mahommedan conquest; it may lay claim, therefore, to some antiquity, and in any case is a curious appendage to the testimony of Josephus on this subject. There are rags and shreds of yarn, with glass beads and paras, left as votive offerings by the Arabs ([75]). Not far from the N. W. angle is a passage, descending by steps to a vault or grotto beneath, for we were uncertain which of the two to call it, being covered with so thick a coat of whitewash, that it is difficult to distinguish whether it is built or hollowed out. It appeared, in great part at least, a grotto; the roof is covered, but the whole is rude, ill-fashioned, and quite dark; the sheikh, who was not informed that we were Christians, a circumstance which our guide was not aware of, furnished us with a lamp of butter. Towards the farther end of this dark vault lie the two corresponding leaves of an iron grating, which formerly prevented all nearer approach to the tomb of the prophet; they have, however, been thrown down, and we advanced so as to touch it; it was covered by a ragged pall. We were obliged to descend bare-footed ([76]), and were not without some apprehension of treading on scorpions or other reptiles in such a place.

The view from the summit of the edifice is extremely extensive in every direction, and the eye rests upon few objects, which it can clearly distinguish and give a name to, though an excellent idea is obtained of the general face and features of the country. The chain of Idumean mountains, which form the western shore of the Dead Sea, seem to run on to the southward, though losing considerably in their height; they appear in this point of view barren and desolate. Below them is spread out a white sandy plain, seamed with the beds of occasional torrents, and presenting much the same features as the most desert parts of the Ghor. Where this desert expanse approaches the foot of Mount Hor, there arise out of it, like islands, several lower peaks and ridges of a purple colour, probably composed of the same kind of sand-stone as that of Mount Hor itself, which, variegated as it is in its hues, presents in the distance one uniform mass of dark purple. Towards the Egyptian side there is an expanse of country without features or limit, and lost in the distance. The lofty district which we had quitted in our descent to Wady Mousa, shuts up the prospect on the S. E. side; but there is no part of the landscape which the eye wanders over with more curiosity and delight than the crags of Mount Hor itself, which stand up on every side in the most rugged and fantastic forms; sometimes strangely piled one on the other, and sometimes as strangely yawning in clefts of a frightful depth. In the midst of this chaos there rises into sight one finished work, distinguished by profuseness of ornament, and richness of detail. It is the same which has been described as visible from other elevated points, but which we were never able to arrive at; it bears N. E. half N. from this spot, but the number and intricacy of the vallies and ravines, which we supposed might have led us to it, baffled all our attempts. No guide was to be found. With the assistance of the glass we made out the façade to be larger to all appearance than that of the temple at the eastern approach, and nowise inferior to it in richness and beauty. It is hewn out of the rock, and seemed to be composed of two tiers of columns, of which the upper range is Ionic; the centre of the monument is crowned with a vase of a gigantic proportion; the whole appeared to be in a high state of preservation; it may perhaps be an ornament to the northern approach to the city, similarly situated to that on the eastern side from Mount Hor. Petra is intercepted and concealed by the prominences of the mountains. An artist who would study rock scenery in all its wildest and most extravagant forms, and in colours, which, to one who has not seen them, would scarcely appear to be in nature, would find himself rewarded should he resort to Mount Hor for that sole purpose.

We had employed just one hour in the ascent, and found that our return to the place where we had left our horses occupied the same time; as the day was closing we were reconducted by Abou Raschid near to the palace, and from thence proceeding in a N.E. direction, quitted the ruins. On leaving Petra the track rises considerably, and is slippery and dangerous; our attention was particularly excited on this side, by remarking with how much care the scanty soil had been banked up into terraces, and disposed into fields and gardens; every nook that could furnish footing for a single plant is turned to account, proving that Strabo was not mistaken in speaking of the horticultural advantages of this city; the inhabitants seem to have made the most of it. At present, the barren state of the country, together with the desolate condition of the city, without a single human being living near it, seem strongly to verify the judgment denounced against it ([77]). It appeared to have been our chief's intention to have carried us for the night to some camp at a greater distance; however, it so happened that we had scarcely quitted the district of the tombs, when we passed near a small camp, consisting of a few tents only. Two men rushing out from them with impetuosity seized our bridles, and carried us by main force to lodge with them; before we could dismount they had contrived to loose the corn bags from behind our saddles, and were fighting with one another, disputing who should fill them. The contest was so much in earnest that the most elderly of the persons engaged was thrown down, and the corn bags which he had secured, snatched from him by force. It will hardly be credited that the object of so much contention was the furnishing necessaries from their own stock, gratis, to persons whom they had never seen before. A sheep was slain, and our supper was as usual: thus finished our first day's visit to the ruins of Petra.

Little more than a general survey had been taken, and that imperfectly. When we proposed returning, the principal objections that were started, were the difficulty of finding provisions for ourselves, and provender for our horses; this was remedied by the purchase of a sheep on our part, together with whatever else was necessary for the ensuing day; it will appear strange to those who have had no experience in Arabian manners, that the same people who had fought with one another a few hours before, for the privilege of providing what we wanted at their own expense, from the moment that payment was talked of, and money shewn to them, became greedy and imposing to the highest degree, and resorted to every method of extortion that they could devise; this is, however, entirely in the Arab character; generous and prone to hospitality at first, and as long as there is no talk or appearance of a recompence, but from the moment it is discovered that any thing can be got, they not only lose all liberality, but even common honesty, and a scene of fraud, double-dealing, and extortion begins; so that, in fact, a poor man may pass better, and upon a more friendly footing than a rich one. The result of the second day's operations has been thrown into the preceding description of Petra. We remained there till night, and took our last farewell with reluctance, leaving unexplored, the great temple which we had seen from Mount Hor; the arch thrown over the chasm of the eastern entrance; the obelisk on one of the commanding heights; many of the ravines and valleys in the entrances of which were tombs, and which promised much if well examined; the insulated and conical mount with steps; the height which we supposed to have been the acropolis, and in short, enough to have employed us four days more at least, but nothing could obtain a further extension of the time allotted. We returned to the same camp where we had passed the night before.

There were great apprehensions of robbers who would carry off our horses in the dark. It was stated they would probably be the Annasee Arabs, who are continually lurking about in the neighbourhood; and it was reported in the morning that two fellows had been seen, who finding that persons were on the watch, made no attempt to do any mischief.

May 26. At day break we quitted the camp and proceeded towards Shobek; the weather throughout the day was excessively cold. An European would find it difficult to believe, that on the 26th of May, in a latitude more southern than the Delta of Egypt, we were suffering great inconvenience from cold, with the wind from the westward. The very elevated situation we were on was in some measure the cause of this, but does not seem quite to account for it; the gusts were so violent, and the cold so bitter, that our people once alighted in the middle of the way, for the purpose of kindling a fire.

Arriving at Abou Raschid's camp, no impatience was expressed at our delay; here we were joined by Sheikh Yousouf and Sahlem; and taking leave of Abou Raschid, who sent his mace-bearer with his iron mace to ensure for us the same reception as if he was himself of our company, ([78]), we proceeded to Shobek. We gave our intrepid friend four hundred piastres, and Mr. Legh presented him with a brass blunderbuss, having a spring bayonet, with which he was much pleased; he kissed us all at parting.

May 27. In the morning we quitted Shobek. On our way, this day, we passed a swarm of locusts that were resting themselves in a gully; they were in sufficient numbers to alter apparently the colour of the rock on which they had alighted, and to make a sort of cracking noise while eating, which we heard before we reached them (Volney compares it to the foraging of an army). Our conductors told us they were on their way to Gaza, and that they pass almost annually. In the evening we arrived at Ipseyra, sometimes called Bsaida; it is a miserable village, and the people a fanatical and surly set. We here met the man who had conducted Sheikh Ibrahim to Wady Mousa, as old Yousouf would not attend him farther than this place; the guide seemed to say that Buckhardt made a very hasty survey of the ruins.

May 28. We went to the tents of Sheikh Sahlem, passing on our way the village of Tafyle, and several others in the district of Djebal; they are generally in picturesque situations.

May 29. In the morning we took our leave of Sheikh Sahlem. On our way we passed several shepherd's boys, who were playing on double pipes similar to some of those represented in the tombs of Egypt. We descended into the Wady El Ahsa, and bathed in the hot spring, which the Arabs call the bath of Solomon the son of David. Crossing the deep ravine and river El Ahsa, we entered into the district of Kerek. El Ahsa is probably the Zared of Scripture, the boundary of the Edomites and Moabites. On our ascent from the valley of the El Ahsa, which occupied two hours, we killed, by the road side, a black scorpion, at least four inches long. About noon we reached a camp belonging to the father of old Yousouf's bride; he is the sheikh of a village called Khanzyre, less than a mile from the camp. The next day we proceeded to Kerek. As we entered Yousouf's quarters, the throats of three kids ranged in a line were cut before us, to celebrate our return. The people were employed bringing in the harvest. We found the sheikh's house very full of Annasee Arabs, who were come with their camels from the eastward to procure corn. They had brought a mare as a present to old Yousouf who had not of late been on good terms with their tribe; he gave, in his turn, six camel loads of wheat and six of barley, a sword of value, and a benish for the chief. The wife of the sheikh's brother was dying of a fever, in a little room which opened into the court, and was so thronged that it was difficult to obtain a sight of the scene: she was lying on the floor speechless, and round her were women and girls, some squatting, and others leaning over her, so thick together that they could not move without treading on one another, or on the sick person, who was hardly visible from the numbers that surrounded her; the whole multitude were uttering the most piercing and piteous cries, nearly to the same tune as at a funeral. Old Yousouf and another male of the family were seated in silence at the lower end of the room towards the door. At our particular request, the troop of mourners were expelled, and the woman left quiet; knowing of no other remedy, and hearing that she was weak from fasting, Mahommed, the soldier, prescribed chicken broth, upon taking which, she recovered surprisingly.

To the S. W. of the castle of Kerek, about a mile distant, is a source the name of which is a memorial of the occupation of this country by the crusaders; it is called Ain-el-Frangee, or the Franks' Fountain.

June 1. In the forenoon we set out on a journey for the purpose of examining the southern extremity of the Dead Sea, under the guidance of an old man of the family of Yousouf Magella, who made us pay him thirty piastres, under the pretence that an escort of three was necessary, at ten piastres each. We left the town by a more easy descent than that by which we first arrived; at the bottom we fell in with a small caravan of horses and mules, who were setting out for Hebron and Jerusalem. We pursued the same road by which we had arrived at Kerek from Hebron. A spot was pointed out to us by Soliman as the scene, in his younger days, of the slaughter of thirty men of Kerek. We could not learn the story very satisfactorily, but it seemed to be the result of a civil war amongst them; it was not far from where we had ourselves been accosted by the armed men, whom we had supposed robbers, and certainly a fitter place for an attack of thieves could not easily be found. We had previously passed many camps; in one of these we were desired to observe a very large herd of cattle collected, which we were informed was a spoil just brought in from the Haouran near Djebal-el-Druze, where they had been robbed by some men in Ismayel's employ. As soon as we came to the pass, which commands an extensive prospect of the Dead Sea, we could observe the effect of the evaporation arising from it, in broad transparent columns of vapour, not unlike water-spouts in appearance, but very much larger. We did not deviate at all from our old route as far as the brook Dara; here the little Hebron caravan halted to eat, and repose for a few hours. They implored us in the most earnest manner, as we valued their safety, not to mention in the huts of the Ghorney's below, that we had seen them, as it would infallibly lead to their being assaulted and robbed; adding, that so small a company could seldom pass that way with safety. From this point we began to take a new course, making a pretty direct descent towards the plain of the Ghor. An open grove of the acassia and doom tree was thinly sprinkled on the first portion of our way; of these a great number were apparently either dead or dying, from what cause we did not learn, possibly their foliage had been stripped by locusts. All this tract might be, and probably has been irrigated, for it would be easy to dam up the brook, and conduct it in almost every direction. The form of fields, and even the marks of furrows are to be seen; and some ruins like those of cottages, or of a small hamlet. Lower down there is, very clearly, an ancient site; stones that have been used in building, though for the most part unhewn, are strewed over a great surface of uneven ground, and mixed both with bricks and pottery. This appearance continues without interruption, during the space of at least half a mile, quite down to the plain, so that it would seem to have been a place of considerable extent. We noticed one column, and we found a pretty specimen of antique, variegated glass; it may possibly be the site of the ancient Zoar. Near these remains the Dara opens from its glen into the plain to the northward, by a nook, where there is a wall of rude brick, with an arched door-way, which, as it seemed not to promise much, we did not examine. The brook so far fertilizes this part of the plain, that it is scattered over with thickets of the acassia and doom plant; we observed another shrub also, the branches of which have an inclination downwards, and are of a dull green with little or no foliage; it bears a fruit about the size of an almond in its green husk, and not very dissimilar in colour, but having several seams or ribs like those on the fruit of the green pippin. When it ripens, the skin retains its roughness without, but becomes soft and juicy like a green gage, and has a sort of sweetness mixed with a strong bitter; by culture it might perhaps be improved to a pleasant fruit; some said it was eatable, but others asserted that it was poisonous, and that children were frequently disordered, or even died after eating it; there is a stone within it, and the smell is sickly and disagreeable. The hare and the partridge of the desert abound throughout this thicket, portions of which are cleared and cultivated. In the very heart of it, not visible in any direction beyond a few yards, unless by the smoke issuing from it, is the village of the Ghorney's, who are by profession Mahommedans, but are looked on by the faithful as little better than absolute infidels, as they seldom, if ever, exercise the forms of their religion. They hire themselves out as herdsmen and shepherds, and are notorious robbers. Their abode has more the appearance of a village in India or the South Seas, than of any we have seen in the east. The weather being now excessively hot, the people were nearly naked; the children quite so: we were well received and few questions asked of us, but our guide shewed great mistrust of our hosts, laying all our goods together close to our heads, where we lay down to sleep.

June 2. On the first dawn we left our guide, who wished to purchase tobacco to take to Kerek, and turning rather to the eastward of north, made our way through the thicket towards the sea beach. We were here surprised to see, for the first time, the oskar plant grown to the stature of a tree, its trunk measuring, in many instances, two feet or more in circumference, and the boughs at least fifteen feet in height, a size which far exceeded any we saw in Nubia; the fruit also was larger and in greater quantity. There is very little doubt of this being the fruit of the Dead Sea so often noticed by the ancients as appearing juicy and delicious to the eye, while within it is hollow, or filled with something grating and disagreeable in the mouth. The natives make use of the filaments, which are enclosed in the fruit, and which somewhat resemble the down of a thistle, as a stuffing for their cushions; and they likewise twist them, like thin rope, into matches for their guns, which they assured us required no application of sulphur to render them combustible. Nearer the sea, the vegetation consists principally of the tamarisk and cane, so high and so thickly set, as to render many parts wholly impassable. The rotten and marshy ground, formed probably by the stagnation of deposited water, during the winter season especially, renders the passage very difficult. The foliage has a salt dew hanging upon it, which gives to the hand the same greasy sensation and appearance that is acquired by dipping it in the sea itself. We saw frequent tracks of the wild boar.

A narrow, pebbly beach, separates the jungle from the sea; it is very hard and firm to the tread, and continues the same along the water's edge, which here turns westward, and forms a bay; as the land lies lower here than in other place, the water encroaches more or less on the shore according to the season; the highest point which it ever reaches being marked by an extensive deposit of timber of all sizes. It dries off into shallows and small pools, which in the end deposit a salt as fine and as well bleached, in some instances, as that in regular salt pans. The western horn of this bay is formed by a sharp promontory, projecting forward into the sea, in a direction nearly from south to north; that is to say, such is the relative bearing of the extremities, for between them there is a considerable concavity in the line of shore where the salt-water stagnates and evaporates. We found several persons peeling off a solid surface of salt, several inches in thickness; they were collecting it and loading it on asses. Towards the same part the ground is treacherous and deep, and only glazed over with a thin crust, not unlike the sediment of mud which the Nile in some parts leaves on its shores. The promontory is not entirely of high land, this being confined to a steep, white ridge running like a spine down the centre; this ridge presents steep, sloping sides, seamed and furrowed into deep hollows by the rains, and terminating at the summit in sharp, triangular points, standing up like rows of tents ranged one above another; the whole is of a substance apparently partaking of the mixture of soft and broken chalk and slate, and is wholly unproductive of vegetation. The height of the eminence varies from ten to about thirty feet, becoming gradually lower towards its northern extremity. At its foot, all round, is a considerable margin of sand, which varies in length and breath according to the season, being much narrower in summer than it is in winter, when we have reason to suppose, that in rough weather, at least, the waves almost wash the base of the cliff. At the northernmost point of the cape some rotten branches are standing up, so encrusted with salt deposited upon them by the spray, or the evaporation, that they have the appearance of straight branches of fine white coral. The total length of this promontory or horn of the bay may be about four miles, computed from the observation, that we employed an hour and twelve minutes in riding along it at a walking pace. Following the line of coast round the angle, the same cliff presents an opposite face of similar appearance and equal height, running two miles or forty minutes in a S. W. by S. direction. Here we first collected lumps of nitre and fine sulphur, from the size of a nutmeg up to that of a small hen's egg; it was evident from their situation that they must have been brought down by the rain, and that their great deposit must be sought for in the cliff ([79]). It is probable that persons come to collect these substances; at least it was the only mode that occurred to us of accounting for the prints of human footsteps which we saw here, and those of asses somewhat farther on; as this place can not fall into any ordinary line of communication. The direction of the cliff is between S. W. and S.; we quitted its foot, where the sand is in some places deep and distressing to the horse, and followed the edge of the beach, which diverges from the cliff to the S. W.; as the water subsides, which being always shallow towards the strait, retires rapidly in this part, a very considerable level is left, which is encrusted with a salt that is but half dried and consolidated, appearing like ice in the commencement of a thaw. All this space is soft, and gives way nearly as deep as the ancle, when it is trod on. We reached the narrowest part of the channel of communication between the sea and the backwater (which we have called the strait) in just two hours, from the foot of the cliff, our direction having been about S. W. The strait is formed by a low promontory projecting from the opposite or western shore; and, fortunately, just as we arrived at the narrowest part, where the ford is indicated by boughs of trees, we observed the small caravan from Kerek landed on the opposite side; and as we could discern the species of animal, as well as the people on their backs, we were all agreed in estimating the distance about a mile. As there were asses of the party, the depth cannot be great. We searched for the shells mentioned by Seetzen, as proving that there are living creatures in the lake, but found none excepting snail shells, and a small spiral species, invariably without any fish, or the appearance of having had any for a long time. Dead locusts were found in very great numbers; they had not become putrid, nor had they any smell, as when cast up by any other sea (vide Volney); they were completely penetrated and incrusted with salt, and had lost their colour. The sight of such a multitude of carcasses of creatures who had perished in passing over these waters, might seem to lend some countenance to the tale of the ancients, " that no living

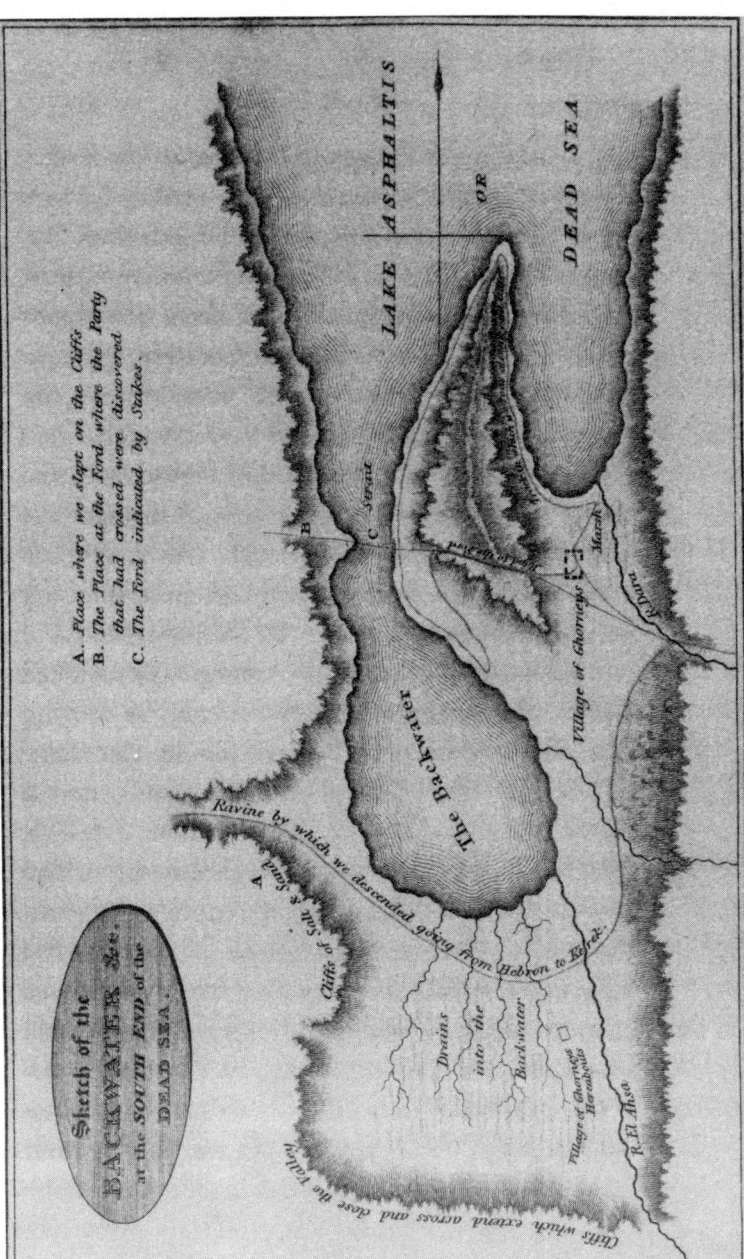

thing could attempt the passage over it with impunity;" were it not a spectacle sufficiently common upon other shores, as Sicily, and about el-Arish; and we had another, still better proof to the contrary, first, in a pair of Egyptian geese, and afterwards in a flight of pigeons which passed over the sea. Leaving the narrowest part of the strait, we followed it to its southern extremity, where it opens into the back-water, and also the shore of the back-water itself to some distance. The high water mark was at this season a mile distant from the water's edge. We were told that this back-water is never dry, and that the ford is not at any season impassable.

It is remarkable how few living things, as birds, or insects, or reptiles, are to be seen on this lake; the want of vegetable matter and fresh water is probably the reason. Having returned from the edge of the back-water, we ascended the cliff, which is steep but practicable, and then we gained a great table-land on its top, where we fell in with the track of those who had passed from Kerek to the ford. In two hours we reached the banks of the Dara, where we found our guide. In the evening, we arrived late at some tents, where Sheikh Yousouf was encamped; we found here a man from Szalt, and two men from Herak in the Haouran, near the Druze country, who had come to reclaim the cattle robbed from them by Ismayel's people([80]), according to what we had heard before. In the morning we removed to Ismayel's tents, when the cause of the stranger was pleaded, but it was before a most partial and interested tribunal, for Yousouf was the accused as well as the judge and arbitrator. He decided accordingly; offering at the utmost to restore half the number that had been stolen. He accused them of having been in some shape the aggressors, but explained himself so little, that we did not learn what provocation he alluded to, it was surprising to find that two places lying so very wide of each other, should have any disputes to settle; there was much arguing and prevarication. Towards noon we returned to Kerek.

June 5. In the afternoon we proceeded on our journey to the northward, accompanied by Sheikhs Yousouf and Ismayel, Dawood, his nephew, and the two men of Herak, together with the man from Szalt. We passed over a fine country, flat, and higher than Kerek, keeping in a N. N. E. direction; the corn was luxuriant in all directions, and the reapers were working. Several sites which we passed, proved that the population of this country was formerly proportioned to its natural fertility. In about two hours we reached Rabba, formerly Rabbath-Moab, afterwards Areopolis; the ruins are situated on an eminence, and present nothing of interest, except two old ruined Roman temples, and some tanks. The whole circuit of the town does not seem to have exceeded a mile, which is a small extent for a city that was the capital of Moab, and which bore such a sounding Greek name. We were yet more surprised not to find any traces of walls about it. We passed the night at a small camp near the ruins; it is the only *Christian camp* we have ever been in; they told us there were altogether five encampments of Christians. They were poor people, but connected with families in Kerek; occasionally they take their turn in the town, and send others to take theirs in the camp. A deep gully behind their tents led to the Dead Sea. This evening, about sun-set, we were deceived by a dark shade on the sea, which assumed so exactly the appearance of an island, that we did not doubt of it, even after looking through a telescope. It is not the only time that such a phænomenon has presented itself to us; in two instances, looking up the sea from its southern extremity, we saw it apparently closed by a low, dark line, like a bar of sand to the northward; and on another occasion two small islands seemed to present themselves between a long sharp promontory and the western shore. We were unable to account for these appearances, but felt little doubt that they are the same that deceived Mr. Seetzen into the supposition that he had discovered an island of some extent, which we have had opportunity of ascertaining, beyond all doubt, does not exist. It is not absolutely impossible, however, that he may have seen one of those temporary islands of bitumen which Pliny describes as being of several acres in extent, and from which he adds, that the Egyptians drew their store of resinous matter for embalming their mummies.

June 6. This morning we visited the ruins of Beit-Kerm, distant from Rubba about one mile and a half to the north. The principal feature of them is a great building, evidently Roman, resembling that which we took to have been a palace at Petra; perhaps this is the temple of Atargatis, at Carnaim, as it is called in 1 Maccabees, v. 43. or Carnion, b. 2. xii. 26. A great number of tanks prove that this was once a populous place ([81]). There were four camps near the ruins; we lodged in one; the men of Herak renewed their discussions and remonstrances with Yousouf, for having returned to them but forty head of their cattle. These were driven along the same road by which we travelled, and the drivers generally halted when we did. Two hours and a half north from

Beit-Kerm there is a slight eminence, which forms a conspicuous object from all the country round, and is called " Sheikh Harn."

June 7. During this day we visited several elevated heights, each commanding very fine views of the Dead Sea, which both comprehended the back-water at one end, and the Plains of Jericho at the other. Jerusalem and the Frank Mount were also discernible, and from the different bearings which we made, we ascertained for a certainty that the length of the lake, Asphaltis, including the back-water, does not exceed thirty miles at the utmost, though the ancients have assigned to it a length of from seventy-five to eighty miles. From the first height the bearings were as follows; Jerusalem, N. W. $\frac{3}{4}$ N.; Frank Mount, N. W. $\frac{3}{4}$ W.; Jericho, N. by W.; east end of the back-water, S. W. by S. From the second height, Sheikh Harn, E. $\frac{1}{4}$ S.; the first-mentioned hill, N. N. E. $\frac{1}{2}$ E.; the Strait leading to the back-water, W. S. W. $\frac{3}{4}$ W.; the village of the Ghorney's, S. W. by W. $\frac{1}{4}$ W.; the hollow of the bay W. S. W. $\frac{1}{4}$ W.; Jericho, N. $\frac{3}{4}$ W.; the extremity of the back-water, S. W. $\frac{1}{2}$ S. Jerusalem and the Frank Mount were not visible, it being very late in the day.

On reaching the tents we found the men of Herak out of all patience at Yousouf's injustice in making so little retribution; they called us aside to assure us that he was no better than a robber, and hoped that we would publish and confirm their complaints at Damascus. "We will drag him by the beard," said they "to Mezeereeb." But it would be no easy task to force the lord of Kerek out of his district.

June 8. We proceeded to the northward, and in about two hours arrived upon the brink of the Wady Modjeb the ancient Arnon; on looking down, it has more the appearance of a precipice than a road, and although the Roman way coincides with the modern track very near to the brink, and again about half way down it, it must have been in a very different state, at least from that by which we descended, and which is not only extremely steep, but so interrupted with rocks and stones, that we were obliged to dismount and lead our horses full half way down the descent. In this rocky space there is only here and there a straggling turpentine tree; about half way the declivity is more earthy and shelving; hereabouts we recovered the Roman highway. It is not here as above, completely paved, but at regular intervals a line of stones is carried across the road in the manner of a step, to prevent the washing away of the earth from above, and to serve as a resting place in the descent. On the right hand of the road, a shallow tank of considerable size, walled round with thick and good masonry, is placed on the side of the hill; and below it, at only a few yards distance, are the remains of a large square building which we took to be a Roman military station; there was another above on the brink of the precipice. We found several mile-stones; all those which were legible, were of the time of Trajan. The valley of the Arnon is less shrubby than that of most other streams in this country, which is probably ascribable to the violence and frequency of its torrents. There are, however, a few tamarisks, and here and there an oleander growing about it; it is not more than three paces wide where the Roman road comes down upon the stream, and there remains a high single arch, measuring twenty-eight feet nine inches in perpendicular height, and thirty-one feet six inches in space; the remnants of the other arches of the bridge have all disappeared. The descent occupied one hour and a half. In our ascent up the opposite side, we followed mostly the ancient road, and found some more Roman mile-stones; one of Marcus Aurelius. We found the road on this side as steep as it was on the other, and it was remarkable in this pass, that from either side looking to the other, there appeared no possible mode of ascent. We had now passed from the land of the Moabites into that of the Amorites. It is observable that as far as the eye could follow the course of the stream from the heights, the valley is neither of a size or nature that could ever have admitted of cultivation, or have given room for the placing of any village or city on its banks, which makes it probable that those places, which were supposed to stand upon the river, were in reality only in the adjacent district.

We found the territory of the Amorites a plane down, of a smoother and evener turf than that of Moab, and with much fewer stones scattered over it. We soon recovered the ancient road, and in forty-five minutes reached Diban, the Dibon of Scripture, Numb. xxi. 30. and Jeremiah, xlviii. 18. The extent of these remains is considerable, but not so large as Rabba. The ruins present nothing of interest. In the afternoon we arrived at a camp in the Wady Wale, pitched on the banks of the river, which this year seems to have swollen to a prodigious degree; the oleanders are here more numerous than we have ever seen them; some which is very rare bore a white flower, the rushing of the waters had rooted many of them up, and the whole were thrown aslant by the course of the torrent, the marks of which were seen upon them to the height of fifteen feet. On the left bank stands a stone about ten feet high, four feet wide at the base in its broadest part, and not more than one foot at the narrowest; it has been set up an end by art, being placed contrary to the natural direction of the strata, and at right angles to the stream very near the bank. We supposed it to be one of those ancient bound stones of which we read so frequently in Scripture. Across the stream, but at a greater distance from its channel, is another similar stone, bearing obliquely on the path, its broadside parallel to the stream. There are no signs of sculpture on them, nor is there any appearance of their having ever been wrought, with the tool ([82]). There is in this same valley another rude work, that may be referred to a remote period; it is higher up by perhaps a quarter of a mile than the two bound stones. A knoll, of very moderate height, rises detached near the centre of the valley, upon the right bank of the rivulet. On its summit are the remains of a very large quadrangular platform, constructed of rude stones laid together without cement. It is possible that this may be one of the " altars of the high places." It is still a place in some measure consecrated; there is a tomb at the top with paltry Bedouin votive offerings hanging about it. About a mile lower down the valley, are the remains of a Roman bridge of five arches; all are fallen, and nothing but the foundation of the piers is left. Near this bridge are other ruins. These were the first objects in our days' journey, on the ninth. From hence we passed upwards out of the valley; near the ancient paved road there were several mile-stones, one of which was of *Severus*. We passed, at the foot of Djebal Attarous, which probably may be Nebo, although it is far from opposite Jericho. We now entered a fertile plain of corn, and stopped at a camp near the ruins of Mayn, which both the name and the neighbouring hot-waters seem to identify with the Baal Meon of Scripture; it stands on a considerable eminence. In the afternoon, we went to a height which commands a fine view of the Dead Sea, and is very near on a parallel with its northern extremity. Here we took the following bearings; Jericho, N. W. ¾ N. Mouth of the Jordan, N. W. ½ N.; Rama of Samuel, N. W. by W.; Djebal Attarous, S. W.; Frank Mountain, W. N. W. ¾ W.; Sheikh Harn, S. ½ W. Below us was a ruin of a square form which we could not get at; from its position we thought it might possibly be Herodium. At sun-set we returned to the camp near Mayn, from whence there are a great number of ruined sites visible, and amongst the the rest Heshbon, bearing N. E. ¾ N.

We engaged a guide from our tents, who undertook to carry us to the sources of hot-water; our route was S.W.; in less than half an hour we reached another tall stone, set up apparently as a boundary mark, like those in the Wady-el-Wale. The direct track is continued from this first, round the southern side of a rocky knoll rising to some height, and in a great measure detached from the surrounding hills. Some remarkable objects, of which we got a glimpse, induced us to pass round on the other side of this knoll; they are rude sepulchral monuments of the same nature with those we discovered on our road from Szalt to the Jordan on our last tour; yet, as the former are rude throughout, without any mark whatever of the tool about them, whereas the others have universally a door in one of the smaller ends, it is possible that they may date from a remoter period, or have belonged to a still ruder people. Their proportions vary considerably, as does their aspect, though the construction is uniform; one flat stone is laid in at the bottom, and this there can be little doubt covers the grave of the deceased; and, as there is no appearance of the tombs ever having been violated, it probably protects them to this day. They would be a highly interesting object for excavation, as it might possibly lead to the ascertaining of the form of some of the weapons and warlike apparel mentioned in Scripture. It is worth noticing, that however remote may be the period to which these sepulchres are to be referred, the stature of those contained in them, is so far from gigantic, that it seems to have amounted to no more than the middle size of modern times.

Not only this rocky eminence, upon which we first observed them, is covered over on all sides with these barbarous structures, but some few are scattered in the fields upon a lower level, and a great many upon the sides of the surrounding hills, insomuch that not less than fifty were in sight at one time. We were puzzled to think to what city this necropolis belonged; Mayn being more than a mile off, in a straight line, would seem too distant. Some which we had passed on our left hand the afternoon before, called Dher, were now visible, upon an eminence at no great distance to the north. Passing on, we found ourselves in an ancient highway, not paved, but edged with stones, and possibly prior to Roman times. Arriving at the brink of a deep descent, towards the Zerka Mayn, we found the track steep, winding, and long. In about two hours from Mayn we reached the bed of the Torrent Zerka Mayn, which we crossed, and kept along it in a western direction. We saw ten animals which the Arabs call Meddn or Beddn; they are of the goat species, as large as asses, with long knotty horns which stand upright; some had beards; in colour they resembled the gazelle. In four hours from Mayn we had reached the place where it was necessary to dismount, the appearance beyond being that of a precipice. Through this, a narrow path has been contrived in a zig-zag direction, which makes the descent tolerably safe. In the last stage of the path there is a fine burst of the Dead Sea at the end of the ravine, with a view of the Frank Mount, and Bethlehem open beyond it; the former bearing N. N. W. Looking down into the valley of Calirrhoe, it presents some grand and romantic features. The rocks vary between red, grey, and black, and have a bold and imposing appearance. The whole bottom is filled, and in a manner choked with a crowded thicket of canes and aspines of different species, intermixed with the palm, which is also seen rising in tufts in the recesses of the mountain's side, and in every place whence the springs issue. In one place a considerable stream of hot-water is seen precipitating itself from a high and perpendicular shelf of rock, which is strongly tinted with the brilliant yellow of sulphur deposited upon it. On reaching the bottom we found ourselves at what may be termed a hot river, so copious and rapid is it, and its heat so little abated; this continues as it passes downwards by its receiving constant supplies of water of the same temperature. In order to visit these sources in succession, we crossed over to the right bank, and ascending by the mountain side, we passed four abundant springs, all within the distance of half a mile, discharging themselves into the stream at right angles with its course. We judged the distance from the Dead Sea, by the ravine, to be about one hour and a half. Macbean says, that there was a cognominal city at Calirrhoe; in which we think, from the very nature of the place, he must be wrong, since there is not space or footing for a town in the valley as far as we saw it. That Herod must have had some lodging when he visited these springs is true, and there are sufficient remains to prove that some sort of buildings have been erected. The whole surface of the shelf, where the springs are, is strewed over with tiles and broken pottery; and what is most surprising, within very few minutes, without any particular search, four ancient copper medals were found; all were too much defaced to be distinguishable, but they appeared to be Roman. Our Arab guide here took a vapour bath according to the practice of the country; a bed of twigs and broom was laid across a crevice, whence one of the springs issued at the height of a foot or two from the water; on this he laid himself, wrapped in his Abba, and only remained a few minutes; the effect of the steam upon him was soon very evident. We observed another of these sweating beds a little further down. We had no thermometer, but the degree of heat in the water seemed very great; near the source it scalds the hand, which cannot be kept in for the space of half a minute. The deposit of sulphur is very great, but the water is tasteless to the palate. A very singular plant grows near the hot sources, of the bulk and stature of a tree; its foliage does not seem to differ from that of the common broom. It bears a pod hanging down from it, about a foot or fourteen inches in length, fluted with convex ribs from the end to the point; we never met with this before. After bathing, we returned by the same road, and passing our old camp at Mayn, proceeded to the great encampment of the Benesuckhers near Madeba. We arrived at night-fall; there were more than two hundred tents scattered over a great extent of ground; we alighted at that of the chief " Ebn Fayes," which was at least one hundred feet long. The chief, and his brother, the same who was with us on our former Djerash expedition, and from whom we escaped to Szalt, received us outside their tent ([83]). They were dressed in handsome silk caftans from Damascus. Sheikh Yousouf had previously been invested with an ermine pelisse ([84]), and made an odd figure, having his red tanned sheep-skin underneath it. The three close sides of the tent were allotted to the visitors, the two chiefs sitting on the open side scarcely within the cover of the tent. The elder brother, who has a hair lip, called for his one-stringed fiddle and played to us, singing at the same time. On our enquiring the purport of his song, he said it was the "death of his father," who we learned had been killed in battle; the notes, though but little varied, were plaintive and harmonious ([85]). There was within the tent a messenger from Damascus, whom we had once seen at Kerek; he had arrived in the course of the afternoon to summon or invite Ebn Fayes to go to Damascus to the pashaw. It was supposed his object was either to make some arrangement with the Benesuckhers for the safe conduct of the hadj to Mekka, as the Annasees under Sheikh Narsah were in rebellion; or to endeavour to reconcile the division which had taken place between the Benesuckhers, that they might be a check against the Annasees. To the accidental presence of this man, the reception we met with was probably owing; and we were lucky in the absence of Abdel Khader, the prime minister, our former enemy. The wooden dish in which our supper was served, was of a size to require four iron handles, and was brought in by three persons.

June 11. This morning, we were told that Ebn Fayes was already on his way to Damascus. His brother remained with us. We requested of him a guide for Oom-i-Rasass, which after some hesitation and talk of danger and enemies, was promised, and an agreement in money made; we were to pass by Madeba as we advanced. After breakfast we proceeded. At Madeba, the only object of interest was an immense tank ([86]). At three we reached Oom-i-Rasass (Mother of Stones). We found the ruins very extensive, and evidently Christian; there were the remains of a stone wall which enclosed the whole city; the cross is often to be met with, but there is no architectural remnant worthy of notice. Mr. Bankes, with his janissary, took a second tour in search of inscriptions, while we remained under the wall. While walking about the ruins, an armed Bedouin made his appearance and robbed him of his abba. Excepting in our journey to Palmyra, we here saw more camels than we had ever before met with.

June 12. We reached Heshbon in the evening, where we found Sheikh Yousouf, the man of Szalt, and the young prince of the Benesuckhers; our first object was to see the ruins, and to inspect the celebrated pools; but just at starting we received a message from Ebn Fayes, to demand payment for permission to proceed; we sent word in reply, that we had already paid him on a former occasion; in answer, we received a message to this effect, tell them, said the young man, " that the first that moves from the tent receives this ball (presenting a pistol) through his body." The firman was now mentioned; he said he cared nothing for firmans; that he considered them only fit for those who were weak enough to obey them; that *he* was Grand Seignior, and every thing else here, and that we must pay. While thus detained, a man brought some wheat to parch ([87]), and to our surprise we observed the ears of an unusual size, one of them exceeding in dimensions two of the ordinary sort, and on one stalk ([88]). Mr. Legh procured some, which he brought to England; it has succeeded very well; we have since learnt that it is not wholly unknown to botanists; it is a bearded wheat. The annexed drawing is from nature, though to prevent delay in printing this book, the plant was unavoidably gathered too early (July 20) to convey a correct idea of its size when at maturity. After some delay, Ebn Fayes seeing we were not inclined to give in, sent word that we might proceed. We found the ruins uninteresting, and the only pool we saw, was too insignificant for one of those mentioned in Scripture. In two of the cisterns amongst the ruins

Heshbon Wheat.　　English Wheat.
Weight.
103gr or 1dr 2st 3gr　　42grs or 0dr 0st 2gr 2gr

Length of Straw.
5ft 1in　　4ft 2in

Number of Grains in the Ear
84　　41

HESHBON WHEAT.

Miss Strickland del.　　On Stone by V. Bartholomew.

we found about three dozen of human sculls and bones (⁸⁹).

June 13. We left Heshbon, passing by a stream which, if followed, would probably have led to the pools. We then proceeded along the road to Szalt, and in about four hours arrived at a place called by the natives Arrag-el-Emir. Here are the ruins of an edifice constructed of very large stones, some of which are twenty feet long, and so broad that one stone constitutes the thickness of the wall. The ruin is situated upon a square platform or terrace, of some extent, with a stream below. From the situation, and from the circumstance of large beasts, in relievo, being sculptured about it, Mr. Bankes believed it to be the palace of Hircan, who, according to Josephus, being driven across the Jordan by his brother Alexander, king of Jerusalem, had built a palace in this neighbourhood, surrounded by hanging gardens, traces of which are yet visible. There are many artificial caves in a large range of perpendicular cliff near it; some of these are in the form of regular stables, in which feeding-troughs still remain, sufficient for thirty or forty horses, with holes in the live rock for the head fastenings. Some of the caves are chambers and small sleeping apartments, probably for servants and attendants. There are two rows of these chambers; the upper one has a sort of projecting balcony across the front of the chambers. There is one large hall finely proportioned, with some Hebrew characters inscribed over the door-way; the whole is approached by a sort of causeway. We spent the whole remaining part of the day here, and slept at an adjoining camp. On the hill, immediately above the palace, are the remains of a small temple much in ruins.

June 14. We advanced to Szalt, passing through a richly wooded and picturesque country; we arrived early in the afternoon, and lodged in the castle. We remained at Szalt until the 16th, when we proceeded three hours in the direction of Amman. Near this place we passed the night in a camp belonging to the party of the Benesuckhers hostile to Ebn Fayes, and we employed the chief part of the next day in examining the ruins of Rabbath Ammon, afterwards Philadelphia, and now Amman. They stand in a long valley, a stream running through them, which has been arched over. The ruins are extensive, but there remains nothing of much interest excepting the theatre, which is very large and perfect, and a small odeum close to it. There are the vestiges also of many other Roman edifices, as well as of Christian churches. We did not find any inscriptions.

June 17. We passed the night at an Arab camp, about three miles distant on the road to

Djerash. Here old Yousouf was again accused of having stolen cattle from the people; it was said to have happened four years ago. After much dispute he ended the argument by saying that " he was one of those people who never returned any thing after it was once in his power."

June 18. At dawn of day we advanced. In about two hours Yousouf took leave of us to return to Kerek. He had made strong demands for money, both for himself and his nephew Daoud, though at Szalt we had made him a present of two hundred piastres over and above his agreement. He also tried to make us give an exorbitant sum to our guide for Djerash, but failed. Notwithstanding all this it must be admitted that he strictly and honestly adhered to his contract with us; and it is doubtful whether we should ever have succeeded in reaching Wady Mousa in safety, if it had not been for him. His only dishonesty towards us was borrowing money from Mr. Bankes, and refusing to repay it; but where all are rogues, and cheating and imposition are reckoned honourable and fair, and do not at all hurt the character of a man amongst his companions, one must not expect too much.

We crossed the Zerka, the Jabbok of Scripture ([90]), the northern boundary of the Amorites about noon, and at two in the afternoon reached

Djerash. We employed this and part of the next day in making those measurements of the public edifices which we had left unfinished before; most of them were Christian churches. Among many new inscriptions which we found, was one recording the dedication of one of the churches to a Christian saint. Macbean, in quoting Eusebius, says, "that the Christians, just before the siege of Jerusalem by Titus, were divinely admonished to fly to Pella;" and Strabo notices, "that it abounded in water;" from Ptolemy he adds, "that Pella was situated thirty-five miles to the N. E. of Gerasa." Macbean also quotes from Ptolemy and Josephus, "that Gerasse was at the east side of the sea of Tiberias;" these authorities seem to shew that the ruins at Djerash are those of Pella rather than Gerasa. In short, nothing but the similarity of names would lead one to suppose that they are Gerasa.

June 19. Intending to proceed to the valley of the Jordan, by the way of a place called Rajib, where we expected to find the ruins of Ragaba, we quitted Djerash in the afternoon, and passed through Katty, and another village where there are some Roman remains in the mosque, about half an hour beyond it. We entered a very picturesque country, most beautifully varied with hanging woods, mostly of the Vallonia oak, laurestinus, cedar, common arbutus, arbutus Andrachne, &c. the latter in some instances was nearly six feet in cicumference; at times the grounds had all the appearance of a noble park; in short, nothing could exceed the beauty of this day's ride; there were some few spots cultivated with corn. As we advanced the wood became more thick; and at dark we stopped at a small open space covered with high grass and weeds. We went with our guide to a small distance to endeavour to shoot some wild boars; we hid ourselves close to the water, where all the trees were marked with mud left by the hogs in rubbing themselves. We heard them plainly advancing, but one of the horses unluckily making a noise, they all ran off. These animals we were told are very numerous here. We returned to our bivouack. Our guide refused to go for water, fearing the serpents in the high grass. Mr. Legh, in the night, feeling something move underneath him, rose to see what it was, and found an adder coming up to him from under the edge of his blanket, attracted no doubt by the warmth of his body, as the night air was very cold; having a knife by him he cut the reptile in halves. In the morning we found another close to our sleeping place.

June 20. We started at dawn, and descending still through a thick wood, arrived at ten, at the village of Rajib, which contains no ruins whatever; though we had previously passed in the wood a Roman architrave, in a small open space, where our guide told us there had once been a village; no other vestiges of which remain. Rajib is situated a little without, and below the woodlands. At noon we began a rapid descent towards the valley of the Jordan, and reached it in two hours. We saw nine wild pigs in our way; they were all in one herd; four hours more, in a northerly direction, brought us to the Bysan ford, and we arrived at that town after dark.

June 21. We went to Tiberias, and the 23rd visited Mount Tabor on our way to Nazareth. Maundrell over-rates the view from this eminence; we saw nothing striking except the beautiful plain of Esdredon. In a cave, amongst the ruins of the town, on the top of Tabor, we noticed many travellers' names; and amongst others, that of Mr. Wright, who visited this place when first lieutenant of the Tigre with Sir Sydney Smith, and who afterwards died in the Temple at Paris; Sheikh Ibrahim's name was also there. For Nazareth and its neighbourhood we refer you to Maundrell.

June 25. Went to Acre. During our stay at Acre we witnessed an instance of unfeeling barbarity. On going to breakfast at the consul's, his Greek servant, who had been very ill for some days before, was lying outside the door, and actually expired on the floor before us as we entered the room, unattended by either medical or any other assistance. The corpse lay neglected for some time, before any one could be found to take it away, all refusing to touch it lest they should be at the trouble and expense of burying it. At last the Turkish authorities interfered and the body was removed. As we have now been more amongst the Arabs, and have had better opportunities of studying their manners and habits than on our former short journey to Palmyra, some farther observations upon them become necessary. The love of liberty created in the wandering Bedouin, by his erratic habits, is instinctively cherished by him from his very infancy; impatient of every species of controul, and proud of his indepedence, he disowns and scorns the cultivating Arab. We found these people still deserving of their character for hospitality, but we never heard of the celebrated story of *bread and salt*, mentioned by Volney; if the mere eating of bread and salt with an Arab was a security from imposition, Sheikh Sahlem, when threatening us, would have said, " had you not ate bread and salt with me, &c." instead of "had you not Shiekh Yousouf with you;" for we had feasted with Sahlem in his own tent, before we had the difference with him. Mr. Bankes was imprisoned, and Sir William Chatterton robbed of his breeches at Palmyra, after eating bread and salt, and we had feasted with Ebn Fayes at Heshbon, before his ill treatment of us. It would certainly be a most noble commendation to advance in their favour were it true. There is a great deal of good breeding amongst them, a sheikh arriving at another's tent, seats himself opposite his friend to avoid all appearance of pre-eminence, so that either side of the tent is occupied, while the end, the "post of honour," remains vacant. When Mr. Bankes presented the Sheikh of Souf with a dress, he immediately sent it into the harem, without looking at it in the presence of the donor; and the people of Kerek, on our arrival, although our appearance must have been so novel to them, abstained from asking any questions. But although civil, they had a great contempt for us, and observing how aukwardly we ate with our hands, for we never, during the whole tour, saw a spoon, or knife, or fork, they remarked amongst themselves, " Poor fellows! they don't even know how to eat; they eat like camels." If an Arab chief gives you coffee first he takes none after, not choosing to drink after a Christian. Thieving, pilfering, low cunning, lying, and cheating, are not considered as dishonourable acts amongst them; we were all of us robbed of some of our effects. On one occasion, Mr. Bankes's drawing of the grand temple at Petra was purloined, and after some days' negociation, he was allowed to purchase it back again, they having confessed all the time that they had it. Mr. Legh's Bible was also pilfered in the same manner, and never recovered. Mr. Bankes's two paint boxes were also stolen, and many other articles were lost. Our diet, while we were with them, varied according to the wealth or poverty of the tribe; sometimes we had pillaw of rice, or of wheat mixed with leban (sour milk), sometimes mutton boiled the moment the animal is skinned (^{92}), and generally in leban, a custom alluded to in Scripture (^{93}). This mode of cooking renders the meat very delicious and tender; far preferable to meat boiled in water: the milk enriched with the juice of the meat is poured on the pillaw of rice or wheat (^{94}). Sometimes we had melted butter, and bread baked on an iron plate in the form of a pancake to dip in it. The staple of the Arabs food, however, is leban and bread. The milk was usually presented in a wooden bowl, and the liquid butter in an earthenware dish (^{95}). The party being seated round, dipped their bread in, endeavouring to make it imbibe as much as possible. The Arabs were very expert at this, pinching the thin cake in such a form as to make a sort of spoon of it. This mode of eating is alluded to in Scripture at the feast of the Passover ([96]). Occasionally a bowl of milk only was presented to us, which was passed round in rotation. Once we had milk sweetened and curdled to the consistency of liquid jelly, too thick to be drank, and very aukward to be taken up with the hands, though it was the only method of eating it. A rich dish of rice and cream was once given us as a great treat. All the way between Kerek and Petra, we had meat served up alone, without bread or even pillaw of rice or wheat. We could not at all reconcile ourselves to this diet, which we found used in this district only. When the Arabs have an over supply of leban, they have a method of preserving it by pressing out the more liquid parts, and drying the curds, which may then be kept for some time; this substance has the appearance of soft chalk, when mixed with water it makes an agreeable acid drink.

When we had pillaw of grain, it often served also for a candlestick, the candle being fixed in the middle of the dish. An Arab, when he wishes to pay you very particular attention, pulls your meat to pieces with his fingers and throws it to you. We never saw roasted meat among the Arabs, except at Narsah's tent at Palmyra. They have no fruits or vegetables; their wandering life depriving them of such enjoyments. It is their custom from time immemorial, to lodge and feed all travellers and their horses for one night free of all expense; as the practice is general, it is equally beneficial to all. We never once paid for food or corn during the whole of our journey, and the expenses of the whole party, eleven persons and as many horses, amounted to one thousand five hundred piastres; a piastre is worth nine-pence of our money, this was from the fifth of May to the twenty-fifth of June. Each owner of a tent takes it by turns to feed the strangers that may arrive. Their jokes were sometimes rather rough; on one occasion, an Arab put a living scorpion inside my jacket ([97]), luckily, some time after, I had occasion to make the usual daily search for vermin, when I discovered the reptile. At the Ghor, when we asked if a poisonous fruit was good, they said it was.

The women weave carpets and cloth for their tents, which are mostly black, and curtains which are striped white and black. Goat's hair ([98]) is manufactured for this purpose. The women have hard work, they grind the corn with a hand-mill, bring the water and wood, cook, and in short do all the drudgery, while the men sit down and smoke all day. The children guard the flocks, the girls always having a bundle of wool at their backs for spinning ([99]). The form of the tents is oblong. We frequently observed negroes in their camps, apparently not slaves; and some had the short woolly hair of the Africans. It may not be amiss here to mention, that, though we never had any apprehensions of personal safety from the Arabs, yet there are some grounds for the dread these people are held in throughout Syria, as we met with many dead bodies concealed in the country frequented by them; we saw twenty in one of the Roman tombs near Nablous, the mouth of which had been shut up with stones; three in one of the theatres at Om Keis; twenty four skulls, &c. in the theatre at Bysan, and subsequently twenty two in the ruins at Heshbon. Whenever we enquired about these proofs, the Arabs always owned they were the remains of people whom they had murdered, and they did not appear to be in the least ashamed of the deed. One in particular at Om Keis was stated to be a soldier. To keep your arms on in a tent, is considered very ill bred, as implying a distrust in the protection of the roof you are under; and whenever we forgot to disarm, the Arabs always requested us to do so.

These people are frequently without water,

and sometimes even that which they have is dirty and bad; nevertheless they are "lords of the desert," pay no tribute, and have nothing whatever to do with governours of any description.

The desert, as one of the ancient authors, I think Diodorus, observes, is their fort, whither they retire as to a place of certain safety on any appearance of attack. The state and equipage of the sheikhs is maintained by means of a revenue derived from a tithe which they exact for all the cattle, the camels excepted ([100]). This tenth of the innumerable herds and flocks, yields the chiefs a very handsome income. The supper in Sheikh Narsah's and Ebn Fayes' tents was bountiful in the extreme; and, as this profuse hospitality is extended to all strangers, there must needs be ample store to meet so great a demand.

It is surprising, that in so monotonous a life, they have no amusements, no games, no athletic employments, to make a little change in their custom of squatting down and smoking all day. All their carpets, cushions, sacks, and in short, every thing they have are covered with vermin, so that it is impossible to avoid them. We used to kill from off our clothes from forty to a hundred every day; and of a night, we frequently observed the Arabs searching and shaking their linen over the fire, the vermin making a cracking noise as they fell into the flames. Old Yousouf used to make a singular figure, with his sword drawn, detaching them from his back. At one time my sides were quite raw from scratching. On settling our accounts, both for this last journey, and the previous one from Tiberias, we found the expences of each, much less than we had anticipated.

July 12th. We embarked on board an imperial brig belonging to Venice for Constantinople, as the consuls on the coast, the merchants, and both Mr. Bankes and Mr. Leigh agreed in opinion, that it would have been madness to have gone to the coast of Asia Minor at this season of the year, when the pestilential air forces all the inhabitants of the coast to quit their habitations, and retire to the mountains during the summer. We have, therefore, deferred this part of the tour for a short time. Our friend, Mr. Legh, left Acre for this place by land, a short time before we did, intending to visit Palmyra, Baalbec, Damascus, and Aleppo. Mr. Bankes went by water to Egypt, with the intention of penetrating into Abyssinia by way of the second cataract. We were truly sorry to part with such excellent companions.

LETTER VI.

Departure from Constantinople for Scutari.—Cross an arm of the sea of Marmora, and proceed through Kisdervent. —Isnik.—Lefke.—Bilejik. — Shuhut.— Eski-Shehr. —Sidi Gazi.—Khosru Khan.—Bulwudun.—Isaklu.— Ak-Shehr.—Ilgun.—Khadun Khan. — Ladik.— Konieh.—Karabignar.— Erkle.— Olukooshlah. —Takehur.—Kolinkboaz, to Tersoos,—thence through Pompeiopolis, and several other ruins, to Chelindreh.

CYPRUS, 10th December.

HAVING equipped ourselves with a tolerable Turkish travelling costume, a firman, a translation of which herewith, and two biruldies for post-horses; the fees for the former, were fifteen piastres; and the latter forty-four. We crossed over from Constantinople in the afternoon of the 29th of September, to Scutari, accompanied by a Tartar whom we had agreed to pay ten piastres per day, and to allow a sum for his return to Constantinople from Athens; we had with difficulty reduced the latter allowance from four hundred, which he demanded, to two hundred piastres; the journey being only eight days, and for which he had a separate biruldi, for three horses, gratis. We had only engaged this man at so high a price, in the hope that he might assist us in enforcing the orders we had for our horses free of expense, which would have amounted to much more than his wages. Besides the Tartar, we had only one servant, and scarcely any baggage.

Our intention was to have pushed through the heart of Asia Minor, from Scutari to Tersoos, and from thence to the coast, through Cilicia, Pamphylia, Lycia, Caria, and Ionia to Smyrna, visiting the different antiquities that came in our way. From Smyrna we intended to pass on to Pergamus and Troy, cross the Dardanelles, and proceed to Athens by land, to which place we had directed our baggage to be forwarded from Constantinople. We should have preferred purchasing our animals, and selling them again at the end of the journey; in this manner the daily expenses would have been restricted to provisions only, while the travelling firman, if properly worded, would have obtained fodder gratis. But this plan would not have admitted of the expedition we wished; we, therefore, used the post-horses. We found, however, that this method was as expensive as if we had paid for the horses' hire; for although the biruldies state the horses are to be supplied free of expense, it is customary to fee the postmasters, which our Tartar did to such a degree, including every body who chose to ask him for money, that when we included his wages, and the expense of his return to Constantinople, the daily amount at least equalled what the hire of the horses, without a Tartar, would have come to. We were detained at the post-house, at Scutari, till sun-set, before we could procure horses, when we proceeded through a beautiful country, the road passing generally near the sea of Marmora. We traversed the villages of Gaobin and Bendick.

September 30th. At two in the morning we arrived at Ghiviza, said to be the Lybissa of antiquity, the place where Hannibal was buried. We remained here only an hour, and at day-light reached the ferry, whence we crossed over an arm of the sea of Marmora to a coffee-house detached from the village of Ersek, where we were to receive fresh post-horses. At the upper extremity of this bay are the ruins of the ancient Nicomedia. This ferry is used to shorten the road, instead of being obliged to go all round the bay; we, therefore, missed the sight of the ruins of Nicodemia, which we did not much regret, as Messrs. Bayley, Godfrey, and Wyse, had visited them from Constantinople while we were there, and on their return reported, that they did not present sufficient remains to attract the traveller out of his way.

We reposed till about ten o'clock, and then advanced through a picturesque country. In six hours we arrived at a village called Kisdervent, where we again rested for about two hours. The natives of this village are entirely Greeks; they appeared an industrious people. It is situated in a romantic valley, with a stream running through it; there is a profusion of wild shrubs as well as gardens, and mulberries for the silk worms. We remained about two hours, and then advanced. Towards sun-set we quitted the valley and crossed some hills, when we came in sight of the lake Ascanius, which we bordered till ten at night, and then reached a considerable place, situated at its eastern extremity, called Isnik, or Tchinisli, on the site of the ancient Nicæa. The present town occupies but a very small portion of the ground enclosed by the ancient walls, which are in a tolerable state of preservation, and at the gate are several Greek inscriptions. There is little else of interest at Nicæa except the walls. In 1097 the place was taken by the famous Godefroi de Bouillon. The plain of Tchinisli is extremely rich and beautiful, has fine gardens, and is well watered.

October 1. In the morning we ascended a hilly country, whence, in seven hours, we descended into the town of Lefke, having first crossed a considerable river over which there is a bridge. This river appears to be a branch of the ancient Sangarius, which discharges itself into the Euxine Sea. An inscription by the road side, as we descended, shewed we were in the old way. We slept this night at a village called Bilejik, four hours beyond Lefke. The next day, in eight hours we arrived at Shuhut, situated in a beautiful valley, from whence we crossed hills, and in ten hours more arrived in Eski Shehr.

October 3. At six o'clock we proceeded on our journey, through a country consisting of open, naked plains, and at noon stopped at Sidi Gazi. In this place are many ancient fragments, such as pieces of columns, friezes, altars, and inscriptions. We remained one hour, and then ascended through a woody country into park scenery, where we found a stag standing in the road; he allowed us to come so near before he retired, that the Tartar dismounted to fire at him. At six we passed a road-side fountain, at which were several antique fragments; one bore a Greek inscription and the cross.

We stopped for the night at Khosru Khan, a miserable place, the houses being mere huts, built of rough stones and timber; and here we first came to the flat roofs. There are in the neighbourhood many remains of columns, an altar with a female figure, and another bearing a Greek inscription. The next day our road conducted us through a woody country ; at eight we breakfasted at a fountain built with stones, on some of which were Roman sculpture, and a Greek inscription. Towards noon we passed two ancient cemeteries, consisting of grottos cut out in the rock; we examined some of them, but found them very much decayed and without plaster. Near to the last was also a Mahommedan burial-ground, but no village in sight. On our right we saw a curd camp; the tents were black like those of the Arabs. At four we reached a dirty place, situated at the beginning of a plain called Bulwudun; this plain is in many parts swampy, and must be unhealthy in the summer. We proceeded at five, and at dark we came to a causeway. At ten we reached Isaklu, a considerable place, in the neighbourhood of rich gardens.

October 5. We proceeded through a fertile plain, bounded by a range of hills close on our right. The plain is well watered, and in the distance to the left are swamps and lakes; in five hours we arrived at Ak-Shehr, a large town surrounded by fertile gardens. To give some idea of the figure which a rich Turk makes in travelling in this country, we give a sketch of the family and attendants of a pashaw whom we met on the road this morning on his way to Constantinople. The procession commenced with several black slaves on horseback, followed by the harem of young and handsome women in a tackterwan; to this succeeded another, with female slaves, some black, some white; and after them were several respectable looking Turks, on horseback; to these succeeded the tackterwan of the pashaw, who was lolling on a sofa between cushions; soldiers, and other attendants, closed his train. Two Tartars, bound to Adana, also passed us from the capital. From Ak-Shehr we proceeded through a poor country, and in six hours reached Ilgun, where we remained for the night.

October 6. The road led us through a country of downs; in seven hours we reached Khadun Khan; here are some Roman ruins, basso-relievos, inscriptions, a lion, fragments of columns in the burial-ground, &c.; the cross generally accompanies the inscriptions. Beyond this place, to the right of the road, are two old altars with Greek inscriptions, and fragments of columns, used as mere modern grave-stones; the Turks called them the five brothers, who they say were buried here, after having fallen in a civil war, at what period was not mentioned. In three hours from

Khadun-Khan we reached Ladik, where we remained for the night. The Mahommedan burial-ground of this place contains many columns, friezes, and inscriptions of the lower empire. These Christian epitaphs are frequently used as head stones of the Turkish graves, the cross being left very perfect and unmutilated upon them, and the stones placed as at Christian graves, except that the head is towards Mekka.

October 7. This morning we proceeded through plains, and travelled eight hours, arriving at noon at Konieh the capital of a pashalic; it is at present a large town, environed like most of the cities of Turkey by rich gardens. The citadel is in the centre, encloses a great part of the town, and is surrounded by a wall and fosse. The walls are built out of the fragments of the ancient city, and contain basso-relievos, Greek inscriptions, altars, lion's heads, sphinxes, eagles, and differently formed large crosses. This was anciently Iconium, the capital of Lycaonia, where St. Paul preached and made many converts to Christianity ([101]). The fosse, surrounding the walls without, is partly filled with rubbish, the rest is a shallow swamp with much verdure. We observed in it some beautiful specimens of the flowering rush. The post-house where we lodged was outside the walls; we did not, therefore, enter the citadel, as we were informed the pashaws permission was necessary; and such was the cowardly conduct of our Tartar, Mustaffa, that we could not persuade him even to ask whether there were any antiquities within the walls: he said, that we must not think of such things in Turkish towns. Unfortunately we had no other interpreter. From the little information we could receive, it appeared that there are no other remains in the citadel, than such fragments as we had seen on the outside walls; from the number and variety of these, we may judge that Iconium was once a handsome city. The inhabitants of Konieh appeared a fanatical people; they were very rude, and the Tartar was quite afraid of them.

At four o'clock we procured post-horses, and proceeded until eleven at night through rich but uncultivated plains, not meeting with a single habitation till we reached the small village where we slept.

October 8. At daylight we advanced through open plains, having some villages in sight and partial cultivation. At nine we stopped at a village to refresh the horses, there being no barley where we slept. Here we remained till noon, and then proceeded through fine plains without cultivation. At sun-set we arrived at Karabignar, situated near some volcanic mounds. We were informed that the principal one has a lake in the centre; that near to the town has two ruined Roman towers on it. The village consists of miserable houses, and the post house was unusually dirty. There is a handsome khan and mosque which was built by a sultan who made the pilgrimage to Mekka; both are now in a ruinous condition.

October 10. This morning a Kiah-bey arrived and several Tartars, whom our attendant allowed to take all the best horses, so that we could not get off till ten o'clock, and then with some miserable animals which could scarcely move : one had died in the stable that morning. The manner in which these poor creatures are treated and worked by the Tartars and surugees (hostlers) is extremely cruel, but we had never observed any thing half so bad as at this post house.

Shortly after we had left Karabignar, we passed close to an insulated circular mound of conical form, surrounded by a natural fosse, partly filled with salt water; the ground is covered with ashes and scoriæ to a considerable extent. From thence the plain became again more level. About two o'clock, we observed three surugees returning on the road, with several post horses which our Tartar wished to get in exchange for our bad ones. The surugees, who are accustomed to this, immediately on observing us turned out of the road, and made a circuit to avoid us; they were pursued in vain by Mustaffa on the best of our poor animals, which falling with him, he was obliged to return.

At five we passed a neat village, entirely deserted by its inhabitants, in consequence of the oppression of the government. On seeing this recent instance of a people obliged to abandon their homes, we easily accounted for the general depopulation of the country, and the very great extent of rich plain which appears uncultivated. In this neighbourhood we observed many Turkomen's tents or huts; they are remarkably neat and clean, made in a circular form, with canes arranged in the shape of net-work; there is a dome roof on the outside of the cane-work, which appears well adapted for admitting the air in hot weather. At night a curtain of canvas, or cloth, is let down. Some Curds were passing the night here; further on we observed some camels left singly to die on the plain; this, it appears, is a constant practice. If a camel falls sick, or is exhausted with age, so as to be unable to proceed with his burthen, it is left behind to take its chance. Some days afterwards our surugee left one of our post-horses in this manner, but he had the chance of finding the animal again on his return the next day, which could not be the case in the instance of a caravan of camels. At eight o'clock at night we arrived at Erkle or Ellegria, situated by the side of the plain in an enclosed country, with beautiful hedges, willows, fields, and gardens, which we passed through for an hour before we reached the town. Erkle appears to agree in situation with the ancient Tyana, which was in this part of the country, and is the only place sufficiently large to be called a town, between Konieh (Iconium) and Tersoos. We however did not remark any remains of antiquity in the neighbourhood. The situation is extremely rich and well watered; the town is neater than usual, and has a good khan and mosque. The governour had put all the surugees in prison for having occasioned the death of a post-horse; it was with difficulty our Tartar could get one released to procced with us, and it was not till eleven o'clock on the tenth that we were clear of the town.

We soon quitted the beautiful gardens of Erkle, and entered into a hilly country. We passed several rivulets of fine, clear water, and at two in the afternoon a village; from hence we ascended into a country of a different nature, and as naked as the plains; the latter must stand at a considerable height above the level of the sea, as, after a moderate ascent, we observed that the highest points of Mount Taurus on our right, with large patches of last year's snow, were but little above us. At sun-set we stopped at a small place called Olukooshlah, where, besides the post house, there are only a few huts and a khan for the hadj; the country is bare. The next day we could not procure horses till ten o'clock; an hour's journey brought us to some trees and gardens, shortly after which we came to a river, and continued by the side of it till sun-set, except for about one hour which was occupied (about two o'clock) in passing over a projection of the mountain, presenting perpendicular cliffs to each side of the river, and rendering it impossible for the road to continue in the ravine. On the sides of the highest parts of these mountains are rich vineyards; the natives bring the grapes down to the road in small baskets, to sell them to the passing traveller; the grapes are of an unusually rich flavour. When we joined the river's side again, we found the scenery gradually increase in beauty. The stream winds through a narrow valley between the mountains, whose sides are sometimes sloping and covered with fir-trees, and sometimes present perpendicular cliffs. We found many fragments of breccia, porphyry, serpentine, and black and white marble, the production of this range. At sun-set we arrived at a picturesque bridge of one bold arch thrown across the stream; below it are the ruins of another, probably Roman; there is also a fountain of remarkably cold water. Here we deviated to the right from the course of the river; the road became rugged, and the scenery less picturesque; the summits of the hills were singularly pointed. At eleven o'clock we arrived at a post house called Takehur, situated in a wild place, surrounded by rugged hills and fir trees.

October 12. We proceeded at eight o'clock, but had only advanced a few paces when we came to an open rupturé with our Tartar; we had often told him to be less liberal with our money in fees at the post houses. At Takehur he complied with the increasing demands of the post-master, though we had desired him to desist. When we rebuked him for it, he said he would return with the horses, and let us make a bargain for ourselves. As we knew that the post-master would exact more when he found that we ceased to have the protection of the Tartar, we were obliged to desire him to go forward. He, however, in a peremptory manner, ordered the surugee to return with our baggage, and we proceeded alone with our servant. Shortly, however, the post-master and surugee, the former mounted on our own Tartar's horse, and armed with his pistols, appeared in our rear, uttering violent threats and menaces, and ordering us to stop. When they overtook us, we were obliged, after some disputing, to give up the horses; but as we could not submit to be ordered back, and by a person in our pay, who was sent to obey us, we preferred walking on foot to returning to the post house, where we should have been exposed to the ridicule of every body. We continued to advance in spite of the solicitations of the postmaster, who soon left us. After proceeding for about two hours, our Tartar came to his senses again, and rejoined us with our horses and baggage.

About one hour's journey from Takehur, we observed that the road was cut through the rock with some labour, and by the side of the stream, near a small fall of water, there is a large square tablet bearing a Greek inscription, but we found it impossible to get near enough to copy it. The rock is cut away in other parts to form the road. The Turks call the place Kolinkboaz, or passage cut with a hammer, and there can be no doubt that it was one of the Tauri Pylæ, or Ciliciæ Pylæ of the ancients. About noon we came to a guard house and fountain, where the roads to Tersoos and Adana separate; the former is the principal one, being the route to Aleppo, Syria, and Mekka; the latter, which turns to the right, we followed. It soon became very rugged and crossed numerous ravines; we had been the whole day upon a gradual slope; at three o'clock we came upon a plain by a more rapid descent; we had on our left a Turkish castle on an eminence. About four o'clock we passed a piece of a column of very handsome porphyry.

Shortly after this the road turned more to the right, and we passed an old Roman castle on the left. About five we came upon the side of a ravine enclosing a very considerable river, perhaps the Cydnus, and descended into the great plain of Tersoos at dusk. At eight we stopped for the night at a very small village. From three to six, the country was covered with bushes, amongst which we observed the myrtle in great quantity and perfection, sometimes seven or eight feet high; the arbutus, Vallonia oak, oleander, carob, caper plant, &c. &c. The plain of Tersoos is destitute of trees.

October 13. At five we proceeded, and at seven reached the khan in Tersoos, having crossed the Cydnus over a considerable bridge.

COAST OF KARAMANIA.

Tersoos the ancient Tarsus, lies about a mile to the S. W. of the Cydnus; it has no good buildings, and is but ill supplied with the necessaries of life. When the officers of the Frederikstein visited Tersoos, they remarked the savage looks of the natives; but we found them a civil, quiet, and well-disposed people. The difference may be attributed to the present Pashaw of Adana, to whose government Tersoos belongs, and who is a mild and just man. According to the report of Mons. Peretier, the French consul, he has taken such measures to punish theft, even in the smallest degree, that no such thing as a robbery is ever heard of in this district; both Mons. Peretier and Mons. Guys his assistant, are dressed as Franks, in which costume they pass freely in the streets without the least annoyance from any body; while Mons. Guys was shewing us about the town, we observed that the women, seeing by our companion that we were Franks, generally contrived to let their veils slip aside whenever we passed any that were in the least good-looking; on the contrary, when we were alone, and taken for Turks, they always covered their faces in a hasty manner, and appeared frightened.

About a mile to the north of the town, the river, previously of a considerable depth and breadth, falls over a bed of rocks about fifteen feet in height, whence it separates into several small channels, turning mills, and watering beautiful gardens. These streams afterwards unite in one, and so continue to the sea. We were told that the inhabitants do not drink of the water of the river, deeming it unhealthy. Many of the principal houses are supplied from wells, but we saw many of the people filling their jars from the tributary streams. The antiquities of this place are but few; fragments of friezes, columns, and Corinthian capitals are scattered about in various parts of the town. The governour lately made excavations for stones to build with, when many columns, &c. were found, shewing the abundance of antique remains which must still exist under ground. There are two gates, one at S. W. and the other at the N. E. part of the town; they are simple arches, but were once decorated. To the N. W. of the town, traces of the ancient wall are distinguishable, and a citadel tolerably perfect to the north. We only saw one inscription in Greek, on a stone which forms part of the elevation of the side pavement of the street, in going from the khan to the N. E. gate. It is not very perfect; the letters are inverted, and it is in a situation which renders it difficult to copy.

The commerce of Tersoos, at present, consists chiefly in cotton, of which the neighbouring plains afford an abundant supply. The khan was so full of merchandize and its proprietors, that we could not obtain a room in it, but lodged on a stage under the piazzas. Goods from Egypt, &c. for Adana, are landed at the scala, and thence transported by camels. Monsieur Peretier's daughter was residing with her father at Tersoos. They export great quantities of cotton. The Armenian church is reported to have been the dwelling house of the father of St. Paul, who was a native of Tarsus; but there is as little probability of this being the real place of his abode, as there is of the church of Tiberius having been that of St. Peter.

Strabo states " that the Cydnus ran through the heart of the city." As the Cydnus is now a good half hour's walk from the modern town, some idea may, from this circumstance, be formed of its original dimensions. We are told also that it was powerful, populous, and maintained the dignity of a metropolis. In Beaufort's work, it appears that the officers of the Frederickstein were informed that the ruins of a theatre, covered with bushes, lay near the river; this would in some measure corroborate the statement of Strabo; but we inquired in various quarters about this theatre, without being able to obtain any information concerning it. We need hardly remark that the Cydnus is famous for the meeting of Marc Anthony and Cleopatra, and for having endangered the life of Alexander the Great, by his bathing in it; we bathed in it above the falls, and found the water unusually cold, but felt no ill effects from it. Though it was now the middle of October, the heat was so great that the thermometer, on the day we arrived, stood at ninety-two degrees in the shade, and during the week we were at Tersoos, it was never below eighty.

October 20. We had some difficulty in coming to a decision about the continuance of our journey, whether it should be by sea or by land; the exorbitant prices demanded for vessels, in consequence, perhaps, of this being the time of shipping the cotton, occasioned us to make the final arrangement for proceeding by land. We had six horses for forty-five piastres per day, it being considered as four days' journey to Selefketh.

At noon we left Tersoos, taking with us a good supply of Bastourma (hung beef), prepared and cured by the Turkomen, who bring it to Tersoos for sale. Our other articles of provision were musty biscuits, and very indifferent brandy distilled from figs; no cheese could be procured. We had been informed that the country through which we were to pass was thinly peopled, and very ill supplied with provisions. We proceeded by the road to Kazalu and the Scala; in about two hours and a half we turned out of it to the right to a small miserable looking village. At three o'clock we reached an artificial mound, noticed in Captain Beaufort's work; we found pottery and other remains on its summit, but no distinct foundations. Here we had a fine view over the plain; the village of Kazalu with its gardens; the coffee-house at the Scala, and the sea with three or four vessels at anchor. We passed on to the westward through the plain, which was partly cultivated with cotton, and through the ruins of a town which appears to have been constructed of large stones, but there is only part of a building standing, which is of Turkish architecture, perhaps a mosque. A little further on, to our left, was another artificial mound, with remains of a fort on it, having square towers at the angles. A third height of the same kind was in sight still further to the westward. Before sun-set we stopped near a small mill turned by a pretty little stream, the ground was covered over with dwarf wood. The plain, between the sea on the one hand, and the foot of the mountains (hitherto well clothed on their sides with wood) on the other, was now considerably decreased in breadth.

October 21. At eight in the morning we advanced on our journey, shortly after which we were environed by gardens of fig, orange, lemon trees, vines, &c. growing in the most luxuriant manner, the ground being here well watered with rivulets; in the midst of them was a village; the people had been mostly sleeping in the open air, as we found their beds, mats, quilts, &c. under the trees. This cultivated tract, however, is very limited in its extent, as we almost immediately passed again into the same kind of dwarf woodland which we had quitted in the morning.

We shortly passed another artificial hill, with ruins of large stones. From the position of these mounds, at such regular distances, it seems likely that they may have been thrown up for fortifications, and for the purpose of commanding a view of the plain and sea.

About ten we crossed a considerable stream, and shortly after reached the ruins of Pompeiopolis. Time and the weather have given the columns a black and dismal appearance, and they are surrounded with dark looking bushes. Forty four columns, of a bad style, are standing, out of about two hundred; but what is that to Palmyra or Djerash where two hundred and forty still stand with their capitals and epistylia? the remains of perhaps two thousand! With the exception of the colonnades and some sarcophagi which are scattered about without the walls, and are of large dimensions, we found little to interest us. The theatre is in a most ruinous state, as is the ancient port, filled with an accumulation of earth. The remains of the town are so blocked up with bushes and briars, that we had more trouble in making our way through them than they deserved. At noon we again advanced; the same sort of wood scenery continued, in which we saw the myrtle in great perfection, the fir, the arbutus, carob, bay-tree, turpentine, and the Vallonia oak. Some of the bushes were frequently entwined to their very summits by the wild vine: there were other shrubs whose names we were unacquainted with. The rivers are occasionally bordered by the oleander, but it was not in blossom. We crossed two streams, the last of which has a bridge of Turkish construction.

About two o'clock P.M. we joined our conductor, who had remained behind at Tersoos to procure barley for the horses, and had arrived last night at the place where we found him. He had come a different road, and said that the man whom he had left with us had misled us. Shortly after we stopped at another large bridge over a considerable river. At five we stopped for the night on the banks of another, whose stream is so rapid, that two bridges, constructed over different parts of it, have been washed away; it was, however, fordable in one place. The water of this river is of a very white colour, as if its course had been through a calcareous bed; the plane tree as well as the carob are of a considerable size near the banks of the stream. A castle stands at the foot of the hills a-breast of Pompeiopolis; we did not examine it.

October 22. At seven o'clock we were on the road; we shortly passed an artificial mound with ruins on it; the country was more open and in parts boggy. We passed several places where the natives tread out their corn, and near them were stages on which they sleep: these stages are raised on high poles for the sake of air in the hot summer nights. At nine we breakfasted near a river, which we crossed at ten, and then entered again into a country of dwarf wood: the road occasionally turned to the sea beach, for the purpose of crossing rivulets which are fordable only at the bars near their junction with the sea. The sea was, however, generally hidden from sight by high mounds of sand. At noon we quitted the plain country, and crossed a small rocky hill on the coast, which appears to have been inclosed with walls in ancient times, and was probably a boundary between Cilicia Campestris and Aspera. On its western side we came upon a sandy bay of the coast, at the discharge of a large river, which winds so extremely near its junction with the sea, that its course bends almost back into parallel lines. On the right is a bridge over the river, and near is a village on a hill. The stones have been collected in heaps over this part of the country with great labour and perseverance, proving that in former times there must have been a considerable population, the foundation of small square towers, probably posts of communication, are visible here and there. Higher up, across a romantic ravine, is a Roman aqueduct of picturesque appearance, its height is so great as to require a double tier of arches. Here we came upon a very stony coast; our conductor lost his way, having crossed the river at its mouth instead of the bridge; a little deviation inland, however, brought us again into the right track, which was very rugged and stony. We found, hereabouts, troughs cut in the rocks, and holes through them to tie cattle to; the land also was cleared as much as possible for pasturage, by heaping up the stones.

At ten o'clock we reached some considerable ruins; they stand upon an elevated spot, fronting the sea, and consist of several buildings within walls; the first we examined, beginning to the north, appeared to have been a theatre, both from its semicircular shape, and its sloping appearance within; we could observe several pieces of seats scattered about, and part of one of the vomitories. At its S. W. angle is a smaller building, with some circular foundation in front of it; facing these buildings is the largest of the ruins, at the N. E. angle of which are the remains of a spiral stair-case. The whole edifice is of very considerable size, and has been ornamented within with arched recesses on all sides. Whether it was a great Christian church or a palace is uncertain. To the east of it is a small temple; its internal form is that of a cross; it is surmounted with a dome, very neatly built, and has four arched recesses. On either side of these recesses are small chambers, which give the whole a square external form. At each angle of the recesses are Corinthian pilasters, and over each arch a cross is sculptured in relievo. In front of this building appeared a vast paved terrace, which proved on examination to be only the top of an immense reservoir of water, into which there is a descent by steps. Being dry, it appeared like a vast hall; it is forty-five paces long, and twenty wide, and is divided into three long arched divisions by two rows of six piers each; its depth appeared to be above forty feet. Near the S. W. angle of this tank is a small edifice which seems to have had a semicircular back and ends. Over the door-way is a Greek inscription of five lines, not very perfect, but in such a state that a Greek scholar might perhaps be able to transcribe it. There are several small tanks amongst the ruins, and in one of the buildings in the eastern part we saw an immense mill-stone. We know not the ancient name of this place; the natives call it Aukullah. The tank and great building agree in position with those mentioned in Captain Beaufort's book, as lying four miles east of Ayash, and two west of the river Latmus, which is certainly the river we crossed at noon. In Macbean's Dictionary we find that the river Latmus had a cognominal town, and as there are no ruins nearer to the river, these may perhaps be the ruins of Latmus.

At two we proceeded over a stony road; the grand aqueduct from the Latmus still continues, across the ravines it is necessarily constructed on arches. We passed a burial place called Shedelah, apparently of early Mahommedan date. At four we descended into a sandy bay, where, finding some wells of water, we stopped for the night. We conversed at these wells with some natives, who called the place Ayash. Here were a few uninhabited huts, and we were told of a village at half an hours' distance above. We were surrounded by ruins and Cyclopean walls of large stones, as well for the support of buildings as for terracing up the land for culture. We employed the remainder of the evening of the 22nd in examining the ruins which lay near us, intending to visit the remainder in succession, as we passed on to the westward the next day. The principal object was a tomb built of a square form, with an arched porch on one side, and a square door at the opposite side. There were composite pilasters at the angles, a lion's head frieze, and a pointed roof with pediments, within, the ceiling is arched; the chamber has four places for bodies below, and five in an elevated sort of stone bench above. There are two other tombs of this description in ruins near it, and close to the sea shore is a large Christian church. The canopy of the altar place has the remains of three saints painted on it; the centre one, by the difference of dress and shape, appears to have been intended for a female; perhaps they represented the trinity. The side walls are mostly fallen, but over the door in front, a cross is sculptured in relief, thus and some visitor has scratched near it, a flag on a staff, probably a banner imprinted by some crusader. Farther to the west are the ruins of another church, with part of a mosaic ceiling. Near this place the grand aqueduct passes on two different levels; beyond it is another tomb of the same description as that first mentioned. It has six elevated recesses for corpses, and one larger over the door. The chamber is six and a half paces by five; the porch two and a half deep; near it are many large sarcophagi.

October 23. We started early on foot, the horses following; we soon ascended an ancient paved way, lined with many of those square tombs described yesterday, more or less perfect, as well as with many large sarcophagi. Some of these are very beautifully ornamented in relievo; one in particular represented an eagle treading on a serpent, and holding a wreath on each side, supported at the other ends by cherubs, with a rose over each wreath. Another had an ox's head suspending wreaths of vines, pomegranates, grapes, &c. Some had tablets for inscriptions, and some were inscribed in large Greek characters covering the whole of one side. Besides the tombs and sarcophagi, we found some pieces of rich frieze as well as several altars; and there were edifices which appeared not to have been tombs but habitations, some of which looked modern. This paved road finally brought us to a sandy bay, and an isthmus which separated a rocky promontory from the main line of rugged coast.

Here the great aqueduct again appears, though much in ruins; and near it are the remains of a palace, the façade of which is one hundred paces across. It has had a colonnade in front, of sixteen pillars; the pedestals only remain; a great many shafts of columns are made use of as modern fences on the isthmus. At the back of the palace, on the side of the hill, appears to have stood a theatre, but it is more ruined even than that of Pompeiopolis. On the promontory are many ruined buildings; one of these has three columns of a portico in front of it still standing; the shafts and capitals are of a single piece, and of good marble: they are of the Corinthian order. According to Captain Beaufort, these are the ruins of Eleusa or Sebaste; and the building on the promontory, supposing it to have been once an island, which is very possible, was perhaps the palace of Archelaus. That on the main has, however, been by far the more considerable edifice.

Passing on westward to the next eminence, we came to a large temple of fluted columns, standing in a very conspicuous situation. In ascending to it from the ruins of Eleusa, there is a place in the road, where one sloping, slippery stone of marble, constitutes the whole width, between a perpendicular precipice of some height on one side, and a tree on the other; we dismounted, and led our horses up it; but the poor baggage horse who could not be so easily lightened of his burthen, fell over the precipice, fortunately without injury, the baggage breaking his fall: this gave us time to examine, at leisure, a tomb standing near the sea shore, to the westward of the temple. It is square and has a pyramidal roof, but is only that of a Mahommedan saint; it has an oriental inscription over the doorway, and in the chamber within is the usual built grave with the cap of a dervis sculptured on it; the head is placed towards Mekka. It has, however, been built out of Roman ruins; one of the stones had the letters B. A. inverted; Captain Beaufort, by his description of this tomb, does not seem to have been aware of the real character of it.

From hence we ascended by the ancient paved way which brought us up to a castle: here we entered by an arched way into a street of ruined walls and buildings, passing on our left a magnificent palace. It has had three arched doors and many windows; the interior is divided into various apartments, supported by columns, which have all fallen. Their capitals are in the form of an inverted bell, and have four crosses enclosed in circular wreaths sculptured on them; they appear, therefore, to be of Christian times; they have a heavy, ugly appearance. There are others ornamented with a variety of decoration. At the east end the building finishes in the form of a half dome; this would look like a church, were it not for windows in that part, and that the building has had upper stories supported on piers. From hence we descended through rough, ruined buildings, and lines of innumerable large sarcophagi; one in particular was beautifully decorated with processions of figures in basso-relievo, bringing offerings to an urn. A great many have crosses, and some have inscriptions upon them. It would appear from the former circumstance, that they are generally of no earlier period than the lower empire. There are also plenty of sepulchral grottos cut in the rock, and many of these also bear inscriptions.

The valley into which we descended leads to the sea shore, where stands a fine old castle, with the remains of a pier projecting into the sea, and the ruins of a building at its extremity. On the hill, to the east of the valley, are the ruins of a considerable town; and on the sides of that to the west, are the remains of houses cut out of the rock itself. On the upper part of these hills stands a sarcophagus, singularly placed on the top of a ruined building; a large hole has been forced into the end of it. As it stands on a base no greater than itself, no footing could be obtained for the purpose of forcing the lid off, and the hole must have been made by means of a ladder. Somewhere on this hill is a modern village; the inhabitants whom we met called it Ichuran. Crossing over the foot of this western hill we came up on a sandy bay, in front of which stands another castle on an island. A low rocky point extends both from the island and the western side of the bay, and, perhaps, it was once connected with the main land. At the east side of the sandy beach, several springs of fresh water issue from the rocks close to the sea; here we stopped to breakfast in sight of both the castles: these are the ruins of the ancient Corycus. It was the first spring of running water we had met with since we crossed the Latmus, between which and the Calycadnus there is no river, and this is the reason why so many vast aqueducts and reservoirs were required for the supply of the different ancient cities.

We conversed with several of the natives, and inquired particularly for the saffron cave of Strabo; they told us we should come to it in our road, but there is no doubt they were deceiving us. We had observed, from the heights, towers at regular distances along the coast. At eleven o'clock we proceeded on our journey over a rough road; the coast to the westward forms many bays and inlets. In the first of these we found a small vessel lying at anchor, which had brought iron, coffee, &c. to sell among the natives. The promontories between these bays are excessively rugged, and the road is so bad, being composed of hard, slippery marble stones, that we were generally dismounted: the poor baggage horse was scarcely able to proceed, and fell several times. The natives of Ichuran, to the number of seven, had followed us, either prompted by curiosity to see what we were about, in consequence of the enquiries we had put to them at Corycus, or for the worse purpose of robbing us if an opportunity offered. They were very wild-looking people, and our conductor did not like them. He gave the musket he was carrying to our Tartar, and desired him to be on the alert, and shoot the first who should assault us. They were, however, only armed with long knives, and we were well supplied with fire arms. According to Strabo and other ancient authors, the inhabitants of this country were noted for their piratical excursions in ancient times; they followed us during the chief part of the day. In one of the principal vallies through which we passed we had observed five caves; we examined the two principal, in hopes of discovering the Corycian saffron cave, but were disappointed. A continuation of very bad road brought us at last into an extensive plain, which terminates to the south in a long, low promontory, extending far into the sea. When we descended into the plain, we passed on our left the ruins of a town in a valley. It agrees with the situation of Pershendy by Beaufort, and we contented ourselves with his description of it, as none of the buildings, except three arches of an aqueduct, seemed to invite a closer examination, or any loss of time. We continued in the plain to some distance, part of which is cultivated with cotton, and beyond it with watermelons, with a few temporary huts. We observed that the men in this country were employed in spinning wool, which is the occupation of the women in every other part of the Levant; it was spun in thick yarns. According to Macbean, quoting Varro, cloth was the manufacture of the country in former times.

The dwellings continued till we came to a morass, where the road passes over the rocks close to the edge of the marsh, which extends in some places as far to the south as the eye can reach, filled with canes, rushes, &c. Before we quitted the plain, we passed, at some distance to the left, the ruins of a large building; part of its walls remain, and the frame of its door-way, constructed of large stones. About five o'clock we stopped for the night near a miserable village, where, by the edge of the morass, there is a large building built out of the ancient ruins; a foundation remains on the other side of the road.

October 24. Proceeding at day-light, our road continued so bad that we were obliged to lead the horses, but having shortly arrived at the extremity of the morass, we were enabled again to enter into the plain, and to mount our horses. Passing on we came to a small mound which has the remains of ancient buildings upon it; on the other side of the road were a few sarcophagi cut in the rock. We next came to an arm of the Ghiuk Sooyoo river, the ancient Calycadnus; this river winds extremely, and is by far the most respectable stream we have seen in Asia.

Three hours' journey from where we slept brought us to Selefkeh, one of the ancient Seleucias, which we entered, passing over the river by a bridge of six arches to a small khan. Selefkeh at present is a poor, miserable village, but in a fine situation; the castle stands on the top of a round hill, at the foot of which is the village, and the ruins of the ancient town extending to a considerable distance. After breakfast we went to inspect them. We first came to an old brick ruin of large size, formerly lined with plaster; near this, on the S. E. side of the castle hill, has been a theatre, now only distinguishable by the shape of the earth, and by two of its vomitories, at present converted into habitations. On the slope where the seats once existed, tobacco is now cultivated. In the plain to the eastward are two large buildings; the first shews nothing but its walls; the most distant has been a large Christian church constructed of solid masonry. The semicircular eastern end is perfect, and one fluted Corinthian column in the front is standing; it may have been formed out of a more ancient temple. There are many other indescribable ruins, and to the west of the theatre, quarries and excavated tombs. We afterwards ascended a hill south of the town, having been attracted to it by large ruins, which we had observed before we reached Selefkeh. The road we followed has formerly been paved, and towards the summit cut through the cliff to some depth. We found ruins covering a considerable extent of ground; the principal buildings have been churches, of which the farthest had the east end in tolerable preservation. The windows were adorned with handsome white marble columns, of the Corinthian order, one of which remains perfect. There are a few coarse sarcophagi, and no less than five large tanks, four of which we examined; the first was forty paces long, by twenty-six wide; the second, fifty, by twenty-six; the third, thirty, by sixteen; the roofs of these have fallen in, but some of the columns which supported the third, remain in their places; the fourth was only nineteen, by sixteen; the roof is vaulted and supported upon three rows of four columns each. From this hill is a commanding view over the plain, the sea, and the winding Calycadnus, which suddenly breaks upon the view from between two cliffs to the north of Selefkeh.

Our conductor was taken ill at this place with spasms in his stomach; the beginning of a disorder with which all our party were more or less afflicted before we reached Chelindreh.

October 25. At sun rise we continued our course to the westward, having with difficulty prevailed on our conductor to proceed further. No animals could be procured in Selefkeh; nor had we the means of providing ourselves with a vessel to undertake the journey by sea. The road led over the hill and through the ruins which we had visited the preceding day, and thence into the plain which we followed for about two hours, and then arrived at some ruins near the sea shore, where has been a small bridge leading to them over a marsh.

The principal object has the appearance of a

small fortress. We had previously crossed a dry torrent, near which were the remains of an aqueduct. We continued about an hour at this place breakfasting and examining the ruins, and then proceeded. Quitting the plain country, and passing along a rocky coast, we came first to an extensive necropolis of sarcophagi cut in the rock. In about an hour more, we came to the ruins of another ancient village, and still farther on to a bay of the coast, having a large Turkish fortress standing on its western promontory; to the south projects a curved isthmus and peninsula; in the cove which it forms lay a polacca brig, which had come from Egypt with salt, and was taking in wood to return. We conversed with some of the crew. From hence we passed into another bay sheltered by an island: here two other vessels were taking in wood. At the head of this bay are ruins of a town, and of buildings on the island. Both these anchorages become nearly land-locked by the curved projection of the point Lissan El Kahpheh. We now ascended a high bluff, very stony and overgrown with firs. We descended on the opposite side amongst romantic cliffs and ravines into a valley. At half-past two we stopped for the night at a small source of fresh water, the only one we had seen since we started. Here an open stage is placed for the accommodation of travellers, there being no inhabitants in the neighbourhood. The valley is inclosed by two high cliffs; on the top of that to the right is a ruined building; there are other hills to the left, which intercept the view of the sea. We went on foot to examine the building, leaving our Tartar, servant, and conductor with the horses. With much difficulty we proceeded to the ruin; the ascent was very steep, and in one instance we were stopped by a perpendicular precipice; after searching some time we found a fir tree placed against the rock, by which we climed up; as we advanced we piled up heaps of stones to serve as marks for our return. The building appeared to be a Turkish castle for the mortar was comparatively fresh. Here we had a commanding view of the sea, together with the island of Cyprus; seeing some tents and people on a neighbouring hill, we thought it prudent to retire quickly, being unarmed, and the natives of these parts having no good character. We reached our party at sun-set in a state of violent perspiration: we supped on rice, which we had brought from Selefkeh, where we had not been able to procure a fowl. We passed a night of drizzling rain, wind, thunder, and lightning, in the open air; we had all a violent, feverish heat and thirst, which obliged us to be constantly applying to the fountain to drink; and this probably contributed to increase a disorder in the stomach, with which we were all more or less afflicted, in consequence, as we supposed, of the badness of the waters coupled with our indifferent diet. In the morning the rain increased, but the weather became serene towards eight o'clock.

We had quitted our night's lodgings at seven. The valley opens at the further end on a deep bay of the sea-coast, from whence, in about two hours, we ascended a mountainous and ugly country, interspersed with fir-trees. The sea was generally intercepted from our view; as we descended, we came to a few scattered huts, and some little cultivated land, with cattle. We stopped at one of these huts about three in the afternoon; the owner of the hut we saw nothing of, but we got admittance into a very neat little room, which, together with another containing a store of straw, and a shed for cattle, formed the whole building. In the immediate neighbourhood of these huts are small portions of land, very neatly cultivated, and threshing grounds, the whole terraced up with much care and pains, though now, abandoned for the winter season, like the cottages in the mountains of Switzerland. Our servant Luigi's illness increased here considerably, and he was in a high fever.

October 27. We advanced at eight, constantly ascending and descending in a rough mountainous country; we had much difficulty in finding the track, for road there was none. Towards three we came down upon a large plain, beyond which, at half-past four, we arrived at Chelindreh. This place, which now only consists of a custom-house, and three or four houses where the Tartars, from Constantinople, usually embark for Cyprus, was anciently called Celenderis, some of the ruins of which remain, principally tombs, and one square cenotaph, consisting of an open arch on each side, with Corinthian pilasters, and pyramidal roof. A bath is also distinguishable.

Two vessels were lying in its little port, which has formerly been protected by a large castle on the point, now much in ruins; there is a tank within it. There is no running fresh water within some distance of Chelindreh; but there is the ruin of an aqueduct, which formerly conveyed it to the town.

October 28. We sent for horses to the nearest post-house, there being none at Chelindreh; it was three hours' distant. When they arrived, we had some difficulty in settling a bargain as far as Anamour, but having completed it for six piastres each horse, per day, we were thinking of proceeding, when the disorder which had attacked all our party (fever and dysentery) increased among us in so alarming a degree, that we were obliged to abandon all thoughts of finishing the tour for the present, and resolved to hasten to Cyprus for medical aid, as we were totally unprovided with medicine, or any of those comforts so requisite in such an emergency.

Our guide, in order to obtain relief from his burning fever, had caused himself to be blooded with the point of a nail sharpened for the purpose. We were all much exhausted by lying on the bare ground, and by want of nourishment, for we found it impossible to procure even a fowl. We had some rice and biscuit, but our appetite was entirely gone. This unfortunate termination of our journey must be attributed, besides the privation of wholesome food, for we had lately eaten scarcely any thing but rotten biscuit and dried beef, to lying out in damp nights on the ground, with very insufficient covering, and to the unwholesome waters which discharge themselves into the sea along the coast we traversed, and which vary in their properties, according to the soils from whence they flow; but there was no choice; and though we were sometimes apprised of the baneful qualities of particular streams, nevertheless we were obliged to avail ourselves of them. On some occasions we slept on the margin of stagnant swamps, where it was next to impossible to escape inhaling disorder from the *mal aria* of such situations. It is a coast, therefore, where a traveller must be fortunate indeed if he escapes without suffering material injury to his health.

On arriving at Cyprus, the rest of the party soon recovered, but I was confined to my bed for fifteen days before I was pronounced out of danger. I could never have recovered had it not been for my friend and travelling companion, who never quitted my bed-side, though the physician on several occasions refused even to enter my room until it had been sprinkled with vinegar; and our servants would not sleep in the same apartment: therefore, had it not been for my friend, I should have been without attendance. While detained here, we were very sorry to learn that Mr. Bankes had a severe attack of fever at Yaffa.

Towards the middle of December, as it was too late to renew our attempts in Karamania, and we were much enfeebled by illness, we embarked for Marseilles in a French brig, of one hundred and twenty tons, and after a passage of seventy-six days, during constant gales of wind, we reached that place, where we performed a quarantine of twenty days, and then proceeded to Montpellier to recruit our health.

SOME ACCOUNT

OF

CUCHUK ALI,

IN

A LETTER

FROM

John Barker, Esq. to his Excellency the Earl of Elgin, dated Aleppo, the 20th. November, 1800.

MY LORD,

Mr. Manesty has lately informed me that he had solicited your excellency's attention to the intimation I made to the honourable company's agent at Constantinople, of the expediency of the public Tartars being permitted by the Porte to pass through the territory of Payass on their return to Aleppo from the capital, instead of being forced to take an indirect route, whereby the transmission of the honourable company's correspondence is not only considerably retarded, but their packets are likewise exposed to be damaged, and even lost, by the messenger being compelled to traverse the Gulf of Iskenderoon, in very indifferent barks of the country.

Your excellency having recently entered into correspondence with the Pashaw of Payass, I deem it incumbent on me to lay before you a detailed account of the extraordinary character of your new correspondent, and my proceedings to cultivate his good-will for the benefit of the public service.

While yet at Constantinople, I was admonished to beware, in my passage hither, of passing through the territory of Cuchuk Ali, Governour of Payass, who had then in his prisons the Dutch Consul of Aleppo, whom he arrested as he was returning from the capital, although possessed of imperial firmans for the exercise of his office at Aleppo, and at a period that the Porte was in peace with the Dutch republic.

The proceedings of Cuchuk Ali on this occasion will serve to elucidate his character, and which will be set in a very strong light by the consideration, that there had for many years previous to the detention of the person in question, subsisted between him and the pashaw habits of the most cordial friendship, and reciprocation of mutual gifts, according to oriental customs.

On the arrival of the Dutch consul at Payass, Cuchuk Ali gave orders that he should be put into chains, and stript of every thing besides the apparel he wore; but the pashaw avoided, with great circumspection, any occasion of coming to an interview with his prisoner; for it is a peculiarity worthy of remark, that this tyrant, whenever he orders a bad action to be committed, retires from the view of it, and carefully shuts himself up in a solitary apartment.

The sum fixed for the consul's ransom was twenty-five thousand piasters, but not being able to furnish more than seven thousand five hundred, he underwent, during the space of eight months, every species of ill treatment. All means were tried to force him to embrace the Mahommedan religion, and to extort from him the money required for his release. To which ends they would at one time confine him in a damp dungeon, without light, and often without sustenance for four and twenty hours; at another they would threaten him with immediate execution, and once even, to shew that their menaces were not wholly nugatory, two innocent wretches who had been arrested under similar circumstances with himself, were impaled before him for having delayed, as he was informed, in producing the money for their ransom. At length, fortunately for this poor man, the arrival at Payass of a caravan from Smyrna, proceeding to Aleppo, furnished Cuchuk Ali an occasion of extorting his ransom from the merchants, by obliging them to advance the money on the bond of his prisoner, and then delivered him into their hands as a slave which he had sold them.

In the year 1789, Mr. Fowles, master of an English vessel in the harbour of Iskenderoon, went with four of his men to water at a place in the territory of Payass, called Jonas's Pillar, where they were seized by Cuchuk Ali and thrown into prison.

A great sum having been required for their release, before the necessary arrangements could be made for its payment, the master was driven by despair to put a period to his existence by precipitating himself from a high tower in which they were confined, and all the rest soon after perished, except a boy of twelve years old, named Charles Edwards, who was then sent as a present by Cuchuk Ali to the afore-mentioned Dutch consul, his late prisoner. I am ignorant of what steps were taken by the mission at Constantinople to obtain from the Porte the necessary satisfaction for this act of violence, but it is certain that none was ever given by its savage perpetrator.

Two years after this a French ship from Marseilles, richly laden with merchandise for Aleppo, was, by the captain's ignorance of the locality of the Bay of Iskenderoon, carried under the walls of Payass, where the captain with part of his crew, under the persuasion of being anchored at Alexandretta, landed in search of the consulary establishment, and were conducted to the governour, who received them with every mark of hospitality. But while he was entertaining them with a sumptuous repast, his men were occupied in taking possession of the vessel, which he immediately unloaded, and sunk, and sent the crew by land to the French consul at Alexandretta. Remonstrances were made by all the European agents at Aleppo, and in a particular manner by the pashaw's then intimate friend the Dutch consul, to whom Cuchuk Ali replied, " My dear friend, you know very well " that consistently with the friendship subsisting " between us, property, and life itself are indif- " ferent matters; nay, I swear, by God, that for " your sake, I would sacrifice my only son " Dadah; but I entreat you not to drive me to " the extremity of denying you that which it is " impossible for me to grant."

" My dearest friend, place yourself in circum- " stances like mine. I am in disgrace with my

"sultan without having given just cause for his
"displeasure. I am threatened to be attacked
"from the four quarters of the earth. I am with-
"out money; I am without means; and the ever
"watchful providence of the Almighty sends me a
"vessel laden with merchandise. Would you lay
"hold of it or not? I know very well the Franks
"will claim restitution of this property from the
"Sublime Porte, and that is precisely what I
"want, because an opportunity will then be af-
"forded for soliciting my pardon."

On the receipt of this letter, all hope of recovering any thing by amicable overtures being
vanished, the French consul made application to
his superior at Constantinople and obtained several
imperial commands on the subject. Three caravellas were likewise sent to Payass to enforce
Cuchuk Ali's obedience. He retired to his mountains; the caravellas fired a few guns against an
empty hut and a ruined fortress, and in a very
short time having consumed their stock of provisions, they gladly accepted such as were ten-
dered them by Cuchuk Ali, who soon obtained,
through the customary means of liberal presents
of French watches, and of fine French cloths,
the good will of the commanders of the expedition sent against him. Such was the satisfac-
faction at the rebel's munificence, that they not

only contracted with him engagements of great private friendship, but even awarded him their intercession in his favour with the Porte; and the dignity of an additional tail was conferred upon him on that occasion, with a fresh order, *pro forma*, for the restitution of the property. In compliance with which order, Cuchuk Ali wrote to the French consul at Aleppo, that he was ready to obey the commands of the Sultan, but, that the cargo of the ship in question having been converted into use, he offered in compensation, as an equivalent, to make over to the proprietors of the goods, sundry plantations belonging to him in the territory of Payass.

The Porte has on various other occasions sent pashaws with great forces to subdue this rebel, but whether owing to the natural barriers that are formed by the high craggy mountains, covered with thick woods, wherein he takes refuge, or to the species of accommodation above described, the Porte has never been able to subdue him, during forty years' existence, in open contempt of its authority. This man, in the early part of his life, was a simple bandit inhabiting the mountains of Payass, at which time that place was a populous and flourishing town of trade.

Cuchuk Ali laid the foundation of his present power by making nocturnal excursions from the mountains to rob the gardens in the vicinity of Payass. Some gardeners, in order to be exempted from these depredations, began by stipulating to pay a trifling annual tribute; others entered into similar engagements, and from a rotolo of coffee, or a few rotolos of rice, the whole town became at length compelled to furnish a stated contribution. Cuchuk Ali become head of a band of forty or fifty robbers, now aspired to render himself master of the place. He began by waylaying the chiefs of the principal families, and in the course of a few years he succeeded in exterminating every individual of such as possessed any power at Payass, or in its vicinity. One person only of those unfortunate families whose adherents he could neither subdue by open force, nor corrupt by bribery, for some time contended with him for supreme authority, till at length Cuchuk Ali, having lulled his suspicion of treachery by giving him his daughter in marriage, murdered him with his own hand, and has often been heard to warn his own children of a male infant proceeding from that marriage, counselling them to crush the crocodile in the egg, lest he should one day revenge on them the blood of his father. Cuchuk Ali with a very inconsiderable number of dependants, which do not, I am well informed, exceed two hundred men, has by a system of the most barbarous cruelty for many years past, impressed terror on the minds of the people of this neighbourhood, and given much disquietude to the Porte, between whom and the rebel there exists a reciprocal desire to be on a footing of friendship, founded on mutual advantages, which ever prevents their continuing long on terms of ostensive hostility. Cuchuk Ali's territorial government may naturally be supposed such as to afford him but very slender means of drawing wealth from the miserable wretches inhabiting his dominions; his revenues proceed therefore in a great measure from the casual passage of travellers through his territory, whom he lays under such kind of contribution as he thinks they would rather bear, than be obliged, by not coming to him, to take a very incommodious route. Sometimes his rapacity and natural brutal inclinations lead him to exceed the bounds he means to prescribe to his impositions, when the Porte declares its displeasure, forbidding travellers to pass through Payass, and thus, as soon as the rebel finds his coffers in need of fresh supplies, the Porte succeeds in forcing him to supplicate for his pardon, which is seldom long withheld, on account of the Porte's necessity of procuring a safe passage for the grand annual caravan of pilgrims from Constantinople to Mekka, who are obliged either to pass by Payass, or make a very disagreeable and expensive journey through the mountains of Armenia.

When this caravan comes into Cuchuk Ali's territory, it yields him a very considerable revenue, for he taxes every individual according to his own caprice, but, however, always upon the system above described. On its approach to Payass, Cuchuk Ali sends some of his household to compliment on his arrival the chief of the caravan, a personage of great distinction, who dismisses the rebel's emissaries with presents for him. Horses are presented which Cuchuk Ali sends back, with a hint that they would be preferred when completely accoutred in all the usual gold and silver trappings. They are then again presented to the rebel in that form. In short, much time passes in negociating and stipulating the precise tribute required; and when at length the measure of his rapacity is filled up, the caravan is *permitted* to proceed on its journey.

In order the better to dispose the pilgrims for his extortion, Cuchuk Ali is always careful to prepare for them, as a beacon of his power and his cruelty, the spectacle of two bodies impaled, transfixed on the gate of Payass. It happened, a few years ago, that his prisons were empty when the caravan of Mekka was approaching Payass; the rebel was somewhat puzzled at so unusual an obstacle, and he imparted his embarrassments to a convivial companion. " The caravan," says he, " will be here to-morrow, and we have not yet prepared the customary execution. Look ye, pick me out two from among my servants." His friend expostulated, and while he was endeavouring to avert his design, by assuring him that every thing would proceed in due order without the formality in question, Cuchuk Ali, still ruminating and stroking his beard, exclaimed, " I have it, go fetch Yacoob the Christian, he has been for four months in bed sick of a fever, he can never recover:" the poor wretch was instantly dragged from his bed, impaled, hung up, *in terrorem,* and served to impress the pilgrims with infinitely greater horror and alarm than if the bodies of ten malefactors had been exposed to their view.

When it is considered that the forces of the wretch, who is the subject of this narrative, do not exceed two hundred armed men, it becomes a matter of surprise, even to those who are well acquainted with the impotency of this government, that such a bandit should have so long braved the controul of the Porte.

He is perfectly conscious of his own weakness, and the little arts he puts in practice to conceal it are characteristic and curious. Whenever any personage of distinction comes into his territory, which is inaccessible but through immense woods; in order to deceive the new comer in an estimation of his forces, he disposes his men in the thickets, so as to pass in review like soldiers in theatrical scenery. Thus the reports of an ocular witness become fallacious, and the power of Cuchuk Ali is extolled and exaggerated all over the Turkish dominions.

He has fabricated a cordon of buildings along the eminences of his mountains, which appears, from far, like towers, and are even reported to be as many castles. They are in reality nothing else than little rude edifices, composed of two thirds of mud and one third of chalk, which a night's heavy rain frequently damages. Cuchuk Ali is, however, prompt to repair them, and they continue to inspire with dread, the traveller who is compelled to approach them.

Such is the character of the being whom I have found means to propitiate, whereby, during eighteen months that I have been honoured with the management of the Honourable East-India Company's concern at Aleppo, I have procured the secure transit through Payass of upwards of thirty Tartars, charged with conveying their correspondence from this place to Constantinople; and though I cannot flatter myself with the hopes of turning my possession of the rebel's good-will to so great an advantage as that of engaging him to restore the groups of eighty thousand piasters which he has seized belonging to British dependents, I esteem it a very great happiness, to have accelerated the transmission of every packet committed to my care, at least three days; as it is evident the Tartars' journies would necessarily have been prolonged that time, and often, in the want of boats wherewith to traverse the Gulf of Iskenderoon, much longer, if I had not cultivated the friendship of the Governour of Payass, in order to secure their free passage through his territory.

I have the honour to be,
&c. &c. &c. &c.
(Signed) JOHN BARKER.

NOTES

AND

SCRIPTURAL REFERENCES.

Note Page
1. 14.—Some remove the land-marks.—*Job*, xxiv. 2.
2. 31.—Whoso sheddeth man's blood, by man shall his blood be shed.—*Genesis*, ix. 6.
3. 33.—If we go, what shall we bring the man? there is not a present; what have we?—1 *Samuel*, ix. 7.
4. 60.—The revenger of blood himself shall slay the murderer.—*Numbers*, xxxv. 19.——Ye shall take no satisfaction for the life of a murderer.—31.
5. 75.—They cried out and cast off their clothes, and threw dust into the air.—*Acts*, xxii. 23.
6. 172.—And the people took their dough before it was leavened, their kneading troughs being bound up in their clothes upon their shoulders.—*Exodus*, xii. 34.
7. 172.—And, behold, there was a cake baken on the coals.—1 *Kings*, xix. 6.
8. 173.—Shall inhabit the parched places in the wilderness, in a *salt* land, and not inhabited.—*Jeremiah*, xvii. 6.
9. 174.—They that are delivered from the noise of archers in the places of drawing water.—*Judges*, v. 11.
10. 178.—She being desolate shall sit on the ground.—*Isaiah*, iii. 26.
11. 179.—And Samson lay till midnight, and arose at midnight and took the doors of the gate of the city, and the two posts, and went away with them, bar and all.—*Judges*, xvi. 3.

Note Page
12. 184.—For ye are like unto whited sepulchres, which indeed appear beautiful outward, but are within full of dead men's bones.—*Matthew*, xxiii. 27.
13. 216.—As the cold of snow in the time of harvest.—*Proverbs*, xxv. 13.
14 217.—They are wet with the showers in the mountains, and embrace the rock for want of a shelter.—*Job*, xxiv. 8.
15. 241.—In the name of our God we will set up our banners.—*Psalm* xx. 5.
16. 241.—In that day shall there be upon the bells of the horses, Holiness unto the Lord.—*Zechariah*, xiv. 20.
17. 243.—Concerning Damascus. Hamah is confounded.—*Jeremiah*, xlix. 23.
18. 257.—The wrath of a king is as messengers of death.—*Proverbs*, xvi. 14.
19. 258.—And ram-skins dyed red.—*Exodus*, xxv. 5.
20. 260.—For the king of Israel is come out to seek a flea, as when one doth hunt a partridge in the mountains.—1 *Samuel*, xxvi. 20.
21. 262.—Greet ye one another with a kiss of charity.—1 *Peter*, v. 14.——And poured it upon his head and kissed him.—1 *Samuel*, x. 1.
22. 263.—Butter and honey shall he eat.—*Isaiah*, vii. 15.
23. 263.—He worshipped the Lord, bowing himself to the earth.—*Genesis*, xxiv. 52.
24. 264. When I lift up my hands toward thy holy oracle.—*Psalm*, xxviii. 2.
25. 266.—Also Vashti, the queen, made a feast for the women in the royal house.—*Esther*, i. 9.
26. 266.—Thirty milch camels with their colts.—*Genesis*, xxxii. 15.
27. 274.—And put them in the camels' furniture.—*Genesis*, xxxi. 34.

NOTES.

Note Page

28. 275.—Neither let me give flattering titles unto man. For I know not to give flattering titles.—*Job,* xxxii. 21, 22.

29. 275.—If I and my cattle drink of thy water, then I will pay thee for it.—*Numbers,* xx. 19.

30. 275.—Who can stand before his cold.—*Psalm,* cxlvii. 17.

31. 275.—Feed me, I pray thee, with that same red pottage. Then Jacob gave Esau bread and pottage of lentiles.—*Genesis,* xxv. 30, 34.

32. 276.—The boar out of the wood doth waste it.—*Psalm,* lxxx. 13.

33. 278.—Except they wash they eat not.—*Mark,* vii. 4.

34. 278.—And she took flour, and kneaded it, and made cakes in his sight, and did bake the cakes.—2 *Samuel,* xiii. 8.

35. 279.—The wilderness yieldeth food for them and for their children.—*Job,* xxiv. 5.

36. 281.—They that dwell in the wilderness shall bow before him.—*Psalm,* lxxii. 9.

37. 282.—And pursued them to Hobah, which is on the left hand of Damascus.—*Genesis,* xiv. 15.

38. 291.—A city that is set on a hill cannot be hid.—*Matthew,* v. 14.

39. 295.—And he said unto them, cast the net on the right side of the ship.—They cast therefore, and now they were not able to draw it for the multitude of fishes.—*John,* xxi. 6.

40. 296.—And they arrived at the country of the Gadarenes, which is over against Galilee.—*Luke,* viii. 26.

41. 297.—Neither abode in any house, but in the tombs.—*Luke,* viii. 27.

42. 301.—And they fastened his body to the wall of Bethshan.—1 *Samuel,* xxxi. 10.

NOTES.

Note Page

43. 303. For we have treasures in the field, of wheat, and of barley, and of oil, and of honey.—*Jeremiah*, xli. 8.——The seed is rotten under their clods, the garners are laid desolate, the barns are broken down, for the corn is withered.—*Joel*, i. 17.

44. 305.—And the ravens brought him bread and flesh in the morning, and bread and flesh in the evening, and he drank of the brook.—1 *Kings*, xvii. 6.

45. 306.—Adjeloun is mentioned in *Joshua*, x. 12.—— Sun, stand thou still upon Gibeon, and thou, Moon, in the valley of Ajalon.——It appears, however, on referring to 2 *Chronicles*, xi. 10. that Aijalon was in the land of Judah, which was on the other side of the Jordan.

46. 306.—The five kings are found hid in a cave at Makkedah.—*Joshua*, x. 17.

47. 306.—A high hill as the hill of Bashan.—*Psalm*, lxviii. 15.

48. 320.—Also he built towers in the desert.—2 *Chronicles*, xxvi. 10.

49. 321.—And the stone wall thereof was broken down.— *Proverbs*, xxiv. 31.

50. 326.—And Joshua set up twelve stones in the midst of Jordan, in the place where the feet of the priests which bare the ark of the covenant stood; and they are there unto this day.— *Joshua*, iv. 9.

51. 327.—They are wet with the showers in the mountains, and embrace the rock for want of a shelter.—*Job*, xxiv. 8.

52. 341.—And they shall go into the holes of the rocks and into the caves of the earth.—*Isaiah*, ii. 19.

Note Page
53. 341.—He built even Bethlehem, and Etam, and Tekoa. —*2 Chronicles*, xi. 6.
54. 342.—A vineyard in a very fruitful hill; and he built a tower in the midst of it.—*Isaiah*, v. 1, 2.
55. 342.—Now Hebron was built seven years before Zoan in Egypt.—*Numbers*, xiii. 22.
56. 342.—And Sarah died in Kirjath-arba; the same is Hebron.—*Genesis*, xxiii. 2. There they buried Isaac and Rebecca his wife, and there I buried Leah.—*Genesis*, xlix. 31.
57. 374.—And the stone wall thereof was broken down. —*Proverbs*, xxiv. 31.
58. 380.—Greet ye one another with a kiss of charity.— 1 *Peter*, v. 14.
59. 380.—Now those that sealed were, &c. &c. Hallohesh. Pileha, Shobek, &c.—*Nehemiah*, x. 24.
60. 384.—Neither will we drink of the water of the wells. —*Numbers*, xx. 17.
61. 385.—If a man vow a vow, or swear an oath, he shall not break his word.—*Numbers*, xxx. 2.
62. 393.—And Moses sent messengers from Kadesh unto the King of Edom, thus saith thy brother Israel, behold we are in Kadesh, a city in the uttermost of thy border:

Let us pass, I pray thee, through thy country: we will not pass through the fields, or through the vineyards, neither will we drink *of* the water of the wells: we will go by the king's *high* way, we will not turn to the right hand nor to the left, until we have passed thy borders.

And Edom said unto him, thou shalt not pass by me, lest I come out against thee with the sword.

And the children of Israel said unto him, we will go by the high way: and if I and my cattle drink of thy water, then I will pay for it: I will only, without *doing* any thing *else*, go through on my feet.

And he said, thou shalt not go through. And Edom came out against him with much people, and with a strong hand.

Thus Edom refused to give Israel passage through his border: wherefore Israel turned away from him.

And the children of Israel, *even* the whole congregation, journeyed from Kadesh, and came unto mount Hor.—*Numbers*, xx. 14—22.

63. 393.—And Aaron died there, in the top of the mount.—*Numbers*, xx. 28.

64. 393.—The women came out of all the cities of Israel, singing and dancing.—1 *Samuel*, xviii. 6.

65. 394.—For by wise counsels thou shall make thy wars. *Proverbs*, xxiv. 6.

66. 394.—Forsook the counsel of the old men.—1 *Kings*, xii. 8.

67. 395.—And behold Saul lay sleeping within the trench, and his spear stuck in the ground.—1 *Samuel*, xxvi. 7.

68. 397.—If thieves came to thee, if robbers by night, &c.—*Obadiah*, 5.

69. 397.—Ye are spies.—*Genesis*, xlii. 9.

70. 402.—And he built towers in the desert.—2 *Chronicles*, xxvi. 10.

71. 415.—Flocks shall lie down in the midst of her; all the beasts of the nations, both the cormorant and the bittern shall lodge in the upper lintels thereof.—*Zephaniah*, ii. 14.

72. 423.—O thou that dwellest in the clefts of the rock.—*Jeremiah*, xlix. 16.

NOTES.

Note Page
73. 426.—He that heweth him out a sepulchre on high, and that graveth an habitation for himself in a rock.—*Isaiah*, xxii. 16.

74. 433.—Take Aaron and Eleazar his son, and bring them up unto mount Hor. And Moses stripped Aaron of his garments and put them upon Eleazar his son; and Aaron died there on the top of the mount.—*Numbers*, xx. 25, 28.—— And the children of Israel took their journey from Beeroth of the children of Jaakan, to Mosera; there Aaron died, and there he was buried.—*Deuteronomy*, x. 6.

But after the army (that had so long mourned the dead sister of the general) were thus purified, he led them through the desert, into Arabia; and arriving in a place (which the Arabians account for their metropolitan city, in times past called Arce, and at this present, Petra) which is environed with a high mountain, Aaron ascended the said mountain, and Moses shewed him the place where he should yield up his soul unto God; and in the sight of all the army standing on a high place, he put off his stoale, and gave it to his son Eleazer, to whom, by eldership, the succession appertained; and thus, in the sight of the people, he died in that very year wherein he lost his sister, in the one hundred and thirty-third year of his age, in the month of August.
Vide Josephus' Antiquities, book iv. ch. 4.

75. 436.—What shall be the trespass offering.—1 *Samuel*, vi. 4.

76. 437.—Loose thy shoe from off thy foot, for the place whereon thou standest is holy.—*Joshua*, v. 15.

77. 439.—Edom shall be a desolation.—*Jeremiah*, xlix. 17. —See *Ezekiel*, xxxv. and xxxvi.

78. 443.—She had strong rods for the sceptres of them that bare rule.—*Ezekiel*, xix. 11.

Note	Page	
79.	453.	—The whole land thereof is brimstone and salt, &c.—*Deuteronomy*, xxix. 23.
80.	456.	—They violently take away flocks, and feed thereof. They take the widow's ox for a pledge.—*Job*, xxiv. 2, 3.
81.	458.	—Drink waters out of thine own cistern.—*Proverbs*, v. 15.
82.	463.	—Thou shalt set thee up great stones, and plaster, them with plaster; and thou shalt write upon them all the words of this law.—*Deuteronomy*, xxvii. 2, 3.
82.	463.	—And the border went up to the stone of Bohan.—*Joshua,* xv. 6.
83.	470.	—And Saul went out to meet him that he might salute him.—1 *Samuel*, xiii. 10.
84.	470.	—An old man cometh up; and he is covered with a mantle.—1 *Samuel*, xxviii. 14.
85.	470.	—I have seen a son of Jesse the Bethlehemite, that is cunning in playing.—1 *Samuel*, xvi. 18.
86.	471.	—Medeba is noticed in *Numbers*, xxi. 30.—— And we have laid them waste unto Nophah, which reacheth unto Medeba.——And in *Isaiah*, xv. 2. Moab shall howl over Nebo, and over Medeba.
87.	472.	—He reached her parched corn, and she did eat.—*Ruth,* ii. 14.
88.	472.	—And behold, seven ears of corn came up upon one stalk! and in the seven plenteous years the earth brought forth by handfuls.—*Genesis*, xli. 5, 47.
89.	473.	—Let us slay him and cast him into some pit.—*Genesis*, xxxvii. 20.
90.	475.	—Took his two wives, &c. and passed over the ford Jabbok.—*Genesis*, xxxii. 22.——Nor unto any place of the river Jabbok.—*Deuteronomy*, ii. 37.——And the border even unto the river Jabbok.—*Deuteronomy*, iii. 16.——Even

NOTES.

unto the river Jabbok, which is the border of the children of Ammon.—*Joshua,* xii. 2.

92. 481.—And he hasted to dress it.—*Genesis,* xviii. 7.

93. 481.—Thou shalt not seethe a kid in his mother's milk.—*Exodus,* xxiii. 19. xxxiv. 26.—*Deuteronomy,* xiv. 21.

94. 481.—And of the fat thereof.—*Genesis,* iv. 4.——Josesphus says, " it was milk."——*Antiquities,* b. i. c. ii. sect. 1.——And as we have it here used, the milk certainly contained the fat and substance of the meat.

95. 481.—She brought forth butter in a lordly dish.—*Judges,* v. 25.

96. 482.—He that dippeth his hand with me in the dish—*Matthew,* xxvi. 23.

97. 483.—And thou dost dwell among scorpions.—*Ezekiel,* ii. 6.

98. 483.—And all the women whose heart stirred them up in wisdom spun goats hair.—*Exodus,* xxxv. 26.

99. 484.—And he made curtains of goats hair.—*Exodus,* xxxvi. 14.

100. 485.—Concerning the tithe of the herd, or of the flock.—*Leviticus,* xxvii. 32.

101. 494.—And it came to pass in Iconium that they went both together into the synagague of the Jews, and so spake that a great multitutude both of the Jews and also of the Greeks believed.—*Acts,* xiv. 1.

INDEX
TO THE PLACES VISITED.

THE ANCIENT NAMES ARE IN ITALICS.

A.

Aaron's Tomb, 432, 435.
Abou Soliman's tomb, 378.
Abraham, house of, 342.
Achzib, Zib. 196.
Acre, *Accho*, 195, 497.
Acoujah, 373.
Adjeloun, 307.
Aggi Dengis, lake, 230.
Ain el Frangee, 446.
Ak Shehr, 492.
Alaks, plain, 231.
Al-baid (well), 348.
Aleppo, 231.
Amatha, ruins, 297.
Amman, *Rabbath Ammon*, 474.
Anamour, Cape, 528.
Antinoe, 163.
Antioch, Antakia, 229.
Aphroditopolis, site, 135.
Appolinoplis magna, 127.
Arimathea, Ramla, 184.
Armada, 94.
Arrag-el-Emir, *Hircan's p.* 473.
Arethusia, 254.
Arsouf, *Appollonias*, 189.
Arti-musshut, tomb, 370.
Ascanius, lake, 490.
Asdoud, *Azotus*, 179.
Asphaltes, lake, 459.
Assuan, *Syene*, 118.
Athan, village, 322.
Athlite, village, 190.
Aukullah, 513.
Ayash, 513.

B.

Baalbec, 214.
Backwater, Dead Sea, 353, 450.
Bait Forage, 328.
Batroun, *Botrys*, 206.
Bayga, valley of, 320.
Bayruth, *Berytus*, 202.
Beit Kerm, ruins, 458.
Bekaa Mathooalis, 212.
Belus, river, 192.
Bendick, 489.
Beshiri village, 109.
Bethlehem, 339.
Bilejik, 491.
Blanco, Cape, 197.
Boulack, port of Cairo, 162.
Bourkee, ruins, 230.
Bulwudun, *Polybotom*, 492.
Bsaida, Ipseyra, 376.
Bysan, *Scythopolis*, 301.

C.

Cafringee, 306.
Caiffa, *Hepha*, 192.
Cairo, 151, 158.

INDEX.

Calirrhoe, valley of, 467.
Callah-el-Hammam, 299.
Callah-el-Rubbat, 306.
Calycadnus, river, 522.
Candele, village, 224.
Carmel, mount, 193.
Carnack, 137.
Castel Pelegrino, 192.
Castle Jeba, 201.
Cataract, second, 20.
Cedars of Lebanon, 209.
Cesarea, 189.
Chelindreh, *Celenderis*, 524.
Cilicia Campestris, boundary, 510.
Contra Latopolis, site, 135.
Corycus, ruins, 519.
Cydnus, 502.
Cynopolis, site, 155.
Cyprus, 526, 530.

D.

Daboude, temple, 105.
Damascus, 282.
Daphne, site of, 225.
Dead Sea, tour, 331.
Dekki, temple, 98.
Derry, 11, 92.
Dettrass, ruins, 372.
Dgellgood, site, 370.
Dgebail, Sheikh, 286.
Dher, tombs, 466.
Dibdeba, village, 386.
Diban, *Dibon*, 462.
Djebal, Attarous, 464.
Djebal, village, 375.
Djerash, ruins, 308, 317, 475.
Djibel Selsilis, mountains, 126.

E.

Ebsambal, small temple, 28.
———— large temple, 37.
Eden, village, 209.
Edfoo, *Appolinopolis magna*, 127.
Elabahn, volcanic mass, 375.
El Ahsa or Hussan, river, 355, 357.
El Arish, 173.
El Assel, river, 359.
El Bered, or Coldriver, 219.
El Cab, *Eleethias*, 130.
El Darrah or Dara, river, 359.
Elephantina, island, 123.
El Gaig, ruins, 378.
El Hagre, ruins, 376.
El Ibrim, river, *Adonis*, 205.
El Kasab, river, 189.
El Kelb, river, 203.
El Leban, river, 203.
El Mulk, river, 220.
El Petras, river, 189.
Elpha, 22.
El Rubin, river, 182.
El Sazib, river, 203.
El Zowar, 354.
Erbed village, 299.
Erkle, or Ellegria, *Heraclea*, 498.
Erment, *Hermontis*, 135.
Ersek, 489.
Escol, torrent, 179.
Esdier village, 177.
Esdredon, plain, 478.
Eski, Shehr, *Dorylæum*, 491.
Esneh, *Latopolis*, 134.
Eugen, village, 307.

F.

Farras, village, 16, 18.

G.

Gaobin village, 489.
Garbe Dendour, temple, 100.
Garbe Girshe, temple, 99.
Garbe Merie, 101.
Gaza, 178.
Gebail, convent, 205.
Gennesaret, lake, 293.
Gerasa or *Pella*, 476.
Gerizim, Mount, 329.
Gesir Adid, 230.
Gharundel, *Arindela*, 376.
Ghiuk Sooyor, R.*Calycadnus*,522.
Ghiviza, *Lybissa*, 489.
Ghor, 483.
Ghorneys, village, 449.
Gilhad Gilhood, village, 322.
Gourna tombs, 137.
Granite quarries, 119.

H.

Hallawye, 305.
Hamah, *Epiphaneia*, 243.
Hamahta or Mote, site, 371.
Haneunis, village, 175.
Hariatoon, ruins, 340.
Hebron, *Kiriath Arba*, 311, 342.
Hermopolis, 153.
Herodium, ruins, 464.
Heshban or *Heshbon*, 471.
Hindaw, 104.
Hircan, palace of, 473.
Homs, *Emesa*, 254, 276.
Howeeh, site, 370.
Hot Springs, Yarmack, 298.
Houarti, 153.
Houle, Lake, 290.

I.

Ibrim, Primnis, 13.
Ilgum, Philomelium, 493.
Ipseyra, *Bsaida*, 443.
Ichuran, 519.
Isalu, 492.
Isnik, or Tchinisli, *Nicæa*, 490.

J.

Jabok, river, 319, 475.
Jacob's bridge, 286.
Jaffa, *Joppa*, 184.
Jamnia, Yabne, 182.
Jebilee, *Gabala*, 224.
Jellaheen's camp, 342.
Jericho, camp near, 330.
Jerusalem, 329.
Jonas's Pillar, 534.
Jordan, river, 289, 325, 329.

K.

Kaffer Baiter, ruins, 328.
Kalapsche, temple, 5, 101.
Kali-Phee, 391.
Karabignar, 495.
Karamania, coast, 502.
Kasmia, river, 198.
Katty, village, 312, 315.
Kavdas or Abouli, river, 208.
Kazalu, road to, 506.
Kerek, 361, 444, 456.
Khadun Khan, 493.
Khanzyre, 444.
Khosru Khan, 491.
Kiriath Arba, Hebron, 311.

Kishon, river, 194.
Kisdervent, 490.
Kolinkboaz, 501.
Konieh, *Iconium*, 494.
Koroskoff, 9.
Koum Ombo, *Ombos*, 123.

L.

Labyrinth, 340.
Ladik, *Laodiceia Combusta*, 494.
Latachia or *Latakia, Laodicea*, 222.
Latmus, river, 513.
Latopolis, Esneh, 134.
Lebanon, 210.
Lefke, 491.
Lehaddineh Hinde, 391.
Lissan el Kahpeh, 525.
Locusts, 443.
Loudd, *Lydda*, 184.
Lourdee, 224.
Lybian Mountains, 146.
Luxor, 137, 147, 149.

M.

Mackad, site, 370.
Madeba, *Medaba*, 471.
Madfuni, 140.
Madjdala, village, 291.
Mahannah's camp, 260.
Mahanna, ruins, 370.
Majdil, *Magdala*, 299.
Majudal, village, 179.
Makkedah, cave, 306.
Mansouria, island, 126.
Marah, 242.

Markab, village, 222.
Marrowhich, site, 370.
Marseilles, 530.
Mataria, *Heliopolis*, 167.
Mayn, ruins, 464.
Medinet Aboo, 147.
Memnonium, temples at, 147.
Mockatem grottos, 131.
Mons Regalis, 380.
Mount Carmel, 193.
Mount Cassius, 224.
Mount Hor, 433.
Mount Lebanon, 209.
Mount Nebo, 464.
Montpellier, 530.
Mummy pits, 142.
Musshut tomb, 371.

N.

Nablous, *Sichem*, 328.
Nebi Aaroon, 388.
Nebi Hood, village, 313.
Nicomedia, 489.

O.

Offidena, temple, 97.
Olukooshlah, 499.
Ombos, Koum Ombo, 123.
Om Keis, *Gadara*, 297.
Oom-i-Rasass, 471.
Orontes, river, 225.

P.

Panias, *Cæsarea Philippi*, 289.

G.

Gaobin village, 489.
Garbe Dendour, temple, 100.
Garbe Girshe, temple, 99.
Garbe Merie, 101.
Gaza, 178.
Gebail, convent, 205.
Gennesaret, lake, 293.
Gerasa or *Pella*, 476.
Gerizim, Mount, 329.
Gesir Adid, 230.
Gharundel, *Arindela*, 376.
Ghiuk Sooyor, R.*Calycadnus*,522.
Ghiviza, *Lybissa*, 489.
Ghor, 483.
Ghorneys, village, 449.
Gilhad Gilhood, village, 322.
Gourna tombs, 137.
Granite quarries, 119.

H.

Hallawye, 305.
Hamah, *Epiphaneia*, 243.
Hamahta or Mote, site, 371.
Haneunis, village, 175.
Hariatoon, ruins, 340.
Hebron, *Kiriath Arba*, 311, 342.
Hermopolis, 153.
Herodium, ruins, 464.
Heshban or *Heshbon*, 471.
Hindaw, 104.
Hircan, palace of, 473.
Homs, *Emesa*, 254, 276.
Howeeh, site, 370.
Hot Springs, Yarmack, 298.
Houarti, 153.
Houle, Lake, 290.

I.

Ibrim, Primnis, 13.
Ilgum, Philomelium, 493.
Ipseyra, *Bsaida*, 443.
Ichuran, 519.
Isalu, 492.
Isnik, or Tchinisli, *Nicæa*, 490.

J.

Jabok, river, 319, 475.
Jacob's bridge, 286.
Jaffa, *Joppa*, 184.
Jamnia, Yabne, 182.
Jebilee, *Gabala*, 224.
Jellaheen's camp, 342.
Jericho, camp near, 330.
Jerusalem, 329.
Jonas's Pillar, 534.
Jordan, river, 289, 325, 329.

K.

Kaffer Baiter, ruins, 328.
Kalapsche, temple, 5, 101.
Kali-Phee, 391.
Karabignar, 495.
Karamania, coast, 502.
Kasmia, river, 198.
Katty, village, 312, 315.
Kavdas or Abouli, river, 208.
Kazalu, road to, 506.
Kerek, 361, 444, 456.
Khadun Khan, 493.
Khanzyre, 444.
Khosru Khan, 491.
Kiriath Arba, Hebron, 311.

INDEX.

Kishon, river, 194.
Kisdervent, 490.
Kolinkboaz, 501.
Konieh, *Iconium*, 494.
Koroskoff, 9.
Koum Ombo, *Ombos*, 123.

L.

Labyrinth, 340.
Ladik, *Laodiceia Combusta*, 494.
Latachia or *Latakia*, *Laodicea*, 222.
Latmus, river, 513.
Latopolis, Esneh, 134.
Lebanon, 210.
Lefke, 491.
Lehaddineh Hinde, 391.
Lissan el Kahpeh, 525.
Locusts, 443.
Loudd, *Lydda*, 184.
Lourdee, 224.
Lybian Mountains, 146.
Luxor, 137, 147, 149.

M.

Mackad, site, 370.
Madeba, *Medaba*, 471.
Madfuni, 140.
Madjdala, village, 291.
Mahannah's camp, 260.
Mahanna, ruins, 370.
Majdil, *Magdala*, 299.
Majudal, village, 179.
Makkedah, cave, 306.
Mansouria, island, 126.
Marah, 242.

Markab, village, 222.
Marrowhich, site, 370.
Marseilles, 530.
Mataria, *Heliopolis*, 167.
Mayn, ruins, 464.
Medinet Aboo, 147.
Memnonium, temples at, 147.
Mockatem grottos, 131.
Mons Regalis, 380.
Mount Carmel, 193.
Mount Cassius, 224.
Mount Hor, 433.
Mount Lebanon, 209.
Mount Nebo, 464.
Montpellier, 530.
Mummy pits, 142.
Musshut tomb, 371.

N.

Nablous, *Sichem*, 328.
Nebi Aaroon, 388.
Nebi Hood, village, 313.
Nicomedia, 489.

O.

Offidena, temple, 97.
Olukooshlah, 499.
Ombos, Koum Ombo, 123.
Om Keis, *Gadara*, 297.
Oom-i-Rasass, 471.
Orontes, river, 225.

P.

Panias, *Cæsarea Philippi*, 289.

INDEX. 559

Palmyra, ruins, Tedmor, 267.
Payass, 531.
Pella or Gerasa, 317, 476.
Pelusium, 171.
Petra, 405.
Phiala, lake, 287.
Philæ, 1, 106.
Pompeiopolis, ruins, 508, 510.
Pyramids, 156, 406.

R.

Rabha, Rabbath Moab, 457.
Radimore, 164.
Rajib, Ragaba, 478.
Ramla, Arimathea, 184.
Rastan, village, 254.
Reashy, 313.
Rhoda, island, 162.
Ruad, Aradus, island, 220.

S.

Sabour, temple, 95.
Safot, 291.
Saida, Sidon, 199.
Sammack, 385.
Sasa, village, 285.
Scorpion, rock, 300.
Scutari, 487.
Selahieh, village, 169.
Selefkeh, Seleucia, 522.
Semmack, 296.
Sermein, 240.
Sepulchres of Petra, 428.
Shedelah, 513.
Shekune, khan, 343.
Sheikh Daoud, tomb, 304.

Sheikh Harn, 459.
Sheikh Jaffa, tomb, 371.
Shobek, 378, 380.
Shuhut, 491.
Sidi Gazi, 491.
Siout, 153.
Sipheer, village, 342.
Solomon's pool, 340.
Souf, village, 307.
St. Simon, ruins, 231.
Suadeah, Seleucia, 227.
Surugees (hostlers), 498.
Syene, Assuan, 9.
Szalt, Amathus or Machærus, 321.

T.

Tabaria, Tiberias, 295.
Tabathat Fahkil, 304.
Tafyle, village, 444.
Takehur, post-house, 500.
Tarichea, walls of, 300.
Taurus, mount, 499.
Tchinisli or Isnik, Nicæa, 490.
Tedmor, village, Palmyra, 267.
Teffa, temples, 103.
Tehene, village, 154.
Tekoa, ruins, 341.
Temple of the Sun, Djerash, 317.
Temple of the Sun, Palmyra, 269.
Temseida, castle, 206.
Tentyra, temple, 151.
Terra Santa, Damascus, 282.
Tersoos, Tarsus, 502.
Thebes, 137, 149.
Tiberias, 300.
Tomb of Jacob, 294.
Tortosa, walls of, 220.

Tortura, *Dora*, 190.
Touman, khan, 240.
Tourneen, 231.
Tripoli, 206.
Tsour, *Tyre*, 197.
Tyana, 498.
Tyrian's ladder, 197.

V.

Vermin, 485.

W.

Wady el Ahsa, 373, 444.
—— Modjeb, *Arnon*, 460.
—— Mousa, 402.
—— Zeit, 327.

Wady Wale, 462.

Y.

Yabne, *Jamnia*, 182,
Yarmack, hot springs, 298.
Yead, village, 214.

Z.

Zeit, Wady, 327.
Zerka, river, *Jabbok*, 319, 475.
Zerka, river, 190.
Zerka Mayn, torrent, 466.
Zib Achzib, 196.
Zoar, site of, 448.

THE END.